MUSIC AND GENDER

MUSIC AND GENDER

Edited by

Pirkko Moisala and
Beverley Diamond

Foreword by Ellen Koskoff

UNIVERSITY OF ILLINOIS PRESS
URBANA AND CHICAGO

Library of Congress Cataloging-in-Publication Data
Music and gender / edited by Pirkko Moisala and Beverley Diamond ;
foreword by Ellen Koskoff.
p.   cm.
Includes bibliographical references and index.
ISBN 0-252-02544-X (cloth : acid-free paper)
ISBN 0-252-06865-3 (paper : acid-free paper)
1. Women musicians.
2. Sex in music.
I. Moisala, Pirkko.
II. Diamond, Beverley, 1948–   .
ML82.M74   2000
780'.82—dc21   99-6791
CIP

Marcia Herndon
1941–97

In the midst of this project, we lost a dear
friend, a mercurial colleague, and an inspiration to many of the authors in this volume. We
wish to honor her and give her the last word
by closing this anthology with her final article.
Like much of her other work, it is a challenge
to music scholarship—a challenge to investi-
gate gender as a whole and necessary system in
every society, a system embracing a variable
range and number of gender roles and definitions. In her vision gender is a fundamental
dynamic field that responds to specific social
situations and needs. In her vision all human
identities would have a respected place.

Contents

Foreword

Ellen Koskoff

Beverley Diamond and Pirkko Moisala, in their ground-breaking volume *Music and Gender,* have given us an impressive collection of fourteen articles based on the current research of an unusually diverse set of scholars from the United States, Canada, and Europe. In addition, these essays are creatively framed by a fascinating and unusual introduction written by the editors and authors and an epilogue by Marcia Herndon, who died during the completion of this work. This epilogue provides not only a deeply moving ending to the collection but also an apt one. Marcia's work over the past decades was an inspiration to many of us, especially the members of the Music and Gender Study Group of the International Council for Traditional Music, many of whom are represented in this volume.

The essays, presenting an eclectic mixture of disciplinary approaches (ethnomusicology, historical musicology, feminist studies, music composition, education, popular music studies, music technology, and sociology), are organized into four large sections, "Music Performance and Performativity," "Telling Lives," "Gendered Musical Sites in the Redefinition of Nations," and "Technologies in Gendered Motion," each of which is introduced by a short introduction placing the essays in their scholarly and methodological contexts.

Some essays are historically framed (Margaret Meyer's work on ladies' orchestras and Jane Bowers's on Mama Yancey); many are based on fieldwork (e.g., Michelle Kisliuk's study of the BaAka Pygmies, Helmi Järviluoma on musicians in Finland, and Ingrid Rüütel on Estonian traditional musicians). Some describe musical cultures "outside" the cultures of their authors (Beverley Diamond's work on Maritime Canadians, Ursula Reinhard's on Turkish women, and Cynthia Tse Kimberlin's on Ethiopian and Eritrean musicians); others look inward (Boden Sandstrom on women mix engineers and Karen Pegley on the gender dynamics of a music class). Some essays examine music and text (Naila Ceribašić on popular music in the context of war and Andra McCartney on the work of Hildegard Westerkamp), whereas others consider the gendering of languages and behaviors surrounding music (Linda Dusman on the gendered context of electroacoustic performance). Some are wide ranging (Marcia Herndon's cross-cultural examination of gender and musical systems), and others are specific to one musician (Pirkko Moisala's portrait of the Finnish composer Kajia Saariaho).

Major themes emerge throughout the four sections: the implications of gender on recent and rapid social, political, and economic change; the performative nature of gender and other identities; constructing the self or selves through life stories; and the gendering of music technology. All the essays, though, share a central core: each focuses on the ways in which gender and musical identities intersect, intertwine, and inform one another within specific contexts.

Music and Gender is perhaps the first ethnomusicological collection to combine a variety of methodologies that mirror, in a way, the recent history of scholarship within feminist and music studies, a scholarship falling into three overlapping historical periods, each marked by different research and analytical paradigms. The first wave—what I refer to here as women-centric scholarship and perhaps best represented in works such as those by Farrer (1975), Cormier (1978), Bowers and Tick (1985), Briscoe (1986), Pendle (1991), Marshall (1993), and Neuls-Bates (1996), among others—dealt with the near invisibility of women's musical activity in the scholarly literature, concentrating primarily on collecting, documenting, and notating women's music, thereby contributing to a more holistic view of the world's musical cultures.

The second wave, influenced primarily by the disciplines of history, anthropology, and folklore—what I refer to here as gender-centric scholarship—began to refashion the question of women's music, framing it instead within the broader context of gender relations. Anthologies by scholars such as Koskoff (1989), Keeling (1989), Herndon and Ziegler (1990), Cook and Tsou (1994), and others examined various societies' gender arrangements and gender styles, seeing music creation and performance as contexts for reinforcing, changing, or protesting gender relations.

The third, most current wave of literature, heavily influenced by postmodern scholarship in feminist theory, gay and lesbian studies, cultural and performance studies, semiotics, and psychoanalysis and best represented in works by Solie (1993), McClary (1991), Citron (1993), and Brett and Wood (1994), among others, has sought to understand the links between social and musical structures and the ways in which each can be seen as embedded within the other.

Music and Gender both celebrates these forebears by including essays that connect to each of these three preceding scholarly periods and, at the same time, moves forward into uncharted territory. It does so by simultaneously embracing two underlying premises. First, women, men, gender, identity, music, culture, and so on are not, and never have been, fixed categories; each must be placed within its own unique and changeable context. Second, and perhaps more important, authors and their views on such subjects exist in dynamic contexts as well, so that the author's subject position must also be acknowledged in the work.

To that end the editors and contributors to this volume took a bold step: they conducted fieldwork on themselves, providing in their introduction a sort of "self-ethnography" that clarifies the subject position of each author vis-à-vis her own work. This openness and honesty marks, perhaps for the first time in the literature devoted to gender issues in music, some insight not only into the workings of individual authors and their perspectives but also into the collaborative process of scholarship itself.

The hallmark of the ethnographic method is fieldwork, that process in which mediation, negotiation, and collaboration take place in real-time, dynamic contexts between people often engaged in spirited dialogue. One of the unexpected benefits of this process, seen strikingly in this introduction, is self-realization, especially on the part of the editors, who had to engage honestly with differences of all kinds in this collection. Using dialogue as a fundamental principle of interaction, the editors and authors, via e-mail, conversed throughout the writing, editing, and organizing of the book. Known collectively as "the conversation," these exchanges provided an ongoing stream of questions, problems, and insights that not only continuously informed individual authors and their own contributions but also enlivened the work as a whole.

Situating the fourteen essays within the larger context of "the conversation" also provided an interesting and creative solution to the problem of the multiple differences in approach, method, and data found within them. In engaging in fieldwork on themselves, the editors have problematized the differences between and among authors, considering issues such as the meaning of gender itself (in the languages of some of the European authors, there is no such word or concept); the assumptions of American, white, middle-class feminists (some see feminism as a political movement, while others do not, leading Moisala, one of the editors, to devise her own term, *genderist,* to describe her position); the slipperiness of changing and multiple identities constructed over lifetimes; and the notion of "the field" as a context for examining one's own as well as others' assumptions. All these issues are cast into the light of discussion and bandied about with, thankfully, no fixed conclusions as to one right way of seeing or doing things.

We may ask whether such honesty is necessary. Do we really need to know every significant detail of the authors' thinking as it changed and developed over time through dialogue with the others? Are we really interested in the individual differences that emerge? I answer yes—especially if the presentation is done well, as it has been here. Indeed, these exchanges are part of what makes this book come to life. By its end we know just as much about the authors as we do about their work. Filled with personal anecdotes, inconsistencies, humor, and self-insight, these glimpses reveal much about the process of collaboration, the creative development and manipulation of streams of thought over time, and the acknowledgment of unresolved differences. No one view is privileged over any other, and readers are invited to join the chorus. Thus, the many differences presented in this collection, which might have resulted in an organizational weakness, have instead been transformed into a strength that no one could have predicted, ultimately resulting in a volume in which the subjects and the subjects' positions are totally and believably integrated.

We need more thinking and writing such as this, work that openly addresses the assumptions of authors and their contexts, for such work can become more than just the sum of its parts: with all its diverse threads moving and entwining simultaneously, it can approach the richness, honesty, and excitement of real life.

REFERENCES CITED

Bowers, Jane, and Judith Tick, eds. 1985. *Women Making Music: The Western Art Tradition, 1150–1950.* Urbana: University of Illinois Press.

Brett, Philip, Elizabeth Wood, and Gary C. Thomas, eds. 1994. *Queering the Pitch: The New Gay and Lesbian Musicology.* New York: Routledge.

Briscoe, James R. 1986. *Historical Anthology of Music by Women.* Sound recording. Bloomington: Indiana University Press.

Citron, Marcia J. 1993. *Gender and the Musical Canon.* New York: Cambridge University Press.

Cook, Susan C., and Judy S. Tsou. 1994. *Cecilia Reclaimed: Feminist Perspectives on Gender and Music.* Urbana: University of Illinois Press.

Cormier, Holly, comp. 1978. *Women and Folk Music: A Select Bibliography.* Washington, D.C.: Library of Congress.

Farrer, Claire B. 1975. *Women and Folklore.* Austin: University of Texas Press.

Herndon, Marcia, and Suzanne Zeigler. 1990. *Music, Gender, and Culture*. Intercultural Music Studies, 1. Wilhelmshaven, Germany: F. Noetzel Verlag.

Keeling, Richard, ed. 1989. *Women in North American Indian Music: Six Essays*. Society for Ethnomusicology Special Series, 6. Bloomington, Ind.: Society for Ethnomusicology.

Koskoff, Ellen, ed. 1989 [1987]. *Women and Music in Cross-Cultural Perspective*. Urbana: University of Illinois Press.

Marshall, Kimberly, ed. 1993. *Rediscovering the Muses: Women's Musical Traditions*. Boston: Northeastern University Press.

McClary, Susan. 1991. *Feminine Endings: Music, Gender, and Sexuality*. Minneapolis: University of Minnesota Press.

Neuls-Bates, Carol. 1996. *Women in Music: An Anthology of Source Readings from the Middle Ages to the Present*. 2d ed. Boston: Northeastern University Press.

Pendle, Karin, ed. 1991. *Women and Music: A History*. Bloomington: Indiana University Press.

Solie, Ruth. 1993. *Musicology and Difference: Gender and Sexuality in Music Scholarship*. Berkeley: University of California Press.

Introduction
Music and Gender: Negotiating Shifting Worlds

Beverley Diamond and Pirkko Moisala

Considering Our Intellectual and Social Location

In recent decades many societies across the world have undergone extreme social, political, and technological change. As it often does, music has played a role in negotiating the places of individuals, groups, and nations caught up in these radical transformations. Just as typically, gender has informed the language of these innovations as well as their implications. In this book we attempt to examine where these discourses—discourses of music, about music, of gendered bodies, and about gender—have intersected in the experiences of the diverse groups and individuals that have experienced the rapid changes of recent decades. To accomplish this goal, the contributors to this anthology, along with many other scholars of the 1990s, have assumed that culture is not a static and rigid phenomenon but a fluid and relational one, performed variously depending on situational contexts and contingencies.

To some extent, then, this volume parallels other "postcolonial" explorations of gender that acknowledge the displacements and movements, as well as the disjunctures and collisions, of people, technologies, histories, and ideas in the late twentieth century. The history of feminist study within the discipline of music shapes the issues somewhat differently, however. Although a decade ago many observed that music scholars had done little to explore gender issues and enter the discourses of feminism, few would now deny the impact of gender-related explorations on virtually every aspect of music study. The publications of the past decade, however, indicate how difficult it has been to articulate a theoretical agenda that interests scholars with culturally relative perspectives in the context of vastly different music cultures.

The earlier multiauthored anthologies that have provided a solid ground for the studies in this anthology are cases in point. In a landmark introductory essay, Ellen Koskoff (1989) articulated a twofold agenda for socially grounded studies of music in plural cultural contexts: she urged us to ask how concepts of gender constrain and shape music making and how music making serves as a vehicle for the construction of gender. Her formulation was forward looking for several reasons: she rightly emphasized "concepts," the constructedness of categories, and the need to avoid essentialism. Several contributions in Koskoff's anthology prefigure current studies that emphasize the dynamics of whole systems and the performative nature of gender constructions. The first publication of the International Council for Traditional Music's Study Group on Music and Gender, Herndon and Ziegler's *Music, Gender, and Culture* (1990), explores issues connected to musical performance and issues created by the gender of the investigator. The retrospection implied by the latter set of issues similarly paved the way for the present volume, which is even more reflexive.

For the most part, however, the essays in both these volumes contribute compensatory ethnographies rather than interpretive insights or tested theoretical models. The diverse approaches and subject matter demonstrate what ethnomusicologists know well: that both the abstract nature of musical sound and the huge range of practices that constitute the human organization of sound render questions about music's "meaning" more complex and difficult than similar questions about languages of words or images. Scholars addressing this complexity have often had to use culturally relative methodologies and concepts.

Nevertheless, many of the contemporary and subsequent contributions to feminist theory in music were framed within the North American academy and addressed a culturally specific tradition: either Euro-American concert music or American vernacular and popular musics. Some of these contributions filled lacunae in our knowledge of women's work, providing the valuable service of "looking after" women's music and women musicians by "remembering them through the methods historians apply in their attempts to objectify the past" (as Jane Bowers and Judith Tick [1987, 3] expressed it in their pioneering anthology). These studies of the late 1980s and early 1990s addressed institutional patterns and problems of access (Bowers and Tick 1987; Citron 1993; Marshall 1993), queried canon construction (Citron 1993), and offered new ways of reading canonic musical texts (McClary 1991; Solie 1993; Cook and Tsou 1994), among other things. Each anthology brought new theoretical insights to music study. In addition to offering more direct explorations of such subjects as sexuality, the conjoining of racism and sexism, and gender ideologies expressed within structures of power, Cook and Tsou (1994, 3) emphasized their feminist positioning as they sought to "demonstrate that musicology can have its own distinctive a presence in the larger realm of feminist studies." Solie's (1993) anthology focused on a single but enormously complex issue: difference. The importance of positionality and subjectivity was further explored in the first book to present a range of gay and lesbian perspectives in music study (Brett, Wood, and Thomas 1994). Theoretical arguments became more sophisticated, but the cultural relativity of theory itself was still largely ignored.

The current volume builds on these studies but differs in several regards. As stated at the outset, the subjects represented here are culturally plural not only in relation to one another but within themselves. Musical communities are depicted as intercultural, interactive, and responsive to the sweeping changes currently affecting every human society.

As regards our political position, we propose not one correct notion but many possibilities: we demonstrate how the "right" strategies in the struggle for social equality (and here we recognize the interrelatedness of issues of gender, race, class, age, etc.) always depend on the situation. In other words, this anthology opposes a homogeneous approach in gender studies. It includes various positions within feminist and "genderist"[1] studies, revealing mechanisms by which gender is experienced, performed, contested, and masked by both researchers and those with whom they study. We hope that this range of positioning will build a greater understanding of cultural and situational differences and, eventually, encourage new participants in the study of gender and music.

The variety of approaches also reflects the diverse backgrounds of this anthology's contributors. Trained within different national traditions of scholarship (though all North American or European and mostly within "music" schools) and working within yet more varied cultural contexts, the contributors were eager not to hide or ignore points of disjuncture but rather to use them to extend theoretical debates. The following sections show how we engaged in an international "conversation."

Reflecting on Ourselves as Subjects

The Conversation

> *Why can't we give different solutions the right to exist, [recognizing] the right to negotiate gender in many possible ways both inside the life worlds we study and inside our scholarly discourses?*
> —H. Järviluoma

We circulated a set of questions inviting the contributors to share stories about their personal and professional perspectives, as well as opinions, theories, or reflections on the themes for the individual sections of the anthology. The questionnaire was a springboard for an e-mail conversation that spanned three continents and five countries. Although we communicated in English, the first languages of the participants included German, Finnish, Estonian, and Croatian.[2] Our professions are similarly diverse; whereas both editors, as well as Reinhard, Kimberlin, Herndon, Kisliuk, Rüütel and Ceribašić, are ethnomusicologists, Bowers and Myers are trained as historical musicologists, Järviluoma is a music sociologist as well as an ethnomusicologist, McCartney is a composer and musicologist, Pegley is currently a popular music studies scholar but formerly was a professional trumpeter and music educator, Sandstrom is a sound engineer in addition to being an ethnomusicologist, and Dusman is a composer.

It is fair to ask whether the pleasure of this "conversation" was greater than the result or whether we were simply pandering to the current fashion for dialogues within feminist and postmodern scholarship.[3] We hoped that the process had the potential for more open-endedness and greater depth as we struggled over ideas. The responses to our questionnaire seem to indicate that many of the contributors endorse such a process and regard dialogue as a way to get beyond lip service to plurality, a way to encounter our differences and search for their rootedness. The observations and anecdotes we shared with one another demonstrate that many of us regard the personal and the professional as integral and indeed inseparable.

Like any conversation, ours was not systematic but had the advantage of immediacy and interactive energy. Many of the anecdotes reproduced here will enable readers to know some of the personal roots of the contributors' ideas. We touched on differences in the relationship between genderings and music in the different cultures in which we worked, on the variable concepts of gender itself, and on the enterprises for exploring it. We discussed the concept of the "field"—both the field of music and the cultural context for the research presented here, all of which employs ethnographic methods in one way or another. We ranged rather spontaneously over issues of class, ethnocultural context, gender, and aspects of identity that are rarely invoked in the postmodern litany—the identity of being a musician, for example. The conversation demonstrated what Reina Lewis (1996, 15) has said with reference to some of these categories: "We can transform our understanding of each term by analysing its articulation with and through the other." Many of our stories and exchanges explicitly or implicitly explored the language of the questions themselves. What exactly was meant by "experiencing," by "gender," or by "gender in relation to music"?

In some cases the group discussion raised issues directly relevant to the themes of the section introductions. In such cases quotations from the e-mail conversation appear here. For the most part, however, each introduction to this anthology's thematically organized sections attempts to situate feminist or other music scholarship in relation to the issue signaled by the section's title. These issues—performance/performativity, life writing, nationalism, and technological development—are vast and urgent, currently engaging scholars from a wide spectrum of academic disciplines. Our intention is not to control or represent fully these large and complex areas of inquiry but rather to suggest some useful networks of thinking that feminist music students and scholars may choose to pursue, as well as to indicate how the specific essays in this anthology are related to these broader contexts of intellectual inquiry. The networks of ideas that we invite readers to contemplate are sometimes counterpointed with excerpts from the authors' dialogue. The effect of bouncing from the specific and anecdotal to the general and abstract conveys something of the process by which ideas often flow and develop, something of the vitality and edge that stimulate engagement.

The section introductions definitely owe much to all the women who contributed, but at the compilation stage the editors took responsibility. We have tried to identify both those issues where consensus emerged and those where radical differences of opinion are evident. Both the points of agreement and the divergences, which are not homogenized or erased, should stimulate readers' further interpretations.

Many Views on Studying the Relationships of Gender and Music

The musical traditions described in this anthology engage gender, either overtly or covertly, in many different ways. In some instances the symbolism of a genre or style is in itself heavily overlaid with gendered concepts, concepts that may be reflected in song lyrics, performance style, or the discourse about the genre or style. In other cases the discourse about a genre may be less overtly gendered, but practices of "appropriate" behavior (rules about who performs what role and how) reflect attitudes about gender that are widely shared, often in the guise of "natural" rather than constructed genderings. This is the case with the BaAka pygmy rituals studied by Kisliuk, the fiddle tradition of Maritime Canada described by Diamond, and the world of electroacoustic composition with which McCartney deals.

Of course, scholars formulate a wide range of questions in relation to these subjects. Where the gendering is less overt, or even hidden, feminist scholars sometimes attempt to reveal the mechanisms by which gender and other hegemonically asymmetrical constructs are masked within cultures; sometimes they work more as salvage artists, recovering the work of women who have been hitherto ignored or examining the strategies of individuals who renegotiate or defy "appropriate" gendered behaviors through their musical participation.

Bowers is among those who regard the celebration of women's successes in less than encouraging situations to be a major objective of feminist research. She states: "I am continually concerned with women's agency in music—especially with their music making in heavily male-dominated fields such as blues and jazz, to take a couple of examples. I am more interested in history than theory, and in women's roles and position in society and the influence of those on their music-making, than in feminist criticism. My scholarship is very woman-centered."

Sandstrom shares Bowers's woman-centered approach and—along with several other authors—stresses the importance of teaching skills to other women, linking both her research and teaching with her own rough road to success as a sound mix engineer: "Once I became successful in this field, I started a sound engineering class for women to help bring women into the field. Some of the women that took my class are working in the field today. I discuss the differences of how we learned sound compared to men. . . . I understood the problems I encountered learning a gendered field and wanted to devise a way to teach women information I knew they could understand and wanted to know."

These statements thus indicate that the various ways in which music and gender are related to scholars' experiences within specific cultural contexts may indeed affect their research objectives. Furthermore, our contributors prefer different labels for the theoretical positions they adopt concerning these research objectives. In particular, the connotations of *feminist* and *feminism* are contentious.

Diamond labels her work "feminist" since, for her, the word acknowledges a political commitment she regards as important in the North American academy.

At this point, my work (especially the project I wrote about in this anthology) is so committed to understanding the ways in which "difference" is regarded, so engaged in trying to sort out the relationship between lived experience and symbolic systems, that I would have to say feminist ideas influence virtually everything I do.

Currently I am really struck by the power of recent emphases on "performativity" as it relates to gender and music. Approaches that essentialize dichotomies of male and female distress me a lot although I recognize that we still need descriptions and critiques of how these dichotomies have been enacted in various societies. But there have always been strong women (and men) who define themselves outside of the conventions and I really like to see their agency celebrated. This is not just a celebration of diversity but a use of my position as a university teacher to disrupt the presumed naturalness about who or what is important.

Herndon, on the other hand, contests the feminist label as being a North American, white, middle-class construct, though she does not completely reject it.

Some people feel strongly that feminism and feminist theory provide an ideal locus for music and gender studies. I fear that, taken on without careful examination, feminist theory could skew our understanding of those margins or fringes that may hold the best lenses for understanding gender dynamics in relation to music—the western model does not even fit all social groups in the "west." Fringes may look, feel, and be very different when the investigation moves outside of middle-class white analysis. Why can't we believe in the possibility that non-western peoples have systems of understanding, bodies of knowledge, and ways of negotiating human questions, limitations, and predilections? There is not now, nor ever will be, an answer.

Several European authors regarded feminism as an American ethnocentric concept, perhaps partially echoing Herndon's sentiments. Moisala has proposed the term *genderism* as an alternative, since she finds that the use of *feminism* often confuses acknowledged political purposes and unacknowledged cultural biases: "When reading American feminist musicology, I often feel that attempts to raise the status of women scholars and attempts to develop gender studies in music are mixed up. Scholars are not aware of their culture-bound biases. Research is always political, I agree, but one should be aware of both his/her own position and cultural background. Ethnomusicology could give music scholarship a helping hand in this matter, could it not?"

Negotiating the Categories and Codes of Identity

Given the complexity and constraints encountered in any individual's self-representation, it is not surprising that several contributors asserted the importance of different "identity" categories at different stages of their careers. Herndon, whose broad-ranging scholarly (and personal) experience included work with Cherokee communities, American symphony orchestral musicians, Maltese Islanders, and Tibetan refugees, explained how the categorization used to make sense of her presence varied with the cultural context.

> Working with the Eastern Cherokee in North Carolina and Tennessee, gender was less important than ethnicity, being known as a halfbreed, a "local," and not someone who came merely to take (knowledge, information, secrets, insights) away. . . . In Malta, I was less important than my expensive Nagra tape recorder. I was only the genderless operator of the tape recorder. This was part of a cultural fiction devised in order to allow a female into the bars and other performance venues for music. Since they knew I was not a Maltese prostitute (and only prostitutes sang in public), after I did sing in public, they created an elaborate "story" about how I was an objective researcher (not a person?) who should be cooperated with, talked to freely and so on.

Dusman asserts that being a "musician" was itself the most important identity category for her. "I think about the idea that 'being musical' is an identity that develops before a consciousness of sex. And so when discriminatory things happened to me, I didn't identify them as being based on gender—I identified them as happening because I wasn't a good enough musician yet, that I needed to work harder at my music." The prioritization of the category "musician" not only affected her self-esteem but caused her to think of herself in divided terms. "There was the 'me' that was a musician, that didn't have much to do with the 'me' that was involved in relationships, or the 'me' that was in my family. . . . So it is only during the last three or four years that I have been working on integrating these separate parts of myself, allowing myself to speak as a woman composing music, as a woman investigating how people respond to music, as a lesbian thinking about my relationship with music in performance."

Other authors also speak about a related division of self: their perceived need to "erase" their gender to do the work they chose to do. Sandstrom, for example, states: "I didn't realize it at the time, but through my association with sound equipment and my role as a mix engineer, I became somewhat gender neutral and to a certain extent race/ethnic neutral. I participated in events that I would normally not have access to. . . . I am interested in seeing a time when one's access to participating and communicating is not dependent on losing your gender because of your job."

Järviluoma, Ceribašić, and Diamond all describe their assumptions of gender neutrality in the early years of their professional work, assumptions shaped by the traditions of their disciplines. Such assumptions clearly frame the social interactions in their professional lives in rather unusual ways. Several contributors were or are aware that they were regarded as improper persons because of the ways in which they "negotiated" gender through denial or the use of categories inappropriate for the cultural context. Moisala, for example, reflects candidly on the ethnocentrism of her earliest work with Gurung women in Nepal and her personal learning process, in which both the culture she has studied and that of her own nation are influential.

> During my first field work at the age of 21, I was upset about the low position and status of women in Gurung culture. I paid attention to things such as who does all the household work. In other words, I looked at the position of Gurung women with the eyes of a young European feminist. But in the course of the past 20 years and several other field trips, I have learned to observe the gender relations in the Gurung culture differently, hopefully, understanding more from the actor-oriented view the balance-seeking dynamism of the Gurung gender system and, as a result of that, I nowadays question many "women's issues" in a way which some other feminists might regard as unorthodox.

Järviluoma, on the other hand, makes the important point that our awareness of experience and our signification of it is inevitably marked by blind spots and erasures: "It is very much possible that we only can articulate the things that are least important when we try to describe how we experience gender in the field. The most forceful motivations of our psyche may be the ones which remain blind and deaf spots, because we have intensively repressed them." Her insistence that we acknowledge blind spots relates to the issues of "framing" or "ideation" that Herndon raises in her previously quoted statements. These themes are implicitly referenced in the stories that several authors exchanged about the development of their awareness of gender issues in relation to music, stories indicating that, as Järviluoma reminded, us "gender is an attitude." Most of us were not conscious of such issues at the early stages of our careers, although several remember the prescriptions and proscriptions by which they were defined as female. For many, the growth of their gender awareness was marked by specific, decisive events or occasions, often in the company of other women. Sandstrom found a community at the Michigan Womyn's Music Festival; Järviluoma, among her own female relatives in Finland; and both Bowers and Dusman, in the women's studies programs in their universities. Bowers relates:

> As far as studying gender in relation to music, that came much, much later. I went to a women's college, but most of my music professors were men, except for the person who taught the freshman course and the orchestra conductor and we certainly didn't discuss women composers or anything having to do with women in music. Since the college had high intellectual standards, we all were encouraged to excel academically, though. There were no men to inhibit our discussion of anything in class. In fact, I chose a women's college because I had gotten tired of listening to boys talk so much in high school. I guess I wasn't too impressed with most of what they said. . . .
>
> It was after I completed my Ph.D. and was teaching at a university that a friend suggested I might like reading Virginia Woolf's *A Room of One's Own*. That was what really got me fired up about looking into women composers. I thought that if there were many women writers we didn't know anything about, there were probably women composers too. And Virginia Woolf was so provocative in the way she compared the social conditions of women's and men's lives. . . . When I was teaching at the Eastman School of Music, Joan Kelly-Gadol came to the University of Rochester and talked about studying the history of women in a very exciting way. She also referred me to Linda Nochlin's wonderful article about the question, "Why have there been no great women artists?" That opened up another whole line of thinking about women and art to me. I got a lot of my methodology from women's historians such as Gerda Lerner, with whom I took a course in the mid-70s.

Dusman also experienced important shifts in her gender awareness during her early professional years:

> I think my female-consciousness began when I started working in the computer-music studio, however, because I was aware immediately that I had a kind of fear of electronics that my male colleagues didn't share. I

know now that when things weren't working for them, they just solved the problem and didn't tell anyone that there had been any problems (some of them told me this in later conversations). But when I had problems, there was this knee-jerk reaction in my head that it was because I was a woman. I want to make clear that this was never stated by my faculty mentor, yet I know I must not have dreamed this up on my own. All ideas come from somewhere, right? . . .

When I got a faculty position at Clark, where there is a strong Women's Studies program, I found feminist theory to be a common interest with my colleagues and a critical catalyst to my ability to "come out" as a lesbian.

McCartney's experience in an electroacoustic studio is articulated a bit differently, but it is not unrelated to Dusman's isolation:

My initial experience with music technologies entailed feelings of loneliness and an uncomfortable sense of not belonging that was present enough to discourage me, yet subtle enough to sometimes make me wonder whether I was over-reacting. I discovered that there was a MIDI Users' Group in Peterborough, Ontario, where I lived at the time. I was surprised to find that I was the only woman member the group had ever had. . . . At one point, a speaker handed out outlines of his talk to everyone except me, walking past me as if I was not there, perhaps assuming that I was accompanying one of the other members.

The ability to negotiate situations that are isolating or antagonistic was a recurrent theme in our dialogue. McCartney, for example, now seeks out environments that are "woman friendly" and feels her "increased confidence and knowledge," as well as her research on gender and technology, have helped her to cope with more threatening situations. Sandstrom similarly sought out new alliances while establishing her sound-engineering business in defiance of norms and expectations.

In a somewhat more complex account of negotiation, Pegley contrasts her experiences as a professional performer and as a music educator:

As a teenager (from a white, middle-class family on the East coast of Canada) I wanted to play my trumpet for a living. When I entered university to study music, I was fortunate to have the opportunity to perform with a local professional orchestra. Ironically, however, I wanted even more to play with a local big band but the band leader stated that no females were ever going to perform in his group. Eventually he broke this rule and let me in, but not before I was pretty torn by it all. Playing in a symphony, unfortunately, was not always that much easier: one summer, while studying abroad in a collegium musicum, I found myself to be the only female in the section and the only English-speaking player. Often in sectional rehearsals conversations shifted languages and I had little time to mentally translate. Occasionally, I was told by my male colleagues that nothing important had been discussed and not to worry about it, which left me frustrated, particularly when I was supposed to be leading the sectional. Yet I was good friends with these men and spent a lot of social time with them. Our friendships [encouraged] me to try and appreciate their position of never having had to negotiate with a female performer in their section. At times I felt marginalized but driven to continue. Somehow, through all of this, I felt like I had the "right" gender, but the "wrong" sex.

In my music education training my sex was not an issue, but, to my surprise, my gender was a problem. I felt that I was being encouraged to be "softer" in vocal timbre and gesture, and dress in more "appropriate" (i.e. "feminine") styles within the classroom. Once again, I found the translation difficult. As a music educator, ironically, I was the "right" sex, but the "wrong" gender.

Pegley uses the concept of translation to help her process of negotiation. This concept is similar to the sort of "code switching" described in situations recounted by Moisala, Herndon, and Järviluoma in relation to negotiations of gender in the field. The Nepalese community in which Moisala worked engaged in code switching because it did not accept her as a woman until she fulfilled their gender expectations. Not until she was recognized as a woman could she properly study women's music.

During my first field trip, I did not fulfill the image or expectations the Gurungs had of a woman: I did not follow the duties and norms placed on women in Gurung society—I did not carry water, clean and prepare the mud floor before my husband woke up; I did not have bracelets but had trousers and short hair. Consequently, I was treated as the younger son, *kancha,* and allowed, for instance, to participate in an all-male meal but, at the same time, it was not possible for me to enter the female musical world. Nine years later, I achieved the full status of woman in the eyes of the Gurungs, because I had a male child with me. During that field trip, tens of Gurung women visited my room; we exchanged our life stories and spoke about music.

Herndon reminds us of the sometimes difficult, sometimes amusing situations that arise when the anticipated gender codes are not shared:

> The only gender problem I had was when I hired a Maltese singer who had lost his job on the docks to help translate difficult song texts. I did not know he was also a gigolo—he didn't know that I didn't know his second profession. He arrived dressed for gigolo work—skin tight pants, white shirt with red ruffles open to the navel, gold chain around his neck, lots of aftershave. When I explained what I wanted (translation help) he sat down and got to work for eight hours, and then I took him to his home village in the car. When we arrived, he said "Is that all?" I assured him it was and he continued to be a confused, but willing, translator for the next six weeks.

Järviluoma describes how she accepted a controversial "appropriate" gender role in the field:

> In 1988, when I started the participant observation of the group I am writing about in this anthology . . . I was 28 and the group consisted mostly of men who were between 50 and 75. There was a lot of negotiation going on between the group and me. I think that we tried to find a form to the relationships which wouldn't endanger anyone's work—theirs or mine. The director developed a solution: he renamed me as the "princess." After the second rehearsal I attended, he called me "princess" and this went on until the end of the research period (7 months). The term was used only by him and only inside the group. When outsiders were present, he used my first name. It is not innocent that a certain category is chosen to describe the researcher or the consultants. It tells about the delicate selection of codes that both the musicians and I had available during the different stages of the process.
>
> I read, at some point, a book called *Women and Social Interaction*. It said that women are often treated as mascots, sometimes helpers, [as if they are] often in need of fatherly protection. This can also be USEFUL to women researchers. Often it is not.
>
> We discussed my being named a "princess" in a qualitative research course at the University of Tampere. What were the features that go firstly with the category of "princess" and secondly, with a "researcher"? Many thought that the researcher category included a certain degree of seriousness, the irrelevance of gender, objectivity. "Princess" seemed to deny and minimise the features that were connected to the "researcher" category. She was a creature from fairy tales, not dangerous, only a pretty little girl.

The knowledge of the princess does not threaten anyone; thus she does not threaten the knowledge of the musicians.

But I would add that, similarly, the knowledge of the folk does not threaten the knowledge of the princess either. The term "princess" is not neutral; it has moral [obligations]. You have to treat princesses with respect; she belongs to royalty. Thus the people who use the term are categorised as "gentlemen." This meant that, for instance, rough jokes were not told when I was present.

"Princess" also belongs to the category of "proud and happy family" and the category of "the longed for baby girl." . . . Young women were sincerely welcomed to the group and appreciated, but at the same time borders were kept with the names. A few years later when I visited the group they had a 14-year-old playing keyboards. She was, naturally, called "princess." I was called by my first name then.

Järviluoma reports that the discussion at the University of Tampere raised many questions: "Does the princess go to the loo? Does she have a body, desires, and the right to be many-faceted? One of the discussants asked if it would be possible to call a male researcher a prince."

Järviluoma's and Herndon's stories have humorous moments but also imply serious issues. As was noted in our dialogue, the gender expectations that female researchers must negotiate in social situations essential to their work are different (usually more constrained) from those encountered by male researchers. Because the strategies we employ to negotiate such situations are not widely discussed within professional communities, the subject and its scholarly implications are still too often ignored in the academic world.

Furthermore, the very notion of the constructedness of gender categories asserted in the stories by Dusman, Bowers, Diamond, Pegley, and McCartney—all of whom are English-speaking North Americans—contrasts with the concepts in other ethnocultural and national circumstances. Moisala alluded to this when she spoke about developing an unorthodox view relative "to some other feminists" in the company of Gurung women. She elaborates on this:

Gender is[,] like music, defined by culture, time/history, situation, and experienced/performed by an individual. As ethnomusicologists, that's what we should emphasize theoretically: cultural relativism before feminist theory. Even though feminist theories have emphasized differences for a long time, I still feel that most of it is very ethnocentric. It has created its own discourse of truth in which "other voices" are only mentioned but still not allowed equal power and opportunity to speak and participate. Too often, the political aims of western feminists silence the other voices.

Ceribašić reminded us that the ethnocentricity of concepts is embedded in language. She observes a more literal kind of "translation" than the one described earlier in relation to behavioral shifts: "The notion of gender in the English language hadn't any parallel, until recently, in Croatian. Now the term 'gender' is translated by the word 'rod' which indicates lineage and parentage (family structure), and which isn't fixed with regard to gender. It is hard, therefore, to translate other words derived from the noun 'gender' (for example, the phrase 'gendered structures,' translated word for word, sounds very odd). In short, until recently in the Croatian language and culture . . . only the concept of sex existed."

International feminist discourse has inspired other cultures to redefine their vocabulary in regard to gender. Nonetheless, culturally embedded connotations most often remain, as Moisala writes with regard to Swedish and Finnish gender concepts.

In both Swedish and Finnish, there used to be only one word, *kön* and *sukupuoli,* respectively, to indicate both sex and its gendered dimensions. It means that the meaning of these words was closer to sex than gender. In Finnish, we speak nowadays about *sosiaalinen sukupuoli* (social "sex") when referring to gender while sukupuoli refers to sex only and, similarly in Swedish, a newly constructed word *genus* is used in addition to kön. These concepts, however, still maintain something about the primary ways to think about sex and gender in these cultures.

Kisliuk reminds us of the word's history in English, where it seems to have arisen first as a way to describe a particular grammatical aspect of certain languages. She suggests that English grammar's lack of this aspect allowed the word *gender* to expand (relatively recently) to mean the social construction of sex roles.

The ways in which language and culturally embedded concepts articulate understandings of gender clearly militate against a homogeneous view of theoretical issues in gender and music studies.

Gender and the Field

The social and geophysical locations of the research represented in this volume diverge widely. From the closed spaces of North American classrooms or studios to African public squares and Croatian airwaves, neither the sites nor mediations of music are homogeneous in any way. Sandstrom, Dusman, Pegley, and McCartney work with North American colleagues or students, Rüütel and Myers work with Europeans in various national contexts, Ceribašić researches her Croatian compatriots, Diamond investigates Maritime Canadians, and Järviluoma and Moisala work with fellow Finns, but Kisliuk, Reinhard, and Kimberlin describe encounters with otherness in their residence with BaAka Pygmies, Turkish women, and Ethiopian musicians, respectively. Bowers and Diamond study genres that are not "theirs" but that are central to the identity of their country. Herndon describes systems she understands as a result of various inter- and intracultural projects.

It may be not just this diversity, however, but the fact that gender has been so fully implicated in contemporary critiques of otherness[4] that leads several contributors to problematize the concept of "fieldwork" altogether. The imperialist associations of folk music research that objectified cultures defined as "other"—or even segments of one's own—while contributing to discourses of national identity was a source of discomfort for some. Järviluoma was especially articulate about this issue as she described her "love-hate relationship with field research" poised between the fascinating and problematic aspects.

> The history of field work in the Finnish tradition of research on folk music is long and impressive. I stepped into that world in the late 1970s. I joined the field research trips led by professor Erkki Ala-Könni. He is perhaps the last member of the old school of folk music collecting and studying in Finland. These trips made me think intensively of the concept of "field," about the history of folk music collecting and studying, about the history of ethnomusicology. As Foucault might have pointed out if he had known what we did during those trips, the history of Finnish ethnomusicology is as polluted as the histories of other human sciences. They are part of the disciplinary technologies of modern society.

Like many feminist scholars, she eventually reconciled her conflicted relationship with fieldwork by reframing her role within an intersubjective encounter:

> I started to teach at the university in 1986—things like field technology and field methodology. I had already been reflecting deeply on the problematics of field research; however, as Foucault again says, peoples'

practices change much more slowly than their thoughts. My practices were very much the same as they had been in 1979. The old concept of "field" was working inside me as if it had a life of its own.

[Since that time], I [no longer] try to make myself invisible in the research process. I can't step outside ethnocentrism. I have to try to live with myself. I like Roy Turner's definition in his article "Deconstructing the Field" (see my article): the field constitutes an attitude, a point of view which will force an intersection of the interests of the inquirer and the life of the subject. I have taken this idea further and said that the researcher, just as well as the field, can be seen as an attitude.

Whereas Järviluoma implies a problematization of the division between insider and outsider, other contributors addressed this dichotomization more directly. On the one hand, Herndon recognized that her relationships and responsibilities changed depending on her relationship to the various communities in which she worked. Ceribašić's work on her own culture, on the other hand, makes no separation between the "field" and her "own culture." Several contributors, including Kisliuk and Moisala, describe a process in which they began as complete outsiders but acquired a measure of insider stature within the communities in which they worked. Moisala's was perhaps the most transformative since, in the eyes of her Gurung friends, she changed from a badly interpreted outsider/insider, a young man (*kancha*), to an accepted older sister (*didi*) during her latest field trip to Nepal.

In conclusion, we suggest that the candid personal stories that emerged in our dialogue are integrally related to important theoretical issues such as the concept of "field," the choice of identity roles in relation to professional work, and the pedagogical and intellectual engagements we make within the institutions where we work. The cultural relativity of research methodologies, including the comfort or discomfort that different scholars feel with categories such as "feminist," is demonstrated by these fragments of the personal. Moving our usually untold experiences from the privacy of our memories to the printed page is, we believe, an important step in giving "different solutions the right to exist."

NOTES

This introduction was prepared with the assistance of Marcia Herndon, Helmi Järviluoma, Naila Ceribašić, Boden Sandstrom, Karen Pegley, Andra McCartney, Linda Dusman, Michelle Kisliuk, and Jane Bowers.

1. Some of the European contributors to this volume prefer this term.

2. This linguistic diversity forced us to clarify meanings and nuances of English-language terms—often with surprising results; in addition, the non-English speakers sometimes construed English terms differently and made English-speakers more aware of cultural biases. One instance was Ceribašić's coining of the phrase "gender sensible" in contexts were Americans would probably have used "gender sensitive." Often the Croatian formulation was much more apt.

3. Within ethnomusicology, examples include the dialogues between Diamond, Cronk, and von Rosen that precede each chapter of *Visions of Sound* (1994) or the Keil-Feld conversations in *Music Grooves* (1994). Specifically focusing on the dialogic process is Dennis Tedlock's and Bruce Mannheim's collection *The Dialogic Emergence of Culture* (1995).

4. Studies such as Trinh T. Minh-ha's *Woman Native Other* (1989) or Gayatri Chakravorty Spivak's *In Other Worlds: Essays in Cultural Politics* (1987) were among the most important contributions of the late 1980s. Such issues as women's complicity with imperialism (see, for example, Reina Lewis's *Gendering Orientalism: Race, Femininity, and Representation* [1996]) have been addressed more recently.

REFERENCES CITED

Bowers, Jane, and Judith Tick, eds. 1987. *Women Making Music: The Western Art Tradition, 1150–1950.* Urbana: University of Illinois Press.

Brett, Phillip, Elizabeth Wood, and Gary C. Thomas, eds. 1994. *Queering the Pitch: The New Gay and Lesbian Musicology.* New York: Routledge.

Citron, Marcia J. 1993. *Gender and the Musical Canon.* Cambridge: Cambridge University Press.

Cook, Susan C., and Judy S. Tsou, eds. 1994. *Cecilia Reclaimed: Feminist Perspectives on Gender and Music.* Urbana: University of Illinois Press.

Diamond, Beverley, M. Sam Cronk, and Franziska von Rosen. 1994. *Visions of Sound: Musical Instruments of First Nations Communities in Northeastern America.* Chicago: University of Chicago Press; Waterloo, Ont.: Wilfrid Laurier University Press.

Herndon, Marcia, and Susanne Ziegler, eds. 1990. *Music, Gender, and Culture.* Intercultural Music Studies, 1. Wilhelmshaven, Germany: F. Noetzel Verlag.

Keil, Charles, and Steven Feld. 1994. *Music Grooves: Essays and Dialogues.* Chicago: University of Chicago Press.

Koskoff, Ellen, ed. 1989. *Women and Music in Cross-Cultural Perspective.* Urbana: University of Illinois Press.

Lewis, Reina. 1996. *Gendering Orientalism: Race, Femininity, and Representation.* London: Routledge.

McClary, Susan. 1991. *Feminine Endings.* Minneapolis: University of Minnesota Press.

Marshall, Kimberly, ed. 1993. *Rediscovering the Muses: Women's Musical Traditions.* Boston: Northeastern University Press.

Solie, Ruth, ed. 1993. *Musicology and Difference: Gender and Sexuality in Music Scholarship.* Berkeley: University of California Press.

Spivak, Gayatri Chakravorty. 1987. *In Other Worlds: Essays in Cultural Politics.* London: Methuen.

Tedlock, Dennis, and Bruce Mannheim, eds. 1995. *The Dialogic Emergence of Culture.* Urbana: University of Illinois Press.

Trinh T. Minh-ha. 1989. *Woman, Native, Other.* Bloomington: Indiana University Press.

Part 1

Music Performance and Performativity

Although the study of performance has always been central to ethnomusicology, the past two decades have arguably witnessed the most vigorous development of methodologies and approaches.[1] Early ethnomusicological landmarks include McLeod and Herndon's *Ethnography of Musical Performance* (1980) and Behague's *Performance Practice: Ethnomusicological Perspectives* (1984). That stage involved the definition of elements of "performance": spatiotemporal framing, the role of an audience, and the nature of the "texts" of such events. Scholars have been fascinated by the ways in which performances vary with context and the means whereby value systems are both mirrored and challenged by such events. More recent work has been less concerned with the boundaries of "performance," seeing everyday and more formalized discourses as interconnected and often rather fluid. Some scholars now examine performance not as the product but as the process of realizing other social goals for example, as part of the negotiation of identity, the symbolic mapping of space and relationship, or the transformation of consciousness.[2]

The essays included here represent three very different approaches to the study of performance. Those by Kisliuk and Järviluoma are process oriented, regarding performance not as bounded and discrete but as fluid and contingent, created in the moment as an interactive event involving all participants, including the researcher. Furthermore, they treat musical performance as "performative,"[3] an activity that accomplishes something as performers adopt a social position, reinforce some aspect of their identity, or generate or reflect tension and change.

Kisliuk's work emerges from the New York University school of performance studies, a group usually associated with American theater scholar Richard Schechner (1988, 1990) as well as with the British ritual theorist

Victor Turner (1986). Here, however, even the more formalized events—"ritual processes," in Turner's language—are not cast, as they once were, either as enactments of stable forces or as containments of transgressive behaviors (or unmanageable power). Rather, like that of Margaret Drewal in *Yoruba Ritual: Performers, Play, Agency* (1991), Kisliuk's approach rejects concepts that imply a static quality in favor of a performer-centered model that foregrounds the agency of the actor.

Kisliuk deals with effects of modernization for the BaAka pygmies; she examines shifts from a forager economy to one mixed with an agrarian market economy while emphasizing that cultural interaction in the contemporary world cannot be reduced to changes in mode of production. Her work provides a valuable example of the contribution that specific, detailed ethnography can make to our understanding of the mechanisms by which gender identities are negotiated.

Using a discourse analysis method developed by Harvey Sacks, Järviluoma explores how gender concepts are maintained and produced in the process of everyday music rehearsals. Her approach centers not only on the fact that categories carry collective meaning but also on the fact that categorization itself is in constant flux in interactional situations. She focuses on the discourse of an amateur *pelimanni* music ensemble of a small country town in Finland, investigating the means by which women are constructed as marginal. She—like other contributors in our dialogue—also reflects on her own negotiation of gendered expectations.

Reinhard's article, which focuses largely on musical texts rather than performance events, may seem out of place in this section. Nevertheless, her exploration of the causes of regionally variable attitudes toward gender representation, the weighing of historical contingencies against other factors, allows us to view musical pieces themselves as part of a dynamic system. By examining a relatively stable repertory, her study acknowledges that in some circumstances continuity is regarded as a necessary response to the pressures of change.

In each case, then, the complexity of factors that impinge on performance decisions and the agency of participants is emphasized.

Notes

1. This period is partially congruent with the flourishing of performance practice studies in historical musicology, although its emphasis on issues of authen-

ticity and historically accurate interpretation differ substantially from ethnomusicologists' concerns with the social production of performance.

2. Many music ethnographies pay close attention to the specificity of particular performance events, their contexts, and the layering of their meaningful components, including the contradictions that they embody. The following are recommended as important models of contemporary ethnomusicological approaches: "Three Fiestas," in Turino 1993 (94–116); "The Gig," in Cohen 1991 (103–34); chapters 1, 2 and 6 of Seeger 1987; and Sugarman 1997.

3. Although far from the earliest usage of the term, a definition often cited by feminist musicologists is that of Judith Butler (1990, 136): "Such acts, gestures, enactments . . . are *performative* in the sense that the essence or identity that they otherwise purport to express are *fabrications* manufactured and sustained through corporeal signs and other discursive means."

References Cited

Behague, Gerard. 1984. *Performance Practice: Ethnomusicological Perspectives.* Westport, Conn.: Greenwood.

Butler, Judith. 1990. *Gender Trouble: Feminism and the Subversion of Identity.* New York: Routledge.

Cohen, Sara. 1991. *Rock Culture in Liverpool: Popular Music in the Making.* Oxford: Clarendon.

Drewal, Margaret. 1991. *Yoruba Ritual: Performers, Play, Agency.* Bloomington: Indiana University Press.

McLeod, Norma, and Marcia Herndon. 1980. *The Ethnography of Musical Performance.* Norwood, Pa.: Norwood.

Schechner, Richard. 1988 [1977]. *Performance Theory.* Rev. ed. New York: Routledge.

Schechner, Richard, and W. Appel, eds. 1990. *By Means of Performance: Intercultural Studies of Theatre and Ritual.* Cambridge: Cambridge University Press.

Seeger, Anthony. 1987. *Why Suyá Sing: A Musical Anthropology of an Amazonian People.* Cambridge: Cambridge University Press.

Sugarman, Jane. 1997. *Engendering Song: Singing and Subjectivity at Prespa Albanian Weddings.* Chicago: University of Chicago Press.

Turino, Thomas. 1993. *Moving Away from Silence: Music of the Peruvian Altiplano and the Experience of Urban Migration.* Chicago: University of Chicago Press.

Turner, Victor. 1986. *Anthropology of Performance.* New York: PAJ Publications.

Performance and Modernity among BaAka Pygmies: A Closer Look at the Mystique of Egalitarian Foragers in the Rain Forest

Michelle Kisliuk

The music of African forest peoples, or "pygmies," has for some time held a special place in the ethnomusicological imagination. In the varied and impressive writings of Colin Turnbull (1961, 1965, 1978, 1981, 1983), Alan Lomax (1976), Robert Farris Thompson (1989), and Simha Arom (1978, 1991), the yodeling, hocketing sound of pygmy singing has served as an icon of social and musical utopia and an image of egalitarianism.[1]

At the heart of my initial interest in this topic was the incomparable sound of pygmy singing. Before ever going to the Central African Republic (Centrafrique), I heard recordings and read descriptions like this one by Simha Arom:

> the beauty of the songs, the characteristic timbre of pygmy voices, at once rough and warm. . . . this music is collective and everyone participates; there is no apparent hierarchy in the distribution of parts; each person seems to enjoy complete liberty; the voices swell out in all directions; solo lines alternate in the same piece without any pre-set order, while overall the piece remains in strict precision! It is this, perhaps, which is the most striking thing about this music, if one had to sum it up in a few words: a simultaneous dialectic between rigor and freedom, between a musical framework and a margin within which individuals can maneuver. This, moreover, reflects perfectly the social organization of the pygmies—if only mentioned in passing—and it does so perhaps not by chance. (Arom 1983, 29–30; my translation)

A seductive vision of pygmy song as an "emblem" for utopian human potentials as well as for quintessential origins surfaces repeatedly in both popular and scholarly literature. As a student I read with both wonder and skepticism Alan Lomax's characterization of a socially and musically egalitarian paradise among pygmies:

> The Bushman and Pygmy people living close to the source of man's known beginnings have a music that might have come from the Garden of Eden. In their complementary, chiefless, egalitarian, and pacifist societies, men and women, old and young, are linked in close interdependence by preference and not by force. Here, where bands of gathering women bring home most of the food, group singing is not only contrapuntal but polyrhythmic, a playful weaving of four and more strands of short, flowing, canon-like melodies (each voice imitating the melody of the others), sounding wordless streams of vowels in clear, bell-like yodeling voices. (Lomax 1976, 38)

Part of what attracted me to study among pygmies was the very suggestion that the structure and performance style of their singing might be consistent with an overall egalitarian lifestyle. As I read about pygmies and their music, however, I wondered to what extent the real people embody the images that scholars, artists, and journalists have enthusiastically claimed they do, and I designed my research to address this question. My field research in Centrafrique spanned nine years as of 1995, including a two-year stay. During those core two years, 1987 through 1989, I became familiar with and participated in the contemporary repertory of hunting dances and women's dances in the area where I lived (the Bagandou region of southwestern Centrafrique). Early in my research I learned that the BaAka in this area have some dances exclusively for women, and I began my efforts to understand the performance style, aesthetics, and micropolitics of BaAka social life by singing and dancing with the women. Having read—and then observed—that pygmies have a relatively egalitarian society (Turnbull 1961, 1965; Bahuchet 1985; Hewlett 1986; Lomax 1968; Arom 1978), I wanted to know in detail whether and how such egalitarianism might take shape in performances controlled by women. In this essay I focus on this issue and aim to summarize what I learned.

Along with the question of egalitarianism, "modernity" is also a theme in my study. I choose the concept of modernity in part to underline that BaAka and other forest peoples—so often imagined as representing a mythical past—are living as you or I within the modern world. Sociologist Anthony Giddens (1990, 15) affirms that although "modernity," as defined by rapid and sweeping change, was established in postfeudal Europe, it is now world historical in impact. Giddens (1990, 5–6) also points out that pervasive notions of social evolutionism (crucial to the colonialist and missionary ideologies that surround and pervade BaAka experience) have masked the workings of modernity outside Europe, especially among so-called "hunters and gatherers."[2]

BaAka

The BaAka[3] (sing., MoAka) pygmies live between the Sangha and Oubangui Rivers in southwestern Centrafrique and extend as far south as Impfondo in the Republic of the Congo. They live mostly in densely forested areas, and their culture is based largely on a hunting and foraging lifestyle. During the past few decades, however, these pygmies (like most other pygmies of equatorial Africa) have become more involved in farm work, either as seasonal laborers for village-based farmers from other ethnic groups or, increasingly, on their own small subsistence plantations cut into the dense forest. Like most forest peoples, the BaAka are generally disfranchised from the African nation-state they inhabit. They do not vote or hold identity papers, and they rarely attend school or receive government health care; on the other hand, they do not pay taxes, nor are they expected to obtain visas or passes to cross borders in the region (which includes Centrafrique, Congo, and Cameroon).[4] Forces currently impinging on their lives include international lumber interests, evangelical missionaries, and African commercial hunters who use shotguns and sell smoked game meat in the city.

I focused my research in a rural community called Bagandou, south of the capital and next to the border with the Republic of the Congo. The Bantu-speaking people of Bagandou are mostly from the Bangando ethnic group.[5] The Bagandou have a long-standing, hereditary exchange relationship with the BaAka of the region. Various terms have been used to characterize this relationship—clientship, parasitism, vassalage, and even slavery (see Bahuchet 1985, 554–55). These broad but contradictory terms betray the complex and changing nature of relationships between pygmies and their neighbors across equatorial Africa. Many Bagandou villagers consider themselves to be virtual relatives of BaAka and emphasize that they have had this clan-based patron-client relationship for hundreds of years. Justin Mongosso, a farmer from Bagandou (now my husband), has been my teacher and research consultant since 1986. Though Justin is not typical, he is an example of a villager who has a mutually positive and affectionate relationship with BaAka.

The Idea of Egalitarianism

Marina Roseman, an ethnomusicologist who works with a rain forest population in Malaysia, has a working definition of egalitarian social systems. Citing Fried, Collier, and Rosaldo, she characterizes them as societies "in which the labor or obedience of one adult cannot be coerced by another adult. Members retain the prerogative of withdrawing from untenable relationships or coercive commands" (Roseman 1984, 413). Although this description is generally true for BaAka as I know them, relations between BaAka and villagers (*bilo*) are not egalitarian. Chandra Jayawardena (1968) suggests that egalitarianism is notably present among people who share a "lower-class" status. He states that "notions of human equality are dominant in a subgroup to the extent that it is denied social equality by the wider society or its dominant class" (Jayawardena 1968, 414). If one were to view BaAka and Bagandou villagers as subgroups of a single regional society, as Grinker (1990) and others view Efe pygmies and neighboring groups in Zaire, one might explain BaAka egalitarian values as having arisen in reaction to their oppression by their neighbors. This raises historical questions, however: how recent are the current BaAka/bilo relations, how have they been changing, and to what extent are egalitarian values among BaAka independent of their relationship to bilo?

The concept of egalitarianism can imply a static state of affairs, whereas real life is in constant motion and defies such categories. It is a tricky task, then, to discuss egalitarianism when we really mean an egalitarianism relative to and perhaps more developed than our own. Remarkably, moreover, the anthropological literature has usually set aside the question of gender when discussing egalitarianism, although Eleanor Leacock and others (Strathern 1987; Bell 1987) have rightly insisted that the issue of gender "in egalitarian society is inseparable from the analysis of egalitarian social-economic structure as a whole" (Leacock 1981, 133). And, Leacock adds, "concepts based on the hierarchical structure of our society distort both" (ibid.).

A Performance Approach

Before outlining my case study, I will briefly explain the approach I take here—what I call a *performance* approach—which overlaps with epistemological issues in current feminist scholarship (e.g., Abu-Lughod 1990).[6] The search for nonobjectivist (and anti-imperialist) scholarship brings ethnomusicology into the movement taking place in many corners of the humanities and social sciences. The task of placing oneself in the epistemological center of inquiry (and bearing necessarily "partial truths" [Clifford 1986]—if any) as a step toward nonobjectivist scholarship poses various questions particular to musical ethnography. Whereas anthropology has wrestled with issues of reflexivity (then postmodernism and deconstruction—see, for example, Rosaldo 1989; Tyler 1986; and Visweswaran 1994) over the past several decades, such issues are ironically still relatively dormant in ethnomusicological discourse, even though they take a particularly penetrating and postmodern turn when applied to the study of performance.[7] When we participate in performance—as ethnomusicologists have for decades—self/other boundaries are undeniably blurred.

A performance approach, as I define it, suggests that ethnographers be as explicit as possible about the conditions that delimit their inquiries. A problem with much conventional ethnography is the tendency to generalize into theory based on a specific interpretive situation. A focus on experience helps to situate readers within the fluctuations and complexities of research, social life, and performance and then leads to theorizing partial truths from those particularities. This requires writing in a way that evokes this immediacy and particularity: beginning with their own perceptions, such ethnographers weave narratives based on the *conversations* within which they are engaged. This does not imply, as some critics have contended, that power relations are somehow level in such conversations. To the contrary, power relations are continually shifting, multileveled, and resonant with history and circumstance. A focus on conversation (or dialogue)—during which power relations are in fact negotiated—obliges researchers and writers to address and examine those relations.

There are at least three interdependent levels of conversation (both literal and metaphorical) in a fully performative ethnography: (1) ongoing conversations between the field researcher and the people among whom he or she works; (2) the researcher's "conversations" with the experiences and materials of performance, such as song, dance, and storytelling, and by extension, issues of politics, social life, and aesthetics; and (3) the ethnography—a textual representation and evocation of the first two levels of conversation, written as a narrative metaconversation among the ethnographer, his or her virtual readers, and the material and ideas addressed. In this essay I use the approach just outlined to address the question of performance and gender in the ever-changing world of BaAka.

BaAka Gendered Performance

Women play central roles in the rituals and protocols surrounding the Ba-Aka net hunt, including *bobanda,* a ritual performed to counteract hunting failure (see McCreedy 1994). Moreover, although the literature on BaAka social organization (e.g., Bahuchet 1985, 93) cites only three specialized status roles in BaAka society (the older or eldest sibling, the master hunter, and the healer/diviner—*kombeti, ntuma,* and *nganga,* respectively), BaAka also accord status to the master of a dance or song repertory, the *ginda.* Unlike the other three roles, which are usually filled by men, a ginda can be a man or a woman, depending on the dance. Like the other special roles among BaAka, however, the ginda holds a status relevant only within the context of that person's particular specialty.

A focus on gender relations during performances of BaAka dances illuminates how BaAka negotiate power within dynamic circumstances. Ongoing, informal negotiation and disputed expectations are part of BaAka social dynamics and are highlighted in performance. An "egalitarian" sensibility, coupled with individual autonomy, makes for a cultural climate of constant negotiation (Dumont 1986; see also Turnbull 1961). In the context of the women's dances, *Dingboku* and *Elamba,* gendered wills intensify the social fray.

Dingboku is performed by women in a line (often several lines made up of women related by residential camp or clan). They stand linked at the shoulder and then step forward and back, swiveling around as a line. In one instance in 1989, BaAka were invited to perform at a funeral for a villager in Bagandou. During a break between rounds of a dance called *Mabo*—a mixed-gender net-hunting dance—some women began Dingboku. The men in control of the drums refused to cede the floor, and Dingboku has no drum accompaniment, only singing. As another round of Mabo got underway, the women headed their Dingboku lines into the road and ran them through the middle of Bagandou village, otherwise quiet in the midday heat. More often, however, the women succeed in gradually gaining the floor for their dances, though male drummers sometimes resist by playing inappropriately and provoking protest. This can threaten the women's initiative but rarely quells it. Dingboku is usually danced as a kind of introduction to Elamba, a newer, solo dance form in which the dancer wears layers of raffia skirts (*melamba*), showing her poise and self-possession as she struts and swings the skirts.

That some men object to the women's dances is not entirely unreasonable considering these dances' relative exclusivity.[8] Subtle interference could

Dingboku in a BaAka camp. Sandimba is at the far end of the line. Photo by Michelle Kisliuk.

BaAka women take Dingboku into the road in Bagandou village, surprising some young villagers in front of them. Photo by Michelle Kisliuk.

Moluebe dances Elamba at Masilako camp, 1992. Photos by Michelle Kisliuk.

be a strategy for offsetting that special spotlight on the women, the men's effort to "keep themselves egalitarian" (Roseman 1984, 434). Men do not have a dance comparable to Elamba, in which women openly display their skills, solo, in front of everyone (men dance solo only anonymously, covered by a full-body mask). Moreover, the teasingly assertive Dingboku songs—mostly women's commentary on sexual relations—involve a humorous slant that mocks men and may even provoke their resistance. One Dingboku chant proclaims loudly and repeatedly the attributes of an erect and pointy penis and then moves into a cadence with the words "the penis is no competition / it died already! / the vagina wins!" (*eloko tembe ya polo / a mou wa laï! / eneke ganye!*). During this chant I saw BaAka men watch passively, if a little glumly. When I later described that chant to some Central African students unfamiliar with pygmy culture, however, those men were aghast that BaAka men would—as they saw it—put up with such humiliation.

Most Dingboku songs have few words, and at first I did not understand the shorthand meanings; one song says only *eeya 'me 'te-o* ("eeya, not me-o"). One afternoon in camp, Djakandja—the daughter-in-law of the camp elder—came to sit with me on my shaded bench, and I asked her about this song. She explained the story: A teenage girl was accused by her parents of

having sex with men in the woods, but she protested that she was only collecting firewood in the forest. The Dingboku ensemble sing-songs the girl's
answer, seeming to defend her independence, "eeya, not me-o, eeya, not me!"

During the 1988 dry season many BaAka converged near Bagandou to
help with the village's coffee harvest, setting up temporary camps in the
nearby brushland. One Sunday an unusually big *eboka* (drumming, dancing,
and singing event) took place. About three hundred people attended this
dance, including thirty or so onlookers from Bagandou, drawn by the sound
of the drums that echoed to their village homes. My campmates and I attended this dance together, and I recorded this event on videotape.

After several hours of the hunting dances Mabo and Ndambo, a large
group of women—about thirty in all—finally began to organize Dingboku.
Sandimba and Djongi knew the dance best and gestured cues to the other
women indicating how they should link up in line and how to proceed. For
fifteen minutes they tried to establish two lines within the hullabaloo of
chatting, milling around, and extemporaneous drumming. Finally throngs
of men, and some women, stood aside to watch. People from my camp and
their relatives from various other camps made up the first line of thirteen
women, arms locked around one another's shoulders. Facing them across the
dance space, the Bongomba women from the host camp and their relatives
made up the second line, a bit longer but more ragged.

Inexperienced with the dance, the Bongomba women had some trouble
consolidating their line. At moments of confusion a man named Sambala
stepped in, wearing a raffia skirt over his trousers as decoration. He stood
between the two lines shouting and flailing his arms, trying to get the Bongomba women to follow his directions. They largely ignored him, continuing to arrange themselves. Individuals periodically disengaged from the line,
deciding to take a position among different friends, while others joined from
outside. Some older women at the sidelines also attempted to direct the
dancers, but like Sambala they too were duly disregarded.

As the women in the first line waited for the second line to be ready, they
stood patiently for several minutes, arm over arm in unself-conscious ease.
Then Sandimba started up a Dingboku song, "Dumana." Although the Bongomba women were still not ready, Sandimba's group began moving. A few
grandmothers and mothers with babies entered from the side individually
to face the line and dance playful steps. Linked in line, Ndami, Mbouya, and
Djakandja tilted their heads as they advanced with the others, singing "dumana" and smiling.

"Dumana" is often the opening song in Dingboku, and it means simply "sex," the only word in the song. The entire Dingboku performance can, in fact, be seen as an aesthetic abstraction of lovemaking. Each Dingboku song has one pair of vocal parts (divided randomly among the dancers), a format reproduced in the dance, which usually consists of two lines moving forward and backward. Like other BaAka songs, the texture of interlocked voices and rhythms in "Dumana" might also be seen as a performed example of BaAka egalitarianism—or at least nonauthoritarianism—wherein each voice and body acts in semiautonomous interrelationship with the others.

After several trips across the dance space, Sandimba left the melody and called out the spoken part of the song, "eeya 'me 'te-o!" The women shouted a rousing response, "'me 'te!" ("ame ote" ["not me!"], pronounced "ameh oteh"). Their feet pounded the solidly packed earth in time, and they ran with the chant, pitching forward as they went, until the two lines met. Then Sandimba's line circled around to face in the same direction as the other line, with only a foot or so between the two, and all the women ran together, first forward and then backward. *Mandudu* leaves bobbed on buttocks, and dust rose from the tramping feet.

The dancers were tired from running, and after some rearranging Sandimba called up a final, slower song. The lines faced each other and moved as a group across the space at close range, one line stepping forward, the other backward. This song has no words, only singing sounds, with a lush interlock and harmonious overlap. The performance coalesced now to a solid groove, the slowed stepping and lush harmonies making some of the women seem to fall into a dreamy, trancelike state while they stepped and sang. In the midst of this euphoria, some drummers began quietly to play the triplet rhythms for the hunting dance, Mabo, falling into time with the Dingboku song. Maybe the drummers wanted to participate in this fine mood, or else they jealously hoped to move the event along into Mabo. The effect, intentional or not, was to articulate a cross-rhythm that heightened the intensity of this transcendent moment.

This song continued for several minutes. The women rocked forward and backward with each step, moving across the dance area that brimmed with onlookers. Then Sandimba shouted the ending call, "Hoya!" The group answered "Ho!" and the lines fell apart with laughter and excited chatting. While Dingboku was breaking up—and it had been a success, judging from the joviality—Sambala confronted Sandimba with unsolicited advice, shaking his finger at her in admonition like a Bagandou villager would. She and other women around her listened casually and mirthfully, and even Samba-la had to smile, unable to take himself so seriously. Sambala's intercession in the organization of the dance looked to me like an effort to draw attention away from the women while at the same time appearing to supervise them. Some men, however, such as Djolo, Sandimba's husband, were sincerely helpful during the women's dances and even sang along encouragingly with the risqué songs.

The milling and chatting crowd slowly started preparing for Elamba. Sandimba led the women in singing the Elamba song "Mama Angeli," while Djongi, the local leader of Elamba, stepped around the periphery of the wide dance space in search of a soloist. Several candidates refused, and Djongi was obliged to make another trip around the circle. She stepped coyly in time to the drums and bounced melamba in her hand with a beckoning motion. A tipsy man mimicked her movements. The potential dancers were reluctant to accept the skirts because there was such an enormous crowd, with many bilo in attendance; the risk of inspiring jealousy if one danced well, or scorn if one did not, was great. Hewlett (1986, 321) has noted that "prestige avoidance" is a BaAka value. The phrase is apt here insofar as it implies not a static or constant "egalitarian" state but one possible socioaesthetic choice in dialogue with ever-changing circumstances.

Djongi stopped in front of Ndami, but the young woman sat motionless, looking straight ahead. Djolo approached to help coax her to agree to dance, as did her comother Tengbe and her oldest brother, Tina. Even a woman from the village stepped in to add her influence. They began to tie the skirts around Ndami's waist as she sat there unresponsively, frozen by stage fright, deep preparation, or both. After a good deal of coaxing, it was clear that Ndami had resolved to dance. A second young woman from another clan was also ready. The two soloists stood and then began tracing their steps around the dance space, one clockwise, the other crossing counterclockwise. They stopped occasionally to gather their poise and then continued stepping in their respective circles. Later in my research I asked about the aesthetic of this section of the dance, and one woman described it this way:

> She walks like this because she prepares her steps to show the public. She advances, goes forward. So, the chest region is where she finds [the center of] her steps, to dance like that; to dance in front of others with neither fear nor embarrassment. She goes forward like that, then stops and stands like that, she looks, she glances her eyes over that way. That is what gives her the go-ahead to dance, that it suits her at that moment to dance:

"Let me go ahead and dance. I'll show the people what it's like." (Diwa at Masilako, June 1992)

The two dancers began embellishing their stepping, lifting their knees high and making the skirts bounce twice behind them with each step. Often during an Elamba performance, female spectators will enter the dance space, one or two at a time, as the soloist dances. After briefly performing comical caricatures of the dancer's movements, the interlopers take the soloist by the wrist, lift her arm in a playful salute to her "superior" effort, and then exit. Most of these jokers are mature women, some of whom dance into the circle while holding their babies. Sometimes men briefly enter the circle. During this performance several interlopers entered the space, including one old woman who mimed a brief parody on all fours, backside in the air. Pandemonium temporarily broke loose when the drumming faltered and the dancers halted. The beat was soon restored, however, and Djongi stepped in to smooth Ndami's skirts and reestablish her stage presence. The other dancer, more mature than Ndami, was particularly skilled. When she stopped still to regain control of the moment, several onlookers came to honor her with coins and other small gifts. Ndami stepped up beside her, and she too was honored, attracting a swarm of relatives who claimed the tokens given to their "child." Even two men from the village came up to honor the style of each dancer with coins.

Now the second dancer began the Elamba hip-swinging movement, in double time, and when Ndami noticed, she began her own Elamba movement, bending her knees, leaning forward at the waist, and swinging the skirts—a spot-lit, "super-feminine" style of dancing, as my friend Justin from Bagandou once described it. To the extent that gender identity is, as Judith Butler (1990, 271) suggests, constituted through "the stylized repetition of acts," this Elamba movement is a crystal-clear example of a BaAka construction of the feminine. It was the peak of the dancing, and Sambala urgently coached the singing women to break into an *esime,* a rhythmic section that intensifies the dancing. They immediately took up "Masambati," an esime song about a widow who, in accordance with an old tradition, marries her sister's husband.

The sun was setting. Many jokers came up right next to the dancers to honor and parody their movements, but the dancers succeeded in keeping their cool. Even among this unusually raucous crowd the young women, unfazed, managed to embody the Elamba aesthetic, performing their self-possession.

An Initiation and Some Unforeseen Lessons

To best learn and understand Elamba, I traveled to Mopoutou, in the Republic of the Congo, to meet the "mother" (ginda) of Elamba, a woman named Bongoï. She, with the help of her husband, Kuombo, initiated me into the dance. Only girls and women who have been initiated are allowed to dance Elamba, and I concluded that my own participation was essential to my learning. Anyone outside a ginda's family must pay a fee to become initiated, thereby becoming the ginda's metaphorical "child." After consulting with Justin (who was traveling with me) and then negotiating with Bongoï, I paid a fee (somewhat high because of my relative wealth) of one cloth wrap, a double spearhead (*ndaba*), a bead necklace, five hundred CFA francs (about $1.50), razor blades, and some safety pins (items popular as earrings).

In the middle of the day, behind some village houses, I underwent the first stages of initiation into Elamba, along with some of Bongoï's little nieces and her youngest daughter, Mekano. The younger girls went first, giggling at the stinging sensation of the "vaccinations" (*kesa*). Double sets of tiny, parallel razor-blade cuts were administered to important points on the body for Elamba dancing: the back of the neck above each shoulder blade, the lower back above the hip bones, the sides of the knees, the backs of the ankles, and the tops of the feet between the big toe and second toe. Rubbed into the cuts was a black mixture of cinders from the wood of special trees, palm oil, and palm salt. The vaccinations are meant to ensure the dancer's agility in the treated body parts, but the procedure, which leaves tiny scars, must be renewed periodically because the effects are said to wear off.

At my request, Justin sterilized a new razor blade, and then Bongoï administered the little cuts to me. Kuombo coached her, remarking at my "white" blood and carefully disposing of the leaves used to wipe the blood. I gathered later that a sorcerer who obtained my blood could do me damage. Kuombo wanted the disposal of the blood to be public, so that if, coincidentally, something bad were to befall me, no BaAka could later be unjustifiably accused by the villagers of wrongdoing.

Bongoï told me that I was now her student (*ebemou*) and that when she came out of mourning (her oldest daughter had died a month earlier during childbirth), she would coach me to dance at the same level of skill that she herself possessed. We both agreed that I should go back to Bagandou in the meantime and practice Elamba there. She added that this initiation gave me authority to teach, and she prepared for me the raw ingredients of the medicine so that I could renew my own initiation, as well as vaccinate others. She said that when one gives Elamba to an initiate, one is also giving that initiate future wealth because she will in turn attract her own clients, who will bring her riches. She noted that I, as an initiate, would surely go on to receive riches on a scale far greater than her own, presumably because of my wide access to people and faraway places. I thought to myself that she could intuit but not envision the form that such teaching and "riches" might take in my case—the opportunity to tell about and teach Elamba in a university setting.

When I returned to the Bagandou area after having been initiated, the women took my interest in Elamba much more seriously, and they eventually wanted to see me dance. My first attempt at dancing, however, provided the context for learning something unexpected about BaAka gender relations.

One evening, during a small dance among my campmates, I told them I would dance this time as long as someone else went first; I was still nervous about performing the Elamba solo. To my dismay I saw that the first person to dance would be Motindo, a grown son of the camp elder. He danced a farcical version of Elamba, as I had seen him do several days earlier, when Djongi had tied the skirts on him and he performed what looked like a gawkily dainty parody of an Elamba dancer while everybody laughed. He swung his hips and pivoted in a circle, his angular shoulders bent slightly forward and his wrists raised limply to his flat chest. Afterward Sandimba joked that Motindo had danced like an insect rather than with the grace of the tiny *mboloko* antelope. I was perplexed with this whole incident since, according to Bongoï, men are not supposed to be in the dancing ring, much less wear the skirts and perform. Since the women were giggling and casual about Motindo's performance, however, I was not sure what to make of it. I did feel somewhat annoyed that they seemed not to be taking things seriously, while I certainly was. Later I learned that this was actually a legitimate part of Elamba. I learned that this sometimes comic opening is, among other things, consistent with the brief, waggish entrances during the Elamba solos, where women and sometimes men honor the dancer with exaggerated versions of her movements. Motindo's performance, then, was one way of courteously preparing for a "better" dancer, a means of diminishing the pressure on the true soloist who would follow. Maybe they even had him dance so that I would not be embarrassed, because however bad I might be, I could not be "worse" than Motindo. Had I understood this, I probably would not have insisted, as I did, that yet another dancer go before me. Coming from a relatively competitive and sexist culture, I did not see that Motindo, a man, had good-naturedly made himself look silly so that a woman—in this case, me—could follow and look good.

Social Stress Enacted: Gendered Contention Performed

The dry season lingered on, and as months passed in the camp near the village, the strain of village life began to wear on the nerves of my BaAka campmates, the stress being provoked by the scarcity of food in the dry season and the burden of working for the bilo and often being demeaned by them. With mounting tension and frustration, men tended increasingly to compete with the women's efforts rather than to support them. This tension became especially evident during performances of Elamba. Although my initial interpretation of Motindo's dancing Elamba—thinking it was an insulting parody of the women—on the one hand illustrates how my own cultural orientation obscured my view, my confusion about this aspect of Elamba was in fact not entirely misguided. The playful space for "parody" in Elamba, including the brief, comic interjections by onlookers, can work like a barometer of gender relations among BaAka, showing support or hostility, depending on the broader social circumstances. The following incident illustrates this.

During this lingering dry season, there was a funeral dance in a camp about an hour's walk away from our home camp, in the direction of the forest. Most of the day was filled by Mabo, but an hour or so before dark Sandimba organized the women's dances. During Dingboku she concentrated for some time on the chant "the penis is no competition / it died already! / the vagina wins!" The men stood by watching, some looking increasingly uncomfortable. When the women had enough of Dingboku, Sandimba announced that they would "shandzeh [*changer* (Fr.)] eboka," and they sat down to prepare for Elamba. As a soloist got herself ready, out of sight, the seated women warmed up with an Elamba song. Their singing kept faltering, however, because the men playing the drums paused repeatedly, dropping the beat. Sandimba shook her head in frustration. Twice and then three times the song was interrupted. Finally she shouted, "You all seize the drumming already!" When the response was still feeble, she got up, took a burning log from a nearby fire, and went to hand it to a drummer to tune his drum. Djolo, her husband, then stepped in to oversee the faltering drummers, and Sandimba came back to lead the singing. Finally the drummers fell into gear, and the women began a lush Elamba chorus. The soloist, a woman I did not know, stepped into the open dancing area. She began stepping around the circle, bobbing her breasts—one in each hand—as she stepped and kicking up her feet sharply behind her while flipping her skirts.

Immediately a few men surrounded the dancer in the dusk in what looked like the manner of the comic interlopers. The first to approach her was Elongo, a MoAka who had become involved with Christian evangelism and had recently refused to participate in BaAka dances, calling them "satanic." Dressed in an old uniform he once wore as a guard for the mayor of Bagandou, Elongo waved his old cap around the soloist's head and then placed it on her as she danced past him. Other men who had been drinking joined in. They swept up dust around her, taking attention away while at the same time interfering with her dancing and seeming to devalue the dance itself. One of the men then unmistakably crossed the invisible line of propriety by pulling down the back of his shorts and "mooning" the onlookers, wagging his bare behind in an exaggerated version of the Elamba hip movement. The scene became slapstick when another man came up and whacked the mooner's bare backside with a cloth. The observing women squealed briefly in shocked surprise. During the commotion, Sandimba got up and led the song from the middle of the dancing ring, standing by the dancer and rhythmically waving a gourd shaker, seeming to protect her. The Elamba dancer kept her concentration throughout this onslaught and finished her solo.

Though Sandimba does not have the "best voice," nor is she the "best dancer" in the group, her personality makes her a leader. When initiative might make a difference, she usually takes it, and when someone's behavior is getting in the way of a performance, she often chastises the offender. This time, as soon as the dancer had stepped to the side of the circle, indicating that she was finished, Sandimba briefly but angrily imitated the grotesque actions of those men, saying that they should have kept out. "We were dancing," she said. Then she took it on herself to pronounce the eboka officially over. It was getting dark. Someone from the host camp gave the soloist a big pot and a ladle for her dancing. She smiled and shrugged her shoulders in bashful pride.

After this Elamba dance, in which those men seemed malicious, I asked some women—including the soloist—what they thought about the incident. They said matter-of-factly that those men were just envious of their dance. The women's space appeared to be somewhat immune to men; when the men behaved outrageously, the women mostly ignored them. I nevertheless wondered, given the lengths to which Sandimba had to go to preserve the integrity of the dance, how long the women could continue to be relatively impervious to such malicious envy if it persisted.

The harassing antics of the drunken men during this performance were unlike the other brief, comic interpolations into Elamba by both men and women that I had seen in the past. They were also different from Motindo's parodies of Elamba, which the women themselves had invited him to per-form and which, I learned later, were understood as an optional opening for the dance. In fact, during a subsequent research trip in 1992, I learned from Bongoï's sister, Diwa, that when a man ties on the skirts and dances the *mokele,* the "opening," he is really dancing *Djoboko,* a defunct men's dance that gave Elamba its power. Diwa explained, "They show the steps to the women, as in 'look, dance like this, like that.' The woman says, 'I see the way the man shows me; ah, that's how the dance is. I'll put on the skirts, I'll dance, so everybody will honor me.'" According to Diwa and her husband, in Djoboko the men used to wear melamba and a cloth covering the head. They danced, moving hips and legs, but not in the feminine manner current for Elamba.

We might understand the incident of jealous disruption of Elamba in the light of the increasing frustration of those particular men as they lingered near the village. Considering the shift in BaAka social and economic status when they live near Bagandou, the roots of this frustration become visible. When BaAka are in their forest territory, women and men spend relatively equal amounts of time and effort providing food. When near Bagandou, however, men do much less hunting, an activity in which they take great pride, while women provide most of the food by gathering wild vegetables, getting manioc from village plantations, and working for village women. The men, besides scaling palm trees to bring down palm nuts for cooking oil and attending dances, spend most of their time in the village drinking palm wine and bilo corn whiskey and clearing villagers' fields—for which they are paid in cigarettes, marijuana, and alcohol. Their male identities are therefore suddenly based more on labor and consumption than on production. Ba-Aka men also transport water for bilo households, a task normally performed by village women. BaAka men are thereby feminized in the eyes of the bilo, and perhaps in their own eyes as well.[9] It follows that some of these men might find the women's dances more threatening than they are in other contexts, and under these circumstances my presence and interest in the women may have heightened the men's envy still further.

According to Bongoï, in Mopoutou it is normal in Elamba for women to enter the dancing ring while the soloist performs, to animate the crowd with comic antics, and to honor (*esepheledi*) the dancer. Men in Mopoutou, how-ever, do not usually step into the dancers' area at all. When in 1992 I described to Bongoï's sister, Diwa, what had happened during Elamba that day in

Bagandou, she concluded it must be the Bagandou style, because, she said, in Mopoutou Elamba would never include such behavior. In my brief time in Mopoutou I noticed no gender tension in connection with Elamba. Kuombo, Bongoï's husband, participated in my initiation and in other arrangements, and he was involved in discussing with us the dance and its origins. But his involvement was complementary to Bongoï rather than competitive. Bongoï remained the mother of Elamba. In relatively isolated Mopoutou, the status of BaAka men is not in flux to the extent that it is in Bagandou. Though relations between BaAka and villagers in Mopoutou are even harsher than in Bagandou—bilo regularly beat and otherwise demean BaAka for not doing their bidding—the social and cultural lives of BaAka and villagers remain separate but interdependent. In increasingly cosmopolitan Bagandou, however, several lifestyles are influencing one another in a more volatile way. Police, Muslim storekeepers, Christian missionaries, villagers, commercial hunters, gold and diamond seekers, occasional tourists, and researchers interact with BaAka as they spend time near the village (and often in the forest as well). I noticed similar tensions around women's dances when I visited Bayanga, an area where BaAka social and economic relations are also being directly challenged by other systems. Therefore, during the women's dances in Bagandou, BaAka men could be understood as expressing—among other things—the fluctuations and frustrations of their own status in the changing world of the village. I do not mean necessarily to link gender tension with inequality, but such tension does suggest a time of flux, a struggle between parties to reconstitute relationships.

Refining Tools for Understanding Cultural Processes: Pygmies as a Case in Point

As quoted previously, Judith Butler notes that gender identity is constituted by "the stylized repetition of acts." She adds, however, that "the possibilities of gender transformation are to be found in the . . . breaking or subversive repetition of that style" (1990, 271). Dingboku and Elamba could be seen as subversive insofar as women performatively define and assert their gendered experience within a relatively egalitarian but still male-dominated environment. Nevertheless, BaAka also show a flexibility and malleability of gender roles and gender relationships, various kinds of "subversive repetition" in response to changing circumstances, from Motindo's goofy dancing to the abject parodies during this last Elamba. This is one example of how BaAka are responding performatively—and therefore grappling conceptually—with the constancy of change and thereby with the modern condition (Miller 1994, 76).

Some BaAka legends (Kisliuk 1991, 1998) and other pygmy legends (Turnbull 1965, 308) support the view that pygmies have long moved in and out of deep forest life in response to historical circumstances. Turnbull's field experience, like mine, nevertheless indicates that social dynamics among pygmies when they are near the village differ from those when they are away from it. Several villagers I spoke with said that BaAka spend much more time near the village now than they did even thirty years ago. It is important to realize, however, that the difference between forest and village social dynamics that seems to affect a BaAka egalitarian balance results from the complex and changing interrelationship of local, regional, and global forces that meet at the village level (and seep into the forest) rather than—as the ongoing academic debate about "pygmies" implies—exclusively from a shift in the mode of production or subsistence.

The "hunter-gatherer (or forager) debate" as applied to pygmies is centered in a conflict between scholars such as Serge Bahuchet, on the one hand, and Robert Bailey and the Harvard Ituri Project, on the other. Bahuchet, using genetic, linguistic, and botanical evidence from Centrafrique and Cameroon, maintains that pygmies occupied the equatorial forest exclusively until the Bantu expansion of about two thousand years ago (Bahuchet, De Garine, and McKey 1990). Based on archaeological and nutritional data from central Zaire, the Harvard group argues that it would have been impossible for pygmies to have survived in the forest solely by hunting and gathering and concludes that they must have always traded with non-pygmy agriculturists or else cultivated foods for themselves (Bailey 1990).[10] Some BaAka legends uphold this latter view as well (Kisliuk 1991, 1998). Since these researchers base their arguments on different groups of pygmies in widely separate forests, however, their debate seems at heart less technically ecological than ideological: is autonomous egalitarianism a basic type of human social life—does it now or did it ever exist—and are pygmies a living example of it? These researchers tend to conflate the ideas of an autonomous hunting-gathering lifestyle and an egalitarian social structure. Turnbull also tended to conflate those ideas in his writing, and this conflation seems to have set the stage for considerable theoretical and interpretive confusion about the lives of pygmies.

Most BaAka currently do some farming as well as hunting and gathering (as do other pygmies and various other ethnic groups in Africa), sometimes participating in a marginal market economy and sometimes not. To reduce culture to its mode of production, or to conflate the two, even when considering long-term historical patterns, obscures the issue. Understanding is better served, as Raymond Williams (1980, 34) suggested, by moving "away from the notion of a fixed economic or technological abstraction, and towards the specific activities of men [and women] in real social and economic relationships, containing fundamental contradictions and variations and therefore always in a state of dynamic process." Williams's vision here foreshadows a feminist (or anti-objectivist) critique of scholarship. A fully performative method addresses social and cultural processes in a manner different from what is still the mainstream in fields including anthropology. Despite efforts to the contrary, ethnoaesthetics and related approaches are not fully performative but still periodically impose scientistic models and use objectifying language that distances the researcher while simplifying complex human processes. The result is often a reduction of lived experience to "grand theory" or "key metaphor," resulting, if unintentionally, in a scholarship that defuses the power of expressive culture.

An extreme but relevant example is Alan Lomax, who attempted to introduce a quantitative, and thus in his view scientific, methodology to the study of aesthetic anthropology (see, e.g., Lomax 1976, 9). He moves toward a provocative but disturbing reduction of worldwide music and dance to quintessential examples and simplistic analyses taken out of context. Underlying Lomax's "Cantometrics" system is a binary opposition between "pure" folk musics, springing from an imaginary time and place wherein "every human community dwelt in its own self-generated bubble of sound" (Lomax 1976, 8)—pygmies being the favorite example—and "degraded" cultural environments that are either "highly cosmopolitan, acculturated, or in a process of rapid change" (1976, 16). With this opposition Lomax set himself up for a "net of reifications," as Steven Feld has noted (1984, 405). Although Lomax is extreme, even the most current of ethnomusicological scholarship often returns to typifying and circumscribing culture, echoing a will to authority that is embedded in the patriarchal history of Western scholarship (see, e.g., Feld 1988). The "pure" versus "degraded" model of culture that lies at the heart of this tenacious paradigm has infused governments, dominant populations, and missionaries with attitudes that are often used to justify exploitive policies (see Kisliuk 1991, 1997, 1998).

As examples in this essay illustrate, most BaAka are aware of the choices before them and are responding in varied ways to the challenges of reinventing who they are and who they hope to become. The performance of gender identity and the negotiation of relative power continue to be a focal point for understanding how BaAka are constituting their futures—just as we do our own.

Glossary

Beboka	plural of eboka
Bilo	Diaka term for nonpygmy black people (sing., *milo*)
Eboka	music and dance event or a piece in the music and dance repertory
Esime	rhythmic "get-down" section in many BaAka beboka
Ginda	the master teacher of an eboka
Malamba	a raffia skirt (pl., *melamba*)
Mandudu	leaves that BaAka tuck in the back of a g-string for a festive look while dancing—most popular among women
Milo	see *bilo*
MoAka	singular of BaAka
Ndambo	a BaAka eboka associated with spear hunting

Notes

This essay is based on chapter 7 of my book *Seize the Dance! BaAka Musical Life and the Ethnography of Performance,* © 1998 by Oxford University Press, Inc., and is used by permission of Oxford University Press, Inc.

1. The term *pygmy* should be read here as "so-called pygmy." *Pygmy* is a problematic term that often carried a derogatory or belittling connotation until Colin Turnbull's loving celebration of the Mbuti pygmies of Zaire (1961). Nonetheless, it is the only term in English inclusive of the many socially, culturally, and historically similar peoples of the African equatorial rain forest, including the Efe, Mbuti, Twa, Baka, and BaAka, among others. These current or former seminomadic hunters and foragers name themselves in many different languages but often use the general expression "forest people" (literally, "offspring of the forest") to distinguish themselves from their village-dwelling neighbors. I use "forest people" and a variety of other terms, but the term *pygmy* also becomes apt when invoking issues and attitudes that engage "pygmies" as a social and cultural category, defined both regionally and globally. *Pygmy* as a racial label is inaccurate, however, and therefore I lowercase it.

2. Kamala Visweswaran (1994, 87) takes exception to this totalizing, Eurocentric viewpoint, and I agree with her objection: "If there are difficulties in periodizing the modern for any given disciplinary formation, the question of modernity in the Third World is no less vexed, and extends the formulation to which

modernity, where? The point here is not to announce, as have some, that modernity is everywhere, but to ask, as does Geetha Kapus, 'How are we placed?'"

3. I have chosen the spelling *BaAka* instead of *Aka,* the root word used in much of the scientific literature to refer to these pygmies of the western Congo Basin (e.g. Bahuchet 1985; Hewlett 1991). BaAka themselves never say "Aka" but use prefixes to form either *MoAka* (sing.) or *BaAka* (pl.), and I feel most comfortable using terms closest to theirs. BaAka have varying accents; some call themselves "Biaka" (a spelling I formerly used), and others say "Bayaka." The spelling used here accommodates these accents while indicating the prefix-root structure of the term (the second *A* after the prefix is capitalized so that readers will pronounce it). The BaAka language, classified as a Bantu language, is called "Diaka."

4. BaAka, like other Centrafricains, are sometimes jailed merely on the strength of accusations and are held without trial while providing manual labor for local authorities.

5. The variation in the name's spelling—Bangando versus Bagandou—resulted from transliteration by French colonialists, and the latter is now the official spelling.

6. The following three paragraphs appear in similar form in Kisliuk 1997. I also discuss this approach in more detail in Kisliuk 1998.

7. See Turner 1986, 75–6. Exceptions to this lack of attention to experience in ethnomusicology include efforts by Chernoff (1979), Seeger (1987), Turino (1990), Titon (1994), and Keil and Feld (1994).

8. I should note that there is also a men's version of Dingboku, sometimes called *So.* It is rare in Bagandou but current both in Mopoutou (Congo) and westward in Bayanga. The one time that I did see So—at a dance during this same season— the women were dancing Dingboku while a visiting ginda from the Congo led the men in So (the songs had no words, only singing sounds). The result was a cacophony, as each group ignored the others' claim to the dance space. Frustrated, the ginda switched to the hunting dance, Ndambo, but the women continued their Dingboku. Eventually the competition ended when Mabo overtook and incorporated both groups.

9. An article by Grinker (1990) on the Efe pygmies of Zaire and their Lese neighbors goes so far as to say that the Lese villagers, both men and women, see the Efe as female and use female terminology to describe Efe men and women. He does not explore, however, how the Efe see the situation.

10. According to the Harvard group, pygmies lived on the periphery of the forest, exploiting both forest and savanna (in Hewlett 1986, 64), and retreated into the forest at the time of the Bantu expansion. That the two sides of the debate are talking about different equatorial forests and different pygmies, and that some of the scientists who hold the revisionist view still assert that pygmies offer a window on a prehistoric world of hunting and gathering (see Bailey 1989),

throws into question the basis of the whole argument. See Pratt 1986, 48, for a discussion of similar debates about "hunter-gatherers" in the Kalahari.

References Cited

Abu-Lughod, Lila. 1990. "Can There be a Feminist Ethnography?" *Women and Performance* 5, no. 1:7–27.

Arom, Simha. 1978. *Anthologie de la musique des Pygmées Aka.* Compact disc. OCORA 558.526.27.28.

———. 1991. *African Polyphony and Polyrhythm: Musical Structure and Methodology.* Trans. M. Thom, B. Tuckett, and R. Boyd. New York: Cambridge University Press.

Bahuchet, Serge. 1985. *Les Pygmées Aka et la forêt centrafricaine.* Paris: Société d'Études Lingustiques et Anthropologique de France.

Bahuchet, Serge, Igor De Garine, and Doyle McKey. 1990. "Wild Yams Revisited: Is Independence from Agriculture Possible for Rain Forest Hunter-Gatherers?" Paper presented at the eighty-ninth annual meeting of the American Anthropological Association, New Orleans, La.

Bailey, Robert C. 1989. "The Efe: Archers of the African Rain Forest." *National Geographic,* November, 664–86.

———. 1990. "Implications of New Research Findings for Understanding Human Ecology in the Tropical Rain Forest." Paper presented at the eighty-ninth annual meeting of the American Anthropological Association, New Orleans, La.

Bell, Diane. 1987. "The Politics of Separation." In *Dealing with Inequality,* ed. Marilyn Strathern, 112–29. Cambridge: Cambridge University Press.

Butler, Judith. 1990. "Performative Acts and Gender Constitution: An Essay in Phenomenology and Feminist Theory." In *Performing Feminisms,* ed. Sue-Ellen Case, 270–82. Baltimore: Johns Hopkins University Press.

Chernoff, John Miller. 1979. *African Rhythm and African Sensibility.* Chicago: University of Chicago Press.

Clifford, James. 1986. "Introduction: Partial Truths." In *Writing Culture: The Poetics and Politics of Ethnography,* ed. James Clifford and George E. Marcus, 1–26. Los Angeles: University of California Press.

Dumont, Louis. 1986. *Essays on Individualism.* Chicago: University of Chicago Press.

Feld, Steven. 1984. "Sound Structure as Social Structure." *Ethnomusicology* 28:383–410.

———. 1988. "Aesthetics as Iconicity of Style, or, 'Lift up over Sounding': Getting into the Kaluli Groove." *Yearbook for Traditional Music* 20:74–113.

Giddens, Anthony. 1990. *The Consequences of Modernity.* Stanford, Calif.: Stanford University Press.

Grinker, Richard Roy. 1990. "Images of Denigration: Structuring Inequality between Foragers and Farmers in the Ituri Forest, Zaire." *American Ethnologist* 18, no. 1:111–30.

Hewlett, Barry. 1986. "The Father-Infant Relationship among Aka Pygmies." Ph.D. diss., University of California, Santa Barbara.

———. 1991. *Intimate Fathers: The Nature and Context of Aka Pygmy Paternal Infant Care.* Ann Arbor: University of Michigan Press.

Jayawardena, Chandra. 1968. "Ideology and Conflict in Lower Class Communities." *Comparative Studies in Society and History* 10, no. 4:413–46.

Keil, Charles, and Steven Feld. 1994. *Music Grooves: Essays and Dialogues.* Chicago: University of Chicago Press.

Kisliuk, Michelle. 1991. "Confronting the Quintessential: Singing, Dancing, and Everyday Life among Biaka Pygmies (Central African Republic)." Ph.D. diss., New York University.

———. 1997. "(Un)Doing Fieldwork: Sharing Songs, Sharing Lives." In *Shadows in the Field: New Perspectives for Fieldwork and Ethnomusicology,* ed. Gregory F. Barz and Timothy I. Cooley, 23–44. New York: Oxford University Press.

———. 1998. *"Seize the Dance!" BaAka Musical Life and the Ethnography of Performance.* New York: Oxford University Press.

Leacock, Eleanor. 1981. "Women's Status in Egalitarian Society." In *Myths of Male Dominance,* 133–82. New York: Monthly Review Press.

Lomax, Alan. 1968. *Folk Song Style and Culture.* Washington, D.C.: American Association for the Advancement of Science.

———. 1976. *Cantometrics: An Approach to the Anthropology of Music.* Berkeley: University of California Extension Media Center.

McCreedy, Marion. 1994. "The Arms of the Dibouka." In *Key Issues in Hunter-Gatherer Research,* ed. Ernest S. Burch and Linda I. Ellanna, 15–34. Oxford, U.K.: Berg.

Miller, Daniel. 1994. *Modernity: An Ethnographic Approach.* Oxford, U.K.: Berg.

Rosaldo, Renado. 1989. *Culture and Truth: The Remaking of Social Analysis.* Boston: Beacon.

Pratt, Mary Louise. 1986. "Fieldwork in Common Places." In *Writing Culture: The Poetics and Politics of Ethnography,* ed. James Clifford, 27–50. Los Angeles: University of California Press.

Roseman, Marina. 1984. "The Social Structuring of Sound: The Temiar of Peninsular Malaysia." *Ethnomusicology* 28:411–45.

Seeger, Anthony. 1987. *Why Suyá Sing: A Musical Anthropology of an Amazonian People.* New York: Cambridge University Press.

Strathern, Marilyn, ed. 1987. *Dealing with Inequality: Analysing Gender Relations in Melanesia and Beyond.* Cambridge: Cambridge University Press.

Thomas, Jaqueline M. C., and Serge Bahuchet, eds. 1983. *Encyclopédie des Pygmées Aka.* Paris: SELAF.

Thompson, Robert Farris. 1989. "The Song That Named the Land: The Visionary Presence of African-American Art." In *Black Art: Ancestral Legacy: The African Impulse in African American Art,* exhibition catalog, 97–138. Dallas: Dallas Museum of Art.

Titon, Jeff Todd. 1994. "Knowing People Making Music: Toward a New Epistemology for Ethnomusicology." *Etnomusikologian vuosikirja* [Yearbook of the Finnish Society for Ethnomusicology]. Helsinki: Finnish Society for Ethnomusicology.

Turino, Thomas. 1990. "Structure, Context, and Strategy in Musical Ethnography." *Ethnomusicology* 34:399–412.

Turnbull, Colin M. 1961. *The Forest People: A Study of the Pygmies of the Congo.* New York: Simon and Schuster.

———. 1965. *Wayward Servants: The Two Worlds of the African Pygmies.* Garden City, N.Y.: Natural History Press.

———. 1978. "The Politics of Non-Aggression." In *Learning Non-Agression,* ed. A. Montagu, 161–221. Oxford: Oxford University Press.

———. 1981. "Mbuti Womanhood." In *Woman the Gatherer,* ed. Frances Dahlberg, 205–20. New Haven, Conn.: Yale University Press.

———. 1983. *The Mbuti Pygmies: Change and Adaptation.* New York: Holt, Rinehart and Winston.

Turner, Victor. 1986. *The Anthropology of Performance.* New York: PAJ Publications.

Tyler, Stephen. 1986. "Post-Modern Ethnography: From Document of the Occult to Occult Document." In *Writing Culture: The Poetics and Politics of Ethnography,* ed. James Clifford and George E. Marcus, 122–40. Los Angeles: University of California Press.

Visweswaran, Kamala. 1994. *Fictions of Feminist Ethnography.* Minneapolis: University of Minnesota Press.

Williams, Raymond. 1980. *Problems in Materialism and Culture: Selected Essays.* London: Verso.

2 Local Constructions of Gender in a Finnish Pelimanni Musicians Group

Helmi Järviluoma

I have been interested for a long time in the multiple meanings of *pelimanni* musicianship. *Pelimanni* is a Finnish expression for a traditional instrumental musician. The concept has evolved during three or four hundred years of interaction and negotiations between different groups of people, and the word is still used.

In this essay I discuss the ways in which the meanings of pelimanni musicianship, particularly its gender nuances, are maintained and produced in the ongoing process of local, everyday interactions among musicians. My study is based on work that I began in 1988 with an amateur pelimanni ensemble in Virrat, a small country town in central Finland. I will focus on the ways these musicians construct and maintain gender in conversations during rehearsals; I pay more attention to the group's music elsewhere (Järviluoma 1997).

I will test the usefulness of the "membership category device" concepts developed by the sociologist Harvey Sacks in studying constructions of gender. According to Sacks (1966, 1974, 1992), much of the knowledge needed for communication is organized in "membership categories." These social categories, therefore, form an important cultural resource. Anyone can be labeled in several appropriate ways. For example, depending on the situation, I can appropriately be described as a "violinist," "teacher," "mother," and so on. These descriptive labels, in turn, can be grouped into larger categories (membership categorization devices, or MCDs); for example, in relation to the descriptive labels just mentioned, the MCDs would be "amateur musicians," "university personnel," "family." I will not provide the total array of Sacks's concepts, but a glossary of the ones I use here appears at the end of this essay.[1]

Sacks designed the membership categorization device concepts to help analyze the ways in which people produce and understand descriptions of one another. Category analysis sounds very "masculine" if we think that labels, names, and "isms" are linked to a phallogocentric desire to stabilize, organize and rationalize our conceptual world, but Sacks did not intend to reproduce rigid categorizations. On the contrary, his approach tried to show how these categories are constantly renegotiated through everyday interactions.[2]

My interpretation of these concepts is also indebted to feminist theories. With Luce Irigaray (1994, 54), I believe that "the gender of the words is related to the question of the gender of the speaking subjects"; the gender hidden in the word is valued differently and unequally on the basis of its perceived masculinity or femininity. *Pelimanni*, like the German word *Spielmann* or the Swedish *spelman*, is a masculine label used generically to refer to people. Musicians are not called by the more gender-specific terms *pelinainen* (*Spielwif*) or *peli-ihminen* (*Spielmench*). My analysis begins from the acknowledgment that the idea of otherness is always there, inscribed in every presence and utterance.

Another aspect of this becomes apparent when researchers talk about music as being "contaminated" by ideology. (Paradoxically, this is often music that the researcher does not like.)[3] Gendered terms often enter the discourse when, for example, "folkloric" music is discussed. For instance, John Shepherd (1993, 64) describes musical folklorism as part of an attempt by male culture to take control: "The discursive constitution of preferred notions of language and music, together with the idealization of classical music and the sanitization of folk music, can all be read as an attempt by male culture to control musical culture by eradicating the tensions between artifice and the material." In Finland generic metaphors sometimes similarly imply a process of feminization. Folkloric music, more specifically choral arrangements of folk songs, has been described as the "castrated tomcat of musical culture" (Juhani Similä, in Kurkela 1989, 9); that is, folk music has lost its power and phallic energy during its processing into "folklorism." The metaphor implies that "sanitized" folk music is a feminized creature, tiptoeing in its folk dance stockings. This way of mapping gender onto musical change has also been discussed by Leo Treitler (1993, 28), who has found that, throughout European history, *effeminization* becomes the synonym of corruption, "deterioration from what is by nature manly."

These approaches to interpretation reflect my belief that contextualization of conversation and writing is necessary whenever we want to discuss meaning. To explore this issue further, I include here entries from diaries and journals in which I wrote about experiences that happened while I was writing this essay. Hence, I suggest that my own situation—living in a foreign country and having powerful dreams—was influential in shaping the ideas expressed herein.

I will return to these issues later, but first I turn to the history of the folk music revival in Finland and the place of women in that movement.

The Revival of Finnish Traditional Music

The pelimanni, or folk music, movement started in Finland in the late 1960s and early 1970s, following a period of extremely rapid urbanization: a transition from an agricultural society to a service- and small-industry-oriented society.[4] Changes took place abruptly, with significant cultural consequences both for the people who moved to towns or immigrated to Sweden and for those who stayed in the emptying rural areas.

A revival of rural culture took place throughout Scandinavia in the 1970s, but although protests against urban values were ubiquitous, the meanings and motives of the revival were not necessarily the same in different countries or regions (Järviluoma and Mäki-Kulmala 1992). The Finnish folk music movement was originally a cultural manifestation dominated by middle-aged rural people, more specifically rural men (Laitinen 1989). Every rural community established its own pelimanni ensemble, carrying the name of its municipality and consisting mostly of middle-aged or elderly men. Konsta Jylhä, the leading figure of the Kaustisen Purppuripelimannit ensemble, a composer and "man of the people," started a process that has been called the most therapeutic in Finnish music history: following his efforts, anyone was able to call himself, or even herself, a composer (Laitinen 1977, 84).[5]

In other Scandinavian countries, younger generations were equally interested in such things as fiddle playing in old and "authentic" styles (see Ramsten 1985). In Finland, however, young people were not particularly interested in traditional music until the 1980s. Since then there have been considerable changes, including more varied constructions of gender within young groups. The celebration of the luxuriant femininity of Värttinä, a "neofolk" group[6] that has become world famous, or the performances of the so-called avant-garde traditionalists[7] and their relationships to gender are interesting in this regard.

The latter promote improvisation, orality, and creativity as the basis of all musical activities. Usually trained in the Department of Folk Music established in the Sibelius Academy (the "cradle of fine art music") in 1983,[8] these folk musicians have established cooperative links with contemporary artists, including modern dancers. Most performances incorporate elements of different world musics.

The avant-garde traditionalists are positioned differently from the pelimanni musicians. In Finland researchers would not readily dismiss the music of avant-garde traditionalists, themselves part of the academy, as sanitized or castrated folk music.[9] As previously described, however, the rest of folklorism has been viewed as castrated—as a form of culture in which the musician's choices are seen as restricted. In the mid-1980s researchers quite openly ridiculed pelimanni groups, which they claimed played like army units, responding mechanically to their conductor's orders. It was at that time that I resolved to look at these groups not from the top down but from the bottom up. Even though researchers in the 1990s are more empathetic (see, e.g., Kurkela 1989, 9), we still lack adequate understanding of the practices of the pelimanni groups.

The Ensemble Virtain Pelimannit

The ensemble with which I worked, Virtain pelimannit,[10] was born in 1972, in the middle of the productive years of the Finnish folk music revival. The group is affiliated with the adult evening college of Virrat, a typical venue for pelimanni activities. It

A Dream while Writing

"I was at a railway station, dressed as a boy. I had a cap. I was inside a wagon. I intended to change trains quickly, to travel in another direction. Instead, however, I peeped into my home. My father was there, saying that my sisters had already gone. They had been searching for pencils but had not found them—they were annoyed. I shrugged my shoulders, but I suddenly knew that it was I who had all those pencils. Some of them were already quite short but still sharp and usable. I went to the train contemplating the meaning of the pencils. I was astonished: I had always had them but had not considered it important."

If a woman intends to write, she feels guilt about her desire to master the language. That's why she has to imagine away her own involvement into this desire for mastery (Hélène Cixous). This is a central problem for me. Why is it so hard to write? Why is it so easy to hide behind patriarchal authorities; why is it so difficult to consider my own ideas meaningful?

In my dream my sisters—maybe they are part of me—were searching for pencils in my father's place. Part of me knows already: I have pencils. I don't need to fetch them from my father. I have the means to express myself without going back to Father.

meets once a week during the fall and winter terms and occasionally during the summer for performances. The ensemble is proud that it is one of the most active performance and dance music groups in the town: the members say they go anywhere they are asked to go and charge moderately. Apart from producing their own dance and music events, they play in events organized by town associations, political parties, school dances, and summer music festivals. They consider themselves servants of the community. Their activities resemble those of the English brass musicians whom Ruth Finnegan (1989) has described.

In the year that I gathered most of my data (1988–89), from one to four women participated along with the approximately twenty-three men in Virtain pelimannit. The most active female pelimanni—a shop assistant—played mandolin, and the other women, who played only occasionally with the group, were accordionists. Altogether there were five violinists, a couple of mandolin and mandolin-banjo players, a tubaist, and around fifteen accordionists.

The members' occupational backgrounds ranged from the working class (builders, bus or taxi drivers [seven of them], etc.) to the middle class (teachers, an office manager, and a forestry supervisor) and agriculture (three male farmers). The age spectrum was wide. The majority ranged from fifty to sixty-four years of age (more than 50 percent), one-third of the musicians were between forty and forty-nine, and a few were around seventy. The youngest member was a twenty-year-old woman who attended only three times before her nursing studies started in a bigger town.

Their music falls into three categories: first, and most substantial, various kinds of dance music, such as waltzes, tangos, schottisches, polkas, marches, and hits of the 1930s through the 1950s—in other words, the music of their own youth and childhood; second, traditional Finnish music; and third, their own compositions. Only a couple of men in the group had composed their own tunes.

The musicians had undergone practically no formal music education, but most of them had learned to read music either on their own or through earlier involvement with a brass band. The tunes were learned during rehearsals from music copied by the conductor. After fifteen years of playing music together, their repertory consisted of more than 270 tunes, all neatly filed.

The leader, Yrjö Raja, was formally educated as a teacher and taught woodwork and music at the adult evening college. He had previously enjoyed an active music career as a brass-band leader and a fiddler, and several times he had won the Finnish national championship in traditional mandolin playing.

The Gendering of Finnish Musical Practices:
From Kantele to Two-Row Accordions

Like the group in Virrat, most of the big rural pelimanni ensembles consist mostly of middle-aged people and include few women. Finnish women of that generation rarely became instrumentalists. When I studied the musical culture of the early decades of this century in three villages in northern Ostrobothnia, I found little mention of women playing musical instruments. "It was believed that playing was a sinful activity and that particularly restricted the participation of women even if they wished to play," one of my interviewees said (in Järviluoma 1986, 85–86). In addition, men had more free time: while they gathered together in the evenings to tell stories and play, "women mostly worked."

Certain instruments were considered appropriate for women, however, particularly the *kantele* (the Finnish national instrument, a type of zither) and mandolin. Women could also play the bark horn in the woods or the zither and saw, but female fiddlers or accordionists were few. Although it is now common for Finnish women to play brass instruments, a woman playing a brass horn was completely unthinkable in an early twentieth-century village: "She would have been considered a really astonishing and deviant person"; "Women mostly sang hymns" (in Järviluoma 1986, 28).

Herding calls were exclusively women's music and an important area of musical expression—"real evening symphonies," as one informant described them (in Järviluoma 1986, 85–86). Lullabies, round-game songs, and lamenting (in Karelia)—and dancing, of course—have also been important. The voice is an instrument that is always there. You do not have to take it down from the wall and stop working while using it.

It is interesting that, in present-day Virrat, the two-row accordion has become popular among young and middle-aged women. The instrument is light and suits women's fingers, but I believe that there is also something "resistant" involved in this preference. In Virrat and neighboring towns there are some women very actively involved in traditional music; they belong to a generation slightly younger than that of the majority in the Virtain pelimannit. One active female pelimanni,[11] for instance, is directing many two-row accordion groups in the Virrat region. One of the groups, in the community of Kurjenkylä, consists of talented young girls. Therefore, I must stress that within the world of traditional music, women have sometimes been more involved than they are in the context I describe here. I must also say that the attitude of the Virrat pelimanni group toward this particular "girls' group" is extremely positive.[12]

Next I will try to show how the musicians—including me as a visitor—collectively maintain, produce, or resist the discourses of femininity and masculinity in the course of everyday musical activities. I think that we can talk about femininity and masculinity as conceptual categories or cultural devices, but only as a starting point. After that it is important to see how people use such categories (see also Wieder 1974, 40–45). The discourse of the pelimannit is partly shaped by these categories, but it also helps to re-shape the concepts.

How is gender, then, present in my data—my observations in my field diary and my tape-recordings of conversation and music making? Here I focus on three specific recorded rehearsal situations, one dealing with choice of repertory, another with aesthetic value, and the third with coffee making.

An Interaction Concerning Repertoire Choice

In the Virrat pelimanni ensemble rehearsals, the conductor has a particular way of involving the members of the ensemble in choosing the next tune to be played. He names the musicians one by one and asks them to "shout" the name of the tune they wish to play next. Sometimes they suggest a tune without a specific invitation, but the women never did so, at least when I was present. Before examining an instance of this practice, however, it is necessary to consider the group's various conversational styles.

During discussions within the ensemble, the women rarely participated in the general communal chatter. They talked quietly with the people sitting next to them. Is this the maintenance of marginality or a different type of discourse? Arguably it is part of the "construction of femininity." The history of "silent" women is too long for us to see this as just an arbitrary coincidence.

Finnish linguists and conversation analysts (see Hakulinen 1987, 65) have shown that men talk more in mixed-gender conversations, participating with greater frequency and in longer segments. Obviously the conversation of women in all-female contexts exhibits different patterns, but already in mixed classrooms girls learn to be silent or talk minimally in "official" situations.

In the interaction concerning repertory choice, we see what happens when the leader addresses Anna specifically, asking her to "shout":

Extract 1 (9629:135)[13]
  1 Leader: HI shout Anna shout (. . . .) (*pause*)
  2 Anna: Not me (. . . .) pick (to shout) somebody else now
  3 Sulevi: Well "Nights in Firenze" is here next (. . . .).
  4   (—)
  5 Leader: The favorite tune of Martti Vesijärvi,
         "Nights in Firenze."

The conductor's invitation to shout (line 1) opens up a range of possible responses, one of which is chosen by the person responding; in conversation analysis terms, the invitation has a "sequential implication": it delimits alternatives for the next speaker, who opts for one of these. The conductor's call for "shouting" and the naming of a tune clearly form a linked sequence, or an "adjacency pair"—just as you must return a greeting or answer a question, you must either name a tune or pass your turn to somebody else when you are asked to shout. Anna chooses the second option and relinquishes her turn in favor of somebody else (line 2). In terms of communication ability, that is a perfectly acceptable solution.

Anna's rejection of the request to name a tune could be interpreted as a sort of resistance to the "masculine power" involved in the situation. On the rare occasions when there were more women at a rehearsal, however, they sometimes participated more often than Anna, both in conversation and also in the construction of collective humor (I have two such examples in my recordings). The "resistance hypothesis" thus implies that although the other women were seemingly more assertive than Anna, they were actually yielding to the male-dominated discourse style.

Nevertheless, I think that Anna's refusal reflects her self-image as a partial outsider, one whose wishes are not worth being heard and whose musical preferences are thus not realized by the ensemble. The invitation to shout is a rare opportunity. The repertory of the band is large, including around 270 pieces of music, as mentioned before. Some melodies had been forgotten for years when somebody "shouted" them back into circulation. Men never voluntarily relinquished their turn to shout, although sometimes they lost it because they spent too much time deliberating. In the previous example, Sulevi took the opportunity immediately and named his choice.

I tried to discuss the issue of silence with Anna in a subsequent interview. I started by asking whether she had any musical preferences: did she, for instance, prefer to play old dance music or traditional music? She said that her taste was catholic. I took up the question of making one's musical wishes heard in the group:

Extract 2 (Interview by H. Järviluoma, Aug. 1995)

1	H.J.:	But there was in any case (P) the group was
2		such that that, part of it was very active
3		and they did all sorts of (.) were acting as
4		chairman
5	A.:	Yes there (—) (.)
6	H.J.:	And then again (.) some were (P) when I
7		sometimes thought about that (—) uh that you
8		for instance when, well, ((the director)) said
9		please tell now these favorite tunes, or ((as he said))
10		"shout" [*he always*
11	A.:	[Yes
12	H.J.:	So you very seldom (.) shouted (.) anything or
13		$you didn't make suggestions.$ ((laughs))
14	A.:	((a laugh)) Yes
15	H.J.:	So I was thinking about it, why was that
16		(P)
17	A.:	I am always a bit timid out there ((a laugh))
18	H.J.:	Yes (P) But was it not a pity when one
19		could have (. . . .) Would you, did you have any such
20		favorite tunes which you would have
21		$wanted to play$ [or was it
22	A.:	[there almost—was played
23		almost
24	H.J.:	YES
25	A.:	every kind of (music) ((a laugh)) (P) so that there
26		were books almost so they had been almost
27		uh played
28	H.J.:	YES. So they came (from there) in ANY case
29	A.:	yes
30	H.J.:	yes (P) yes it was
31	A.:	Well it was naturally not (easy) to go there
32		suddenly uh when I had not been playing at
33		home (P)
34	H.J.:	*yes*
35	A.:	but it was terribly nice to be, no, no they did not
36		(P) quite quite quite nice it was to be and it was
37		as if somebody was pulling me with a
38		string that "go there now"
39	H.J.:	yes
40	A.:	yes ((a laugh))

I cannot analyze Anna's answers without considering my interview questions. I start by saying that some members in the group were very active. When I start to talk about the others (line 6), who could be characterized as the "passive" members, I speak indirectly, pausing and then relating an experience involving Anna (lines 7–13). I seem to be creating a membership categorization, a polarity within the ensemble Virtain pelimannit between "active members" and "other members."[14]

I focus attention back on the group (line 18) when I ask Anna about her inability to request her favorite tunes. She claims that the large repertory (mostly handwritten sheets compiled into "books") was played thoroughly in any case. Anna's comment in lines 31–33 is interesting. Here she carefully raises an issue that she obviously feels is behind her silence: she had not been playing her instrument at home when she first joined the group. This suggests that her silence has to do with features[15] she is attaching to the category "musician": she seems to withdraw slightly from the center of that category because she was not a musician when she first joined the group. Maybe she considers "shouting," naming a tune, as a right and obligation of "musicians." Nevertheless, she straightaway constructs herself as an integral part of the group (lines 35–38), stressing how nice it is to be in the group and saying that it felt as if somebody had pulled her "with a string" to the rehearsals.

I started the discussion by implying that she was a member of the "passive" part of the ensemble, but she herself finished by constructing

Reflections while Writing

I'm an alien in England when writing this article, in a language that is not my own. Tämä on minun kieltäni. In spite of that difficulty, something has changed in my situation since I left Finland. For a short while I will be less a mother. I will have less responsibility. This country is Other for me, and it is in the realm of the Other that you can enjoy irresponsibility. Roland Barthes came to this conclusion when wondering whether there is not some reverse racism when you love a foreign country, "one is tired of the same, one exalts the Other" (1989, 303–4; cf. Engh 1993, 77).

But my work also makes me critical of our preoccupation with otherness. An influential ethnomusicology textbook said clearly in the 1960s that the only possible way for an ethnomusicologist to gain sufficient objectivity was to study musics other than his or her own (Nettl 1964). Even now, in England, the question ethnomusicologists ask me is "What is your research area?" and they mean it geographically. When I answer, "A rural community in mid-Finland," that is somehow not an acceptable answer. If herself as a willing and regularly participating member. Her construction does not equate the pelimanni ensemble with the category "musician," not even if the category "officers" is combined with it—an association I made in lines 2–4. Indeed, this implies a fact that became clearer and clearer during the interview: for her, a pelimanni group is an inclusively defined social group that includes musicians, coffee makers, ticket sellers, and so on.

Anna has been a member of the group right from its inception in 1972. The other women were not active members, as she was. In the beginning, however, she could hardly play her instrument, mainly holding her mandolin in her arms. Instead she was there for all the activities, and she would be the first to volunteer to sell tickets at performances and so on. She was a "pelimanni," even if her musical input was minimal.[16]

you study musicians who live only about 100 kilometers from your home, it is deemed too much of the same.

Ethnomusicologists and anthropologists have become increasingly aware of the power relations implied by the study of a clearly defined Other, be it primitive, tribal, non-Western, nonliterate, nonhistorical—the list could be endless. Gayatri C. Spivak, referring to Foucault on the problems of teaching so-called postcolonial literature, has put it as follows: if marginality is constituted as an area of investigation, this is only because relations of power have established it as a possible object (Spivak 1993; cf. Turner 1989, 27). I am not saying that ethnomusicologists should stop studying other cultures; it is important to stress this. I am saying that the polarity that has grown between studying the Other and the Same still needs to be questioned. The practices of ethnomusicologists are changing more slowly than their talk.

The implications of this categorization remain elusive, however. Because instrumental "musicians" have historically constituted a male-dominated category, one could view her more open-ended category construction as more gender neutral than the one with which I began. Conversely, however, her category construction maintains the marginalization of women, accepting their restricted musical participation.

Conversation about Visual Image

The second event to be analyzed concerns the negotiation of the visual image of the group in performance. This dialogue took place during an annual meeting of the folk musicians' association of Virrat. Preceding this exchange, the head of the association gave a general description of the pelimannit's activities during the previous year, saying among other things that the group performed dance music in Virrat anytime they were asked, without looking "at race or gender or other aspects." The phrase was partly intended as humor, but at the same time, it says something important about the organization's willingness to be open toward different societal groups.

The association chair thus used a "boundary-crossing code" (see Järviluoma 1995, 1997), a type of discourse important in identity negotiation. Soon after this, however, he set boundaries within the group: he claimed that the group's males differentiated themselves from the female members by means of visual image.

Once again, there are larger contextual issues influencing the shape of this exchange. It is well known, for example, that many rock bands do not totally exclude women but use them on stage "to enhance their visual image, usually as backing vocalists dressed in glamorous outfits" (Cohen 1991, 81). As Sara Cohen observes in her study of Liverpool rock culture, women were considered a threat to the coherence and smooth functioning of rock bands. One female musician herself admitted that she judged female performers more harshly, assuming that "they are there to add glamour and not for their performance abilities" (Cohen 1991, 201–22, 208).

In the Virtain pelimannit, on the other hand, the women in the group do not have particularly glamorous outfits: they wear exactly the same gray trousers, shirt, velvet vest, and tie as the men. In the earlier years, especially in the late 1970s, when the group still used the "official" national costume of Virrat, women wore the ladies' Virrat costume, which was certainly different from the men's costume. By the late 1980s, however, during frequent discussions about clothing, no one ever suggested that women and men should wear different clothes on stage.

This is related, in part, to an aesthetic preference for a large group to be dressed uniformly, a look that the conductor described as "handsome" or impressively beautiful. Sometimes he expressed this in a way that recognized the contribution of the less-competent players (including some women), even if they could not, for example, act as musical leaders (KPK 1988, 54:54). Nevertheless, the women's importance in enhancing the appearance of the group was often brought up explicitly, even if humorously.

Extract 3 (KPL Y) A = the head of the association (one of the musicians); B = the conductor

1   A: It's great that we have more of the fair sex (P) now (—) we have more girls than [before]

2		normally, generally, we have only one and now there's four (P) and (P) it's great
3		that Hillevi has come back to the gang after being some years [away
4	B:	[The
5		pelimanni group's appearance has become better
6	A:	much better
7		((*laughs*))
8	A:	And so we can state that we others grow old gracefully. This is really a marvelous
9		gang. That's it and now to the meeting—

Let us look at the ways in which the sexes were described. Women were addressed as a category, qualitatively identified in terms of beauty: the phrase "fair sex" is literally "the more beautiful sex" in Finnish. The women were also named as "girls," implying "not-yet-adultness": in Sack's system, "girl" can be viewed as part of the membership categorization device "stage of life." The conductor added (line 5) to the implication by commenting on the enhanced appearance of the group.

As noted earlier, the rhetoric of both "difference" and "boundary-crossing" are present in this conversation. There is a generic group—"we others" (meaning exclusively men) (line 8)—from which "the fair sex" is differentiated. Nonetheless, the "standardized relational pair" (SRP) presented explicitly here is not qualitatively specified in a predictable way as "beautiful girls" and "ugly middle-aged men." Rather, the men, described as "we others," are "growing old gracefully" (*vanhennutaan arvokkaasti*).

How does this relate to the social meaning of the concept "musician"? The problem of growing old gracefully is a central concern to male rock stars, as Odd Are Berkaak (1992, 202) has shown; they are supposed to stay young and youthfully rebellious all their lives. In the pelimanni musical world, however, men seemingly can deal better with aging; I observed this on various occasions in the course of my research (Järviluoma 1997, 233–38).

I noticed that talking about "the fair sex" was a typical way of opening official mix-gendered situations, even when one would least expect it—for example, in situations where the speaker clearly appreciated the presence of women. Such was the case here: women's presence and participation in the ensemble were acknowledged. Nevertheless, the expression "it's great that we have more of the fair sex" illustrates one of the basic problems that women have with men's acts of "homage." The phrase was used casually but carried meanings that were far from innocent. Mary Wollstonecraft (1992) already recognized this paradox in 1792, noting that, among other things, not only are women given this "empty adoration," but in addition they are supposed to adore the prison in which they are confined.

In the next example the group was organizing a countywide traditional music event. They refused to allow it to be a chaotic carnival: they were planning the program, minute by minute, to accommodate the forty-six groups that planned to participate. One masculine imagination, however, inspired by the thought that a young women's dance group would dance a can-can in the event, threatened their neat structure:

Extract 4 (KPL Y 9630)

1	A:	(—) or tomorrow the letter leaves so THEY ARE, LISTEN
2		FORTY-SIX if they all just come then it god bless takes a day to thresh.
3	B:	Yeah not in [that
4	A:	[Hopefully they don't come all
5		((many people laugh))
6	B:	If many come the tunes have to be lopped off
7	A:	Forty-six groups think about that (.) if they all come then—
8	C:	Where was it once (. . . .) pieces and it was prolonged so damned long
9	A:	YES(. . . .)
10	D:	it easily takes five minutes each tune (. . . .)
11	E:	(. . . .)
12	A:	And the the soloists over and above (P) soloists at that and folk dances at that and
13		else and to the dance dancers has not been given more than four minutes (P)
14		to this village gang and then four minutes (P) to the gang from Vaskivesi[17]
15		too (P) and then well (P) there was such an impressively beautiful[18] picture of those (P)
16		what are they, gymnast girls (.) it was in the newspaper so let's take them too
17		[there
18	F:	[ten minutes (. . . .)
19		((many people laugh a lot))
20	C:	They get half an hour and from the others (. . . .)
21		((unconstrained laughter)) (—)
22	F:	If they perform can-can it takes ten minutes $before anybody can play

23		anything after that$
24	E:	(. . . .)
25	G:	It becomes Värisevät lehdet[19] after that
26		((laugh))
27	A:	It would be good if the girls could perform too.

This conversation extract can be analyzed appropriately in several ways. First, I will use Sacksian MCD terms, and second, I will thicken the description with some other perspectives.

It is possible to read this excerpt via the Sacksian standard pair "willingly gazing men" and "sexy girls." This reading emphasizes the fact that, according to Sacks's "consistency rule," when men discuss girls in erotic terms, they themselves are appropriately heard speaking as sexual human beings. We can read the vibrant body entering the text for a moment and see how desire is articulated here.

In line 14, when discussing the folk dance groups, the conductor used the terms *porukka* and *sakki,* translated here as "gang." These labels do not convey either the gender or the ages of the group's members. The "gymnast girls," however, like the women in example 5 (discussed later), were framed in terms of appearance, gender, and age. They were brought into the discussion by the conductor when he noted their "impressively beautiful" appearance in a newspaper. Their abilities as "dancers"—another potential category actualized only later, at line 27, for example—were not mentioned at this point. The gendered term *voimistelijalikka* ("gymnast girl"), including the morpheme *likka,* a slightly pejorative characterization of a youngish girl, can also be seen as part of the MCD "life stage." Girls were thus constructed as objects of the male gaze and desire, and according to Sacks's consistency rule, the folk dance groups that were mentioned earlier were implicitly categorized as rather dry; here we can see an instance in an everyday discussion in which folk dance was constructed as "sanitized." This construction was reinforced when the folk dance groups were given only four minutes of performing time even though the "gymnast girls'" time was imagined as stretching to half an hour plus ten minutes for recovery. Here men laughed at their own desire.

When the men talked about the gymnast girls, however, they did not confine them within clear-cut boundaries. At line 27, when the laughter stopped, the conductor foregrounded the gymnast girls as "performers." By stating that "it would be good if the girls could perform too," he invoked the category of "amateur performer." In this MCD, pelimannit were considered senior citizens, helpers, who could enable the junior dancers to get publicity leading to performance opportunities.

If we invoke the deconstructionist idea that meanings are partly created through deferral, however, through the void located in the *différance,* we could interpret the extract differently. This humorous exchange also creates what is *not present* explicitly in the language; that is, when the musicians speak as "willingly gazing men," the paradoxical effect is that the ordinary, matter-of-fact masculinity of these men (and women) in their matching gray trousers, ties, and vests does not completely disappear from their mind.

Thus there is no single message in the group's humor (see Silverman and Torode 1980, 143–69). The meaning located in the words can be effaced by nonsense and laughter. Here the humor is based on exaggeration, but often through language games in which words are repeated. It is not only modern writers but also ordinary people who escape the univocal, increasingly pure signifier that in vain tries to force itself on the subject (see Kristeva 1980, 144–45).

Meaning also relies on memories of other performances, other associations. In this regard, it is important to know that the girls' dance group and the pelimanni group are associated with the same adult evening college. Thus the men had seen the group performing before, and so had I. This is how I described their can-can performance at the college's "little Christmas party":

Extract 5 (KPK 1988 48:50)
Stately dresses. Very sensual. The white knickers blink. Four young women from 13–16 years. Also their hair has been properly laid.

Both I and, later, the pelimanni men (see example 4) read the can-can performance in terms of appearance because it was presented as a sensuous performance. The dancers were using clothing and a style familiar from the Moulin Rouge: late nineteenth-century-style dresses and hair and long lace knickers that twinkled when the young women kicked their legs (see Haug et al. 1988). It would, of course, be dangerous to conclude that only one reading of their performance was possible. How did the dancers and their choreographer read this? Further research would be necessary to learn whether they perceived this choreography as a positive "performance of femininity."

Interaction Concerning Practicing and the Kitchen

It is reported that when the late Herbert von Karajan was asked in a press conference why there were no women in the Berlin Philharmonic, he answered that "a woman's place is in the kitchen and not in the symphony orchestra" (*Die Welt* 7 Nov. 1979; in Rieger 1986, 185). Ethnomusicology should not exclude "kitchen work" phenomena from their ethnographies. Sometimes women are told to remain in the kitchen, as Karajan urged them to do, but far more often women willingly assume the kitchen work within music cultures. Women thus have a direct effect on the musical output.[20] In my case, the analysis of women's work in the kitchen during rehearsals also brought up some important methodological questions.

Virtain pelimannit did not have any objections to the basic idea of having women in their ensemble, but my field descriptions of the group repeatedly show that the kitchen was women's space. If there were women at the rehearsals, at least one of them was always involved in making the coffee. Only two of the more than twenty men ever participated. My diary shows that women made coffee by themselves five times out of eleven. Five times a man helped a woman, and once the male leader of the group made it alone (no women were present). One of the consequences of the fact that women are tied to coffee making is that they cannot attend the entire rehearsal. Usually they lose at least a half-hour of practice.[21]

Let us see how this works. In the extract below, during one of the last rehearsals of the year, a big creamcake was bought to celebrate. One of the men, Eero, arrived late. He is an active man who belongs to many associations; he is not only the chairperson of the pelimanni association but also an active participant in sports administration. Anna did not hesitate; she knew what to do. Here, from within the group, we find a qualitatively specified standard relational pair: "men performing duty" and "caring and helping-women":

Extract 6 (KPK 1989, 183:225)
In the middle of everything [the practice] Eero came dressed up in a tie and cardigan (the others had suspected he had been at some sport administrators' event. We had already been talking at coffee break—is anybody else coming, perhaps only Eero, we have to save a small piece of cake for him). Immediately Anna put her mandolin under the chair and left to go to the kitchen.

The division of labor in rural Finland, at least when elderly or middle-aged people are involved, often produces episodes that resemble the foregoing scene. As I noted earlier, Anna was a pelimanni, even if her musical input was minimal. Her kitchen duties were part of her legitimation as a group member. Why has Anna not devoted herself more to playing her instrument in two decades? One answer, though morally objectionable, would be that she is a useful and legitimate member of the group because, and as long as, she puts the needs of men first.

Studies of rock culture have demonstrated that women usually opt to more or less hang around without passionately practicing one instrument or one style of music—they are happily eclectic. As Jaana Lähteenmaa and Sari Näre have put it, maybe women are more able to acquire the skills they need in postmodern society by not sticking to one particular hobby or one monolithic musical style. Instead, they may opt to move smoothly, to shuttle, between different discourses of music, hobbies, and school and thus subsequently have strong abilities to cope with a diverse and rapidly changing world (Lähteenmaa and Näre 1991, 329–35; see also Cohen 1991).[22] With these studies in mind, we could ask whose interests it would have served had Anna become a virtuoso mandolin player at the expense of her woodwork hobby, her membership in the school administrative delegation, or her grandmotherly duties?

Elisabeth Lawless confronted rather similar problems when she studied female preachers in the United States. As a feminist, she interpreted her data as showing that male dominance restricted the career of one particular preacher (Lawless 1992, 307). Later, however, even though still wanting to sustain her interpretation, she deeply regretted that she had not shown her interpretations to the preachers before publishing the book. In particular, the previously mentioned preacher had her own interpretation, one that challenged the researcher's readings of the situation. Lawless thinks that her book would have been better if both interpretations had been included (Lawless 1992, 308–11; see also Koskoff 1993).[23]

This is partly why I returned to Anna and discussed my interpretations with her. When I brought up the issue of losing practicing time, she readily acknowledged it:

Extract 7 (Interview by H. Järviluoma, Aug. 1995)

22	H.J.:	Ym (P) well I sometimes thought about
23		the fact that one loses practicing time
24	A.:	So one does lose (.) does lose but (P)
25		on the other hand one already got some (.)
26		$practicing done too$ [((laughs))
27	H.J.:	[$yeaah$
28	H.J.:	yes (0.4) yes
29	A.:	for a long time

In both cases she stressed that she really did not mind: "It didn't make any difference to me" (line 21) and "on the other hand one already got some practicing done too" (lines 25–26). When I laughed and said yes a couple of times, she added "for a long time" (29): she was a member for a long time, so she had attended many practices.

Remember that I raised the issue. I started not from a gender perspective but rather from the membership category "pelimanni group" and, within that, a specific subcategory, "the coffee makers." Anna was consistent[24] in not choosing to speak about gender either. She spoke as a member of the pelimanni group, a category that, according to Harvey Sacks, can be seen as a "team"—not a loose collection of people like those at a "stage of life" or those who are "redheads." "Pelimanni group" is related to categories such as "family" or "gang" in the sense that membership in these groups presupposes loyalty and a sense of belonging. Probably the "pelimanni women" of the group could have formed a teamlike construct as well, if it had occurred to them and if they had wanted to. But such a construct does not exist in the cultural repertory of Anna, and she did not identify herself by her gender. (Of course, gender was vividly present in our interview because we both were women.)

Anna's comments such as "it didn't make any difference to me" can thus be read as indications of her loyalty to the group. She did not organize the activities hierarchically. On the contrary, near the end of the discussion, in line 37, when she points out that the (male) director of the group also made coffee at times, she created another perspective on the category of coffee makers:

Extract 8

```
37      A.:  But (P) Arvo was himself of the kind (P) that
38           he also made it then
39      H.J.:  YES so he did
```

If the director is part of the coffee makers, it can be regarded as an important group. Thus Anna constructs herself as part of an important activity. Is Anna "an altruistic individualist," as Jaana Lähteenmaa and Sari Näre (1991, 329–35) have called women who make individual decisions but at the same time never stop taking other people into account? Anna was bold and came to the ensemble—dominated by men—without having played her instrument before. She was individualistic, but she took care of others' needs at the same time. Thus we return to the question of women's greater responsibility toward others and what effects this has.

Concluding Remarks

Cities at night, I feel, contain men who cry in their sleep and then say Nothing.
It's nothing. Just sad dreams. Or something like that.

  —Martin Amis, *Author, Author*

My study of pelimanni ensembles has emphasized the positionality of discourses of gender. What is marginal at a certain moment depends on the position of the viewer. It is not enough to stress the sex of the speaker; we have to analyze the different discourses, perspectives, and social interactions that construct the gendered subject.

The fact that the pelimannit I have studied are composed mostly of men must not deceive us into believing that this culture comprises only "cock folk." Already the well-known symbol of Finnish folk music, Konsta Jylhä, whom I mentioned previously, was different. He could cry on the stage[25] and remain, nonetheless, a "man of the people." This is exceptional; Finnish macho men usually cry only in their sleep, like Amis's city men. But the tradition of the pelimannit reveals how men can be defined as marginal in the symbolic order.

In Kristeva's terms, femininity (if it is possible to define it) is simply something that the patriarchal symbolic order has marginalized (Moi 1988, 164). In fact, pelimannit are themselves marginal if we look from a certain position. The music college and the town's male choir stand at the top of the patriarchal hierarchy, representing hegemonic masculinity. The members of the male choir have "their chests full of honorary medals," as the pelimanni conductor bitterly mentions. Furthermore, Virrat itself is marginalized. A female pelimanni from a neighboring town won a medal, whereas no pelimanni from Virrat did so.

With regard to applying Sacksian category analysis to the study of gender construction in the context of music making, I find it to be a useful technique that ought not to be dismissed because of its "masculinity." I tend to subscribe to the position articulated by Toril Moi (1988, 159–60): she considers it important not to banish logic, conceptualization, and rationality as "nonfeminine" but instead to try to develop a society in which these virtues would not be categorized as "masculine." Sacks clearly emphasizes the fact that people belong in many categories that are maintained or (re)created constantly. Categorization was, for him, a culturally methodic (procedural) *activity*, not an inert cultural or semantic grid (see Watson 1994). The model benefits from, among other things, Lena Jayyusi's (1984) developments, which take even more into account how category features are generated in specific situations.

Both women and men in the Virtain pelimanni ensemble constantly negotiate their gender identities. On one hand, they orient to the gender categories of Finnish rural and small-town society and to features conventionally reinforced in these communities. On the other hand, the musicians construct their identities relative to specific situations, and they redefine and resist aspects of the conventional categories.

My bottom-up analysis tries to avoid treating people as "cultural dopes" (Garfinkel 1984, 66–69) and instead attempts to show how they use norms and categories. Categories are not totally abandoned here, of course. I could easily read how the group methodically created and maintained Anna's position as a woman in many ways. On the other hand, Anna herself constructs herself as an individual who in some senses is bolder than other women— she had the courage to stay in the group even though, so far, she could hardly play her mandolin, and she enjoyed the group with all her heart. Men are also negotiating their masculinities in these everyday discussions of subjects ranging from their suitability as coffee makers to attitudes toward their bodies.

I hope that I have managed to interrupt the discourse of music researchers who tend to put all forms of folk music into a homogeneous category, trying to master, neutralize, and reduce it. I suggest that it is useful to see the activities of both pelimanni and trad'n'avantgarde musicians as positive ways of "becoming a minority," escaping the hegemonic order of the majority.

It is much easier to see innovative attitudes in the practices of traditional avant-gardists, but such attitudes are not altogether absent from the practices of pelimannit. A play of signifiers occurs just as much on the grass-roots level of amateur music making as on more professional levels. To label any aspect of these musical practices as "masculine" or "feminine" would be justifiable only as part of that play.

APPENDIX 1: GLOSSARY OF MEMBERSHIP CATEGORY DEVICE TERMS

Category, or Membership Category

Much of the knowledge needed for communication is organized into "membership categories," which form an important cultural resource. Anyone can be labeled in several appropriate ways, for example, teacher, wife, adulterer, mother, or rap fan. Each of these descriptions is a "membership category."

Categorization

This term derives from a distinction Lena Jayyusi has made between membership categories and "membership categorizations." Categorization "refers to the work of members in categorizing other members or using 'characterizations' of them, whereas the former (Category) refers to the already culturally available category concepts that members may, and routinely do, use" (Jayyusi 1984, 20).

Category-Bound Features

Where features are formulated, explicitly or implicitly, as conventionally accompanying some category, we may talk of them as being category bound.

Category-Generated Features

Where features are provided for in discourse as having been situatedly *produced* through their tie to some category, we may talk of them as being category generated.

Consistency Rule

This rule helps to determine the application of MCDs. If a person is identified under a certain category, then the next person in the conversation may be identified by using a category from the same collection of categories.

Economy Rule

This is another rule to determine application of category collections: a single category from a collection may suffice to describe a person.

Membership Category Device (MCD)

Categories can be grouped into larger collections. Members of society have rules for using categories from collections. Thus an MCD is a collection of categories plus rules of application. Any category is a potential member of at least two MCDs; for example, "baby" appears in "family," "stage of life," and "lovers."

Standardized Relational Pair, or Standard Pair (SRP)

Some category pairs that logically belong together can be called standardized relational pairs. SPRs are a certain type of MCDs that include only two categories. We often make sense of the world through standard pairs: men and women, mothers and children, teachers and pupils. Category pairs typically include rights and duties, such as mutual help.

Qualitative Specification

Standard pairs are often qualitatively specified. We speak not only about mothers and children but about "loving mothers and happy children" or "indifferent mothers and neglected children."

Teamlike Device

Certain MCDs include categories that members of a society feel fit so closely together that they form a "team" or social "unit." For instance, "family" is a teamlike unit, but "stage of life" is not.

Appendix 2: Transcription Symbols

Translating these transcriptions presented a range of problems. Ideally such transcriptions incorporate symbolic notation indicating patterns of oral delivery such as pauses and dynamics. The conventions governing the use of such notation in translation have been developed by ethnomethodologists. If the translation here were completely literal, however, it would be impossible to understand. The version here is a compromise that expresses the content but retains some of the markers of the Finnish transcripts (Järviluoma 1997, 159–63).

(. . . .)	Indicates the transcriber's inability to hear what was said
(—)	Elipsis; part of the transcription is omitted
(P)	Pause (numbers in parentheses indicate elapsed time in tenths of a second)
(.)	Micropause
WORD	Capitals, except at the beginning of lines, indicate especially loud sounds relative to the surrounding talk
\<text>	Especially low sounds relative to the surrounding talk
(( ))	Double parentheses contain author's descriptions rather than transcriptions
# #	Squeaking voice
$ $	Smiling voice
underline	indicates an unidentified change in the way of speaking
[	Overlapping talk

Notes

The glossary is based on Silverman 1993, 80–89; Jayyusi 1984; Cuff 1980; Sacks 1974, 218–24. Thanks also to Terry Walker. Several people have offered invaluable comments on earlier drafts of this essay. I thank them all, especially Barbro Klein, Bruce Johnson, Virginia Mattila, Moira Kelly, David Silverman, Jaana Lähteenmaa, and the editors of this book.

1. See, for example, Silverman 1993, 80–89, for a basic introduction.

2. Julia Kristeva has moved beyond the Saussurian concept of *langue* to resituate the talking subject at the center of language analysis. According to her, language comes into being in the process of talking between subjects; therefore, to study meanings we have to examine specific strategies used in different situations (Kristeva 1980). This is similar to the ideas of ethnomethodologists such as Harvey Sacks. One could use concepts of both Ferdinand de Saussure and Sacks to study the Virtain pelimannit ensemble. In seeking to study the system of signs of the ensemble, Saussure would perhaps study the structure of their repertory from the printed sheets. Sacks, on the other hand, would listen to how the rep-

ertory is used in live situations, the sequences in which one member after the other chooses the next tune. Perhaps the most important difference between Sacks and Saussure is that the latter confined himself to imagined examples, whereas Sacks studied real conversations.

3. Often the rejection of the study of certain musics happens simply because the (ethno)musicologist does not like the music. Even popular music scholars exhibit this tendency, as Charles Keil has noticed: because researchers favor the study of "cool" musics over the "corny," such important areas as American polka music have been practically unstudied. The rites of "polka happiness" represent everything that is "corny, dated, two-beat and square" (Keil and Keil 1993, 3).

4. Within Europe, only Bulgaria maintained agriculture as the predominant means of livelihood longer than Finland.

5. In the early 1970s Jylhä was extremely popular in Finland among a wide range of audiences. I was always struck by one particular aspect of his performances: every time he played his composition "Vaiennut viulu" (the "Silent Violin," which hints at the death of a pelimanni), he cried and had to wipe his eyes. This was always highlighted in the media: the music itself was not given much attention (Laitinen 1971, 26).

I listened to one of his concerts in my little rural hometown when I was around ten years old, and I think that the spirit at the moment when Jylhä wept was somehow sacred. A man crying on the stage does not fit the Finnish macho image of men. The whole crowd of 900 people listened earnestly, as though perhaps the man was suffering to save us all.

6. Värttinä, categorized by Louis van Elderen (1994, 63) as neofolk, consists of young female singers plus mainly male instrumentalists. The women usually wear overtly feminine clothing: for instance, long flowery dresses that, to me and probably to many other Finns, evoke slight nostalgia for the dance dresses of the 1940s and 1950s. More important, they write their own lyrics and use folk lyrics that are assertive and do not hesitate to connect young women and sexuality.

7. "Avant-garde traditionalism," or "trad'n'avantgarde," is a term that has been floating in the ping-pong game of Finnish folk music discourse for a couple of years. I cannot recall the moment I first heard it. The first time I saw it in print was in an article by Hannu Saha (1993, 22) about the first director of the Sibelius Academy Folk Music Department, Heikki Laitinen. His aims as a teacher of folk music students were twofold: first, to continue directly from the basic, creative ideas of tradition and, second, to expand the tradition toward avant-gardism. This has led Laitinen and the students of the Sibelius Academy not only to study profoundly the basics of "orality" (or "memory-based" music, as he calls it) in Finnish ("*Kalevala*") rune singing as well as in many other musics and sounds but also to explore different vocal techniques used around the world (Laitinen 1994; Suomussalmi-ryhmä n.d.). For instance, on her solo album, Anna-Kaisa Liedes (n.d.)

includes a track combining Ingrian rune singing, elements of Pygmy singing style, and African drumming all subtly fused together.

8. The founding of the department is usually represented as a sort of triumph in the struggle for recognition of traditional music.

9. Here I talk about the same phenomenon that Bruce Johnson has observed in Australia. His work on the relationships between Australian traditional jazz and the academy (e.g., Johnson 1992) is illuminating in this respect: the introduction of jazz studies courses there has deepened a previously existing fissure in the music world (ibid., 10).

10. *Virtain* is the genitive case of *Virrat; pelimannit* is the plural of *pelimanni.*

11. This woman, Airi Hautamäki, and the groups she leads are currently being studied by M.A. student Katja Riihola, from the Department of Folk Tradition at Tampere University.

12. They seek ways to collaborate with and support each other, for instance, by making joint traveling arrangements to festivals and organizing concerts and competitions together.

13. The extracts are from field recordings. The numbers in parentheses refer to the catalog of the Tape Archive of the Department of Folk Tradition, University of Tampere. KPK refers to the author's field diary. See appendix 2 for an explanation of transcription symbols.

14. We both laughed a lot during this conversation, thus making a potentially difficult topic easier to discuss.

15. See the glossary for explanations of category-bound features and category-generated features.

16. I also asked her whether she had an idea why there were so few women in the group. She constructed herself as bolder than other women. She said that her hobby started when she went to listen to a rehearsal after having heard the sound of music in her yard. She went again, and this time she asked if she could join the group. The musicians said, "Of course, welcome." "They (other women) should have been as bold as I was. I just went there boldly and asked if I could join the gang." She had been part of the group for almost twenty years.

17. This is another community belonging to the administrative area of Virrat.

18. The conductor used the word *komea,* which is usually translated as "handsome." Although "handsome" is usually used for men, however, this term can also refer to women who are somehow impressively beautiful.

19. The name (with diacriticals) means "shivering leaves"; it is a nickname for the accordion composition "Varisevat lehdet" ("Dropping leaves").

20. Today women play in the Berlin Philharmonic, but we can still see instances of the same attitudes. For instance, in Finnish techno musical culture "women folk take care of the food side, some general things and act as managers. Men folk carry the heavy things to their places and then act like 'kings' during the actual techno parties" (a techno activist's statement in Ala-Harja 1997, 54).

21. Nevertheless, although I was a woman researcher in this male-dominated group, I never lost any "practicing time" because of kitchen work. I have analyzed this in detail elsewhere (Järviluoma 1995, 1997). During my fieldwork there was a constant negotiation of the masculine and feminine categories: the group, especially the leader, described me mainly in feminine terms that I would seldom apply to myself.

22. From another angle, though, there are obviously genuine disadvantages in the fact that women are encouraged to divide their attention in too many directions. It is not only a virtue. A woman should at least have a possibility to develop, for instance, expertise on her favorite instrument—which many women also do. For instance, Luce Irigaray (1994, 48) praises the fact that women are more interested in others—is that a sweet trap?

23. As David Silverman (1993, 199–201) has pointed out, from the point of view of validation, it is not necessary to secure the endorsement of the findings from the members of the group studied. Nevertheless—and this would have definitely been the point in the Lawless case—members' readings of the researchers' interpretations offer invaluable data that in turn help in the analysis.

24. See the glossary for an explanation of this term.

25. Kristeva (1980, 144) has talked about several artists having the same "fragile sensitivity."

REFERENCES CITED

Archive Sources
KPL Y   Archives of the Department of Folk Tradition, University of Tampere
KPK   Field diary, Helmi Järviluoma

Literature
Ala-Harja, Päivi. 1997. "Tekno ja teknokulttuuri" (Techo music and techno culture). M.A. thesis, University of Tampere, Finland.
Barthes, Roland. 1989. "One Always Fails in Speaking of What One Loves." *The Rustle of Language*, trans. Richard Howard, 296–305. Berkeley: University of California Press.
Berkaak, Odd Are. 1992. "Barnet, språket og 'den andre stemmen': om førankring av identitet i samtidskulturen" (The child, language, and "the other voice": on grounding identity in todays' culture). In *Den påbegynte virkelighet*. Studier i samtidskultur. Oslo: Universitetsförlaget.
Cohen, Sara. 1991. *Rock Culture in Liverpool: Popular Music in the Making*. Oxford: Clarendon.
Cuff, E. C. 1980. *Some Issues in Studying the Problem of Versions in Everyday Situations*. Occasional Paper no. 3. Manchester: University of Manchester.

Elderen, Louis van. 1994. "Finnish Popular Music, Culture, and National Identity: Some Questions by an Outsider." *Etnomusikologian vuosikirja* 6:50–65.

Engh, Barbara. 1993. "Loving It: Music and Criticism in Roland Barthes." In *Musicology and Difference: Gender and Sexuality in Music Scholarship,* ed. Ruth Solie, 66–79. Berkeley: University of California Press.

Finnegan, Ruth. 1989. *The Hidden Musicians: Music-making in an English Town.* Cambridge: Cambridge University Press.

Garfinkel, Harold. 1984 [1967]. *Studies in Ethnomethodology.* Cambridge, U.K.: Polity.

Hakulinen, Auli. 1987. "Mies, nainen ja kieli" (Man, woman and language). In *Kieli, kertomus, kulttuuri,* ed. Tommi Hoikkala, 52–70. Helsinki: Gaudeamus.

Haug, Frigga, et al. 1988. *Female Sexualization: A Collective Work of Memory.* London: Verso.

Irigaray, Luce. 1994 [1989, Fr.]. *Thinking the Difference for a Peaceful Revolution.* London: Athlone.

Järviluoma, Helmi. 1986. *Musiikki, liikkeet, hillikkeet* (Music, movements, restraints). Tampere, Finland: Department of Folk Tradition.

———. 1995. "Local Construction of Identity: Analysing Category-Work of an Amateur Music Group." In *Popular Music: Style and Identity,* ed. Will Straw, Stacey Johnson, Rebecca Sullivan, and Paul Friedlander, 155–61. Montreal: Centre for Research on Canadian Cultural Industries and Institutions.

———. 1997. *Musiikki, identiteetti ja ruohonjuuritaso* (Music and identity at grassroots level). Acta Universitatis Tamperensis 555. Tampere, Finland: University of Tampere.

Järviluoma, Helmi, and Airi Mäki-Kulmala. 1992. "Folk Music and Political Song Movements in Finland: Remarks on Symbolic Home-coming." In *Music, History, Democracy,* vol. 3., ed. Antoine Hennion, 691–705. Paris: Éditions de la Maison des Sciences de l'Homme and Ministre de la Culture Recherche, Musique et Dance.

Jayyusi, Lena. 1984. *Categorization and the Moral Order.* London: Routledge.

Johnson, Bruce. 1992. *Jazz: A Test Case for Popular Culture in the Australian Academies.* Institute of Popular Music Occasional Paper 3. Liverpool: Institute of Popular Music, University of Liverpool.

Keil, Charles, and Angeliki V. Keil, with photographs by Dick Blau. 1992. *Polka Happiness.* Philadelphia: Temple University Press.

Koskoff, Ellen. 1993. "Miriam Sings Her Song: The Self and the Other in Anthropological Discourse." In *Musicology and Difference: Gender and Sexuality in Music Scholarship,* ed. Ruth Solie, 149–63. Berkeley: University of California Press.

Kristeva, Julia. 1980. "From One Identity to an Other." *Desire in Language: A Semiotic Approach to Literature and Art,* 124–47. Oxford: Blackwell.

Kurkela, Vesa. 1989. *Musiikkifolklorismi ja järjestökulttuuri* (Music folklorism and organization culture). Helsinki: Suomen Etnomusikologinen Seura.

Lähteenmaa, Jaana, and Sari Näre. 1991. "Moderni suomalainen tyttöys: altruistista individualismia" (Modern Finnish girlhood: altruistic individualism). In *Letit liehumaan,* ed. Jaana Lähteenmaa and Sari Näri, 329–37. Helsinki: Suomalaisen Kirjallisuuden Seura.

Laitinen, Heikki. 1971. "Kansanmusiikin uusi tuleminen" (The revival of folk music). *Musiikki* 4:24–28.

———. 1977. "'Kaustislaisuuden' synty. Kaustisen ensimmäiset kansanmusiikkijuhlat ja maaseutukulttuurin paluu 1960-luvun Suomessa" (The birth of Kaustinen spirit). M.A. thesis, University of Helsinki.

———. 1989. "Suomalaisen kansanmusiikkiliikkeen taustasta ja luonteesta" (The background of Finnish folk music revival). *Kansanmusiikki* 2:14–17.

———. 1994. "Music-making as a Research Method." *Ethnomusicology* 38:3.

Lawless, Elisabeth. 1992. "'I was afraid someone like you . . . an outsider . . . would misunderstand': Negotiating Interpretative Differences between Ethnographers and Subjects." *Journal of American Folklore* 105, no. 417:302–14.

Moi, Toril. 1988 [1985]. *Sexual-Textual Politics: Feminist Literary Theory.* London: Routledge.

Nettl, Bruno. 1964. *Theory and Method in Ethnomusicology.* New York: Free Press.

Ramsten, Märta. 1985. "The New Fiddlers: Trends and Revivalism in the Folk Music of the Seventies." In *Folkmusikvågen* (The folk music vogue), ed. Birgit Kjällström, Jan Ling, Christina Mattsson, Märta Ramsten, and Gunnar Ternhag, 193–200. Stockholm: Rikskonserter.

Rieger, Eva. 1986. "'Dolce semplica'? On the Changing Role of Women in Music." In *Feminist Aesthetics,* ed. Gisela Ecker, trans. Harriet Anderson, 135–49. London: Women's Press.

Sacks, Harvey. 1966. "The Search for Help: No One to Turn To." Ph.D. diss., University of California, Berkeley.

———. 1974 [1972]. "On the Analysability of Stories by Children." In *Ethnomethodology,* ed. Roy Turner, 216–32. Aylesbury, U.K.: Penguin Books.

———. 1992. *Lectures on Conversation.* 2 vols. Ed. Gail Jefferson. Oxford: Blackwell.

Saha, Hannu. 1993. "Tuntematon Laitinen" (The unknown Laitinen). *Uusi Kansanmusiikki* 3:4–7, 22.

Shepherd, John. 1993. "Difference and Power in Music." In *Musicology and Difference: Gender and Sexuality in Music Scholarship,* ed. Ruth Solie, 46–65. Berkeley: University of California Press.

Silverman, David. 1993. *Interpreting Qualitative Data: Methods for Analysing Talk, Text, and Interaction.* London: Sage.

Silverman, David, and Brian Torode. 1980. "The Essentialism of Ethnomethodology." *The Material Word: Some Theories of Language and Its Limits,* 143–69. London: Routledge and Kegan Paul.

Solie, Ruth, ed. 1993. *Musicology and Difference: Gender and Sexuality in Music Scholarship.* Berkeley: University of California Press.

Spivak, Gayatri Chakravorty. 1993. *Outside in the Teaching Machine.* London: Routledge.

Treitler, Leo. 1993. "Gender and Other Dualities in Music History." In *Musicology and Difference: Gender and Sexuality in Music Scholarship,* ed. Ruth Solie, 23–45. Berkeley: University of California Press.

Turner, Roy. 1989. "Deconstructing the Field." In *The Politics of Field Research,* ed. David Silverman and Jaber Gubrium, 13–29. London: Sage.

Watson, Rod. 1994. "Catégories, séquentialité et ordre social." *Raisons Pratiques* 5:151–85.

Wieder, D. L. 1974. "Language and Social Reality." *Approaches to Semiotics 10.* The Hague: Mouton.

Wollstonecraft, Mary. 1992 [1792]. *A Vindication of the Rights of Woman.* London: Penguin Books.

Music References

Liedes, Anna-Kaisa. n.d. "Viinarattihin rakastuin." In *Kuuttaren korut,* OMCD 44.

Suomussalmi-ryhmä (incl. Heikki Laitinen). n.d. "Mikonkatu Live." In *Tulikulkku,* KICD 30.

3   The Image of Woman in Turkish Ballad Poetry and Music

Ursula Reinhard

In Turkey music plays a large role in the battle between the sexes. The patriarchal Islamic culture largely forbids women from participating in musical activities. Despite this fact—or perhaps because of it—almost all poetic and musical creativity is dedicated to the love of women. Even love toward Allah is expressed in Sufi music, for example, as though the one offering the prayers were offering his devotions to a beloved woman. Therefore it is illuminating that the most important and challenging song type within Turkish folk music is the long melody called *uzun hava,* which is reserved for love or for desire and lament.

There are various types of Turkish musical ballads whose content refers to women. These vary in form, according to the province. They are always sung by men, and they characterize women positively or negatively, mostly both at the same time.

The first ballad type I will introduce comes from the Black Sea area (see Reinhard and Reinhard 1968, 326ff., 368). Basically this music exhibits the characteristics of Black Sea music, but even apart from the text, it is obvious that these ballads constitute a distinctive type. Turks characterize the music of the Black Sea area as different from that of the rest of Anatolia. The reason for this difference lies in the composition of the population, which consists of Lases (a Caucasian people), Greeks, and only a few Turks. Until Atatürk resettled the Greeks in 1923, Lases and Greeks lived together on this coast and into the Pontic Mountains. The breadth of Lases musical style was stable until around 1963, when good roads were built. The area had been protected since it lay within Trabzon, an offshoot of the Byzantine Empire. This state held off all enemies, above all the attacking Turks, from the sixth century to 1462. The population was Christian and only gradually converted to Islam, a process completed by the seventeenth or eighteenth centuries. At this point

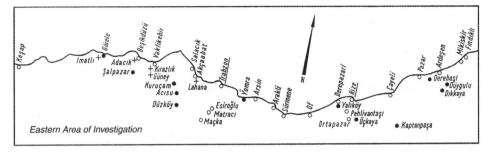

Turkey, eastern Black Sea

the tables turned, and Islamic traditions and customs were maintained there even more strictly than in the rest of Turkey, a difference that still obtains. This is particularly true of customs regarding women, at least superficially, as I will show. The ambivalence between strict and sinful behavior can be clearly felt in the Black Sea ballads. They always concern the kidnapping of girls by love-stricken men, positioning the girls themselves as the guilty party. The girls are typically represented as being Greeks or Armenians, that is, unbelievers in terms of Islam. They lead the young men away from the path of goodness through pleading and persuasion. The couple flee together into the pathless mountains to some pasture, where they make love. Of course, the police, alarmed by the parents, immediately begin pursuit of the couple. The boy and the girl are chased from place to place, looking for somewhere to hide. In the end they are found; the young man lands in prison, and the girl sometimes makes no statement at all and other times lies to the court.

The musical style of the Black Sea area is generally dancelike and much faster and more "temperamental" than music in the rest of Anatolia. This can be explained, as I already mentioned, through the area's diverse population. This holds true also for the ballads. The narrative songs called *destan* mostly have lyrics written by semiprofessional singers and are set to distinctive melodic models that are always modified in performance. The singer accompanies himself on the small Black Sea fiddle called a *kemençe*.

The rhythm is strict and very fast, with a constant meter. Melisma is rare, but the pitches, which often repeat, fall within a narrow range. The songs are always strophic and have four lines. Varied line repetitions can also be heard. The text is syllabic and performed like "chattering," as a form of singing speech. The strophes always have seven syllables, but the rhyme forms are not always those of the seven-syllable *mani*, that is, *a a b a*. Different rhyme forms occur within one ballad.

It is typical for the pattern of strophes to be broken up several times. The reason for this lies with the delivery of the singing speech in a manner common to the epic and ballad singing of many other countries as well. Here numerous lines are grouped together and sung in one rush to the same melody, which is, however, often varied. This gives the impression of a loss of breath, but it is actually a stylistic mannerism. Table 3.1 shows the structure of a typical ballad in this genre. The music of this ballad seems simple, but as this table shows, the decisive element of tension is not melody, as Western-oriented listeners might surmise it to be, but rather the variation of formal units and sections.

I have subdivided the musical example into parts *a* to *h* to explain the function of the "narrative lines" and to show how the musician plays with them. He introduces in the two first strophes the formal parts *a, b, c,* and *d* and uses *c* as a musical "narrative line" for five lines of text. He thus plays the same musical line five times against five different lines of text. The first of nine kemençe-only interludes follows, by means of which the singer divides the ballad of forty-one strophes into ten blocks with eleven instrumental sections, including the prelude and postlude. Only sections *a, b, c* and *d* appear again in the third and fourth strophes. The other sections, *e, f, g,* and *h,* appear in the fifth and sixth strophes. The second instrumental interlude sounds after the seventh strophe. The strophes between the interludes are all sung and played without interruption, in one breath. Therefore, several strophes form one unit, a "strophic block." The narrative lines are built into the strophe and are surrounded by one or at most two different melody lines. Usually the musician uses *c, e,* and *g* as narrative lines, that is, thirty-nine lines for *c,* twenty-nine for *e,* and fifty-three for *g.* In this variant, *c* exhibits a concluding character, *e* has a transitional character, and *g* uses an interval of one-and-a-half steps to produce a feeling of agitation. These parts always deal with the love relationship of the fleeing pair and their common problem, so that one can recognize here the rare case of a text-music relationship. Only four lines show the "peaceful" phrase *d.*

Parts *a* and *b* are always sung at the beginning of a strophic block. They both begin with the highest note and then descend in the order of G–F♯–E–D♯–C♯, thus occupying the range of a tritone, or augmented fourth.

As can be seen from the table, the musician inserts the first interlude after two strophes and then gradually extends the number of strophes in the blocks between the interludes, first to about three or four strophes and later to five and finally to six strophes. With this expansion, the tension increases. The same process can be seen in the number of narrative lines within the

Table 3.1. Typical Ballad Structure in a Performance of Figure 3.1

Feature 1	Feature 2	Feature 3	Feature 4	Feature 5	Feature 6	Feature 7
Prelude	(kemençe)					Only 5 maniforms,
1–2	*a* and *b* and concepts of melody sections *a, b, c,* and *d*	5 lines of *c*	5	2 strophes	In all strophes 7 syllables	*a a b a*
Interlude 3–7	(kemençe) *a* and *b* and concepts of melody sections *a, b, c,* and *d* then *e, f, g,* and *h*	5 lines of *c* and 2 lines of *e* 4 lines of *g* and 3 lines of *g*	15	5 strophes		17 and 6 and 5 different kosmaforms distributed in the ballads with rhymes: *a b c b* and *a b a b* and *a a a a* and 6 mixed forms, *a b b b*
Interlude 8–10	(kemençe) *a* and *b*	9 lines of *c*	9	3 strophes		
Interlude 11–14	(kemençe) *a* and *b*	7 lines of *e* and 6 lines of *g*	13	4 strophes		
Interlude 15–17	(kemençe) *a* and *b*	9 lines of *c*	9	3 strophes		
Interlude 18–21	(kemençe) *a* and *b*	3 lines of *c* and 8 lines of *g*	11	4 strophes		
Interlude 22–26	(kemençe) *a* and *b*	8 lines of *c,* 3 lines of *e,* 4 lines of *g*	15	5 strophes		
Interlude 27–30	(kemençe) *a* and *b*	8 lines of *e* and 5 lines of *g*	13	4 strophes		
Interlude 31–35	(kemençe) *a* and *b*	3 lines of *e* and 5 lines of *g* 4 lines of *e* and 6 lines of *g*	18	5 strophes		
Interlude 36–41	(kemençe) *a* and *b*	9 lines of *g* and 3 lines of *g* 2 lines of *e* and 4 lines of *d*	18	6 strophes		
In strophes 41 2 final lines	part of the scale downward with some bending of some other notes		2	1/2 strophe		
Postlude	(kemençe)					

Key: feature 1 = strophe block numbers; feature 2 = melody lines at beginning of strophic blocks; feature 3 = melodic narrative lines; feature 4 = number of narrative lines; feature 5 = number of strophes containing lines in col. 4; feature 6 = number of poem syllables; feature 7 = poetic rhyme forms

Recording 1027
BALLAD
(Akçaabat, 29.5.63. Voice and fiddle: Hüseyin Köseoğlu, 26)

Figure 3.1. Typical Ballad Structure in a Performance of Ballad 1027 (From Ursula Reinhard and Kurt Reinhard, *Auf der Fiedel Mein . . . : Volkslieder von der Osttürkischen Schwarzmeerküste* [From my fiddle . . .: Folksongs from eastern Turkey's Black Sea coast]. Veröffentlichungen des Museums für Völkerkunde Berlin, Neue Folge, 14. Berlin: Museums für Völkerkunde Berlin, 1968, 368.)

blocks. The singer begins with five narrative lines and ends with eighteen in the final strophic block. The resolution and relaxation of tension in the ballad are achieved through a scale that partly proceeds downward, with a few diversions for the last two lines of the following text:

Poem 1

Strophe No.	Melodic Phrase	Turkish Text	English Translation
Prelude			
1	a	Nasıl parlıyor nasıl	How they shine, ah
	b	Trabzondaki daşslar.	the stones in Trabzon.
	c	Bir kaç dane diyeyim	I want to sing a pair of stanzas,
		Dinlesin arkadaşlar.	listen, my friends.
2		Vali kelizi Vali	The governor is coming,
		Elleri keri bağli.	his hands behind his back.
		Biraz darif edeyim	I want to now tell a bit
	d	Başıma gelen hali.	about what has happened to me.
Interlude			
3	a	Sevdalık ede ede	Giving my love, loving
	b	Geldim ha bu yaşıma.	I have grown as old as I am
	c	Bir güzel yol saşırdı	A beautiful woman lost her way
		Geldi yanı başıma.	And she came to me
4		Ver Allahim sabırlık	Give patience, O God, to him
		Sevdalı yürekliye.	who has a loving heart.
		Sordum kız nerelisin	I asked the girl, "Where do you come from?
	d	Nerden geldin buraya?	and where are you coming from now?"
5	e	Derenin kıyısında	On the bank of the river
		Yıkıyı çamaşırı.	she washes her laundry.
	f	Sordum kız nerelisin?	I asked the girl, "Where do you come from?"
	g	Dedi kıran aşırı.	She said, "From far away."
6		Dedim Urum kızına	To a Greek girl I said:
		Kız annen arar seni.	"Girl, your mother is looking for you."
		Başladı yalvarmıya:	Then she began to beg,
	h	Sen alacasın beni.	"You should take me."
7	g	Ah ne dedimsen ona	No matter what I said to her,
		Ondan kurdulamadım.	I could not save myself from her.
		O kavurun kızımın	Oh, you daughter of a heathen,
	h	Gönlünü kıramadım.	I could not soften your heart.
Interlude			
8	a	Seni yuduren arar	I said, "My little one,
	b	Ufacığıma, dedim.	She is looking for you, the lost one."

c		Gönlünü kıramadım Aldım kabul eyledim.	But I could not soften your heart, and so I accepted your suggestion.
9		O benim güzelimlan Yaylaya gideceğim.	With my beautiful one I want to go to the mountain pasture.
		Daha yeni sevdalı Söyleyi güleceğim.	In continually renewed love, I will sing, I will laugh.
10		Daha yeni sevdalı Sormayın aramızı.	In continually renewed love! Don't ask what has happened between us.
		Nazlı yarin annesi	The mother of the coquettish loved one,
d		Şikahat etti bizi.	she sued us.

Interlude

11	a	O benim ufacığım	Oh, my little one
	b	Zilifini darıyı.	is combing her locks.
	c	Geldi iki jandarma Köyde beni arıyor.	Two policemen came looking for me in the village.
12	e	Aldım ufacağımı Aldım da çıkdım evden. Jandarmalar arıyor Çıkalım habu köyden.	I took my little one and led her out of the house. "The police are looking for us, let us flee out of this village."
13		Dedi bana güzelim Biz gidelim nereye? O benim güzelimlan	Then my beautiful one said, "Where are we going, then?" Oh, with my beautiful one,
	g	Kezerken köyden köye. Köyden köye kezerken Geldik Kemaliyiye.	I'm going from village to village. I'm going from village to village. We've come to Kemaliyi.
14		O benim güzelimlan Orada biraz kaldım. Bir gün bir akşam	Oh, with my beautiful one, I remained there for a while. One day, in the evening,
d		Üsdü aksı bir haber.	I received a bitter message.

Interlude

15	a	Aksı bir haber aldım	I received a bitter message.
	b	Dedim, nedir bu haber?	What kind of message was it?
	c	Jandarmalar geliyor Baş çavuş da beraber.	The policemen came here together with the police sergeant.
16		Hemen çıkdım kabıya Bir sağa sola bakdım. Aldım ufacığımı Hemen oradan kaçdım.	I immediately went to the door, I looked to the right and the left, and took my little one and fled immediately with her.
17		Kel beşime beşime, Deyirim e kız sana. Biraz bu yana geldim	"Follow me, follow me," I said to you, girl. I went a bit
d		Kavuşdım bir ormana.	and reached a forest.

Interlude

18	a	Daha güzel olursın	You will become even more beautiful,
	b	Dara başını dara.	oh, comb, comb your hair.
c		O benim güzelimlan	Oh, with my beautiful one,
		Çıkdık da yaylalara.	I went up to the mountain pasture.
19		Yaylanin cimeninde	On the pasture of the mountain
	e	Yarim dizime yattı.	my beloved slept on my knees.
	c	Odurtuk dinlenirken	Then we sat and listened attentively,
	g	Karanlık da kabattı.	the darkness covered us.
20		Dedi bana güzellim:	My beautiful one said to me:
		Biz gidelim nereye?	"Where are we then going now?"
		Akşamı aldık ele	When it became evening,
		Döndik ordan keriye.	we went back.
21		Şu karşıdan aşağı	From over there the river
		Dere geliyi dere.	flows downstream, the river.
		Saat iki zamanı	When it became two o'clock,
	d	Geldik endik bir eve.	we came to a house.

Interlude

22	a	Aldım ufacığımı	I took my little one
	b	Aldım da çıkdım düze.	and led her to flat land.
	c	Geldik ordaki evde	There we came to a house,
		Yadak serdiler bize.	a bed was made ready for us.
23		Haburadan aşağı	Ah, from here downstream
		Yol iner Badışağa.	the way goes toward Padişah.
		O benim güzellimlan	Ah, with my beautiful one
		Kakdık yatdık aşağı.	I stayed and slept there.
24		Verdiğin şeker beri	The sweets that you gave me
		Aldım güzelim aldım.	I took, I took, my beautiful one.
	d	Bir kaç akşam uykusuz	A pair of nights without sleep
		Kaldım orada kaldım.	I remained, I remained there.
25	e	Dedim Urum kızına	I said to the Greek girl:
		Kız seni ne edeyim?	"Girl, what am I to do with you?"
		Kakaladılar bizi.	We were then shaken,
	g	Uyan, dedi Hüseyin.	"Wake up, Hüseyin."
26		Haçan uyandım bakdım.	I woke up immediately and looked around.
		Aglayı da duruyı.	She stood there crying.
		Bakdım kabıdan biri	I saw someone at the door,
	h	Hüseyin bağırıyı.	he called: "Hüseyin."

Interlude

27	a	Usdam kaç günde yabdın	Oh, master, how many days
	b	Habu kadar yabıyı?	until now have you been building this house?

	e	⌐	Yürüdüm adım adım	One step at a time, I went
			Vardim açdım kabıyı.	and opened the door.
28			Bakdım burda dostlarım.	I saw my friends there.
			Etti bana bu işi	Then came storming in
			Kırdı içeri bakdım	Maçka's police sergeant
			Maçkanın baş çavuşı.	and made me worried.
29			Sevdalığın beşine	Behind my beloved
		⌐	Dökerdim derlerimi.	I broke out into a sweat.
	g	⌐	Kırdı içeri hemen	He had stormed in
			Bağladı ellerimi.	and bound my hands together.
30			Bakdım burda yarimin	I saw how my beloved there
			Eli koynunda kaldı.	pressed her hands to her breast.
		⌐	Düfek bıçak dabanca	Rifle, knife, and pistol,
	h		Nem varısa dobladı.	what I had, they took away.

Interlude

31	a		Haburadan aşağı	Ah, from here downstream
	b		Yol iner Badışağa.	the way goes toward Padişah.
	e	⌐	Aldı vurdıler bize	They took us and pushed us forward
			Hemen ordan aşağa.	quickly going down from there.
32		⌐	Düfeğim omuzuma	My rifle on my shoulder,
	g	⌐	Kola kiderim kola.	I walked and watched attentively.
			Doğrı ordan biz endik	From there downward
			Ordan da karakola.	we went to the police station.
33			Yaylanın çimeninde	On the pasture of the mountain
		⌐	Yata güzelim yata.	I slept once with my beautiful one.
	e	⌐	Ordan haraket ettik	From there we left
			Endik da Akçaabada.	and came to Akçaabat.
34		⌐	Asker ettiler beni	They grabbed me,
	g	⌐	Mekdup yazsam gımume.	If only I could write a letter to someone!
			Aldı çıkdıler bizi	They grabbed us and led us
			Doğrı mutteimume.	directly to the prosecutor.
35			Duruken kabısında	As I stood at the door
			Mutteimum çağırdı.	the prosecutor called to me.
		⌐	Aldı ifademizi	He took down what I said to him.
	h		Beni yardan ayırdı.	He separated me from my beloved.

Interlude

36	a		Yüreğimin derdini	Just as my sorrows had left my heart
	b	⌐	Düketsam kısa kısa.	for a little while,
	g	⌐	Aldılar beni ordan	they took me away from there
			Kedirdiler mabusa.	and brought me to a prison.
37			Mabusane önünden	Outside of the prison
			Arkadaşlar geçiye.	friends pass by.

		Bakmazlar darafıma	But they don't look for me, for Hüseyin,
		Bişe mi, der Hüseyin.	who calls to them, "Anything new?"
38		Olup olmaz sözlerin?	"Have you said good things or bad things?"
		Dedim güzellim dedim.	I asked my beautiful one, I asked.
		Birinci mahkemede	Ah, at the court, there they gave me
	d	Altı ay ceza yedim.	a punishment of six months.
39	g	Habu kadar şeyleri	Yes, so that's how things stand with me.
		Saya güzellim saya.	Count, my beautiful one, count.
		Bir ayı deyçil düşdü	They subtracted one month,
	d	Indi damam beş aya.	now there are only five months.
40	e	İkballerimiz ağır.	Our fate is a hard one,
		Güzellim ne edelim?	but what can one do, my beautiful one?
	d	Hepsini desam bitmez	If I told everything, it would never end,
		Kısa kısa kidelim.	So I will make it short.
41		Cebundaki Yamayı	These patches on my pockets
		Diyorlar yağlık yağlık.	they call an embroidered cloth.
		Bu işte böyle kalsın	Yes, this is how it is and it will stay so.
		Sizlere olsun sağlık.	May you always remain healthy.

Postlude

The image of women in the Black Sea songs reveals ambivalence between love and hate. This tension stems from the torture of sexual desire unfulfilled because of religious and social prohibitions. Rage and hate are expressed in the text by lines such as "I will throw a boulder at your breast," "I will mutilate you," or "the claws of the angel of death should hit you." The desired girl is mocked because she has yellow teeth or crooked legs or because a fire burns in her pants. The songs include phrases such as "filthy daughter-in-law"; "double-believing witch"; "fat girl, you have aroused curiosity in me"; or "when you bite the girls in the cheek, they go right to the police." Nowhere else in Turkey are sexual wishes expressed as blatantly as in the Black Sea area, whose songs include the following remarks: "at two o'clock we'll let our pants down"; "the wood of the bed must not creak"; and "the barrel fell over as we slept together, the parents didn't notice anything." Presents of gold, jewelry, or fabric, which the men use to lure the girls, are important, though the men also become angry over the expense of these gifts. The texts often speak of desperate, hopeless pleading with the father and mother or of the high cost of the bride that precludes any hope for a relationship. The grandmothers play an important and negative role as the oldest person of respect in the family.

In general, songs sung by girls in Turkey (though not these ballads, which are sung only by men) often contain the female protagonist's complaint that she was forcibly given to an unloved man and her request to the one she loves to flee with her. The protagonists also threaten to shoot their men dead if they are untrue to them. In addition, they demand that their men not smoke and that they learn to read and write and go to school. There are self-confident remarks such as "One thousand of your nights have not as much worth as one of my nights."

From all this one can deduce that there is something to the reputation of the Black Sea women, namely, that they are energetic and accustomed to taking on life on their own terms. Their independence was essential in earlier times because many men went to sea. When the men visited home, they did not have the power to determine much. They were treated as inferiors by the hard-working, powerful women. It is even alleged that many women occasionally beat their husbands. Toward outsiders, however, they showed themselves only as strict Muslims who, veiled and in colorful clothing, struggled over difficult mountain paths with large baskets and heavy loads on their backs. These social conditions thus render explicable and understandable the creation of the ballad in terms of both lyric content and agitated musical form.

A second type of ballad from southwest Turkey sounds completely different. I have selected an example in which a young female judge plays a role. She has sinned according to Islam, but the ballad's creator accepts her and is full of love and empathy for her.

Poem 2

Bodrumlular erken biçer ekini	The people of Bodrum harvest their grains early.
Feleğe kurban gitti Bodrum hakimi	You were a victim of fate, you female judge of Bodrum.
Nasıl astın hakim hanım ipe de kendini	How could you hang yourself with a rope, Woman Judge?
Altın makas gümüş bıçak ile doğradılar tenini	They are cutting your body down with a pair of golden scissors and a silver knife.
Çifte doktorlar doğradı o beyaz tenini.	Two doctors are cutting down your white body.
Bodrumun kalesinde kuzgun dolaşır	Above Bodrum's fortress the vultures are flying,

Hakim hanımın kardeşlerine kara haber ulaşır	The brothers of the Woman Judge received a black piece of news.
Nasıl astın hakim hanım ipe de kendini	How could you hang yourself with a rope, Woman Judge?
Altın makas gümüş bıçak ile doğradılar tenini.	They are cutting your body down with a pair of golden scissors and a silver knife.
Hakim hanımın memleketi Kütahya Tavas	She came out of the Province Kütahya-Tavas, our Woman Judge.
Hakim hanım sen eyledin bizleri perişan	Woman Judge, you have made us very confused.
Nasıl astın hakim hanım ipe de kendini	How could you hang yourself with a rope, Woman Judge?
Altın makas gümüş bıçak ile doğradılar tenini.	They are cutting your body down with a pair of golden scissors and a silver knife.
Hakim hanımın evlerinde baykuşlar öter	In the house of the Woman Judge now the owls are crying out,
Yaşı yirmiye varmadan ömrü biter	Her life has come to an end before she was twenty.
Nasıl astın hakim hanım ipe de kendini	How could you hang yourself with a rope, Woman judge?
Altın makas gümüş bıçak ile doğradılar tenini.	They are cutting your body down with a pair of golden scissors and a silver knife.

In 1968, when Kurt Reinhard recorded it in Bodrum, this ballad was not yet old but very popular. That city bears an obvious Greek influence, since it lies across from the Greek island of Rhodos. Many Turkish men obtain their wives from there. The province of Muğla, where Bodrum is located, is well-to-do. When women there appear in public, they are freer than those in the Black Sea area. They are more open and "natural," and they do not feel themselves to be suppressed. This attitude can be explained through, among other factors, the nomadic derivation of many residents, who had not long been permanently settled in 1968. Nomadic women are able to maintain a way of life that is not as restricted as that of, for example, women of small cities, who often appear with lowered eyes and prim behavior.

I want to make only a few observations about the melody of this second ballad type: the ballads of this province consist not of formal sections lined up one after the other but rather of a through-composed melody in several strophes, which are wavelike in form. The melody begins with an ascending third, followed immediately by a descending fifth. This line is then repeated. In the second line the singer begins on the third above the highest note of the first line. The melody again moves immediately downward, so that once more a wave-shaped movement is created. The second line is also repeated. The constant repetition of these two melodic periods creates a four-line strophic song to varying lines of text. The song displays Greek influence in the rich ornamentation of the singing and in the accompanying violin, particularly in its glissando-like "gliding."

In the recording by Kurt Reinhard, after some initial metrical difficulties in the ensemble playing, the female musician, who plays the *deblek* (a tin drum), and her brother, who plays the European violin, agree on a meter of four beats and, at phrase endings, on a meter of six beats. The deblek maintains the meter rather strictly throughout, while the singing and the violin part occasionally depart from it. The violinist accompanies his own singing heterophonically.

One finds other ballad types that concern women, or rather the sociological-religious difficulties in the relationship between men and women, in other provinces of Turkey as well. All these songs have their own styles. The spectrum of their content stretches from traditional to modern problems. A while ago, for example, a ballad about the television series *Dallas* and its love-related tragedies was sung. This is a sign of how vital folk and folklike music still is in Turkey and how this music repeatedly treats explosive, current topics.

In secluded rural areas, particularly in eastern Turkey, young widows are still not allowed to remarry; in the few cases where they may, they are allowed to marry only their husband's brother. Songs concerning this issue are often taught to girls. This custom is especially well expressed in the following example, which was played by a folk singer (*aşik*), a kind of "songwriter" who accompanies himself on the *saz* (a long-necked lute). The conclusion makes it clear that he has described his own experience, for he says, "I am Ali with the lute." He is also the one whom the girl begs in the last lines of each strophe in the refrain, "Oh, you, with your black eyes, come down from the summer pasture." The young woman is dismayed at marrying the much younger brother of her deceased husband because he is a youngster who has slept on her lap; he has lain on her breast like a small cat and chewed his bread for his dog to digest.

Poem 3

Gelin oldum Karabekir iline	I became a bride in the land of Karabekir,
Yedi bayram kına yakmam elime	I did not color my hands with henna for seven feasts.

Kurban olam çiğdem gibi geline	I will sacrifice myself now, like an autumn crocus,
Yayladan gel kömür gözlüm yayladan.	Oh, you, with your black eyes, come down from the summer pasture.
Altına serdiler ipekli döşek	They spread out a silk cloth,
Koynuma koydular bir ufak uşsak	they laid on my breast a little boy.
Öpmesi yok sevmesi yok konuşak	He couldn't kiss, couldn't love, couldn't talk with me.
Yayladan gel kömür gözlüm yayladan.	Oh, you, with your black eyes, come down from the summer pasture.
Ocağa koydular dünkü su idi	They put water on top of the stove, water from the day before.
Çoçuk geldi kucağimda uyudu	A child came and went to sleep on my lap.
Baba bana yapacağın bumuydu	Was it this that you've done to me, Father?
Yayladan gel kömür gözlüm yayladan.	Oh, you, with your black eyes, come down from the summer pasture.
Senin baban karşı köyün ağası	My father is the head of the village over there.
Çok pesime düştü genci kocası	They chased after me, both the young and the old.
Dizime vurdumda gerdek gecesi	I slap my knee [from suffering] during my wedding night.
Yayladan gel kömür gözlüm yayladan.	Oh, you, with your black eyes, come down from the summer pasture.
Ocağa koydular misir darısı	They put on top of the stove corn and barley.
Koynuma koydular kedi yavrusu	They laid on my breast a little cat,
Bana derler bu çocuğun karısı	they called me the wife of the child.
Yayladan gel kömür gözlüm yayladan.	Oh, you, with your black eyes, come down from the summer pasture.
Sabahleyin oğlan gider kuzuya	In the morning the boy goes to his lambs,
Dişi ile ekmek doğrur tazıya	and he chews up bread for his dog to eat.
Aslımı sorarsan Ali sazıyla	If you ask where I come from, I am Ali with the lute.
Yayladan gel kömür gözlüm yayladan.	Oh, you, with your black eyes, come down from the summer pasture.

The text of the song derives from a traditional *aşık* melody model (Reinhard and Pinto 1989, 124ff.). The most important characteristic is the downward flow of the refrain lines in sequences. This flow uses melismatic settings of syllables and words. The song is metrically strict and is accompanied monophonically by the saz to emphasize the meaning of the text and the feeling of despair. Bourdon notes and polyphonic textures are woven in only during the prelude. The song dies out on the last word. It is set in the E mode.

My large amount of material from Turkey repeatedly shows that it is the men who create the ballads in which women play the main role. Many customs and practices thus become clearer. Except in the Black Sea region, music does not exhibit unique characteristics relating to the lyrics; rather, musical models from the general pool of folk music are used.

We still lack research about the degree to which men sing songs in genres that were created by women without acknowledging the originator. Thus far, it is clear only that the musical duties of women include lullabies and death laments.

NOTE

This essay was translated from German into English by Linda Fujie.

REFERENCES CITED

Reinhard, Kurt, and Ursula Reinhard. 1968. *Auf der Fiedel mein . . . : Volkslieder von der osttürkischen Schwarzmeerküste* (From my fiddle: folk songs from eastern Turkey's Black Sea coast). Veröffentlichungen des Museums für Völkerkunde Berlin, n.s., 14. Berlin: Museums für Völkerkunde Berlin.

Reinhard, Ursula, and Tiago de Oliveira Pinto. 1989. *Sänger und Poeten mit der Laute, Türkische Aşik und Ozan* (Singers and poets with lutes: Turkish Aşik and Ozan). Includes two cassettes. Veröffentlichungen des Museums für Völkerkunde Berlin, n.s., 47, Abteilung Musikethnologie 6, Staatliche Museen Preußischer Kulturbesitz. Berlin: Museums für Völkerkunde Berlin.

Part 2

Telling Lives

Musicology has prioritized "telling" lives—the lives, that is, of influential creative artists, the genius figures of European high art—to an extent that is arguably unparalleled in most other scholarly domains. Furthermore, the peopling of European music histories with "great" artists in the "art music" domain and the relative anonymity of other musicians and other musical practices was a foundational but unexamined assumption underlying the formation of historical musicology. More recently, however, we have become attuned both to the perspectives and factors that ascribe historical significance to lives and to the critical problems of "telling"—representing and interpreting—the enormous complexities of human musical experience.

Although biography, oral history, and life writing are hardly new to the discipline of ethnomusicology,[1] many theoretical issues associated with the use of life stories in music study have yet to be engaged. The essays in this section address some of these issues, dealing in different ways with a range of problems surrounding the "truth claims" of individuals, the interpretive frameworks of readers, the shifting contingencies of the stories, and the factors that lead to the erasure of certain kinds of experiential narrative. In all the chapters in this section, the combination of data types, particularly documentary and oral sources, permits us to glimpse the dialogic nature of life writing.

Beverley Diamond addresses the fundamental feminist issue of essentialized identities in relation to the musical life stories of musicians from Prince Edward Island, the smallest of Canada's Maritime Provinces. She argues that we should not "debate" but "relate" essentialist and constructionist discourses of gender to understand how individuals and communities create gendered identities by means of their musical choices, aesthetic values, and stylistic distinctions. By shifting the frame of her own representation in the middle of the essay, she demonstrates how knowledge can be reconfigured from one perspective to another.

Jane Bowers's reflective article on the challenges of writing the biography of blues singer Mama Yancey is rooted in traditional historical methodology. Here, however, Bowers comes to terms with the different forms of African American biography, forms that may reflect established storytelling traditions or construct multiple contradictory selves in accordance with the expectations of interviewers or social contexts.

Pirkko Moisala reveals how gender is constructed at both shared and individual sites of music making and music-related behavior. She demonstrates how the gender identity and subject position of an individual—in this case, the internationally renowned Finnish composer Kaija Saariaho—is mediated by her environment and sociocultural surroundings. Saariaho's gender performance is analyzed in relation to her press reception over almost twenty years.

Margaret Myers's work is a historical study, filling a lacuna about the musical activities of women in European orchestras of the late nineteenth and early twentieth centuries. The breadth and variety of her oral historical data, however, data that contrast markedly with the documentary record, additionally permit an analysis of the mechanisms of invisibility effacing the history of these ensembles and an assessment of the evaluative judgments that have assigned the experiences of women who played in them an unjustifiably low stature in most accounts.

These and other ethnomusicological studies are part of one of the most dramatic of postmodern shifts in scholarship in many different disciplines: namely, the widespread recognition of the need for what feminist philosopher Lorraine Code (1995, xvi) has called "a storied epistemology, one that grants epistemic force to narratives that tell of the construction of knowledge, and of subjectivities, stories which are specifically contextualized within and located in relation to human lives."

NOTE

1. Landmark biographies, from Frisbie and McAllester's (1978) edition of Navajo Blessingway singer Frank Mitchell's autobiography to Virginia Danielson's *Voice of Egypt: Umm Kulthum, Arabic Song, and Egyptian Society in the Twentieth Century* (1997) are prominent, if not numerous, among ethnomusicological studies. Life writing is included in each chapter of one of the most widely used undergraduate ethnomusicology textbooks in English, *Worlds of Music* (Titon 1996);

used to situate and frame a reflexively scholarly anthology, *Music Grooves* (Keil and Feld 1994); and published in collections of oral historical interviews (Crafts et al. 1993).

References Cited

Code, Lorraine. 1995. *Rhetorical Spaces: Essays on Gendered Locations*. London: Routledge.

Crafts, Susan D., Daniel Cavicchi, Charles Keil, and the Music in Daily Life Project, comps. 1993. *My Music*. Hanover, N.H.: University Press of New England.

Danielson, Virginia. 1997. *The Voice of Egypt: Umm Kulthum, Arabic Song, and Egyptian Society in the Twentieth Century*. Chicago: University of Chicago Press.

Frisbie, Charlotte, and David McAllester, eds. 1978. *Navajo Blessingway Singer: The Autobiography of Frank Mitchell*. Tucson: University of Arizona Press.

Keil, Charles, and Steven Feld. 1994. *Music Grooves: Essays and Dialogues*. Chicago: University of Chicago Press.

Titon, Jeff Todd, ed. 1996. *Worlds of Music*. 3d ed. New York: Schirmer.

4   *The Interpretation of Gender Issues in Musical Life Stories of Prince Edward Islanders*

Beverley Diamond

The telling of lives has always been compelling. Its many public modes—written biography, TV documentary, balladry, story telling, cinematic representation, and so on—exhibit vibrant immediacy, "authenticity," and dynamism. Many scholars have been drawn to "oral history," or "life stories," but feminists have found such texts particularly useful for various reasons. Such stories give "others" a voice in history, they problematize the relationship of subject to object, and they are less prone than many other representational genres to erase emotion- or value-laden intangibles. For all these reasons, oral narratives have been particularly rich means of exploring the performance of gender and the gendering of (everyday or more formalized) performance in specific social contexts. Feminists have, furthermore, been astute theorists of experiential narratives, assessing the status of such accounts, the dialogic nature of their construction, and their political positioning, among other things. All these considerations have proven valuable in developing a sophisticated approach to the study of gender.

The telling of *musical* lives seems to have been especially compelling. The journalistic literature on popular, jazz, or classical musicians constitutes the largest section of many music libraries and music sections of book stores. Paradoxically, however, music has been one of the domains where life stories have been resolutely believed to "speak for themselves." The preponderance of literature on musical lives has been, until recently, more concerned with the events of the lives than the events of the "telling," generally ignoring issues of positioning or dialogicism. Undoubtedly because oral narratives are often rich with musical references, ethnomusicology has lately exhibited a surge of interest in "life stories,"[1] and hence a consideration of theoretical issues that emerge in scholarly considerations of such texts in intercultural milieux is timely.

What happens when the telling of musical lives and the telling of lives through musical reference are examined as constructions and interpreted with an awareness of feminist issues such as those just outlined? What can we learn by magnifying one particular (abstract) juncture in one specific (concrete) location: music and gender in the life narratives of musicians in a specific time and place? This essay addresses these questions with reference to a collection of musical life stories recorded in Canada's smallest Maritime province, Prince Edward Island, in the 1990s. These rich narratives reveal that a particular focus on music and gender may enable us to see more clearly the complex web of factors that impinge on the invention of selves in culturally plural social locations.

Several assumptions frame my presentation. First is the belief (which I first saw articulated by bell hooks [1994, 217]) that oral narratives must be heard or read not so much in terms of what the subjects accomplished but in terms of what they desired, not just in terms of what they did but in terms of the individuals to whom they sought to relate by their actions and in terms of both what they actualized and what they excluded about themselves. In these terms, music often plays a major role. Musical preferences or associations, the community of friends with whom one seeks to relate not only when joining a performing group but also when idolizing one star or another, vigorously disliking one style or another, or even passively permitting a certain kind of sound to fill one's space—these are potent modes of expressing desire, establishing relationship, and actualizing the self.

My second assumption is that music and gender are both sites for negotiating an individual place within communities that tend to reinforce certain values and behaviors as normative.[2] That is, musical life stories enable us not merely to construct the socially reinforced or to reflect the individually differentiated but also to understand the relationship between these value systems.

Prince Edward Island and the Canadian Musical Pathways Project

Although I had several long-standing musical acquaintances on Prince Edward Island, I had the privilege of getting to know more musicians and individuals involved in the music scene there in conjunction with a large-scale research project on issues of music and community identity, the Canadian Musical Pathways Project. The project involved case studies in a number of ethnoculturally diverse Canadian communities.[3] Oral history, festival documentation, and archival research were complementary components of each case study. I did much of the interviewing during the summer of 1993, assisted by Roy Johnstone, a well-known Prince Edward Island fiddler whose knowledge of the fiddle community and the issues of concern to that "musical world" were invaluable assets.

The island province, densely populated by Canadian standards but comprising only .5 percent of Canada's population, is unique in several ways, although it is closely connected with the adjacent Maritime provinces of Nova Scotia and New Brunswick. The 1996 edition of the *Canadian Encyclopedia* describes it as "the most rural province in the nation as only 39.9% of the population is classed as urban." First to populate the island were the Micmac, who continue to play an important role in contemporary life. Although European explorers and fisherman have visited the island since the early sixteenth century, Acadians, fleeing neighboring regions of Nova Scotia and New Brunswick after their defeat in the 1750s, were the first resident Europeans. English, Scottish, and Irish immigrants arrived in the late eighteenth and early nineteenth centuries and, from the mid-nineteenth century onward, constituted the majority population. Although significant communities of Dutch and Lebanese arrived on the island during the past century, the ethnocultural profile is more homogeneously British (85 percent) than is that of any other Canadian province. Most consultants from cultures outside the Anglo-Celtic or Acadian mainstream commented on the difficulties of feeling so marginalized. "When I was walking on the street, people looked at me all the time, like 'You are the only person here [who is] different,'" said one. People are "really scared to talk with other people," said another. A third described a refugee camp in Pakistan as a more supportive community than the Canadian one. A fourth declared, "It's not easy to live here when you are an immigrant." Those who managed to stay on the island for a longer period of time had more favorable experiences as networks of friendships built. It must be recognized, however, that the anomalous demographic of Prince Edward Island (PEI) sets it apart from metropolitan regions elsewhere in the country; in Toronto, for example, ethnocultural diversity is so extensive that there is, demographically, no large ethnocultural or linguistic majority.[4] As it has in other parts of the country, recent immigration is rapidly diversifying the PEI community, but it is still relevant to query the ways in which islanders who are in extreme minority situations shape their musical lives in difficult circumstances.

At the time of the study, the celebration of "islandness" was particularly acute in the light of debates over the construction of a "fixed-link" bridge

to the New Brunswick mainland. Although such debates had been periodically renewed over more than a century, this time the fixed-link forces, predominantly the urban business community and transportation industries,
won the day over environmentalists and the majority of rural residents. By
1997 the fourteen-kilometer bridge was open.

Both sides of the fixed-link struggle have positioned their arguments in
relation to the huge international tourist population that flocks to the ocean
beaches, especially on the island's ecologically fragile north shore, and enjoys theater and musical events during the summer months in venues as
small and remote as "Elephant Rock" or as large and institutionalized as the
Confederation Centre. Hence, although the island is nicknamed "Spud Island" by some (with reference to its potato cultivation), the highly "developed" north shore equally stimulates local labels as the "Coney Island of PEI."
It is in this area that Lucy Maud Montgomery's fictional character Anne of
Green Gables, an innocent, freckled girl who constitutes the island's most
public identity symbol, immortalized in an annual musical at the Charlottetown Festival, is said to have lived in a green-gabled house near the sea-
shore. The presentation of Celtic music, dance, and crafts in dozens of venues around the island is a central part of the public image. Local craft
boutiques are advertised along with rural bed and breakfast sites on the dozens of highway signs that dot the landscape. The innocence of Anne and the
promotion of folk music, crafts, and so on constitute a readily evident parallel to the process described by historian Ian McKay with regard to Nova
Scotia, whereby a conceptual "Age of Innocence" is constructed through the
replication of symbols of an idealized folk society. Nonetheless, as the oral
histories indicate, it is negotiable whether these symbols are "static artifacts
testifying to the lost splendours of a vanished golden age," part of the "aesthetic colonization of the country by the city," as McKay (1994, 32, 9) contends about Nova Scotia.

The recorded interviews with PEI musicians were not designed to foreground any particular identity issues, such as gender.[5] We wanted to explore
the discourse through which gender and other identity issues can be articulated rather than to evoke direct discussion and analysis that would over-
emphasize those issues.[6] Furthermore, because the analysis of gender issues
was not the only or even the primary objective of the research, these stories
reveal where and how gender emerges in the self-representations of diverse
individuals who are deeply involved with music making in one way or another. In addition to recorded interviews, documentary research and partic-

ipant observation in music making, both informal and public, helped us get in touch with multiple local musical scenes.

Framing This Representation of Musical Life Stories

Political Positioning

It is increasingly apparent that oral narratives are neither liberal nor reactionary per se; rather, they may be positioned and turned interpretively to different ends. Consequently, it is important to consider the political positioning of my choices, both the choice of the PEI case study and the choice of consultants whose stories are discussed. The homogeneity and British dominance of the island could easily be construed as normative in Canada at the very point where many of us are attempting to make more visible the many other voices that have been muted in earlier Canadian histories. Furthermore, the use of oral history, it has been argued, exacerbates this problem. Dympna Callaghan, for example, refers to the "ideologically occluded connection between feminist experience and white hegemony" in white women's personal narratives. She observes that "whiteness is presented in these texts as personal experience, which reinforces the invisibility on which its dominance relies" (Callaghan 1995, 201). She refers to Gayatri Spivak, whose various subaltern studies have warned us about the close alliance between concrete experience and the micropolitics of self, on the one hand, and "the positivism that serves as the ideological foundation for neocolonialism" (ibid.), on the other.

Despite the risk that the PEI narratives might be read in this way, there are a number of advantages to this choice. First, the maintenance of a hegemonic culture that validates a particular subset of national origins (here the British and Acadian) operates rather differently in an economically marginalized region, and this difference is little understood in contemporary cultural studies. Second, the island's musical mainstream, which is unquestionably constructed as the fiddle and folk-derived songwriting worlds, also differs fundamentally from the commercial mainstream of English-language popular music in urban North America, and this similarly argues for a more localized examination, since the perceived "norms" of Anglo-Canadian gender are often performed differently in the PEI context. The localization of these factors surely decenters the potentially neocolonial message. Finally, because consultants from different racialized and ethnocultural communities participated in the study, the research validates their perspectives and gives recognition to their shared involvement in the performance of island culture, an involvement that must be recognized as enormously difficult given these individuals' ethnocultural isolation from a larger community.

Levels of Acquaintance and Issues of "Discordant Registers"

Notwithstanding this justification (which some may read as a rationalization) for the choice of a case study, I nevertheless encourage readers to ask hard questions about the status of the narratives selected for presentation here.[7] Three levels of "acquaintance" must be acknowledged. Roy Johnstone, a local musician, interacted mostly with close acquaintances as an insider to the fiddle world. I, however, interviewed individuals with whom I had some previous acquaintance as well as new acquaintances who were first approached in conjunction with the project. The latter group includes all the consultants who are relatively new immigrants. In several of these cases, only a single interview with a person of very short acquaintance was possible, and the consultant was challenged with teaching me an impossible amount to make the narrative comprehensible.

Nevertheless, I believe that these differences in the depth of the relationships between interviewers and consultants are problematic only if we erase the conditions of their production. In other words, if we were to discard interviews with cross-cultural awkwardness, we would eliminate many voices of difference. If we were to imply that all interviews are equal, we might similarly ignore the dialogicism that created aspects of the discourse. Although ethnomusicology, like other social scientific endeavors that venture across ethnocultural boundaries, urges long-term engagement with specific communities, the breadth of research in the current project was, in my view, no less valuable, though very different in effect.

More problematic for me was my position as the "author/authority/authenticator"[8] in the representation of the stories of friends and acquaintances. Ruth Behar has written articulately about this problem:

> Torn between these voices, the life historian/author usually settles for a segregated, often jarring combination of the three: the native voice, the personal "I was there" voice, and the authoritative voice of the ethnographer. The difficulties inherent in making music out of these three "voices" or "discordant allegorical registers" . . . also pose the key challenge: by mediating between, or counterpointing, different linguistic

tropes or registers, the ethnographer can potentially create a text that is as much an account of a person's history as it is an account of how such a history is constituted in and through narrative—the native's life story narrative and the life historian's telling of that narrative. (Behar 1995, 149)

Behar refers to a double telling, a concept that influenced my decision to shift my interpretive frame halfway through this essay. In the first part my search for pattern and conjuncture is presented with a somewhat distanced voice of authority, one that draws on a wide range of external sources to validate the experiential patterns revealed in my consultants' stories. Fragments of many stories are used in a way that erases individual personalities and interventions. In the second part, however, the search for motion and disjuncture is presented with more of the "I was there" voice intact. Not all the disjunctures that emerge in this section are interpreted, or at least they are not fixed in their interpretation. Although my double telling is not the solution to discordant allegorical registers, it does at least point to the constructedness of the accounts.

This dual "reading" of the musical life stories also mirrors the tension between essentialism and constructionism to which I alluded earlier. The first reading ventures close to essentialism; the second, to constructionism. The essentialist lens looks for sameness and pattern, ways in which "groups" are constructed as if they share attitudes, values, and lifeways. This lens reveals some of the ways in which a gender dichotomy between male and female is socially asserted though differently reinforced in various musical worlds. Although this analysis is certainly motivated by my political belief that such essentialisms must be revealed as constructed (not natural) and hence mutable, I also recognize and respect the strategic uses of essentialist positions by many consultants. The constructionist lens focuses not on pattern but on flux, change, and disjuncture. These moments in the musical life stories reveal the contingencies of gender identity and the strategies by which we negotiate with the world and assert individuality. Neither story is truer than the other. Both lenses are needed to understand the ways in which concepts of gender operate in relation to the musical worlds we create and perform and to which we respond.

Multiple Narrative Genres, Styles, and Strategies

Different levels of acquaintance, of course, exaggerate the "discordant allegorical registers" to which I referred earlier; as many oral historians have demonstrated,[9] expectations about different ways of "telling," even specific oral genres, are culturally bracketed. Although such bracketing has usually been described in relation to ethnocultural difference,[10] milder forms operate between different musical worlds. Whereas both Francophone and Anglophone island song writers, for example, described detailed personal events in relation to specific compositions (a mode of discourse prevalent at local public events and to some extent perpetuated in the highly personal liner notes produced with their cassettes and CDs), this genre of story (if it may be labeled a genre) is rare in interviews with musicians from other musical worlds.

A different shift in discourse style was from the personal to what might be called the "institutional" voice. This happened when people spoke about their work in a way that seemed to echo the rhetoric of the institution for which they worked or when they spoke "as if" they were a devotee of one thing or another. Consultants from non-European nations, for example, sometimes assumed a teaching posture to try to clarify information about music in their country of origin. The reasons for such shifts are undoubtedly multiple; at times the shifts perhaps helped to mask the deep emotions such conversation evokes, and at other times they were designed to augment the knowledge of an interviewer who clearly needed some sort of introductory encyclopedic account. Another pattern in the shift between a personal and institutional voice was more apparently tied to gender and is discussed further in the second part of this essay. Women in particular would often negotiate a shift between two conflicting perspectives by assuming, from moment to moment, a more personal or more institutional subjectivity. Although there are many contrary examples, I read the many instances of this as indicating the difficulty some female consultants have in negotiating the social constraints they face as women, on one hand, and professional musicians, on the other.

This was but one means of shifting subjectivity. Another, recently analyzed by the linguist Deborah Tannen (1995), is the creation of dialogue in the discourse—speech as if spoken by multiple players and voices. Like changes in style, this peopling of a monologic account with many voices is a means by which consultants were able to reflect the complex, many-sidedness of their experience and their identity. These aspects of performativity will be addressed again later in the essay, but they are signaled here to remind readers of the enormous complexity of interpreting any text in relation to the experience it references.

Gender: Articulated, Enacted, or Symbolically Projected

As mentioned earlier, the project's emphasis on identity issues did not espe-cially foreground gender. This enables us to examine something that femi-nist researchers have not addressed to any large extent: *in what circumstances* and *by what means* does gender (or class, region, language, etc.) emerge as an important issue? When an individual narrates his or her musical life, where is gender explicitly referenced with regard to music, and where is the "discourse" gendered in unconscious ways? What produces gender con-sciousness and what maintains gender blindness?

A tenuous distinction between issues that were "articulated" and those that were "enacted" is perhaps useful. Articulated issues are those that con-sultants identified as being related to gender. Hence, if an interviewee said that her father played the fiddle and, further, that she did not know why women did not play much, the gender issue was regarded as having been articulated. If, however, a consultant simply described male fiddle players without drawing attention to the gender specificity implied by the descrip-tion, the gender issue was considered to have been enacted. The distinction may seem pedantic, but it served as a tool for examining patterns of gender awareness. Although everyone enacted gender issues in their musical deal-ings with other people, only a limited number articulated gender issues, doing so in relation to specific experiential contexts.

The majority of consultants who articulated gender issues were female. Semiotics has taught us that this awareness of an identity construct (such as gender) is often related directly to negatively valued experience. (In com-parison, in interviews with a number of visible minority consultants, gen-der was rarely mentioned, but race was a dominant theme, for it was clearly the issue that most affected their lives as musicians, teachers, or organizers.)[11] In the PEI interviews, articulated gender issues generally related to proscrip-tions on participation in certain kinds of musical activity—fiddling, for ex-ample. In addition, the politics and strategies for commercial success were occasionally discussed using gendered labels.

Sonic detail, however, was rarely described as gendered, although eth-nicity, for example, was often articulated with reference to musical aspects. Fiddlers distinguish Acadian and Gaelic styles with reference to tempo (Ac-adians play faster), ornamentation, and rhythmic "feel." Men and women's styles were never explicitly distinguished, perhaps because historically the fiddle tradition in this region has been male dominated.

To trace enactments of gender, I examined descriptions of the musical tastes or activities of family members and friends, as well as the genders of comusicians and other participants in the musical networks of individual consultants. Among the most consistent enactments of gender, but one rarely articulated as a gender issue, was the representation of parents' musical participation.

The third aspect of our inquiry into the gendering of musical life stories, the study of symbolically projected gender assumptions, was by far the most difficult. The gendering of implicit values, styles, or even "genres" of discourse is unconscious in most instances. Some Euro-Canadian interviews clearly exhibit patterns of dichotomous gender stereotypes: male commitments to innovation, solitary hard work, aggressive aesthetics, rejection of rules, and assertions of music's autonomy from life or, conversely, female commitments to tradition and institutional structures, cooperative learning processes, gentler aesthetics, rule boundedness, and social groundedness. That such dichotomies are perpetuated in many ways via musical choices is evident. More interesting, perhaps, are the subtle means of asserting agency and modes of resistance.

Reading Musical Life Stories for Pattern and Conjuncture

How, then, is gender performed in the texts of the musical life stories of this closely knit network of Prince Edward Islanders? Do they construct for themselves an "idea of Folk" as gendered as the one McKay (1994, 32) posits for the province next door when he argues that "representations of the archetypal Nova Scotian came to emphasize muscle-bound masculinity and prowess" while observing that a large proportion of the collectors and "representers" were women?

Gendered Repertories and Performance Practices

The male dominance of performance in the hegemonic fiddle music world has been extensively described in oral and written sources.[12] Ken Perlman, who has made the most extensive collection of fiddle music on the island, describes the tradition as follows:

> Fiddling was considered by and large to be a man's calling, and those women who were musically inclined were encouraged to take up the pump organ or piano. Part of this was simply an extension of other "di-

vision of labor" attitudes that had men running the ploughs, mowers, and binders, and women learning to spin weave, and cook. But there was also a general feeling that fiddling at dance events was no "proper" activity for a woman. In fact, with the exception of the Evangeline area of Prince County, where Zélie-Anne Poirier has been an active dance player for many years, most women fiddlers plied their art primarily in the privacy of their homes. (1994, 28)

Perlman notes that the few active female fiddlers tended to come from "fiddling families" but that contemporary training programs (county fiddlers associations, at least one of which provides subsidized lessons for children) now encourage boys and girls equally to learn the tradition.[13]

Life stories with Scottish, Irish, or Acadian individuals whose families were active in the fiddle world consistently perform this construction of a male-dominated tradition in references to the fiddle activities of fathers and grandfathers.[14] One woman jokingly confessed, "I always had the impression that it was something that was passed on from father to son. It was like blue eyes or something." She remarked that she had never heard of a woman fiddler in her youth, adding: "I'm sure that's why an awful lot of women didn't play on the island especially, because there was no model for that. Women played the piano or the organ in the church" (RJ/MB 1993).[15] Another fiddler explained the extent of his father's passion with the following story: "As I say, he had a great love for the fiddle. Oh yeah, Dad'd tell me stories 'bout the times he'd be pickin' up people at the airport, fiddle in their hands, put them in the back seat and while he was driving them to their destinations get them to play tunes for him, you know" (RJ/CC 1993). The current director of the Queen's County Fiddlers invokes the male tradition despite the fact that women are welcome in the contemporary organization: "I feel that we are opening up the doors and creating a greater interest in fiddling by giving them the opportunities to learn new tunes, and I think that we're going to retain local styles because that's what we passed down, as they hear [at the rehearsals] their uncles and their fathers play these tunes" (RJ/CC 1993).

In *Belfast People* (1992), Susan Hornby's anthology of oral histories, Angus Leslie MacLean's description of his musical family epitomizes the same style of discourse: "The music, you know, was in all the MacLeans. My grandfather and my father and all the way back" (in Hornby 1992, 205). An Acadian fiddler, one of the younger generation of women who are breaking the conventional pattern, nevertheless recalls, "I think I had an uncle who played the fiddle just for his own pleasure" (RJ/AD 1993).

Some fiddlers regarded their fiddles as female.[16] Angus Leslie MacLean, for example, speaks as if he demanded fidelity from the instrument in return for protection: "The way I'd take care of [my fiddle], I'd keep it nice and tidy and everything, put her out of the reach of anyone that could get a hold of her to play her. I'd do that but I wasn't mean or anything like that. But I wouldn't loan it to anybody to go to play and me not go myself" (in Hornby 1992, 209). Even where a man was not active as a performer, he might still bring the fiddle world to his family:

> There was lots of music in my home, right. It was church music, mostly, but my father was a really enthusiastic singer. My sister and I sang, played organ, piano, but my father was really musical without any training. He didn't play an instrument, but he was just one of those people that just lived for music. And even when he was an old man and had trouble getting around, if there was something musical going on that he could crawl to, he'd go. And he used to sing all the time around the house and around the farm. And he used to jig fiddle tunes. When I was really small, I remember. He loved fiddle music. (RJ/MB 1993)

Or similarly:

> Well that goes back to when I was about three, four, five years old maybe, and I was introduced to fiddling through fiddlers who used to come to our home when I was a kid. And my Dad, although he didn't play, [didn't] fiddle much himself, he had a tremendous love for fiddling, and as a result he frequently invited a lot of fiddlers to our home. So it wasn't unusual to have three, four, or five fiddlers there some evenings playing fiddle, and of course it was just a natural talent to want to listen to the music, and that's the beginning of it. (RJ/CC 1993)

In some instances female partners constituted stark opposition to fiddle music, its negative. This was clearest in the case of one family in which, on one side, the grandfather was Catholic and the grandmother was Protestant.[17] The grandfather in this narrative was a highly reputed fiddler in the 1920s and 1930s, well known for his weekly radio appearances. Both because the consultant's grandfather was a significant figure in the PEI community and because she speaks eloquently about gender in relation to the fiddle tradition, I will quote Roy Johnstone's interview at some length:

> I grew up listening to old-time music and from my earliest recollection I remember mainly visitors coming to my grandparents. They had a lot of

company; they had a lot of relatives, and they had a lot of friends that would drop in, and the visit would always involve or include my grandfather playing the fiddle. And if there wasn't anyone there to accompany him on the piano, then he would just sit in the kitchen and play his fiddle tunes. . . . My grandmother was Scottish Presbyterian before she met him, and she was quite religious. He was very religious himself, but he lived his music a lot, and she still, I think, had ingrained in her that the fiddle was the devil's instrument in some ways. And I know that after they were married—well, he didn't give up playing for dances right after they married, but he sort of slackened off as far as dances were concerned. He played more for their friends and so on at house parties, and then the house parties kind of dwindled off, and then it would just be when people dropped in. And she encouraged him to play for friends and relatives that way, and she also encouraged his playing on the radio. She thought that was marvelous that he could go in and everyone in PEI and half of NS [Nova Scotia] could listen to his playing. She was really proud of that, but anyway the dances were another thing. (RJ/MM 1993)

The belief in the evils of dances was so strong in this family that misfortune was associated with fiddling for dances: "One theory—and I believe that it's probably true—is that my grandparents, well, they had four children altogether, and two of them died, one during a bad flu epidemic. And my grandmother blamed his death on the fact that my grandfather had been playing at a dance somewhere in the country and he brought the influenza bug home or whatever home with him, and so that was the end of his playing for dances, because she was brought up in this strict tradition that didn't believe in dancing" (ibid.). The positive/negative dualism expressed here conflates assumptions about gender and religion, one reinforcing the other. Other references to the fact that Catholic communities produced more fiddlers than Protestant communities imply similar dichotomization on religious grounds.

The idea that fiddling for dances introduced moral and physical impurities into one's existence was not tied only to the strictness of Scottish Presbyterians, however. Other consultants associated it with Catholic women as well. One Catholic fiddler commented that her mother was not much of a fan of fiddling. The same fiddler later noted that the nuns at her school were opposed to fiddling.

For Protestants in particular, the opposition to fiddling was usually related to the perception that it went hand in hand with excessive alcohol consumption and consequent physical aggression. Many interviewees, however, indicated that drinking was not always part of the house-party tradition or even, in some instances, a practice of fiddlers who played for dances. The renowned fiddler and radio celebrity Lem Jay, for example, was described as a gentle man. Fiddlers acknowledged the stereotype of the drunken fiddler but explained that musical skills demanded a largely sober performer. Gary Burrill's interview with Stan Myers, who moved from Martinvale (King's Country) to Boston, similarly describes an abstemious fiddle household:

> I played fiddle all around. There were a lot of fiddlers—we used to have what we called a halfway house. Not an alcoholic halfway house, which is what most people think of. My father being a fiddler, all of these Maritimers used to come. They'd all know we came from that part of the island and there was music at the house, so that's where they'd land. Angus Chisholm, Alex Gillis, Donald MacLeod, Chester MacDonald, A. A. Gillis, Alcide Aucoin, Colin Boyd—that's just naming a few of the more prominent ones that I can remember.
>
> We had the guitar and mandolin and fiddle, and they'd come in and they'd practice. They used to practice more than anything else. My father didn't drink—there was never any booze in our house at all. But they'd take their own little jug—Donald MacLeod and Chester liked to drink tea a little bit, and they'd spruce them up. (in Burrill 1992, 50)

Even though all these fiddlers were male, later in the interview Myers mentions a woman named Georgina Webster, whose father played for fiddle contests on the island in 1926: she "played with me over at WMBR the night they had 'PEI Night,' and she is tops. She is right up there with the best of them. She's extremely good" (in Burrill 1992, 51).

The narratives reenact the "story" of a male-dominated fiddle tradition, but there are suggestions of the ways in which women did find a place in the tradition. They participated most often in events that were safely contained in the concert hall or home, as Perlman noted, but often as piano accompanists, the support for the system. Furthermore, women such as Zélie-Anne Poirier and Georgina Webster managed to excel despite the male orientation of the fiddling world. The fact that Webster is mentioned not in conjunction with the live social events described by Stan Myers but only with regard to radio broadcasts suggests an interesting aspect of the venue restrictions associated with women's fiddling. The asocial space of the recording studio, devoid of the "dangers" of social interaction, is clearly more gender neutral than is the dance hall or even the house party. This may indicate, then, a way in which electronic mediation of a tradition can facilitate changes in the gendering of social performance.

In the course of the PEI interviews, the fiddle tradition was the only Anglo-Celtic or Acadian repertory that was consistently described as a male-gendered world. Small immigrant communities have also occasionally attempted to maintain specifically gendered repertories, but the new context of Maritime Canada has sometimes demanded change. As is consistent with practices in their countries of origin, the handful of instrumentalists in the island's Lebanese and South Asian communities are male, while both men and women maintain some dance traditions (e.g., the Lebanese *debki* dancers in Charlottetown). The Filipino community was preparing to revive a May flower festival among its young girls in 1993. (An interview that touches on this appears in the next section of this essay). A Sri Lankan (Sinhalese) singer and his wife, however, spoke about the *rabana,* a small frame drum widely known in their country, where it is often associated with female performing groups: "You know, some people play rabana with singing [about] current situations. Some interesting stories . . . it's very traditional. The people get together, especially women together. They play rabana around like dancing. It's very nice" (BD/TT 1993).[18] Although the women's performances of these funny, politically astute, topical songs remain largely as a fond memory, he performs this repertory in the occasional multicultural tea houses and at multicultural festivals in Charlottetown. The original contextualization of repertories, including their gendering, becomes secondary to the intense desire to present anything of one's ethnocultural heritage to the larger island community. Such musical practices have sometimes been dismissed as "vestigial,"[19] but such a label fails to recognize the dynamism of small ethnocultural groups. These initial stages of educating a largely ignorant Euro-Canadian community may be a necessary part of a long process that ultimately leads to more extensive revitalization; the Filipino experience discussed in more detail below is a case in point. Gender crossing, as in the case of the Sri Lankan genre, is pragmatically associated with the early phases of such revitalization.

Gendered Patterns of Institutional Commitment

Although not articulated as gender issues, several other patterns—ones that crossed the generically defined musical worlds as well as ethnocultural boundaries—were enacted or symbolically projected as gendered in the musical life stories from Prince Edward Island. One of these concerns commitment to institutional structures. The majority of male consultants described an independent pathway to music. One country musician, for ex-

ample, explained: "I didn't take any serious lessons. I bought some books
and studied them, but most [of] what I learn, I learn by ear" (BD/NM 1993).
The one institution this musician did support was the Island Songwriters
Association. Although many country musicians, both male and female, are
self-taught,[20] the point here is rather that male musicians tended to emphasize this factor as part of their musical life stories whereas female musicians
rarely did so.

An Acadian writer of folk songs who "took a few courses in university
but nothing to speak of" describes his self-taught guitar skills as a pathway
to independence: "I was about twenty years old when I started [guitar]. Yeah,
just picking away. At that point it was just to try to be able to accompany
myself so that I'd be able to sing. . . . I was trying to find some freedom in
being able to be more independent" (RJ/RP 1993). A Scottish fiddler describes
the noninterventionist encouragement he received: "I started about five or
six or seven, somewhere in that area. Jackie Chipman strung up an old fiddle
and he spotted my interest in the fiddle, I guess, and he gave Dad the in-
structions to take the fiddle and just hang it on the wall, and whenever I felt
that I wanted to play it, to let me play it. And I guess I did. . . . I picked up
some tunes fairly early in life . . . all by ear, by listening to imitate from
whatever source" (RJ/CC 1993).

Many women spoke differently about their training and access to music
making. They attributed their skills to teachers or organizations that nurtured
them. The county fiddlers' associations, for example, which undoubtedly
play a major role as teaching institutions for both men and women, were
acknowledged more often in the women's accounts. An Acadian fiddler explains that she joined the Prince County Fiddlers and "took private lessons
at the College of Piping." Recognizing the Roman Catholic church's earlier
opposition to the fiddle, one consultant noted the irony of its current involvement with such fiddle associations: "And now the Catholic church
supports—very strongly throughout the Maritimes—traditional music. There
would be no PEI Fiddler's Society without Father Faber MacDonald or Father
Charlie, and the same for Cape Breton" (RJ/MB 1993). Not only Christian
churches were cited for their support of music. An Iranian-born singer explains how she frequently looked to the Baha'i community to support her
musical endeavors. Their assistance was particularly important to the refugee camp in which she found herself after fleeing her country during the
Ayatollah Khomeini's revolution: "There were again problems. In order to
have the instruments we weren't able to buy ourselves, in a refugee condition, we had to beg the Baha'i family to buy [them] for us. They bought the

organ (harmonium) and the violin. We wanted to have a santur. There was a professional player but he never got the santur" (BD/HM 1993).

Of course the tendencies for narratives about institutional commitment to be gendered were not without exceptions. Interviews with the (currently male) directors of the two largest teaching institutions in the province—the Music Department at the University of Prince Edward Island and the College of Piping, in Summerside—predictably voiced strong support for their respective schools and for the concept of institutional training. Since the College of Piping is perhaps the more controversial institution because some see it as a regimentation of a vernacular tradition, the director's remarks were particularly interesting on this point: "Institutionalization of education isn't a bad thing. It's basically what the educators make of it. . . . I think people are afraid that institutionalization is too structured, too formal, but again, I think that . . . certain instructors have a way of communicating their ideas whether it's in a formalized setting or it's informal" (BD/SM 1993). He emphasized the autonomous teaching styles of instructors and hence the individuality of the process. He later stressed the dynamism of his curriculum: "I feel a real responsibility as a player and a teacher to pass it [the piping tradition] on in a pure form, [but] that doesn't mean that we can't show them new things. I like exposing them to different kinds of things and letting them come to their own conclusion of what's tasteful or not" (ibid.). One might, then, perceive that the grounds on which his commitment rests, emphasis on individuality and innovation, are not inconsistent with the narratives of male consultants cited earlier.

Other instances of women's commitment to institutions emerge in the next section of this essay, where they are examined in the context of fuller and sometimes even contradictory interpretive strategies.

Gendered Pathways

A major premise of this and virtually every other feminist study of "performativity" in the 1990s is that identities are not fixed but changeable and contingent. With my strategically essentialist lens still intact, however, I ask whether these very fluctuations and contingencies are in any way reinforcing dichotomized concepts of maleness and femaleness.

Clearly some women and men follow locally circumscribed career paths. In narratives of lives that range beyond the island and adjacencies, however, the pathways of male and female musicians exhibit a dichotomized pattern. Although several female consultants travel extensively in other parts of Canada and internationally, their music making, for the most part, remains more local and more homogeneous with regard to style and genre. An exception to this pattern is the young Acadian fiddler whose story is presented later in this essay; her move to neighboring New Brunswick allowed her access to classical music, albeit without giving up her first love, fiddle music. Two other female musicians described simply giving up their music when they moved; in one case music was actively pursued again when she returned to the island. A number of male consultants, however, described dramatic shifts and developments in their repertory and style in conjunction with travel to other, less-homogeneous places or places that simply encouraged a different or more varied aesthetic.

It is interesting to compare commodified island music with regard to this theme. Among those who have moved beyond the boundaries of island recognition, the biggest style shifts from one recording to the next have been made by male artists. The two highest-profile songwriters from the island are cases in point. Teresa Doyle writes frequently about PEI history, highlighting several of the island's remarkable women of the past, for example, the Acadian "Belle Marie," who was burned at the stake in 1723, or herbalist Christy Campbell (celebrated in Doyle's song "Stowaway," which is the title song of her third album), whose early 1800s association with the Micmac enabled her to live apart from society's norms. It is significant that one female consultant endorsed Doyle with regard to these songs: "I'm always going to make up something brand new based on where I lived—which is Teresa's ghost thing which is very creative" [BD/BH 1993]. Many male songwriters have also written and recorded significant songs about island history. The significance is not that this is a female pursuit but rather that a local woman narrated her own desires by connecting to Doyle on the basis of this style of "innovation." Doyle is inevitably compared with Lennie Gallant, both award-winning artists who are widely known nationally.[21] Unlike Gallant, who has moved off the island to facilitate his career and has evolved musically toward a rock style since his earliest folk-based album *Breakwater*,[22] Doyle retains an acoustic sound and uses texturally clean arrangements (her albums contain a remarkable number of monophonic numbers). In live performances on the island, she continues to perform traditional folk songs along with her own songs and those of several other island songwriters. Hence, she stays closer to the folk song tradition that thrives locally.

We can see similar generic shifts related to geographic moves in the lives of a number of other artists who are, as yet, known regionally rather than nationally. A songwriter of Caribbean ancestry moved from a folk-based

Celtic-influenced style to reggae when he left the island for a job first in Calgary and later in Vancouver. He has now returned and has found new inspiration and a deeper personal identity in the history of the small eighteenth-century black community in Charlottetown's "Bog" area. He describes his current stylistic synthesis as "rastacadia" music. Similarly, a classical composer who had worked professionally in Montreal for a period of time, writing modernist concert music, had similarly moved away from the acoustic, folk-related music of his earlier years; on his return to the island, he became more associated with the jazz and rock scenes. He describes the style change from Montreal and back as follows:

> But the stuff I write there was more—I don't know what you call it—strident or stark, or more traditional twentieth-century, student compositions. . . .
>
> Well, I haven't written anything in the serious vein for a long time, like five years. And I never feel like I'm going to again. It doesn't bother me. . . . I kind of have gotten back into the pop thing again but with this baggage or this extra [training], so it gives me a different perspective on that music too. The stuff I did do when I first moved back here was all electronic music, or electroacoustic music, even the orchestra piece, because there's no real outlet for ensemble playing, but I enjoyed that. (BD/SF 1993)

There are some interesting differences here, relating in part to the generic worlds in which these musicians engage. Both male and female fiddlers, past and present, seemed to carry their musical preferences with them and reinvent an island (or a Maritime) culture when they were away. The stories in Burrill's *Away* of communities in Boston in the early twentieth century also illustrate this pattern, but so do contemporary stories such as that of Anastasia (recounted below), whose off-island classmates gather for regular *ceilidhs* in their new university community. This is significant with regard to border crossing since, as mentioned earlier, the fiddle tradition is regarded *in itself* as a border zone. It attracts audiences and performers from diverse segments of island society. Its power as a symbol of the "local" then, depends to a large extent on its capacity to represent an identity that transcends ethnocultural, class, or gender specificity. The genre that succeeds in this respect is the one that is the most overtly and consistently associated with constructions of maleness, a fact that merits careful consideration.

To be accurate, however, it is important to note that virtually all musicians on the island are versatile, and audiences are accustomed to hearing musical juxtapositions that might be unusual in larger urban centers. The regular benefit concerts throughout island communities, in themselves one of the strongest indications of community-mindedness and of music's role in it, often feature musical variety. One benefit I attended combined country singers and fiddlers with local comedians. Another featured an array of local bands in a variety of popular styles: bluegrass, country, folk, and rock. PEI Symphony players described the need to cross into more popular genres, and one classical musician described a real love for "the old nostalgic songs." The PEI Songwriters Association asserts both in its newsletter and at public events that it welcomes all styles of composer. Fiddlers may now be classically trained, carrying this particular crossover in both directions. At the annual Heritage Fall Festival, professional Celtic bands play side by side with children from newer immigrant communities who may be just beginning their study of a particular musical or dance style. This border crossing is undoubtedly enabled by the small and closely knit society on the island, one that mitigates clear and simple generic associations with specific subgroups, be they defined by gender or framed in some other way.

The Construction of Essentialism

At the outset of this essay I related the reading of musical life stories for pattern and conjuncture to essentialism. Nevertheless, both when my consultants independently reinforce the "story" of male dominance of the fiddle tradition and when I coordinate similar patterns in the career paths of island musicians, it is clear that these accounts (like all essentialist accounts) are constructions. The implication, however, is that such accounts reflect socially shared bases for living, and although I think this implication has been responsibly presented and defended here, I recognize that issues of sample and interpretation are always assailable in such presentations. Whose consultants? Whose "social"? Shared when? Essentialist constructions are partial truths, politically positioned.

Reading Musical Life Histories for Motion and Disjuncture

As the final paragraph in the previous section implies, although the preceding representations are grounded in specific life-story accounts by specific musicians, they nevertheless tend to exaggerate a dichotomous picture of maleness and femaleness enacted through musical choices. The essentialist lens finds gendered patterns and structures in the interview accounts by either implicitly or explicitly relating them to other sources. There is no de- nying that such patterns are partial truths—sometimes strong truths, as in the case of the male-biased fiddle tradition; sometimes contested truths, as in the gendering of the Maritime concept of the "folk"; and sometimes id- iosyncratic or phenomenological truths. But this partial picture is not an adequate feminist representation of gender and music in oral historical ac- counts. The structuring of the traditions about which they speak does vio- lence to the strength and agency of consultants, to their significant roles within these traditions, and to their personalities, individual identities, and power. It tends to treat individual accounts as if they represented groups.

At one level the solution to this is simply to listen better. As I was writ- ing this article, I heard a speech by the Toronto journalist and activist Susan Cole in which she stated that listening to what women have to say about their lives and believing them is a radical research method. To complement the essentialist lens, then, and in the spirit of Cole's contention, I now try an account that employs what I am calling a "constructivist lens," a frame- work that emphasizes the fluidity and contingencies of gender identity, that searches less for pattern and more for change, less for confirmations of so- cially structured "institutions" and more for points of negotiation, less for consistencies among stories and more for contradictions or disjunctures within them.

In pragmatic terms this shifts the reading of oral historical accounts. I am still struggling with the "how" of this shift. I am inclined to say that it is microscopic—that it looks more intensively at smaller segments of discourse, at the nuance of word choice, the flow of words, the shifts in style or speech genre, the oral performance, and the comprehension barriers between in- terviewer and consultant. It is of necessity a dialogic approach; the presence of the interviewer must not be ignored to the extent that it was in the stra- tegically essentialist representation.

Let us listen to three PEI women's stories through this lens.[23]

Leti LaRosa

A Filipino woman who left a professional job to immigrate to the island in the 1970s following her husband (who came to Newfoundland in 1966 to finish his university training and then stayed, working for Agriculture Canada), Leti LaRosa has assumed the role of cultural ambassador and multicultural research- er on the island. She is also in demand as a caterer. Until 1986 hers was the only Filipino family on the island. I interviewed her during our first meeting at her home, and she had to introduce me both to her life and to many aspects of her cultural tradition with which I was not acquainted. She showed me several photograph albums on this occasion. We shared an academic background, however, a love of research, and an interest in questions of multicultural policy and cultural representation. Involved in several multicultural organizations on a national and international level,[24] she spoke about cultural diversity in a broader manner than did many other consultants.

The significant events with which LaRosa constructs her current identity include two points of dramatic change. Her move to Canada is the first of these. Coming from the northern Batan Islands, she spent most of her life in Manila. Her knowledge of dance stems from her high school days, when she learned over thirty dance genres as part of the physical education curriculum. Trained in mathematics and employed as a professor, she became acquainted with a rich range of cultural traditions in her home country in the course of traveling for teaching assignments across the country. She explained modestly, "We have Spanish, English, and then Filipino, and I can understand and speak some of the dialects. So that's how it is. Because when I was at home I traveled all over the Philippines to give lectures at different universities." She knew that the large (first) wave of Filipino immigrants to Canada between the mid-1960s to the late 1970s, a wave that included her husband and herself (ten years later), was composed largely of professionals, especially medical experts. "My sister-in-law is a medical doctor, and she was working in Newfoundland at the time. She was one of the first professionals that were recruited by the Canadian government to come here and work. Because during that time there were still very few Canadians who were in the field of medicine . . . so they had to get these professionals from other countries. And they got so much from the Philippines." As I heard her, I could not help but think that she must have expected fantastic esteem and easy professional advancement in her new country. Instead, she respected her husband's wish and the Filipino tradition that she not work while her children were growing. She turned partly to cake decorating and catering, teaching international cooking occasionally (without pay) at community colleges, but especially to the performing arts. When I asked with a sigh in my voice whether she would return to mathematics at some point, she replied quite simply, "Probably catering is much better." The dramatic shift from academic professional to unemployed housewife, from cosmopolitan urbanite to isolated minority in a small city, struck me as daunting, but she easily accommodated the change and turned her talents to work that fulfilled both her needs and those of the society in which she now found herself.

A second change and a new opportunity occurred in 1986 when a group of islander men who had been corresponding with Filipino women via a Florida-based pen pal club traveled to the Philippines and returned with new wives. LaRosa comments on this remarkable turn of events as follows: "Most of the Filipinos that are here, they came to marry an islander. So they were uprooted from the Philippines and they were brought here. These guys, they call to the Philippines, meet them, and then marry them, and then bring them up here. And so they didn't bring anything representing our culture." This situation meant that the unique role of LaRosa and her husband, for a time the only Filipino man on the island, was intensified. But the possibility of building a community, however small, now existed. She kept insisting that "you need only about three or four who are really committed." The Filipino population of fourteen adults in 1993, however, was far flung, with three in the western county, three in the east, and the rest in Charlottetown or suburbs.

LaRosa's eagerness to contribute professionally to her new country was realized through the arts: "That's my interest, the performing arts," she asserted straightforwardly. She taught Filipino dances to her own children and others as they arrived. She gathered artifacts of every region of the Philippines in her own home, arranged concerts by visiting artists, and compiled scrapbooks and photo albums to document the emergence of Filipino culture on the island. She accepted a new academic role as community historian.

Her description of Filipino music did not differentiate historical developments, even though her accounts of Canadian events were carefully located by year. The account of the former switched from a personal story to a more formalized and rather extensive instrumentarium:

> We have music from the natives, which is like drumming. And then we have music from other groups of natives, which is like gongs. That is the *kulintang*. And then we have this ukulele, and then we have the guitar. [The guitar] is very famous in the Philippines because we manufacture and export them. And then we have the *banduria*[25] and the mandolin. We have the harp;[26] yeah, some people play harp. And we have the only bamboo organ in the world. That was constructed, I think, during the Spanish time, and now it's a tourist attraction in the Philippines. That's in one of the oldest churches that we have.[27] We have this gong;[28] people when they dance, they use the gong. Then we have . . . well, piano is very popular. Very few Filipino homes that you visit don't have a piano.

The instruments she mentions are, with the exception of the kulintang, adaptations of European instruments, many of which are traditionally used in the plucked string orchestra, or *rondalla*. Of these instruments, only the piano continues to play a role in the everyday lives of Philippine Islanders: "When we have gatherings here, I have a piano downstairs, and one of the Filipinas that we have here, she's a good piano player. She is a doctor at the college. She will come down and will play the piano, and we just all sing. I have a book that was sent to me by the seniors from Vancouver. They have written a book about folklore in the Philippines, and they have all the difficult Filipino songs in different languages. We have seventy-two languages in the Philippines."

Other contact with Filipino music in the diasporic communities living in larger Canadian cities is made via tape and video recordings. LaRosa has been a resource person in this regard as well.

> I order tapes from the Philippines. That's why I'm scared whenever they borrow my tapes. . . . My son has a cassette that can dub tapes. So we just dub tapes whenever, and I just dub the part that they need. . . . Sometimes we go and visit one province purposely to see their show and then, after that, I will ask them "Could you provide me with a tape of that?" and then they will give me a copy of the tape. So I have here a tape from Winnipeg, from Vancouver, from Toronto, Montreal. So whenever we want to learn something we look at all the tapes. We use that as a pattern for learning. The Philippine embassy sent me a big file of [dance] instruction. Just looking at it you go crazy. It's easier to see it on tape.

More recently she has taken an initiative to videotape performances by over thirty ethnocultural groups on the island and to conduct interviews with elders in each community. Her "archive" is slowly encompassing a diverse, pluralistic array of communities.

After 1986 LaRosa enthusiastically began to organize the tiny far-flung Philippine community to participate in public events, aware that regional differences must be respected and utilized for the community to thrive. They collaborated on Filipino Christmas parties and then participated in the Heritage Folk Festival for the first time in 1988, winning the prize for excellence in artistic display only a year later. "Last year [1991] we had the northern part of the Philippines. All the artifacts that we show came from the northern part, and the performance was also from the northern part. . . . Then the year before we had a Muslim performance, and all the artifacts that we showed came from the South, like the big box that is hand carved and inlaid with mother of pearl—that is from the Muslim region." In addition to rotating the regional emphasis, she coordinated the local knowledge about regional dances. "That's *tinikling*. One of the girls here, Sally, she lives in Cardigan. She dances that with Raymond. I taught them how to dance that, maybe three years or four years ago. . . . I used to do it with Raymond when we had Sally for the tinikling and Shioni for the *carinosa*[29] and then Nancy Macneeman came. So we had her for . . . that Muslim dance."

Although most Filipino immigrants to Canada are Catholic, as is LaRosa, it is significant that she endeavors to include Muslim genres in island performances. Furthermore, this sharing of authority has apparently prevented rifts within the small group: "If you become too authoritative and too—you dictate things—it sort of turns the people. What helps is you give them the opportunity and the recognition of whatever they do and that will help them explore more of their talents." Paradoxically, the cooperative spirit that enabled the women to build this tiny cultural infrastructure has now given way to a single male dance teacher who rehearses a children's group on a weekly basis. Although this gendered shift in authority might be read as a patriarchal turn of events, it is in fact LaRosa's strength as a cultural leader that enabled her to pass the teaching role to one of her former students, a move that negotiates solidarity in accordance with her belief in enabling others.

Consistent in LaRosa's construction of her identity is her insistence on having gifts to offer to the larger society. This theme surfaced in her earlier descriptions of her mathematics career; in her concern about her family; in her dissemination of cultural information via tapes, lessons, and so on to her fellow Filipinos; and, in the following statement, in her desire to engage the Canadian mainstream. I had just expressed my own concern about the exoticization of visible minority cultures in Canadian multicultural "shows." I suggested that many such presentations were perhaps too objectified, too staged, and asked whether she shared that view. She replied: "No, we do not share that because we are so proud of our culture and we want to share it with every Canadian, just like the Scottish [or] the Irish are sharing their culture." She reiterated this in conjunction with our discussion of the "Philippine Fiesta," a highly successful event that had taken place just before my arrival on the island in early July. In a five-hour extravaganza that attracted ticket sales of over 300, a Filipino dinner preceded a performance of Montreal musicians and dancers doing thirty-one dances. The audience was smaller than the ticket sales, however, which LaRosa thinks was probably because the event was scheduled on the holiday weekend. I suggested that ticket sales pay the bills, but LaRosa quickly replied: "But we don't want that. We want them to be there. We want them to see what we can offer."

Her concern with representation for the outside community does not preclude initiatives to develop community-based renewal, however. She describes her efforts to revive the Flowers of May ritual—a procession that is presented mostly by the young girls of the community.

> The month of May is a very big month for the Philippines because we call that flower month. [It] involves lots of music because we offer flowers during the whole month of May, every day, and there are people assigned to do that. The children, they really dress up to offer the flowers to the Blessed Virgin and while doing that we sing. . . . It has to be done in the church. When I was growing up, my parents always sent us to the country because it's fun to do it in the country rather than in the city. So we stayed in the country for a month and we [would] do that every day. And the flowers—people bring the flowers. Let's say I would be the one in charge for this week; everyone in town would bring flowers to your place, and there are people who arrange the flowers in different shapes. They cut up, you know, the banana tree. It's soft, so they separate the trunk, and then they shape it in different shapes, like a heart, cross, and then they fill that with flowers and you carry it. It's really beautiful. . . . We have quite a few little girls here now, because that's mostly girls. The boys are not part of that. It's only the girls. And then, at the end of the month, we have a procession. Everybody is getting flowers, and that's all with music. But there we sing it in Latin or in Spanish.

There is, then, a matriarchal inheritance constructed within this tiny community, undoubtedly relating in part to the unusual way in which the female-dominated community was constituted on the island in the first place. LaRosa has found ways to shift her project as membership in her community slowly grew, to negotiate solidarity, and to forge collaborative achievements. Her motivation, however, has clearly been directed to the larger society in which she attempts to negotiate a proud place for Filipino culture.

Barbara Hagerman

Barbara Hagerman, like Leti LaRosa, was born outside the province but much closer culturally, for she comes from an English family in the neighboring Maritime province of New Brunswick. A musically precocious child in a rural community, she enjoyed special attention from her teachers. She eventually studied voice at Mount Allison University, was certified as a teacher, and moved to the island to teach in the school system. A real love for performance led her into conducting, and she now directs a community choir on the island; in addition, she does some solo concertizing, in part with a prominent classical guitarist who teaches part-time at the University of Prince Edward Island. She enjoys a wide network of social contacts both on and off the island, and possibly because of this, she was appointed to a federal grants council. In turn, this activity has made her more aware of cultural policy and the complexities of identity issues in contemporary Canada. I had known Hagerman to a limited extent for some years before asking her to participate in a project interview. In the course of our extended discussion at her home, I felt myself relating strongly to her rural Anglo-Canadian roots.

Hagerman was one of the few consultants who differentiated her parents less on the separateness of their musical tastes and more on their level of confidence in performing publicly. Beyond her immediate family, a variety of women musicians peopled her youth.

> The only thing I can remember when I was little is that somebody was always singing in our house. I can remember 1953, at least—I had been singing in school, I think I was in grade three—the first time we had a Christmas play, and I had been singing there. My dad sang in the choir at church and my mother never sang in front of people, but if she was in good humor, she would sing while she was sweeping or cleaning or scrubbing or whatever. And my aunt Esther played for Eastern Star, and my aunt Helen, when I went to church and stood beside her, she would be singing alto and my grandmother sang alto and my dad's cousin was the piano teacher in town. This was a town of a thousand people. And when I was in grade four, the Women's Institute in the county had a music festival, and there never had been one up till then.

A huge shift occurred in her childhood when a music festival adjudicator came to town. She describes him as a rather strange character, an older bachelor who called himself "professor" and had one glass eye. She explains that he was "so impressed with the raw, natural talent" in this two-day music festival (the first one in the early 1950s) that he gave up his job in Milltown and moved to Woodstock. He went to all the rural schools and organized choirs that he took, at his own expense, to regional and eventually provincial music festivals in New Brunswick. This was a decisive event in her young life, for it provided Hagerman both a mentor and a benefactor (she eventually learned that he was the source of the piano that mysteriously arrived at her house when she was about twelve).

She describes an environment in which she had more intuitive skill in music than her fellows, skills that rapidly led her to learn the church organ, direct the junior choir, and teach her peers, all by the age of fifteen or sixteen. The absence of local support for classical music made her value external authority (ranging from music festivals to God) to a large extent, in keeping with the gendered pattern described earlier.

> Music festival was really important to me because it was the only place where I could make sure that I was doing what I thought was supposed to be done as far as music was concerned. Oh, and I did RCM [Royal Conservatory of Music] exams—like, I won two silver medals in the same year, one for singing, one for piano, one year. So there was all that going on. People were encouraging me in various ways, but I decided when I was fourteen that I needed to know what I was going to do after I was finished school. And if you're smart, you're supposed to go to university, except we had no money and nobody in my family had ever gone to university. But I had been working since I was twelve. . . . Anyway, when I was fourteen, I was in the music festival. . . . I was really religious, and I sort of made this pact with God [that] the next day, [when] I was singing my sacred solo, if I made 90 on my sacred solo, then that would be the sign that I should go into music.

This event, this point of negotiation in her life, set the style of negotiating in other situations as she matured. Hard work and considerable talent had to be tested against external validation. As she became part of the institutional system, responsible for certain aspects of this validation process, she continued to believe that such processes uncover talent in unsuspecting places, however their mandate is defined. Nevertheless, although this might be read as another instance of institutional commitment that I associated earlier with the construction of "woman," it is through her engagement with schools, choirs, funding agencies, and so on that she has negotiated various positions between the local and national, same and other, woman and professional.

Another aspect of her childhood, one she describes as formative, is the fact of isolation. At various points in the interview she mentions occasions where friends ignored her professional identity: she describes, for example, the scene in the staff room of the school where she taught after she played a tape of her solo recital performance. Hagerman says the astonished teachers responded with statements such as "I didn't know you could sing": "I'm thinking, 'Well, what did you think I was here for?'" She expresses frustration because "they just didn't have any concept." At a recent party she said to a friend, "You've never asked me what I do." And she explains the real cost of this musical isolation: "Like, for about twenty years of my life, here, I just gave up. Nobody was interested in what I did, nobody ever asked, and if I mentioned it, they just turned it right off and talked about the hockey game and if they were going to the dance on Saturday night. So I just stopped. It couldn't be part of my life." Both her feeling of isolation and her connecting of that aspect of her adult professional life to her childhood feelings are interesting with regard to gender and music. The isolation aspect may be a function of specific social conditions, but ones that are shared perhaps by more Canadian women artists than has been hitherto acknowledged. The self-conscious return to the theme of isolation in her story, however, is more complex. It reflects, in my view, not merely the frustration she felt over a lack of recognition but the dissonance between her view of her identity and the strongly gendered patterns that were socially reinforced.

Whereas her childhood memories include a mixture of female and male role models (although the "professor" is clearly the first possible career model), her description of her husband's musical tastes makes clear that a gender dichotomy had emerged in relation to music, one that implicates class relations rather prominently: "[He] listened to country and western music when I met him. So he's come along now that he really likes Mahler symphonies. And he likes my singing. Well, he always liked me singing."

An inconsistency in Hagerman's story emerges, however, as she attempts to negotiate between the demure and modest style of femininity that seems especially prevalent on the island and the often competitive, larger-than-life spirit that is certainly a part of her personality and undoubtedly a useful attribute for a classical singer. Reflecting the first tendency, she states her musical goals in life modestly: "I've decided that I'm sort of like the one little candle and that I can't be concerned about [music] nationally and I can't be concerned globally as far as music is concerned. I can't limit myself to classical music because I enjoy the other music probably more—the old nostalgic type of music—but I think that my job has been to try to get people to love music, to make it part of their life."

She regards the carol singing at her large-scale Christmas parties and her ongoing community choir work equally as part of the realization of this goal. Later she describes her teaching activity in a similar fashion: "I'm just going for people, one person at a time." Her involvement *is* national, however, for she is a conscientious member of federal agencies that are in the midst of defining new cultural policies for the nation. Her confidence in such agencies is expressed strongly: "The one thing that I always believe about the Canada Council system, and I've certainly heard every horror story beforehand, but I really believe that the cream rises to the top in anything. And I think it's the job of the council to make sure that there's an avenue for that cream to rise to the top, which I think we're working at." She sees herself as an initiator in this regard, not just a respondent to social forces: "A lot of us are saying that these things [cultural policy] should be questioned, and we *are* questioning, and they're making changes. And it's not only the outside community that's doing it, but it's the board that does it too."

As in the case of other aspects of her experience, the roots of this two-way pull—between local and national, inward and outward, modest and extroverted—also connects to a story from her youth that articulates the previously mentioned musical dichotomy.

> The last time I sang with the symphony, we did an evening at the opera, and I was so proud of that. We taped it, and I took it home to play it for mum and dad and my sister, and they laughed all the way through it. Laughed all the way through it. And I can recall, I think about after the first year at university, I heard my mother tell somebody that they were ruining my voice at university 'cause all of a sudden there was some projection to it. It wasn't dear little sweet five-year old Barbara. God it was hard to take.

She describes a sort of double bind, which parallels LaRosa's to some extent, between her role as woman and professional, responding creatively and situationally rather than uniformly or consistently.

This bifurcated vision, as I read it, allows Hagerman to negotiate the previously described tensions between her roles as woman, professional, and singer. She moves between inside/outside, self/other, local/global, and modest/ambitious to negotiate a complex identity. An interesting aspect of her narrative that may relate to this is her propensity to invent conversation in the course of her monologue. Deborah Tannen is among those who have analyzed this style of speaking, demonstrating how we all animate the many subjectivities that constitute our "selves." Further, she contends: "The act of transforming others' words into one's own discourse is a creative and enlivening one. Following Friedrich . . . , it is a poetic act of the individual imagination. Moreover, and perhaps paradoxically, and this I think is Bakhtin's chief argument, it is a supremely social act: by appropriating each other's utterances, speakers are bound together in a community of words" (Tannen 1995, 202).

Some individuals, however, use this technique more extensively than others, and Barb Hagerman is one of those people. This speech style clearly demonstrates her capacity for dramatic presentation. Beyond that, it illustrates that her performance of her own identity depends on her construction of relationships with a host of colleagues, friends, and associates—an entire social world.

Anastasia Desroches

Anastasia Desroches is a young Acadian woman from the island's French-speaking "Evangeline district."[30] One of several young women who are acquiring prominence as fiddlers, she was working, at the time of the interview, as a fiddler at one of the many restaurants that have live music during the tourist season. She was also doing some performances with the project interviewer, island fiddler Roy Johnstone, and teaching and performing both Highland and Acadian dance, especially at the College of Piping—a school for Scottish music and dance established in Summerside, PEI, in the early 1990s. She planned to continue her studies in music at a bilingual university in neighboring New Brunswick during the fall and winter. Her development as a dancer was primarily with a group called the Lady Slipper Step Dancers, from Kensington, PEI.

One of the things that especially interested me about Desroches's experience was her manner of negotiating both the male-dominated fiddle world and the (to a lesser extent) female-dominated folk dance world. It is not surprising that she and her sisters were all directed to dancing, an activity in which she trained every week for fourteen years. In her case, however, a passionate love of the music accompanying that dancing was the real inspiration: "I just loved fiddle music so much. I had to learn it. I had to have it with me all the time so I could play it."

Desroches distinguishes the music her parents preferred, which she calls "country music," from her own "folk music" and further emphasizes her individuality in the manner she learned the tradition. In this regard, she differs from both Hagerman and LaRosa in that she set herself apart at an early stage through her musical preferences. "The first different style I heard was the Calgary Fiddlers at the Canada Games in Cape Breton, and I decided then that I wanted to learn how to play the fiddle. So that summer, 1987, I got myself a fiddle with my babysitting money, and I just started picking up tunes on my own, learning by ear. Then that fall, I went with Prince

County Fiddlers." Both she and the director of the dance group in which she started continue as members of the Prince County Fiddlers, but this does not seem to be a major social outlet for her: "I go to a few practices, a few sessions with them once in a while," she said.

University became a new site of negotiation, and musical styles were at the center of this: "I was very discouraged from playing traditional music at university, but every Saturday night, a bunch of us would get together and have our ceilidhs. In the girls' residence we had a piano room, and probably twenty or thirty of us from Cape Breton and PEI got together, and we had the guitars and the fiddles and the piano and the flute. . . . But here not so much. I find a lot of the young people aren't too interested in it around here." Desroches finds "self" while "away" but is still able to draw on another self to support the institution she now attends. She is hardly a subversive student, contending that her university studies helped her, improving her bowing technique and enhancing her reading ability,[31] which in turn enabled her to learn tunes more easily. She nevertheless expresses her attraction to fiddle: "And I was just told at the beginning, 'You're not to play fiddle music. Just stick with the classical while you're here. It'll be a lot better for you.' But it was too strong a temptation." She clearly enjoys narrating this small bit of "subversion." "Secretly . . . we had secret get-togethers, but everyone likes fiddle music. Even my teacher. I know she likes the fiddle music, because once she was going to a party, and she wanted to learn how to play some fiddle tunes 'cause it was a party, you know, instruments and stuff like that. And she asked me to teach her some fiddle tunes. I never got around to it."

Like most female consultants from the island, Desroches expresses a strong commitment to the organizations with which she is associated. The College of Piping, where she taught throughout the 1990s, was described as "a really good service" because of the variety of music taught and the recognition it gives to the local town. She continued: "It took a lot of work on behalf of some people to get it going. It's a really good thing, especially for young kids, 'cause that's a lot who's involved. There's a lot of young students who'll promote this stuff in future years."

Johnstone then asked her about the value of competition, knowing that many fiddlers have opposed fiddle contests since they were banned on the island in the late 1920s, in the interests of social equanimity and cooperation. He asked her to compare Highland and step dancing in this regard, perhaps betraying his own preference for the noncompetitive step dancing in the tone of his voice. She, however, took a strong position supporting competition:

Yeah, Highland dancing is kind of [competitive]. It's a thing that's big everywhere. . . . Our dancers will go to all the competitions, like, you know, in all these provinces. Whereas the step dancing—there's some [competition] in Nova Scotia, but in Cape Breton, it's not competitive there at all. . . . I think it [competition] is a good thing. I think especially for young kids, because it gives them a chance to test themselves, and it gives them something to work for. You know, they say, "I have to learn some new steps for this competition," and it's really good for them. They can see where they stand in comparison to other dancers, even if they don't win. It's not important. It also gives them confidence because they got up on the stage and danced all by themselves. And yeah, I think it's a good thing.

Her views echo Hagerman's in the reliance on external sources for legitimation not in the sense of winning but in the sense of place within the larger world.

Johnstone revealed his own bias more directly when he followed up by asking: "You don't think it takes away from appreciation of the tradition in itself?" Like many other female consultants, however, Desroches expressed a situational argument, refusing to see tradition and competition oppositionally: "No, I don't think [it takes away from appreciation of the tradition]. I think it's just a different thing altogether. And I think one rather helps the other. It makes for better dancers, 'cause they try harder for the competition."

Although she was just beginning a professional career in the early 1990s, Desroches has already learned how to negotiate a double position, as woman and musician. To a large extent, her dancing is an acceptable expressive outlet for the former role, while her fiddling resists the constraints of that role. The balancing of respect for classical and folk music reveals the sort of situational decision-making that appears in Hagerman's and La Rosa's stories as well. This strategy has already proven to enable Anastasia Desroches to negotiate the enactments and symbolic projections of gender in her life as a musician.

Conjunct/Disjunct Life Stories

The research for this essay began with the assumption that music is a domain in our lives through which we can express desire, establish relationship, and actualize self. The telling of musical life stories—not as self-evident reports but as constructions, fantasies, creative texts in themselves—reveals those expressions. In the patterns and conjunctures among a wide range of stories, we see more than the individual; they reflect values and beliefs that are socially repeated and therefore performatively reinforced as "normal" cultural values and beliefs. Obviously such values and beliefs may be as comfortable for some as they are uncomfortable for others. In whole or part, they may be supported by some, resisted by others, or juxtaposed with other values and beliefs. In their shifts and disjunctures the life stories suggest how individuality can be negotiated and agency asserted. My twofold presentation of patterns and conjunctures, on one hand, and motion and disjunctures, on the other, reflects my belief that feminist scholars should not debate as much as relate the essentialist to the constructionist, acknowledging both the hegemonic struggle and strategic uses of the former while attempting to validate the latter.

This essay focuses on one aspect of identity—gender—in one specific location, Prince Edward Island. It is not surprising that, in such a closely knit complex of island communities, patterns and conjunctures are quite strongly marked. In this regard, they relate to the high proportion of Acadian and British-origin rurally based residents, to the vigorous celebration of "islandness," and to the phenomenon of large-scale tourism, which affects not only the province's economy but also its cultural self-representation. By exploring how differences (e.g., in gender, ethnocultural background, age, or class) are "narrated" in relation to diverse and even divergent worlds of music, we begin to understand more about the role that music can play in contemporary intercultural contexts while nevertheless insisting that this story is specific and unique. The stories of the three interesting individuals who have a voice in the latter part of this essay may teach us more than just how three strong women negotiate musical positions that enable them to surpass local proscriptions on the concept of "woman"; in addition, they may teach us to listen better—that most radical of research techniques—to individuals whose experience is dramatically various.

NOTES

1. Ellen Koskoff's article "The Music-Network: A Model for the Organization of Music Concepts" (1983) is a pioneering work that remains exemplary in its attempt to interpret as well as represent the musical life stories of a small group of consultants. The widely used undergraduate ethnomusicology textbook *Worlds of Music* (Titon 1984) includes excerpts from life history interviews in each chapter. The editor of that text, Jeff Todd Titon, has also theorized the labeling of experiential narrative, drawing useful distinctions between oral history, life story, and

other terms (Titon 1980). Monographs presenting one or more life stories are too numerous to list here, although I would like particularly to acknowledge the influence of Judith Vander's *Songprints* (1989). The anthology *My Music* (Crafts et al. 1993) has contributed to recent interest in the topic and parallels the objectives of the Canadian Musical Pathways Project to some degree. Charles Keil introduces the interviews for the "My Music" project with a paradox involving "idioculture"—recognizing each person as a separate and unique "culture"—and the mass-cultural forces that help to shape American musical taste (Crafts 1993, 211–12). Although this is not quite the same reading as my "essentialist" and "constructionist" accounts in this essay, the tension between the self and the socially framed is recognized in both our accounts. Ethnomusicologist David B. Coplan (in Marcus 1993) has contributed an interview with Johnny Clegg and other South African musicians to the important series Late Editions: Cultural Studies for the End of the Century, a series that specifically uses interviews and personal narratives as a tool for exploring the "culturally emergent." In Canada a group of musical life stories was published in *Canadian Music: Issues of Hegemony and Identity* (1994), an anthology which I coedited with colleague Robert Witmer. Significant feminist work on experiential narratives includes Cynthia Kimberlin's (1990) work with women musicians and several essays in this volume. Less visible, perhaps, but significant bases within the discipline of ethnomusicology are the many graduate students papers and theses on the musical lives of individuals. Students in my own graduate program, for example, have recently produced studies of Ontario country singer Little Joe Nicholson (D. Gifford); holocaust survivor Chana Erlich (L. Lichtenberg); Hattie Rue Hatchett, an African American musician from Buxton, Ontario (R. Stewardson); and women electroacoustic composers in Canada (A. McCartney).

2. Social norms of gender, asserted as if they are innate or natural, are often described as essentialist. Generalizations about gender that are politically expedient are sometimes said to be strategically essentialist (see Spivak 1993). The belief that concepts of gender are individually or socially constructed and mediated is often described as a constructivist position. See Fuss 1989 for further exploration of the terms and for a sophisticated demonstration of their coimplication.

3. The definition of "community" itself—as well as affiliations such as urban/rural, majority/minority, local/regional/national/international, and so on—was intentionally problematized in part by defining each case study in a slightly different way. Some were bounded by a specific ethnoculture or language (e.g., small, isolated, and rather dispersed French-language communities in Saskatchewan; the burgeoning community of Hong Kong residents of Markham/North York, Ontario; Mennonites in St. Jacobs, Ontario; Latin Americans within the Toronto and Ottawa metropolises in Ontario; or Caribbeans in St. Catherines, Ontario), and some were defined by region (e.g., Prince Edward Islanders or Yukon Territory musicians). Different shared factors cut across different case studies, however.

Tourism, for example, is a major economic factor in Prince Edward Island and St. Jacobs. The challenges of building a relatively new, diasporic community were shared by the Chinese, Caribbean, and Latin American ethnocultural groups. Historical oppression—resulting in struggles for language rights or religious autonomy, for example—resonated in some ways in both the Mennonite and Francophone Saskatchewan projects. In every case study consultants from diverse ethnocultural affiliations and musical worlds were interviewed.

Several field-workers were York University graduate students who chose to interview musicians (and others) in their home communities. Hence, each project involved both "insiders" (in one way or another) and community outsiders, and together the researchers were varied with regard to gender, age, scholarly experience, and ethnocultural affiliations. Consultants were similarly varied, since our aim was to explore the musical pathways of individuals in different musical worlds, many of which were associated with different ethnocultural and institutional milieux. Although most consultants were musicians, individuals who were active as fans, promoters, or organizers were also interviewed.

4. Statistics Canada reports that in terms of ancestral origins, 25 percent of the current population of Canada is British and about 22 percent is French, but statistics vary widely from one province to another. In Ontario citizens of British and French origin together constitute less than 30 percent of the population. Recent demographic shifts have resulted in a large Chinese community (now the third largest, at 9 percent). Saskatchewan and Alberta, however, have large German, Ukrainian, and Scandinavian communities. The largest communities of First Peoples are also resident there. The balance of urban to rural populations also differs widely. Over 80 percent of Ontario's population claims urban residence, whereas only 49 percent of Albertans and fewer than 15 percent of Prince Edward Islanders are urban.

5. Our format, loosely controlled, included questions about the musical environment of each person's childhood—preferred listening of parents and siblings, musical activities at each stage of life, and specific pieces or artists that had been of significance at different life stages. We did ask some specific identity-related questions, often in the form of "relationship" questions, since the pathways idea—the connection to others rather than the separation from others—was a priority. Hence, we might ask, "To whom do you relate your musical preference for X most strongly?" or, "Do you feel that the music in your life connects you more strongly with your islandness or your Gaelic heritage or your Canadianness?" We also investigated how identity aspects affected certain experiences, asking, for example, "Do you think your gender was a factor in your experience of X?"

6. Several unanticipated issues affected the representation of musical experience as gendered. Although we wanted to interview approximately equal numbers of men and women, for example, interviewers (including myself) were slightly biased toward same-sex interviewing. In addition, the gendering of archival

materials differed from one project to another. Saskatchewan was particularly interesting in this regard, since recorded oral history with folk musicians from the 1970s and 1980s included a larger proportion of men, but parish histories of family narratives abounded in this province, and women produced most of these written narratives.

7. Given all this, one might ask why this particular case study is used as the basis for this essay. The reason is largely pragmatic—the interviewing had been done some years earlier and the tape recordings were transcribed and adequately considered. There was also logic in examining the means by which the English-speaking majority in this area genders its musical practices, since some of these patterns are perpetuated in other parts of the country in spite of demographic differences. The incorporation of Acadian and Filipino interview material is a significant choice in that each of the patterns identified are more evidently constructed when viewed comparatively.

8. An earlier study in which this problem was addressed in some detail is my coauthored study *Visions of Sound* (1994)—in which chapters are juxtaposed with dialogues among the coauthors and a somewhat unconventional typographical design allowed us to counterpoint the voices of consultants. Many other scholars have, by the late 1990s, devised creative ways of addressing similar problems. One of my favorites is Billie Jean Isbell's (1995) representation of a miniature "drama" in which she is a minor actor. Another is the novelesque presentation Barbara Tedlock uses in *The Beautiful and the Dangerous* (1992). Feminists have also been instrumental in devising data collection that is less hierarchical than conventional interviewing. See, for example, Shulamit Reinharz's "Original Feminist Research Methods," in her *Feminist Methods in Social Research* (1992), in which alternatives such as group diaries, drama, and associative writing are suggested, among other methods.

9. Ruth Finnegan's studies of West African oral discourse genres are particularly significant in this regard. Furthermore, her *Hidden Musicians* (1989) was a major influence on the conceptualization of the Canadian Musical Pathways Project.

10. Interviews with older First Nations consultants were particularly marked by such differences in expectation. These interviews frequently shifted from personal accounts to the recounting of a formal story, from presentation to conversation. The Yukon case study provided a good example. Several elders from illustrious families of one or more of the five First Nations resident in this territory—the Tagish, Tutchone, Tlingit, Tahltan, and Kaska—had served, on an ongoing basis, as a teacher to Daniel Janke, the researcher who conducted part of this case study. This was important since, as Julie Cruickshank has eloquently observed in *Life Lived Like a Story* (1990, 36), a presentation of the narratives of women elders in the Yukon, her consultants viewed the process of narrative as an ongoing process of making "connections between events in her past and present life." Their narratives were far from linear accounts of experience; rath-

er, they were stories told over a twenty-year period, stories that were rooted sometimes in mythologies and sometimes in personal events. She describes a dialogic process in which one consultant, Angela Sidney, assessed "the kind of context
a cultural outsider needs to be taught before that person can actually begin to
hear what she is saying" (ibid., 21). Elsewhere she has similarly acknowledged that
"oral traditions survive by repeated retellings, and each narrative contains more
than one message. The listener is part of the storytelling event too, and is expected
to think about and interpret the messages in the story" (Cruickshank 1991, 12).
Her representations of the lives of Angela Sidney, Annie Ned, and Kitty Smith
(in particular) indicate, as do Janke's interviews with Angela Sidney's son Pete
Sidney and others, that a different process of telling lives does not imply a separation from cross-cultural engagement within the experiences of those lives. The
complex ways in which mythology and oral history reinforce once another in
traditions of Yukon First Nations people point to difficulties of cross-cultural
comparison and the ethnocentricity of assuming that oral history is constructed similarly from different ethnocultural perspectives.

11. In an exception to the pattern, both male and female Yukon Native American elders often referred to individual male and female music domains and, in
particular, insisted on the appropriately gendered lines of transmission for songs.
Tagish elders regard the passage of songs from uncle to nephew and from aunt
to niece as appropriate. This was the only context in which the process of transmission was described as an important aspect of the gendering of music.

12. This is still evidenced, furthermore, by the fact that, the most representative CD compilation of PEI fiddlers to date (Perlman 1993) presents twenty-five
fiddlers (all male), although two piano accompanists are female. Nevertheless,
younger female fiddlers from both Prince Edward Island and nearby Cape Breton Island, including Natalie MacMaster, Brenda Stubbert, Melanie Chiaisson, and
Anastasia Desroches had recordings on the market by the mid-1990s.

13. Melanie Chiaisson, from one of the island's respected fiddle families, is a
"graduate" of this style of training program. With her father and uncle, she produced her first recording in 1995: *The Road to Rollo Bay,* a cassette produced pri-
vately by the family but distributed across the island.

14. An interesting contrast emerged with the Yukon interviews, where Anglo-
Canadian consultants tended to draw stark contrasts between the musical preferences of their parents. The PEI consultants, however, often simply did not
mention mothers and grandmothers, although in some cases they referred to
them as the opposition (the inverse) of the tradition.

15. Tape references beginning with *RJ* were interviews conducted by Roy
Johnstone, a resident of the island and a fiddler. Tape references beginning with
BD were interviews conducted by the author.

16. Later in the interview McLean also refers to his harmonica as female.

17. The tension between Catholics and Protestants relating to different social norms was sufficiently extreme in nineteenth-century Prince Edward Island to erupt into violence at times. One of the best-known instances of this was the Belfast Riot of 1847, in which several people were killed. Belfast, PEI, is, ironically, a Scottish community.

18. Published performance practice descriptions differ somewhat from that of my consultant. *Grove's Dictionary of Musical Instruments* describes the *raban* [sic] as a larger drum around which women sit and play in unison with both hands.

19. See, for example, Weale 1988, 45.

20. More country musicians were interviewed in the Yukon study than in Prince Edward Island. Similar assertions of autonomous learning by Yukon musicians include references to "woodshedding," "lone maleness," and in the case of one consultant, a style that he regarded as "a bit more yahoo." One consultant described his first winter in the north, in an isolated cabin on unemployment insurance, "just playing guitar continually . . . eight-hour stretches sometimes."

21. An artist who represents an exception to my statement is Angèle Arsenault, who is proudly recognized as an islander, although she has been based in Quebec for some time.

22. An interesting Cape Breton parallel is the acclaimed fiddler Ashley MacIsaac, who in his first multinational production, *Hi, How Are You Today?* (1995), used heavy metal elements and a rock underpinning for many traditional Celtic tunes.

23. All quotations are from taped interviews conducted by the author or Roy Johnstone in 1993.

24. At the time of the interview she was vice president for the Atlantic region on the National Council of the Filipino Association of Canada, had helped to organize a Canada-wide talent festival for Filipino performers, and had participated in heritage festivals in the United States. By 1999 she had also assumed the presidency of the Race Relations Education Association (PEI).

25. A *banduria* is a Spanish plucked lute.

26. She may be referring to the bamboo jaw harp.

27. She is probably referring to the bamboo organ built in 1818 by the Augustinian Diego Cera in Las Pinas, near Manilla.

28. She shows a photo of *agung*, a pair of gongs used for Muslim dances.

29. Frequently used in staged shows of Filipino folk dance, the *carinosa* developed in the late nineteenth century in Catholic communities. The performers model their presentation on the manners of the Spanish aristocracy. LaRosa described this as "like a lady flirting with a man." I did not pursue the issue of performing stereotypic gendered roles in dance performance.

30. The region is named after the Acadian heroine whose bravery at the time of the Acadian expulsion from British North America in 1755 was mythologized by Longfellow, among others.

31. The use of notation is controversial among island fiddlers, many of whom believe that stylistic nuances can be learned only via the aural tradition.

References Cited

Behar, Ruth. 1995. "Rage and Redemption: Reading the Life Story of a Mexican Marketing Woman." In *The Dialogic Emergence of Culture,* ed. Dennis Tedlock and Bruce Mannheim, 148–78. Urbana: University of Illinois Press.

Burrill, Gary. 1992. *Away: Maritimers in Massachusetts, Ontario, and Alberta: An Oral History of Leaving Home.* Montreal: McGill-Queen's University Press.

Callaghan, Dympna. 1995. "The Vicar and Virago: Feminism and the Problem of Identity." In *Who Can Speak? Authority and Critical Identity,* ed. Judith Roof and Robyn Wiegman, 195–207. Urbana: University of Illinois Press.

The 1996 Canadian Encyclopedia Plus. 1995. CD-ROM. Toronto: McLelland and Stewart.

Crafts, Susan D., Daniel Cavicchi, Charles Keil, and the Music in Daily Life Project, comps. 1993. *My Music.* Hanover, N.H.: University Press of New England.

Cruickshank, Julie. 1990. *Life Lived Like a Story.* Vancouver: University of British Columbia Press.

———. 1991. *Reading Voices. Oral and Written Interpretations of the Yukon's Past.* Vancouver: Douglas and McIntyre.

Diamond, Beverley, M. Sam Cronk, and Franziska von Rosen. 1994. *Visions of Sound: Musical Instruments of First Nations Communities in Northeastern America.* Chicago: University of Chicago Press; Waterloo, Ont.: Wilfrid Laurier University Press.

Diamond, Beverley, and Robert Witmer, eds. 1994. *Canadian Music: Issues of Hegemony and Identity.* Toronto: Canadian Scholars Press.

Finnegan, Ruth. 1989. *The Hidden Musicians: Music-making in an English Town.* Cambridge: Cambridge University Press.

Fuss, Diana. 1989. *Essentially Speaking.* London: Routledge.

hooks, bell. 1994. *Outlaw Culture: Resisting Representations.* New York: Routledge.

Hornby, Susan, ed. 1992. *Belfast People: An Oral History of Belfast, Prince Edward Island.* Charlottetown: Tea Hill.

Isbell, Billie Jean. 1995. "Women's Voices: Lima 1975." In *The Dialogic Emergence of Culture,* ed. Dennis Tedlock and Bruce Mannheim, 54–74. Urbana: University of Illinois Press.

Kimberlin, Cynthia Tse. 1990. "'And Are You Pretty?': Choice, Perception, and Reality in Pursuit of Happiness." In *Music, Gender, and Culture,* ed. Marcia Herndon and Susanne Ziegler, 221–39. Wilhelmshaven, Germany: F. Noetzel Verlag.

Koskoff, Ellen. 1983. "The Music-Network: A Model for the Organization of Music Concepts." *Ethnomusicology* 26:353–70.

McKay, Ian. 1994. *The Quest of the Folk: Antimodernism and Cultural Selection in Twentieth-Century Nova Scotia*. Montreal: McGill-Queen's University Press.

Marcus, George E., ed. 1993. *Perilous States: Conversations on Culture, Politics, and Nation*. Chicago: University of Chicago Press.

Perlman, Ken. 1994. "'And It Was Good Pastime': Old Time Fiddling on Prince Edward Island." *The Island Magazine* 35:23–30.

———. 1993. *The Old Time Fiddlers of Prince Edward Island*. Cassette and booklet. Marimac Recordings C 6501.

Reinharz, Shulamit. 1992. "Original Feminist Research Methods." *Feminist Methods in Social Research*, 214–39. Oxford: Oxford University Press.

Spivak, Gayatri. 1993. "In a Word: Interview." *Outside in the Teaching Machine*, 1–24. London: Routledge.

Tannen, Deborah. 1995. "Waiting for the Mouse: Constructed Dialogue in Conversation." In *The Dialogic Emergence of Culture*, ed. Dennis Tedlock and Bruce Mannheim, 198–217.

Tedlock, Barbara. 1992. *The Beautiful and the Dangerous: Encounters with the Zuni Indians*. New York: Viking.

Tedlock, Dennis, and Bruce Mannheim, eds. 1995. *The Dialogic Emergence of Culture*. Urbana: University of Illinois Press.

Titon, Jeff Todd. 1980. "The Life Story." *Journal of American Folklore* 93:276–92.

———, ed. 1984. *Worlds of Music*. New York: Schirmer.

Vander, Judith. 1989. *Songprints*. Urbana: University of Illinois Press.

Weale, David. 1988. *A Stream out of Lebanon: An Introduction to the Coming of Syrian/Lebanese Emigrants to Prince Edward Island*. Charlottetown: Institute of Island Studies.

5   Writing the Biography of a Black Woman Blues Singer

Jane Bowers

The first time I heard Chicago blues singer Estelle "Mama" Yancey (1896–1986) perform, at the University of Chicago Folk Festival in 1983, this tiny, arthritic, and nearly blind elderly woman amazed me with the vitality of her singing and moved me with the power and humor of her lyrics. What strength of character she must have to appear before an audience, I thought, for she had to be assisted to her onstage seat, seemed unable to adjust her position on the chair or to fix her dress so that it covered her knees adequately, and was scarcely capable of adjusting the microphone with her gnarled, arthritic hands. Several years earlier, after Mama Yancey and pianist Erwin Helfer had appeared at the University of Chicago Folk Festival, David Novick wrote that "Mama's voice is frail, like her body, but not thin. . . . Her singing wove through the muted fabric of Helfer's playing with such assuredness that together they created a rich tapestry of emotions that only a zapped-out rock freak could have missed. A moment of stunned silence at the set's end was followed by shouts, whistles, palm-reddening applause, and a standing ovation that forever put those carefully staged stadium demonstrations to shame" (Novick 1979, 7). When she appeared at the Chicago Jazz Festival in 1979, the critic Harriet Choice reported: "Mama Yancey deservedly won the crowd's first of two spontaneous standing ovations for the night. . . . Thousands of young people shouted and cheered for her, not because of endurance, but because Mama Yancey still knows how to tell a story, to sing the blues" (Choice 1979: 6).

Judging from these reactions, it might appear that Mama Yancey had been singing before a large public her entire life and that she was a consummate professional performer. Her life was varied, however, and she did not emerge as a public performer until 1943, when she was forty-seven years old. From that year through the end of her life, she produced only seven com-

Mama and Jimmy Yancey at their apartment in Chicago in early 1951. Photo by Phillip L. Kiely.

mercial recordings, of which two were made after she was eighty-five years old.[1] A theme that runs through a number of interviews with Mama is the role that her father and later her husband—noted blues and boogie-woogie pianist Jimmy Yancey—played in inhibiting and restricting her music making. Thus, during her married life, which lasted until Jimmy died in 1951, Mama was primarily a homemaker. Although she had no children of her own, she devoted considerable time and attention to taking care of her niece and nephew when they were growing up. She also worked occasionally outside her home, doing domestic work and serving as a Democratic precinct captain. In addition, while Jimmy was still living, she sang frequently at musical parties at home from at least the mid-1940s. After his death Mama resumed singing in public only during brief, sporadic periods, and she probably did not sing at all during other periods. It was only after she had turned eighty, when Erwin Helfer began bringing her out again to appear with him in public, that Mama Yancey sang before large crowds. Yet she adapted easily to these new experiences.

Intrigued by her powerful singing, I began investigating Mama Yancey's life during a summer seminar taught by Professor Richard Crawford at the University of Michigan in 1984. After collecting biographical information about her and immersing myself in Mama's song repertory and improvisation styles over a number of years, I decided to write her biography.

Writing Mama Yancey's biography has posed many problems. First, aside from a one-paragraph biography in telegraphic style in Sheldon Harris's *Blues Who's Who* (1979), nothing covering anything near the whole of her life had been compiled. Second, although several articles by Derrick Stewart-Baxter dating from the 1950s and early 1960s (Stewart-Baxter 1954, 1960, 1961) provide some biographical information about both Mama and her husband, his sources of information are uncertain and his data scant. Third, in the various interviews with Mama that are available on tape or in edited print versions, she did not provide much biographical information about herself, and the information she did provide is often contradictory; the same is true of two brief interviews I conducted with Mama in 1984 and 1986. Fourth, since Mama Yancey made only a handful of phonograph records, mostly on small labels, and because her public performances were relatively rare, there is little description of her work in print. Fifth, I have found few public documents pertaining to Mama Yancey.

On a more positive note, I have been able to track down and obtain information from a number of people with whom Mama worked or who attended music-making sessions in the Yanceys' home. After Mama's death in 1986 I was also able to interview her niece, with whom she lived for a number of years. Taken altogether, these printed and oral sources have allowed me to attempt a biographical study of Mama Yancey's life. Still, there are too many holes for a continuous narrative, and there are many problems regarding accuracy. Often I have been unable to double-check information given by one source, and when several sources provide information about the same event, they sometimes conflict. How can I establish "what the facts were"? Marc Pachter (1979, 4) has written about the problems of biographers who are either "inundated by thousands of documents and impressions . . . or starved for the lack of them." In Mama Yancey's case, it is the relative lack of documents, as well as the uncertain nature of some of them, that causes me the greatest problem.

Of course, biographers must not only try to establish the facts; they must also interpret them. They must try to understand their subjects' personalities and values and attempt to learn what lay behind their actions and how they developed in the ways they did. How am I to understand the different stories Mama told to different interviewers or to the same interviewers at different times? Conversely, how am I to understand the themes to which she often returned when telling her life story? Can they be taken at face value, or was a certain self-construction at work? Jeff Todd Titon (1980, 276) has suggested that we look at the kinds of narratives subjects tell about themselves, which may be called life stories, as self-contained fictions that must be distinguished sharply from their historical kin: biography, oral history, and the personal history (or "life history"). Titon argues: "Personality is the main ingredient in the life story. . . . Even if the story is not factually true, it is always true evidence of the storyteller's personality. The most interesting life stories expose the inner life, tell us about motives. . . . The life story tells who one thinks one is and how one thinks one came to be that way" (290). Given that Mama's "life story," as she told it in fragmentary fashion to different people, is one of the principal sources of information about her activities, as well as about her personality and motives, how can I best use it?

First, let me address some of the factual problems in Mama's life story. I will then take up some of the themes elaborated in her life story and attempt to suggest what they may reveal about her personality, motives, and values. Finally, I will consider Mama Yancey's life story from the perspectives of various scholars who have dealt with life-story narratives and autobiography, the personal narratives of male blues musicians, the male blues role, blues women's roles and images, black women's history, and the writing of feminist biography—all for the light they may shed on Mama's experiences, behavior, achievements, and self-representation. In doing this, I will pay special attention to the intertwining of gender with other factors.

The factual problems in Mama's life story do *not* begin with her birth date, as they do in the life stories of many musicians, including her husband. In interviews Mama always reported that she was born on 1 January 1896, and on the basis of U.S. census records from 1900, I have been able to confirm that she was indeed born Stella Harris in January 1896, although the precise date is not mentioned. Mama usually also reported that she was born in Cairo, Illinois, and the census records show her living in this town with her mother, Mary Harris, along with her maternal grandparents and several other family members and boarders in 1900. Nevertheless, she told Barry Dolins (1977, 35) she was born in Chicago, at 3243 South Butterfield, after her parents had come north from Cairo.

There is greater discrepancy about the place where Mama grew up. Because the 1900 census records place her in Cairo, they cast grave doubt on Mama's stories about spending her childhood in Chicago from infancy. In

1964 she told Barbara Dane that her parents had brought her to Chicago when she was six months old; later in the same interview she remembered it as six weeks. In the late 1970s she told Howard Mandel that she was raised in Chicago, and she also told Bob Rusch that she had been in Chicago since she was four months old. In 1984 she told me that she had lived in Chicago since she was seven weeks old.

Another set of stories placed Mama primarily in St. Louis during her youth. Already in 1961 Derrick Stewart-Baxter (1961, 7) reported—perhaps on the basis of information passed along to him by Birch Smith, who may have obtained it from Mama—that Mama had spent most of her youth in St. Louis. In 1964, in the same interview in which Mama claimed to have moved to Chicago at the age of six weeks or six months, she told Barbara Dane that she had known singer-guitarist Lonnie Johnson in St. Louis before she even knew where Chicago was, thus suggesting a prior connection with that city. In the mid-1970s she told Barry Dolins that her first eight years of education had been in St. Louis, where she lived with her mother. And in 1986 she told me that she went to St. Louis to live with her mother and moved to Chicago when her mother passed away. According to this story, she remained in St. Louis long enough to work for Liggett and Meyer Tobacco Company for about a month. When I asked her about the discrepancy between her Chicago and St. Louis stories, she said that she had gone to school in St. Louis and spent summers with her father in Chicago. Unfortunately, school records shed no light on her whereabouts during her youth. The extant Chicago school records do not mention her name, and although St. Louis school records show that a Stella Harris enrolled in the Riddick School in September 1900, the Stella Harris in question seems to have entered the third grade (although the records are by no means definitive) at a time when Mama would have been only four years old. Thus these records may not refer to the young Mama Yancey at all.

Another discrepancy has to do with the death of Mama's mother. Although she told Bob Rusch that her mother died when she was thirteen years old, she told Barbara Dane that her mother died at age thirty-six. Since census records state that her mother was eighteen years old when Mama was born, Mama would have been about eighteen when her mother was thirty-six. Because of this discrepancy, it is unclear when Mama would have arrived in Chicago even if she had moved there when her mother died. In any case, since her stories about her early life in St. Louis are more specific than the ones set in Chicago, it seems likely that Mama spent part of her childhood there.

The dates Mama gave for her marriage to Jimmy Yancey constitute another problem, although fortunately one that has recently been cleared up. Mama variously reported that she got married in 1917 (Rusch), 1919 (Dane), 1921 (Mandel), and 1922 (Bowers). Furthermore, she told Dane she could not remember how old she was when she got married, although she thought she was twenty-one, which conflicts with the year she gave Dane for the marriage. Although she told me she had her marriage certificate in a trunk in her niece's basement, after Mama's death I learned from her niece that the basement had been flooded several years earlier and that she had discarded the trunk's contents after severe water damage. My requests for a search of Cook County's Vital Records also failed to turn up a certificate of marriage until July 1997, when a new search was successful. The marriage license located on that occasion is dated 27 November 1925, and it indicates that James Yancey and Estella [*sic*] Harris were married by the Reverend A. L. Lewis at 3155 Federal Street on 7 December 1925, a date Mama never reported to interviewers.

Surprisingly contradictory are Mama's claims about the places where she sang when she was younger. She told Dane she had not gone to church at all and Mandel that although she often went to church, she never sang in a choir, but she told me that she sang in church choirs in both St. Louis and Chicago. Stewart-Baxter (1961, 7) also reported that she sang for a time in a church choir in St. Louis. Moreover, she contradicted herself regarding the occasions when she first sang with Jimmy at parties and clubs. She blatantly falsified a 1961 trip to California, telling Mandel that she did about four months in the state—in San Francisco, Los Angeles, Monterrey, and San Diego—and telling me that she sang in San Francisco, Los Angeles, and San Diego, "all over California down there." According to Dane (1985), however, Mama traveled only to San Francisco, where she sang at a club Dane had opened for just a few weeks.

In summary, the themes on which Mama elaborated in interviews included her birth date, of which she seemed especially proud; the city in which she grew up; how and where she started singing; and when and where she met her husband. Sometimes she spoke about her parents, and she occasionally mentioned a younger sister who had died as a child. In addition, she had a set of stories she told about Jimmy, the earliest of which centered on his having sung and danced for the king and queen of England and having received a citation from them when he was around thirteen years of age. She also liked to talk about his work at Chicago's "White Sox Park," as she called Comisky Park, and gave various numbers of years for his employment there.

Sometimes she claimed that boogie-woogie pianists Albert Ammons and Meade Lux Lewis had hung around listening to Jimmy play piano at his mother's house, and she said that Jimmy had taught Albert to play and Albert, in turn, had taught Meade. She also maintained that they had adopted Albert, paying fifty dollars for him.

Another theme in her life story was how her father felt about her singing. She told Dane that her father did not want his child to go on stage, sing, cut her hair, or bring him a child and that she never sang or cut her hair until after he died. She told Mandel that her father said that one day she would be a beautiful singer but that he did not want her to be on the stage, and she told Rusch that her father was very strict and held her back. She told me also that her father did not want her to sing in public, but she added that after he died, she told herself that he was gone and would not know what she did, so she began singing. Still, because of her father's attitude, her husband also did not want her to sing. After Jimmy died, she had leeway; she could do what she liked. Although Mama spoke less about her mother than about her father, she did tell Dane that her mother was a guitarist who used to sing and play the blues, and she tried to teach Mama some things.

In another story she related to Dane, she said that she used to play the guitar, but Jimmy told her to throw it into the garbage can; he did not want her to play. She got mad and hit him over the head with it. The theme of Jimmy's restricting her music making, indeed, came up again and again. She said that he did not want her to do anything in the musical line. He did not let her sing at rent parties, and he did not want her to work with him. He even disliked it when she picked things out on the piano. She would sit down and play one tune whenever she got to a piano, and he would take it up, but he would never play it at the Bee Hive or record it. When Dane asked whether her husband wanted to be the musician in the family, Mama agreed and said, "That is where we would have our difficulties, you know." But at home they worked together "constantly." There would be just the two of them and a half-pint (of whiskey).

Mama also loved to tell stories about musical parties at her home. She said that her house was crowded like a dance parlor, and people had to wedge in on a shoehorn on Saturday nights. Her house was *the* house. People would be there every Friday, Saturday, and Sunday and leave Monday morning because they had to get back to work or class. Just when these parties began hinges on when the Yanceys acquired a piano, and the evidence for that is problematic. Yet guests in their home have fairly reliably reported that they attended parties in the Yanceys' home from around 1946 on, and they confirm that these parties extended well into the wee hours of the morning, with some people sleeping over. Complicating the issue of the Yanceys' frequent parties, however, are the claims Mama made to Mandel about going out to parties nearly every Saturday night.

Another theme Mama addressed was how people reacted to her singing. She said that when they went out to parties, Jimmy would always play and she would be the entertainer. If they stayed away, it was a dead party. She said that there was an overflow crowd when she sang at Carnegie Hall in 1948 on a program featuring the Kid Ory Band, and she boasted that her voice was so loud that they took away the microphone. The *Record Changer,* however, reported that it would be no great exaggeration to say that nobody was at that concert, and the editor thought the presence of Mama Yancey was a piece of bad judgment. He stated, "Apparently no one in authority realized that this frail little lady would freeze up completely on the giant stage, and that her particular style of blues delivery would be completely lost as a result" (Grauer 1946, 29). Mama could not have been confusing the audience's reaction to this performance with that of her 1981 Carnegie Hall appearance with pianist Art Hodes, where their set was the high point of the show (Hodes 1984), since she told the story before the later appearance. With regard to a performance with pianist Richard Jones at the Art Institute of Chicago, Mama claimed to have had a powerful effect, telling Dane that "each and everybody was spellbound." She also boasted to me that when Dane called her to come down to the Gate of Horn when she was working in Chicago in the late 1950s, the boss told Mama that she would be working from that day on. According to Dane, however, Mama was never hired at the Gate of Horn; rather, Dane would sometimes ask Mama to come down and sit in with her (Dane 1990).

Mama rarely spoke about recording sessions. Although she responded to questions in Dane's interview regarding her 1943 Session records with Jimmy, most interviewers did not ask her about recording, and she did not volunteer any information. It appears that she was far more interested in listeners' responses to her singing than in putting out songs commercially.

Mama liked stories about traveling to do concerts, however. How she first got together with the faithful pianist of her late years, Erwin Helfer, was one of her favorite themes. According to Mama, she met Helfer when he was just seventeen or eighteen—or maybe it was fifteen or sixteen. He may have come around with a friend of Jimmy's, "Cripple" Clarence Lofton, or he may have come around with some students from the University of Chicago shortly after Jimmy died. In any case, in 1956 she was engaged to sing for the newly formed Indianapolis Jazz Club, and Little Brother Montgomery was supposed to play for her. He got drunk and angry, however, because they had billed the performers as "Mama Yancey and Brother Montgomery" instead of "Brother Montgomery and Mama Yancey," and he refused to go. Mama then asked Helfer to drive her around Chicago looking for someone else to play for her, but when she failed to turn up anyone else, she told him to come along. So he went home and borrowed his father's car, and after picking up some Old Grand-Dad whiskey on the way out of town, they drove to Indianapolis, arriving just in time for the concert.

In talking about performing, Mama liked to tell what she would do if her accompanist made a mistake. For example, she might tell him that if she came to the end of the stage and gave him a dirty look, he would know he had made a mistake somewhere. When I asked her how she chose the songs she sang, she said it was "just someone sitting down and playing the piano," and she picked it up and took it from there. She added, "Those different sounds and different thoughts come in your mind when you're singing blues, see, especially if you have something certain on your mind. . . . Well, those different voices and pains[?] will come to you, you see, and just put the words in your mouth."

Mama rarely discussed her work outside of music with interviewers, although she told me that when Jimmy was living, she was working as a maid at lodges because he did not want her on stage. She worked only sporadically, however, because her husband made their living. Mama also reported that after Jimmy died, she went out and got a job—she was a maid and worked for the Eleanor Lodge Company. And she sometimes spoke about doing precinct work for U.S. Congressman William Dawson, which may have occupied her for some seventeen to eighteen years. She seems to have been engaged in this activity already by 1954, for in that year Stewart-Baxter (1954, 4) reported that Mama was a precinct captain for the Democratic Party in her ward, delivering the vote, looking after poor people, and doing what she could for those less fortunate than herself.

But Mama preferred talking about good times. For example, she told Dane that when they came back from New York and had royalty checks from *Yancey Special,* Jimmy's paycheck, and their check from Carnegie Hall, she wanted to cash them all and "lock up" every tavern on State Street. She added that she had seen a white lady with a Hudson seal coat and said she wanted one. Jimmy told her that if anyone in the world could wear a Hudson seal coat, she could wear one, too. He gave her anything she wanted. She boasted, "I paid $595 for it, and it's right out there at 6357 Stewart right today, and I'm going to have me a stole made out of it." As her comments about "locking up" every tavern on State Street suggest, Mama did not hesitate to tell interviewers about having fun drinking. Yet she seemed reluctant to talk about intimate matters, for early in her 1964 interview with Dane, she hesitated before using the pet name Jimmy often called her, "red ass." Although various people who knew Mama well told me that she could talk roughly at times, she rarely revealed this in interviews. Thus the interview situation seems to have disguised her usual mode of expression to some extent.

Let me now turn to the perspectives of various scholars who have dealt with life-story narratives and autobiography to see what light they may shed on Mama's life story and self-representation. Particularly helpful in connection with Mama's varied tellings of her life story is the viewpoint articulated by anthropologist Harriet Ottenheimer in connection with her work with "Cousin Joe" (Pleasant Joseph), a New Orleans blues singer. Ottenheimer states: "Life-story narratives . . . usually reflect traditional attitudes and occur within established storytelling traditions. Self-conscious, unspontaneous performance pieces, life-story narratives are often repeated by their tellers almost word-for-word. It is as though a life-story narrative, told once, becomes a model or stereotype, guiding subsequent retellings. We don't expect contradictory versions of the same episode from a single narrative" (Joseph and Ottenheimer 1987, 225). In her work with Cousin Joe, however, Ottenheimer found that although most of Joe's narratives were remarkably consistent, and some were repeated almost exactly word for word, "occasionally . . . there were variants which appeared to contradict one another" (ibid.). Although the existence of variant versions in life-story narratives conflicts with our basic cultural assumption that a person's life story will present a complete whole and provide the individual with a single identity, many of those who work with life-story narratives are forced to come to terms with "a *discontinuous* self—one which is constructed through narration and which often appears to include multiple and contradictory selves," for as Ottenheimer points out: "Telling a life story enables one to create a self which need be 'real' only to oneself and to one's listener. Different selves can be created for different listeners and even for oneself in different moods" (Joseph and Ottenheimer 1987, 226).

Elsewhere Ottenheimer submits that if the life story is a form of folklore, then we *should* find variants, since variants in folk tales are expected and even desirable. She suggests that as researchers we need to forgo our expectation that there be a single, true account of a life rather than several conflicting ones (Ottenheimer 1982, 7–8). Indeed, it is not only in orally transmitted life stories that we find evidence of multiple or contradictory selves. Anarchist Emma Goldman, for example, constructed herself in her autobiography, *Living My Life,* as "woven of many skeins, conflicting in shade and texture," according to Goldman's biographer Alice Wexler. In one telling passage, in fact, Goldman recounted how, when artist Robert Henri wanted to depict "the real Emma Goldman" in his portrait of her, she asked, "But which is the real one? . . . I have never been able to unearth her" (in Wexler 1992, 39–41). Wexler further suggests that Goldman "regarded the autobiography as a dramatization rather than an exploration of her life, yet another dramatic performance in a lifetime of performances on a variety of public stages" (1992, 42).

In Mama Yancey's case, some of her varied stories undoubtedly resulted from remembering things in different ways at different times and from forgetfulness. But it also appears that Mama sometimes created "different selves" for different listeners or for herself in different moods. This idea is supported by a comment made by someone who knew her well—that Mama would say anything that popped into her head; she was not concerned with accuracy or consistency. That she spoke impulsively probably accounts for at least some of the contradictions in her stories, such as the different marriage dates she reported. Mama must have whimsically pulled different dates from the air (or simply agreed with whatever date someone else proposed) out of a sense of playfulness with the interviewer's aim of acquiring facts about her, the thought that the exact date was no one else's business, or the simple wish to have fun saying whatever popped into her head. Thus, Ottenheimer's concept of a "discontinuous self" seems useful for understanding Mama Yancey, as does her and Wexler's perception that an autobiography, or life story, may be viewed as a dramatization of one's life, a dramatic performance.

Viewed as evidence about her personality, Mama's varied stories about herself must play an important role in her biography. At the same time, the historian in me would like to establish "the facts." Since my aim is not to record Mama's life story alone, I must, as befits the biographer and historian, "interpret . . . documents, letters, accounts by eye-witnesses, reminiscences, autobiographical statements, and . . . decide questions of genuineness, trustworthiness of witnesses, and the like" (Wellek and Warren 1956, 75–76; in Titon 1980, 281). The aspects of a subject's life story that require interpretation are not limited to conflicting elements. Recent discussions of biographical writing have focused on some of the biographer's problems in interpreting the first-person accounts of the subjects they study. For example, in a special issue of the journal *a/b: Auto/Biography Studies* devoted to feminist biography, Lois Banner points out how various kinds of autobiography serve different purposes. An autobiography may be "a didactic piece, designed to instruct, or a confession, like the many Puritan autobiographies designed to demonstrate personal transformation." Or it may be "a chatty piece, like those . . . of celebrities which stream from the presses and which are designed to sell" (Banner 1993, 161). Pointing to historical connections between the genres of autobiography and fiction, especially the novel, Banner (1993, 162) states: "Roland Barthes may go too far when he writes that biography (assuredly he would include autobiography) is nothing but 'a novel that dare not speak its own name.' . . . But there is much truth in Alix Kates Shulman's discussion of the similarities between crafting a biography, an autobiography, and a novel. In all these forms of writing . . . , characters must be imagined, significance imposed, events interpreted."

In the *Journal of American History,* Jane Sherron De Hart speaks to the way in which one telling of an event may lead to a similar telling and interpretation of it in later accounts. In an oral history project involving pro- and anti-ERA activists, De Hart and her fellow researchers discovered "how quickly after an event the construction of narrative begins, how soon significance is attached to actions, consequences are assigned, labels applied, and hypotheses developed about 'what happened.'" Immediate accounts, constructed sometimes within just days after a decisive vote, prestructured all later interpretations (De Hart 1993, 591). This agrees with Ottenheimer's observation that a life-story narrative, once told, may become a model or stereotype guiding subsequent retellings. An example in Mama Yancey's case might be her story about growing up in Chicago from infancy. Once told—for whatever reason—her original account may have become a model for subsequent retellings.

In a further effort to interpret Mama's life story as well as some of the ways in which she presented herself as a blues singer, I want to turn to two studies of male blues musicians. In the first of these—a study concentrating on male Mississippi-born blues musicians—Barry Pearson concludes that bluesmen used to the interview process made assumptions about what the interviewer wanted to know and how best to fill those vacant spots with information that served their own self-interest. They talked of their life development in congruence with what they thought the interviewer expected, as well as what they believed they should have been. In his analysis of musicians' life stories, Pearson (1977, 21, 23) found that the artists used materials from four major sources: (1) their experiences, especially musical; (2) items or events selected from the traditions of their fellow musicians; (3) items or events associated with stereotyped expectations of coethnic nonmusicians; and (4) materials conforming to mass-cultural or white attitudes and beliefs.

In Mama Yancey's case, the bulk of her narrative material is associated with the first category—her experiences, especially her musical experiences. Perhaps because she did not belong to a closely knit group of fellow musicians, I have not found examples related to Pearson's second category in her material. I am also not sure about the presence of items associated with Pearson's third category—the expectations of coethnic nonmusicians—except perhaps for Mama's predilection for boasting. For a fondness for boasting, an aspect of Mama's personality that is revealed in her life story, has been frequently suggested as a convention of communication shared by many persons of African American heritage. Ceola Ross Baber, for example, has proposed:

> The content and style of presentation typical of bragging and toasting are consistent with other priorities of Afro-American culture. . . .
> Personal power and influence are established through the skillful use of words. Black speakers combine improvisation and mimicry with boasting and storytelling; such devices are extensions of the African oral heritage. (Baber 1987, 93)

In connection with Pearson's final category—materials conforming to mass-cultural or white attitudes and beliefs—Pearson suggests that the exportation of blues into mass-culture markets following a decline in coethnic support made it necessary for the blues musician to become aware of white expectations as well and that a lucrative market partially informed by the white interviewer and critic had obvious implications for how the bluesman portrayed himself—he became something exotic. Although white critics and audiences developed an image of the bluesman that was very much their own creation, it may have gained internal acceptance and ascendancy as blues artists strategically conformed to it (Pearson 1977, 24). Whether blues women as a group have exhibited parallel behavior is uncertain. Pearson (1977 25n4) points out that although certain female artists, such as Memphis Minnie, Big Mama Thornton, and Koko Taylor, have exhibited behavior similar to that of their male peers, they did not constitute a large enough sample for effective study and, moreover, that the interview materials were simply not there. In Mama Yancey's case, I am uncertain whether white expectations influenced the ways in which she portrayed herself to white interviewers or behaved as a blues singer. For example, when she performed in California, she bought a soft mauve long-sleeved sweater with a plain neck and a matching soft mauve skirt. Enhancing her outfit with pearls, Mama presented herself almost like a well-dressed sorority girl, according to Dane

(1990). Photographs of Mama singing in Indianapolis in 1956 exhibit a sober, dignified manner of dress. Perhaps she thought her white audiences expected her to be ladylike, but that does not agree with what they might have expected of a blues woman had they been familiar with the images of such musicians as Bessie Smith and Memphis Minnie. Thus, did Mama's manner of self-presentation reflect her own sense of propriety rather than the expectations of a white audience?

Barry Pearson (1977, 121) also identifies five narrative categories related by bluesmen: (1) the novice's acquisition of instruments, (2) the description of community (including family) opposition or support, (3) the major musical influence or model, (4) early performance jobs, and (5) life as a working musician. Mama's narratives relate to only three of these categories—the second, in that she described the opposition of her father and husband to her public music making, and the fourth and fifth, in that she talked about her performance experiences, although in an incomplete sort of way. In connection with Pearson's second category, I would suggest that whereas blues musicians' descriptions of opposition to their music making may constitute a sort of trope in their narratives, it is nevertheless reasonable to suppose that in many cases there is an element of truth in their assertions. In Mama's case, her assertions certainly sound plausible, especially in the light of a centuries-long tradition of casting aspersions on women who work in the theater. Nevertheless, since I have no means of double-checking Mama's claims, I must entertain the possibility that she invented part of the opposition to explain, either to herself or her interviewers (or both), why she had not become a well-known blues singer. As Pearson (1977, 216–17) points out, the artist's wish to introduce himself to a potential audience may not coincide with the interviewer's goal of gathering historical information.

The second scholar whose work on male blues musicians I wish to consider is Charles Keil. In *Urban Blues* Keil is primarily concerned with the expressive male role of the contemporary bluesman within urban lower-class African American culture. Keil (1966, 1–2) uses the term *role* to refer to something the person who fills it is obligated to express because of the expectations of his or her audience. According to Keil (1966, 20): "The hustler (or underworld denizen) and the entertainer are ideal types representing two important value orientations for the lower-class Negro. . . . Both . . . are seen as men who are clever and talented enough to be financially well off without working. In this sense, a good preacher can be both a hustler and an entertainer in the eyes of his parishioners and the Negro community at large."

Keil sees blues singing and preaching as closely linked, despite the fact that blues singing is ostensibly a secular and even profane form of expression, and he suggests that the blues artist plays a role intimately related to sacred roles in the African American community. He also proposes that the role of blues artist is "all-encompassing in nature, either assimilating or overshadowing all other roles an adult male may normally be expected to fulfill" (Keil 1966, 143), such as those as husband and father. He finds the attributes of the blues role difficult to describe, however, because "a blues singer's personality and life style represent a heightened model or type of Negro masculine behavior in general. The bluesman is in a sense every man: the country bluesman is an archetype of the migrant laborer; the city bluesman, a stereotype of the stud, the hustler." In addition, the man is inseparable from the role, since "the bluesman's work is his life and vice versa" (Keil 1966, 152–53).

How do Keil's speculations about the role of the bluesman relate to Mama Yancey? With regard to the link Keil notes between blues singing and preaching, there is some congruence, since some of the messages Mama delivered in her songs—learning to distinguish right from wrong, to get good treatment for oneself, and to grieve deeply and cope with death and deprivation—sound a lot like preaching. On the whole, however, there is far more difference than congruence. First, because of the sex and gender roles assigned to women in patriarchal society, it is likely that no woman has ever been able to represent either of the ideal types Keil describes—hustler and entertainer—in the same way men have. More specifically, since Mama Yancey either worked outside music or was supported by someone else for most of her life, she would never have been seen as talented enough to get by financially without working. Second, a woman, no matter what her personality and style of behavior, could scarcely represent a heightened model of African American masculine behavior in general. True, if she traveled a great deal, a woman blues artist might with some stretch of the imagination represent an archetypal migrant laborer, but she would be hard-pressed to represent a stereotype of the stud or hustler. As for the bluesman's work constituting his life and vice versa, that would apply only to those musicians who constantly traveled to sing or play the blues. Since Mama Yancey rarely traveled to sing the blues, did not assimilate her familial roles to the blues role, was not masculine in her behavior, and was rather distant from the professional entertainment world altogether, it does not seem possible to use Keil's concept of the role of the contemporary bluesman to explain much about her life or career.

Recently, in an unpublished manuscript, Peter Aschoff has addressed the question of the social role of the bluesman. Acknowledging that there have been many great female blues performers, Aschoff nevertheless argues that the social role of the bluesman is quite gender specific:

> To be a musician who performs the blues is a musical skill/talent and occupation open to all, but to be a bluesman is a social role closed, by definition, to the distaff side. . . .
>
> Just as a woman can, by definition, never be a Catholic priest, a woman can, by definition, never occupy the role of bluesman without gender ambiguity. It is the social and gender ambiguity of women blues singers which causes the mythology of the blues culture to recognize their sexual magic as especially powerful and siren-like. (Aschoff 1995, 51–52).

Pointing out that the term *blueswoman,* the obvious counterpart to the term *bluesman,* does not even exist in the lexicon of the blues, Aschoff proposes that those tough, legendary women who were able to handle the life of a bluesman—Memphis Minnie, Lucille Bogan, and Louise Johnson—were made by life into bluesmen even if they were not born to it. Unlike theatrical and vaudeville blues singers, such as Ma Rainey and Bessie Smith, "real blues women" lived the same life as the men. Thus, while the occupation and role of the bluesman is defined as male, both men and women may occupy the role. Indeed, Aschoff (1995, 54–56) sees blues women as gaining much of their social authority and sexual power from their ambiguous occupation of male social roles and positions. Of course, Aschoff's concept of the bluesman also fails to suit Mama Yancey. Because she did not live the life of a bluesman, she did not even ambiguously occupy a male social role and position.

Have any models been proposed for understanding black female blues singers that would shed better light on Mama Yancey? Does Mama Yancey in any way suit the role that has been retrospectively assigned to women blues singers of the 1920s and early 1930s? To consider this question, I will turn first to an influential article by Hazel Carby about the sexual politics of women's blues during this period. In "It Jus Be's Dat Way Sometime," Carby takes up several themes. One is the way in which both fictional and biographical narratives have mythologized the woman blues singer and used her to represent "women who attempt to manipulate and control their construction as sexual subjects" (Carby 1986, 12). Another is the way in which various blues lyrics sung by these women assert female sexual autonomy and how, for example, the line "I can play and sing the blues" in one song even situates the singer "at the center of a subversive and liberatory activity" (1986, 18–19). A third theme is the subversive activity of the singers' careers, which were carried out despite frequent disapproval by the men in their personal lives (1986, 19). Furthermore, Carby sees the blues singers as occupying

> a privileged space; they had broken out of the boundaries of the home and taken their sensuality and sexuality out of the private and into the public sphere. For these singers were gorgeous and their physical presence elevated them to being referred to as Goddesses, as the high priestesses of the blues, or like Bessie Smith as the Empress of the blues. Their physical presence was a crucial aspect of their power; the visual display of spangled dresses, of furs, of gold teeth, of diamonds[,] of all the sumptuous and desirable aspects of their body reclaimed female sexuality from being an objectification of male desire to a representation of female desire. (1986, 19–20)

Although the moment in which the blues expressed women's power and control over sexuality was short-lived, the women who sang them have become our cultural icons of sexual power, according to Carby (1986, 21).

Carby's perspectives suggest at least one important approach to studying Mama Yancey, that is, through the content of her lyrics. In some of her lyrics Mama represents herself as attempting to control her construction as a sexual object, as in her lines "Make me a pallet on your flo' / So when your good gal comes she will never know," although explicit sex was rarely Mama's focus. In some of her songs Mama also clearly situated herself at the center of a "subversive and liberatory activity," for example, in thinking up ingenious ways to pursue her man after he had left her, daring to have "a [different] man every day of the week," and advising another woman, "Tell your man once, little girl, you do not have to tell him twice." Nevertheless, since in her life story Mama did not focus clearly on these topics, the extent to which her lyrics reveal her personal values is unclear. I will return to this topic later. Furthermore, Mama Yancey did not subversively carry out a career against the wishes of the men in her life, and she never wore spangled dresses, furs, or diamonds like the early vaudeville blues women, nor did she display her body as desirable in performance. Thus, she did not cultivate the image of a "blues queen" and hence she does not suit the role assigned to the popular blues women of the 1920s.

Ann duCille, indeed, has questioned the mythology surrounding the celebrated women blues singers of the 1920s and 1930s in her recent book *The Coupling Convention*. Comparing their images to those of women who produced a different cultural form, which duCille calls the "bourgeois blues"—the cultural commentaries of black women writers such as Jessie Fauset, Nella Larsen, and Zora Neale Hurston—duCille calls into question

> the utopian trend in contemporary cultural criticism that readily reads resistance in such privileged, so-called authentically black discourses as the classic blues of the 1920s and the folkloric fiction of Zora Neale Hurston, while denigrating other cultural forms for their perceived adherence to and promotion of traditional (white) values. . . . I argue that much of the discourse that champions the sexual "self-invention" and "authenticity" of blues queens such as Bessie Smith and signifying sisters such as Zora Neale Hurston does so without examining the reflexive nature of the invention, without interrogating the role of ideology in shaping the period, its artists, and its attention both to the folk and to black female sexuality. (1993, 67, 69)

Although many of duCille's arguments are only distantly related to my questions about the identity of Mama Yancey, I nevertheless find some of her broad perspectives useful. She points, for example, to the danger of erasing the complexities of a wide range of African American historical experiences and replacing them with a single, monolithic construction (duCille 1993, 71). She suggests that probably few black women "lived the kind of sexually liberated lives or held the kind of freewheeling values refracted in the blues" and that like other expressive media, the blues invoke the fantastic (1993, 72). DuCille also problematizes Carby's observation that the blues women invented themselves as sexual subjects. Although lyrics in such songs as "I'm A Mighty Tight Woman" and "Put a Little Sugar in My Bowl" "spoke boldly to sexual freedom and personal choice . . . , they also spoke to the racial and sexual iconography that cast the African woman as a hypersexual primitive" (1993, 74). DuCille suggests that we examine critically the ideology that "made possible the invention of both the explicitly sexual black female subjects sung in the songs of blues women like Bessie Smith and Ma Rainey and the often more covertly sexual subjects written in the fiction of Jessie Fauset, Nella Larsen, and Zora Neale Hurston" (ibid.).

Both Carby and duCille point to the culturally constructed nature of the prevailing images of women blues singers of the 1920s and early 1930s. By citing their studies, I want to draw attention to the pitfalls of using contemporary cultural constructions of women blues singers as analytic tools for understanding the reality of blues women's lives and consciousnesses. DuCille's warnings, in particular, suggest caution in assigning too much agency to a singer's self-invention. In any case, Mama Yancey's distance from these blues women in career choice, song material, professional stature, and physical presentation as a performer suggest that the myths surrounding the early women blues singers will not help us understand her. Her life and work need to be to viewed within another framework.

I think it must have been Mama's distance from the professional entertainment world in particular that prevents the concept of role, with which both Keil and Aschoff are explicitly concerned and to which Carby and duCille also speak in connection with their focus on image and mythology, from being productive for looking at Mama Yancey's life. Instead of filling an expressive role, Mama seems for the most part to have led a rather ordinary life, while certain circumstances allowed her to demonstrate her extraordinary singing talents beyond her own circle from time to time. Although all audiences, including those for whom Mama sang, have expectations of those who perform for them, and Mama delivered especially well those aspects Keil (1966, 16) describes as sound, timing, and the spoken word—although for her it was mostly the sung rather than the spoken word—Mama was no entertainer in the usual sense.

What models have been proposed for studying other groups of African Americans, especially females, then, that might shed greater light on Mama Yancey? How can I best understand how Mama Yancey's identity as both an African American and a woman influenced her life and the ways she presented herself to others?

Darlene Clark Hine's research into the autobiographies of late nineteenth- and early twentieth-century black women who migrated or fled from the South to the Midwest seems to provide one useful framework. Hines has concluded that

> Black women, as a rule, developed and adhered to a cult of secrecy, a culture of dissemblance, to protect the sanctity of inner aspects of their lives. The dynamics of dissemblance involved creating the appearance of disclosure, or openness about themselves and their feelings, while actually remaining an enigma. Only with secrecy, thus achieving a self-imposed invisibility, could ordinary Black women accrue the psychic space and harness the resources needed to hold their own in the often one-sided and mismatched resistance struggle. (Hine 1989, 915)

Black women's self-imposed secrecy and the culture of dissemblance assumed its most institutionalized form in the founding, in 1896, of the National

Association of Colored Women's Clubs, at the core of which was a concern with creating positive images of black women's sexuality. To counter negative stereotypes, many black women downplayed or even denied sexual expression (Hine 1989, 917–18).

Although as far as I know, Mama Yancey never joined the black women's club movement, which fostered a self-conscious culture of resistance, perhaps her reticence to reveal accurate information about herself represents part of the larger black women's culture of dissemblance. What we know of her life does not indicate that she avoided activities that may have provided grist for detractors' mills, as did many of the women about whom Hines reports: for example, Mama may have engaged in some kind of numbers game, and she may also have had an extramarital lover. Nevertheless, it seems that she did not talk with interviewers about these matters. Probably there was a self-imposed secrecy and dissemblance at work that went beyond Mama's presentation of multiple selves. She simply kept silent about some aspects of her life. Perhaps this resulted from her being interviewed largely by whites with whom she wished to "hold [her] own in the . . . mismatched resistance struggle," to recall Hine's thesis.

In a chapter on the power of self-definition in her text *Black Feminist Thought*, Patricia Hill Collins (1990, 91) carries the theme of black women's dissemblance further, discussing the dual consciousness many African American women developed to protect and hide "a self-defined standpoint from the prying eyes of dominant groups." Collins suggests that the struggle of African American women as they lived two lives, one for others and one for themselves, led to their preoccupation with self-definition (1990, 94), and she goes on to propose that black women's efforts to find their own voice have occurred in at least three safe spaces: (1) black women's relationships with one another; (2) music as art, including spirituals, blues, jazz, and the progressive raps of the 1980s; and (3) "the space created by Black women writers" (1990, 96–103).

With regard to Mama Yancey, Collins's first category of "safe space" cannot be probed because Mama's relationships with other black women were never documented. To Collins's second category, however, belong the lyrics of Mama's original blues songs, and these may well be examined as a source of information about Mama's self-definition. Since I have examined Mama's lyrics elsewhere, reading them in relation both to own her life story, personality, values, and gender identity and to blues lyrics sung by other singers (Bowers 1993), I will not discuss this subject in detail here. Let me give one example, however. In her "How Long Blues"—a song that Mama performed regularly and recorded on six different occasions—Mama's text centers on the singer's mistreatment by her man, which is a central theme in blues songs generally, but Mama nonetheless imparts originality to her song by including stanzas that create the character of a good little woman who is tough, has a clear sense of right and wrong, and seeks to teach that to others. Comparing Mama's text to principles she articulated in conversation and to ways in which she is reported to have behaved in real life, I have concluded that we can read her personality and values fairly well in the persona she creates in this song, as well as in other original songs. Thus, the materials of Mama's performance can be viewed as raw materials for her biography. Nevertheless, since her lyrics were heavily mediated by conventions of genre, performance venue, and the borrowing of traditional lines and stanzas characteristic of the folk blues tradition, they must be interpreted just as carefully as her interview narratives must be.

I am still searching for theoretical frameworks that will help me understand Mama Yancey. Indeed, despite my affinity with Mama because of our shared gender, I am even finding it somewhat difficult to write a "feminist biography" about her. I wonder, for example, how I can best respond to Lee Chambers-Schiller's (1993, 217) description of feminist biography—that is, biography that "takes as its particular task the examination and analysis of the gender relations of a culture, the ways in which individuals reflect and resist gender roles, internalize and critique conventional gender ideology, push the boundaries of and accommodate to the limitations that society construes as appropriate female experiences while forming relationships, sustaining life, nurturing the spirit, and creating meaning within a specific historical context." I also ponder how to use what Devoney Looser (1993, 182) describes as long-standing implicit rules for writing feminist biography: "measuring the degree of rebellion inherent in a woman's achievement—as well as gauging her place in a historical line-up of feminist heroines." And I question how best to use Rachel Gutiérrez's (1992, 49) idea that "the woman who stands out is the one who, whether in her role in history, whether determined to challenge conventions, whether feminist or not, somehow becomes an example of independence and creative work."

In the introduction to *The Challenge of Feminist Biography*, Sara Alpern, Joyce Antler, Elisabeth Israels Perry, and Ingrid Winther Scobie suggest that changing the gender of the subject has changed the nature and practice of the biographical craft in several important ways. The first is that a different type of person—one who has not achieved celebrity or lasting fame—is now receiving biographical treatment. Feminist biographers thus are looking at different kinds of achievement, and in so doing they "are not only restoring 'invisible' women to the record but enlarging our perspective of the record" (Alpern et al. 1992, 6). A second major way in which changing the gender of the subject is changing biography is that

> when the subject is female, gender moves to the center of the analysis. Feminists contend that women's lives differ from men's, often in profound ways. Because society tends to value male models of achievement and behavior more than it values female models, a woman's gender may exercise greater constraints on the way her life evolves. Failing to consider this difference distorts, if not falsifies, any account of a woman's life. This is true even when a woman is unaware of or inarticulate about the effects of gender on her life. (ibid., 7)

Moving gender to the center of the analysis may mean placing more emphasis on private lives and on the female life-cycle experience, especially the later stages of the life cycle—mature adulthood and old age. It may also mean investigating the importance of female friendships during major life transitions (ibid., 9).

What does this mean for my treatment of Mama Yancey? First, the very act of my writing her biography, even though she did not achieve the celebrity or lasting (if modest) fame of most male blues artists who have received biographical attention, seems to demonstrate a feminist approach to musical achievement. Second, moving gender to the center of my analysis means that I must bring out the ways in which gender exercised greater constraints on Mama's musical activities than it did on those of her male contemporaries. At the same time, I need to recognize that her marriage did not interrupt her career, since she had not begun a career before her marriage; in fact, her marriage to pianist Jimmy Yancey gave her opportunities to sing as she moved into her late forties and fifties that she would not have otherwise enjoyed. Of course, this sort of privileged access to a particular activity through a husband or other close male relative is typical of many women's experiences. Still, both the extreme male domination of the blues world and Mama's conception of her role as a woman and wife must have deterred her from putting herself forward more as a singer and perhaps from further developing her guitar playing as well. They surely also contributed to the ways in which Mama retreated into private life for long periods of time. Nevertheless, this too needs to be put into historical perspective, for many male musicians in Mama's milieu, including her husband, spent years of their lives working outside music.

Moving gender to the center of my analysis also invites speculation about the relation between Mama's continuing to sing well into old age and characteristic women's life-cycle experiences. Moreover, it suggests the importance of examining the effect that Mama's friendship with another woman, Barbara Dane, had on the resumption of her public singing in the late 1950s and 1960s. Nevertheless, although Dane's influence was incontrovertible, Mama's singing was also revived in the mid-1970s and early 1980s because of her friendship with Erwin Helfer. Indeed, Mama needed a man to play piano for her—she never performed with a woman pianist, and women who played the piano most often accompanied themselves. Thus, the gender of the person exercising an influence on the renewal of Mama's public singing was not a critical factor. Nevertheless, it is worth considering the significance of Barbara Dane in one period of Mama's life, because Dane and Mama admired each other greatly and seem to have given each other important emotional support during the times they got together.

The only interviewer to ask Mama how being a woman affected her work in the blues world was Bob Rusch. Rusch's single question was "You're a woman, and a small woman at that, how did you handle what has traditionally been a male dominated profession?" Mama replied: "I just handle it like I always did when I came here. I found it was a man's world and I go along with it (laughter) you can't beat that. Now what am I goin' to do about it? Do you know I only weigh 98 pounds, what am I going to do in a man's world (laughter). I'm going to try to change it? You got to be kidding (laughter), you got to be drunk" (Rusch 1978, 5). Although Mama's spontaneous response to a male interviewer's question was undoubtedly designed to be humorous, I also take it as serious evidence that Mama Yancey was fully conscious of male domination in the profession and that she did not consider herself up to challenging it. For the most part, she operated "comfortably and creatively" within the boundaries of the constraints of her woman's life (Alpern et al. 1992, 8). Although her lack of challenge to male bluesmen did not in the least make her male dominated, neither was she a spokesperson for women's rights. Nor did her musical activities constitute resistance or rebellion against gender roles. Still, her significant achievements mean that Mama Yancey can become an example of independence and creative work, to respond to Gutiérrez's suggestion. Although I am still searching for ways in which to understand Mama Yancey better, I know that these things are important to consider in writing Estelle ("Mama") Yancey's biography.

APPENDIX: CITED INTERVIEWS WITH MAMA YANCEY, IN
CHRONOLOGICAL ORDER

Barbara Dane (with Pete Welding), 23 September 1964. Barbara Dane Collection, tape A-24 and A-29. Archive of Folk Culture, Library of Congress.

Barry Dolins, June 1976 and March 1977. Excerpted and presented in narrative form in Dolins 1977.

Howard Mandel, ca. 1977. Oral History Program, Jazz Institute of Chicago. University of Chicago Library.

Bob Rusch, ca. 1978. Transcribed in Rusch 1978.

Jane Bowers, 15 June 1984.

Jane Bowers, 2 January 1986.

NOTE

1. In 1943 Mama Yancey recorded four songs with Jimmy Yancey for Session Records, of which only two were initially released, on Session 12–002 and 12–003, a third later appearing on Roots EPL001; these three were reissued on *"The Immortal" Jimmy Yancey, 1898–1951* (Oldie Blues OL 2802); *Jimmy and Mama Yancey/Cripple Clarence Lofton*, vol. 2 (Gannet Gen 5137); and *Jimmy Yancey: Complete Recorded Works 1939–1950 in Chronological Order*, vols. 2 and 3 (Document Records DOCD-5042 and 5043). In 1951 Mama recorded five songs with Jimmy Yancey that were issued on *Jimmy and Mama Yancey: Yancey Special* (Atlantic LP 130) and reissued on *Pure Blues/Jimmy and Mama Yancey* (Atlantic LP 1283) and *Jimmy and Mama Yancey: Chicago Piano*, vol. 1 (Atlantic SD 7229). In 1952 Mama recorded seven songs with Don Ewell that were released on *Mama Yancey Singer/ Don Ewell Pianist* (Windin' Ball 102). In 1961 Mama recorded five songs with Little Brother Montgomery, of which four were released on *Chicago—The Living Legends/South Side Blues* (Riverside RLP 9403) and the fifth on a two-LP set, *Chicago—The Living Legends* (Riverside RLP 9389/9390); all were reissued on compact disc as *Chicago—The Living Legends/South Side Blues* (Riverside OBCCD-508-2). In 1965 Mama recorded eight songs with Art Hodes that were issued on *Mama Yancey Sings, Art Hodes Plays Blues* (Verve/Folkways 9015). In 1982–83 she recorded ten songs with Erwin Helfer that were released on *Maybe I'll Cry* (Red Beans RB 001; reissued on compact disc Evidence Music, EDC 26078), and during the same period she recorded eleven songs with German pianist Axel Zwingenberger that were released on *Axel Zwingenberger and the Friends of Boogie Woogie, Vol. 4: The Blues of Mama Yancey* (Vagabond VRLP 8.88009).

REFERENCES CITED

Alpern, Sara, Joyce Antler, Elisabeth Israels Perry, and Ingrid Winther Scobie, eds. 1992. Introduction. *The Challenge of Feminist Biography: Writing the Lives of Modern American Women,* 1–15. Urbana: University of Illinois Press.

Aschoff, Peter. 1995. Unpublished manuscript, University of Mississippi.

Baber, Ceola Ross. 1987. "The Artistry and Artifice of Black Communication." In *Expressively Black: The Cultural Basis of Ethnic Identity,* ed. Geneva Gay and Willie L. Baber, 75–108. New York: Praeger.

Banner, Lois. 1993. "Biography and Autobiography: Intermixing the Genres." *a/b: Auto/Biography Studies* 8:159–78.

Bowers, Jane. 1993. "'I Can Stand More Trouble Than Any Little Woman My Size': Observations on the Meanings of the Blues of Estelle 'Mama' Yancey." *American Music* 11, no. 1:28–53.

Carby, Hazel. 1986. "It Jus Be's Dat Way Sometime: The Sexual Politics of Women's Blues." *Radical America* 20, no. 4:9–22. Repr. in *Unequal Sisters: A Multicultural Reader in U.S. Women's History,* ed. Ellen Carol DuBois and Vicki L. Ruiz. New York: Routledge, 1990.

Chambers-Schiller, Lee. 1993. "The Value of Female Public Rituals for Feminist Biography: Maria Weston Chapman and the Boston Anti-Slavery Anniversary." *a/b: Auto/Biography Studies* 8:217–32.

Choice, Harriet. 1979. "Carter's Alto, Arrangements Give Fest Memorable Moments." *Chicago Tribune,* 31 August, 4:6.

Collins, Patricia Hill. 1990. "The Power of Self-Definition." *Black Feminist Thought: Knowledge, Consciousness, and the Politics of Empowerment,* 91–114. Boston: Unwin Hyman.

Dane, Barbara. 1985. Telephone conversation with author, 8 October.

———. 1990. Interview by author, 9 November, Oakland.

De Hart, Jane Sherron. 1993. "Oral Sources and Contemporary History: Dispelling Old Assumptions." *Journal of American History* 80:582–95.

Dolins, Barry. 1977. "Rent Party Piano: An Underground Music in Chicago 1913–1927." M.A. thesis, DePaul University.

duCille, Ann. 1993. "Blues Notes on Black Sexuality: Sex and the Texts of the Twenties and Thirties." *The Coupling Convention: Sex, Text, and Tradition in Black Women's Fiction,* 66–85. New York: Oxford University Press.

[Grauer, Bill, Jr.] 1948. "lemME take this chorus." *The Record Changer* 7, no. 7:4, 29.

Gutiérrez, Rachel. 1992. "What Is a Feminist Biography?" In *All Sides of the Subject: Women and Biography,* ed. Teresa Iles, 48–55. New York: Teachers College Press.

Harris, Sheldon. 1979. "Yancey, Estella 'Mama.'" In *Blues Who's Who: A Biographical Dictionary of Blues Singers,* 591–92. New York: Da Capo.

Hine, Darlene Clark. 1989. "Rape and the Inner Lives of Black Women in the Middle West: Preliminary Thoughts on the Culture of Dissemblance." *Signs* 14:912–20. Repr. in *Unequal Sisters: A Multicultural Reader in U.S. Women's History,* ed. Ellen Carol DuBois and Vicki L. Ruiz. New York: Routledge, 1990.

Hodes, Art. 1984. Telephone conversation with author, 2 July.

Joseph, Pleasant "Cousin Joe," and Harriet J. Ottenheimer. 1987. *Cousin Joe: Blues from New Orleans.* Chicago: University of Chicago Press.

Keil, Charles. 1966. *Urban Blues.* Chicago: University of Chicago Press.

Looser, Devoney. 1993. "Heroine of the Peripheral? Biography, Feminism, and Sylvia Plath." *a/b: Auto/Biography Studies* 8:179–97.

Novick, David. 1979. "Chicago Fun Times: U. of C. Folk Festival Returns." *Reader: Chicago's Free Weekly,* 2 February, 1:7.

Ottenheimer, Harriet. 1982. "The Second Time Around: Versions and Variants in the Life Story Narrative of Cousin Joe, a New Orleans Blues Singer." *Louisiana Folklore Miscellany* 5, no. 2:7–12.

Pachter, Marc. 1979. "The Biographer Himself: An Introduction." In *Telling Lives: The Biographer's Art,* ed. Pachter, 2–15. Washington, D.C.: New Republic.

Pearson, Barry. 1977. "The Life of the Blues Musician: An Analysis of the Traditions of Oral Self-Portrayal." Ph.D. diss., Indiana University.

Rusch, Bob. 1978. "Mama Yancey: Interview." *Cadence: The American Review of Jazz and Blues* 4, no. 11:4.

Stewart-Baxter, Derrick. 1954. "Mama and Jimmy Yancey." *Jazz Journal* 8, no. 10:3–4.

———. 1960. "Blues on Record, Part XXII." *Jazz Journal* 13, no. 2:5, 26.

———. 1961. "Blues on Record, Part XXIII." *Jazz Journal* 14, no. 2:7, 40.

Titon, Jeff Todd. 1980. "The Life Story." *Journal of American Folklore* 93:276–92.

Wellek, René, and Austin Warren. 1956. *Theory of Literature.* 3d ed. New York: Harcourt, Brace and World.

Wexler, Alice. 1992. "Emma Goldman and the Anxiety of Biography." In *The Challenge of Feminist Biography: Writing the Lives of Modern American Women,* ed. Sara Alpern, Joyce Antler, Elisabeth Israels Perry, and Ingrid Winther Scobie, 34–50. Urbana: University of Illinois Press.

6 Gender Negotiation of the Composer Kaija Saariaho in Finland: The Woman Composer as Nomadic Subject

Pirkko Moisala

This study is based on the postmodern premise that subjectivity—as well as identity—is an ongoing, discursively constructed process within which gender is a fluid and changeable factor. Gender and gender identity are constantly negotiated in new sociomusical contexts and situations. As Teresa de Lauretis (1988) emphasizes, "woman" is both the Other—an institutionally constructed cultural representation—and a real-life person with individual experiences. I use these premises to examine the category of "woman composer" as both a sociocultural construction and an individually experienced and created identity and performed subject position.[1]

When I was reading the biographies, notes, diaries, and correspondence of women composers of different nationalities and from different centuries and periods of the Western art tradition, including the contemporary, I was struck by the many similarities in their experiences and musical paths, despite the differences in their national and cultural backgrounds. These common aspects, along with the underlying patterns of thought, particularly those relating to creativity and professionalism, are nicely collected and analyzed by Marcia Citron in her excellent book *Gender and the Musical Canon* (1993). Common elements among women composers, however, are not the whole truth; as also noted by Citron, women composers differ in time, place, and possibly foremost, individual experience. Paraphrasing Rosi Braidotti (1994, 162), we can say that the category "woman composer" is a general umbrella term that brings together different kinds of women, different modes and levels of experience, and distinct identities. Furthermore, being a woman composer is internally a heterogenic, multifaceted, and even conflicted process. Gender (in this case, that of a composer), understood as a social process, unavoidably and additionally involves the structures of power and knowledge that produce the subject as an element of that social process (as addressed in Foucault 1984).

In the spirit of Braidotti (1991, 1994) and her epistemology of nomadic transitions based on the perspective of positive sexual difference, I adopt the stance that the identity and subjectivity of a woman composer are discursively constructed in three interconnected domains: differences between men and women, differences among women, and differences within each woman. In each woman composer's life, womanhood is constantly negotiated in relation to gendered conventions and structures, in various sociomusical situations, in interaction with people of the other and of the same sex, within the public sphere of musical life, and as an internal growing process for each composer. The negotiation of gender, "the nomadic mode . . . as an art of existence" (Braidotti 1994, 159), may involve various strategies to present (or perform, if you like) gender or to cover or even mask it.

This essay is my interpretation[2] of the gender negotiation of the Finnish composer Kaija Saariaho, internationally acclaimed from the early 1980s to the present day.[3] I demonstrate, by examining the public's reception of Kaija Saariaho and her own experiences, how the negotiation of gender identity and the presentation of a woman composer take place, as ongoing processes, between the realms of conventional otherness (the socially constructed category of women composers) and real-life experiences of the individual. The analysis is largely based on my interview with Kaija Saariaho[4] and on previously published interviews by others,[5] as well as on critical reviews of her works[6] that I interpret through the aforementioned theoretical lens. I do not mean to "psychologize" her life; instead, I want to emphasize that this interpretation is my own. After having read a draft of this essay, however, Saariaho validated my interpretation while acknowledging that it is a new perspective for her. Furthermore, although gender was an influential factor throughout her life, it was obviously not the only factor influencing her career as a composer. This analysis of Saariaho will also touch on technology and nationality.

The analysis of Saariaho's gender negotiation, her "nomadness," is presented in two parts. The first section discusses gender as a factor in the construction of her identity as a woman composer, and the second focuses on her negotiation of gender in relation to her social environment, particularly the Finnish press. Whereas the former emphasizes internal processes involved in gender construction and identification, the latter is more about the interaction within and among outside institutions and elements. This

Kaija Saariaho. Photo © MIC/Maarit Kytöharju, used by permission.

nevertheless does not imply that these realms of gender negotiation are separate; this organization is simply a means to present the discussion clearly. Gender construction is always simultaneously both an internal and interactive social process. I have not consistently organized the story of Kaija Saariaho chronologically because, in my opinion, the process of gender negotiation does not take place in a linear progression but is rather more like light refracted by a crystal: gender is performed differently depending on the context and situation.

Seeking Identity: Differences Within

Like many other (women) composers before her, Kaija Saariaho already exhibited various artistic talents as a child. She painted and played the piano, the violin, and later on the organ. After she had finished school, she began to study visual arts and graphics, because even though she had a keen interest in composing, she did not believe that she could ever become a composer. Her image of "a composer" and of a "creative person" did not fit her own self-image:

The images I had of a composer made me think that I could not externally or internally correspond to those images. When one, as a child and
music student, reads about great composers, it forms one's image [of a
composer] and, in addition, . . . the image one has about Sibelius. What
kind of understanding you have about overall musicality [is influenced
by the fact that a composer is] an overwhelmingly extroverted creative
person. These were the thoughts which paralyzed me, because I never
could think of enacting these images.[7]

The images Saariaho had about composers and creative people were formed
within the Finnish music culture of the 1960s and 1970s. Jean Sibelius, always pictured as a sturdy old man with a big cigar, was undoubtedly the best-
known composer in that milieu. Neither the music history course curriculum nor the standard concert life included women composers, not even
Barbara Strozzi or Lili Boulanger. At that time Ida Moberg (1859–1947), now
known as the first woman composer in Finland, was completely forgotten,
and the only recognized Finnish woman composer of the time, Helvi Leiviskä
(1902–82), was regarded as being outside the modern, avant-garde musical
circles. The marginalization of Leiviskä, who worked as a librarian at the
Sibelius Academy, did not ease the distance Saariaho felt between herself and
composing. Saariaho felt that "composing and music were such great things
that I, as the kind of poor girl that I was, could not reach them."

Perhaps thanks to Sibelius, who provided the young Finnish nation with
national pride in the early twentieth century as well as during the years of
World War II, the status of composers has always been exceptionally high
in Finland. In Gallup polls or surveys the occupation of "composer" is always ranked among the top professions. In Finnish music culture the title
of "composer" is given rather exclusively to those who have formal training (i.e., a diploma) in composition. Although there are some notable exceptions (such as Aulis Sallinen, the well-known opera composer), an individual with formal training but few if any compositions is more likely to be
considered a "composer" than is someone with a long list of works but no
formal training.

This cultural and musical environment did not provide Saariaho with role
models or encourage her to study composition. The need to compose became
so urgent, however, that in 1976 she insisted that the composition teacher
at the Sibelius Academy, Paavo Heininen, accept her as a student. The way
Saariaho describes her internal calling corresponds closely to the idealistic
notion of an artist who is compelled to make art: "I understood that the only

thing that meant something to me was music, and it felt unbearable to think I could not do that. It was an internal 'must' requiring that I become a composer. Music and I, we had to be together. I do not have any identity without my music." Saariaho was in a position without precedent. Thus, in Marcia Citron's (1993, 68) words, how could she feel validated as a composer? Saariaho had to negotiate her calling as a composer within the male art music tradition in which creativity was situated in the rationalized subjectivity of man (Citron 1993, 57–69). The differences between her image of a composer and her own self-image created an internal conflict, "an anxiety of authorship" (Citron 1993, 55–78), that she initially tried to overcome by attempting to mask her femaleness: "Then at some point of time [at around age twenty], I began to smoke cigars, and I tried to project a stronger image of myself. However, that phase passed quickly. Thereafter, I have no longer had any such problems with my self-image."

The contradiction between Saariaho's image of the composer and her self-image was possibly a central factor in "paralyzing" her creativity at the beginning of her training. This paralysis was, in my understanding, due more to the ambivalence caused by this contradiction than to lack of confidence, for she must have had a great deal of confidence to insist that the composition teacher accept her as a student. In addition to feeling paralyzed, Saariaho describes herself at that time as being "closed." She thanks her first and, in her opinion, most important composition teacher, Paavo Heininen, for helping her to find the way back to her lost creativity. Heininen was a demanding, severe teacher who in a way forced her to become more confident. Among other things, he made her look at the mirror twenty times a day and say, "I can." "In a way, he had to tear certain things out of me, but I think that everything he did was successful, indeed, because I was quite closed at that time. I had such enormous insecurity . . . at that time in my life and also in my work [composing]. It had something to do with my identity as a young woman and with all my human relationships. Paavo did enormous work with me. I felt that he pulled me into life."

Saariaho did not experience her teacher-student relationship with Heininen as gendered, although she admits that she cannot say whether a woman teacher would have made a difference. Saariaho explains that her rediscovered creativity was something she had already possessed as a child. Did she loose this creativity when she faced the cultural representation of "woman" to which creativity is not linked? "Somehow, something within me began to open, and I got into a kind of child's world which was without insecurity and fear. It was not the first time I was in that world with these colors and voices, all these dimensions. I found it again. It was a world of great, free associations in which I had already lived."

The Role of Role Model: Differences among Women

In interviews by women journalists, Saariaho was frequently asked whether she had female role models. With the exception of Helvi Leiviskä, whom she met briefly in the early 1980s and with whom she felt no connection, she did not meet or know about other women composers. As a young woman she compensated for this lack with literary idols: Virginia Woolf, Sylvia Plath, and Edith Södergran (a Finnish-Swedish poet). At the time, when the post-modern project began to reconstruct the "Great Stories of Great Artists," Saariaho found it possible to identify herself as an artist in the romantic sense of the word. The life stories of these women writers attested to the difficulty of combining a "woman's life" with creative work.

Saariaho's process of searching for an identity took place—and possibly still does—within the contradictions not only between the image of the composer and her real-life experiences but also between her conception of a woman's traditional life and her own desire to be an artist. Again, cultural conventions seemed to be irreconcilable with her own experiences. "Woman" as a cultural sign was present in both the social pressures placed on Saariaho (by questions such as "Why don't you have children?" or "Why aren't you married?") and in her own comprehension of the traditional life of a woman implicit in her words. Throughout the interviews of the 1980s, "artist/composer" and "woman" were an irreconcilable dichotomy in her mind. The following terms have been drawn and interpreted from these interviews:

Composing	Traditional Role of a Woman
holistic, far-reaching work	motherhood, children
abstract things, away from reality	everyday things: cooking, housework
egocentric	altruistic
asocial	social

At the very beginning of her career, when she probably felt most burdened by social pressures, this conflict of identity caused feelings of guilt and uselessness. She had found an identity as an artist, but she was not yet free from social expectations. At the age of thirty-one, however, she claimed no longer to have these negative feelings: "Now I only do what I must for my work" (*Helsingin Sanomat* 23 Oct. 1983; all translations from Finnish are my own). Nevertheless, she still thought that "when becoming an artist, a woman must give up many things and withstand, in addition, the pressures of society" (ibid.). This attitude may be influenced by one of Saariaho's composition teachers in Freiburg: "He used half of his teaching time to explain to me that if a woman composer has children, she can no longer compose anything but lullabies. 'I have seen it happen,' he said."

Five years later, in 1988, Saariaho reaffirmed that, according to her own experience, a woman composer must give up a lot: "One cannot have everything, but I feel it is a privilege that I may do just what I want" (*Uusi Suomi* 23 June 1988). This belief, however, changed after the birth of her first child, in March 1990. Within one month she began to compose again. She discovered that motherhood need not exclude composing. Her second child was born in 1994: "[Now] I think that it is unbelievable that someone can claim that [childbirth] has any other effect but a practical one: can I arrange my life so that I have time to compose? The act of composing is so strong that it is hard to deny it."

Saariaho frequently emphasized in published interviews, either explicitly or implicitly (for instance, by refusing to talk about her gender), that she does not want her gender to be an issue and that she no more wants to be called a "woman composer" than she wants to be labeled a "computer composer." She wanted people to experience her music simply as music, not as music composed by a woman: "I don't overlook a woman's perspective, but I consider it a kind of ghettoization if my music is approached like that" (*Helsingin Sanomat* 5 Sept. 1990).

Throughout the 1980s, however, her womanness was very much in the Finnish press. Women journalists, in particular, asked her frequently about the way she experienced her gender in relation to her work as a composer. This gender emphasis in (female) journalism most probably arose from the surge of feminist discussion in Finland around then. Although feminism, as an academic subject, a social force, and a favored topic of discussion, swept powerfully over Finnish culture in the 1980s, the musical life around art music remained one of the last untouched bastions. There was a social mandate for a woman composer serving as an example of a successful artistic woman. Saariaho refused this role. She also distanced herself from feminism: "It is useless to expect any feminist perspective from me, or to explain my music as feminine. One does, however, face one's womanhood every day. One can get temporary attention, but one remains a curiosity. Even though, with us in Finland, equality [between sexes] is so much discussed, there are still some people to whom a woman as a composer is a sacrilege" (*Helsingin Sanomat* 23 Oct. 1983).

In 1994, when Riitta Valkeila and I published our book on women composers (*Musiiken toinen sukupuoli*), there was a great deal of public discussion in Finland about women in music and about the neglect of women composers in music history. Other women composers, such as Anneli Arho, Saariaho's contemporary, who ceased composing to take care of her family, and young female composition students of the Sibelius Academy were interviewed and asked how they experienced their gender in relation to music. They all responded similarly: they said that they did not want to get attention as women composers, and they claimed that gender had nothing to do with their composition work. As a feminist who had worked to get women composers of the past and present known in Finland, I felt offended, but I understood their need to deny their womanness in public.[8]

It is possible that these composers' public denials of their sex or gender was partly based on the confusion of terminology. When interviewers asked whether their sex (there is only one word for both sex and gender in Finnish; the term *gender* is an artificially constructed word translated into Finnish literally as "social sex") had influenced their compositional work, these women may have thought that they were being asked whether their compositions were somehow "feminine" because of their sex, and they therefore denied such an essentialist view. They also may have wanted, as did Saariaho, to distance themselves from the conventionally constructed representation of woman. A more plausible explanation, however, is that the denial of their gender as an influential factor in their composition work was, and possibly still is, a strategy used to survive in the male-dominated Finnish art music culture. Claiming to be a feminist could have been the last nail in one's professional coffin. As Citron (1993, 67) claims, there still is no fully formed female tradition in art music; thus, how could a woman confidently identify herself as a female composer? In the light of my research, it seems that presenting oneself as different from other women composers and emphasizing (neutral) individuality is, for a woman composer, a more effective strategy for achieving acclaim as a composer than using (or wanting to use) women composers as role models—or possibly this is the case only in Finland, where women composers are still a rarity.

Following her own desire to attain recognition as a composer without any gender labeling, Kaija Saariaho does not consider gender when establishing relationships with other composers; rather, she seeks professional contacts based purely on their ability to inspire her artistically: "I have met only a few woman composers; too few, in fact. I cannot regard a person as a 'woman composer.' To me, she is first a composer, and if her work interests me, I am also interested in her as a person. All professional contacts are like that."

Negotiating a Subject Position: Differences between Men and Women

The social contexts—the community of composers, awards committees, conductors, musical associations, concert halls, and so on—in which a contemporary woman composer of Western art music makes her musical pathway are perhaps more male dominated than most other areas in Western cultural life. The gender negotiation of a woman composer takes place in social settings in which power lies almost purely in male hands. In these male-dominated social settings, gender negotiation becomes an additional, demanding task. The female composer must struggle skillfully to find acceptable ways both to negotiate her gender within a musical tradition based on a patriarchal ideology and to negotiate her subject position with male conductors, musicians, and studio workers so as to avoid compromising herself as a composer. This struggle is both external and internal; the social difficulties a woman experiences influence her confidence as a composer.

Kaija Saariaho has worked throughout her career in all-male social surroundings. After the death of Helvi Leiviskä in 1980, she was until recently the only woman member of the Society of Finnish Composers, and after she moved to Paris in 1982, she was the only woman composer working at IRCAM, the Institut de Recherche et Coordination Acoustique/Musique. When Saariaho was asked to recall circumstances during her training and career in which she was treated in a gender-biased manner, she said that gender has always been an influential factor in her career: "Of course gender has been a hindrance. Many did not take a woman composer seriously. When self-confidence is already low, it makes me swallow my tears" (*Helsingin Sanomat* 5 Sept. 1990).

In all-male social surroundings, a woman faces her otherness in many ways. Being treated as "something different" is not always negative or inequitable but may simply happen because of the separate qualities of male and female cultural behavior. In all-male social surroundings, a woman feels like an outsider—in Saariaho's own words, "something different," "an odd bird":

Among my male colleagues [in Finland], I was the only woman. Even though their wives and girlfriends were often present, they were completely another thing. My male colleagues were loyal to me to a great extent but, on some occasions, there were such "male" things, and then I was treated as an outsider. All those friends who are still my friends, they never believed that I could not do something because I was a woman. They really were interested in equality, although they had their own male systems in which my position was rather odd. I felt that there were rules which I did not understand.

In dealing with gender as a factor in their careers, however, women composers must cope not only with all-male social surroundings but also, even today, with prejudices against women composers: "It was quite obvious that people could not place me [as a composer]. 'What are you doing here, pretty girl?' asked one older composer. That naturally did not strengthen my confidence as a composer. I got rather upset, but I could not show it. I don't think it rattled my sense of my calling, but perhaps, after all, it made it more difficult."

In Saariaho's case the difficulties she experienced in the beginning of her career changed, if not diminished, in proportion to the esteem she ultimately earned as a composer. She is now in a privileged position attained by few composers, one in which she can usually choose with whom she works and who performs her works. One of the criteria for choosing the people with whom she works is their gender attitudes:

> I meet so many musicians, my music is played so much, that I meet a variety of people, and some are quite impossible to work with. But those are people with whom I no longer wish to associate. Of course, nowadays, when my music is valued, they are more tolerant of me; people are seldom awful to me now, but that still occasionally happens. I try to wipe such kinds of people and memories out, and if it is up to me, I do not go back to them. Nowadays, I have good opportunities to influence . . . who plays my music and who conducts it.

But are the success and the status a woman gains as a composer the end of the difficulties and troubles she faces because of her gender? Does the gender negotiation, the search for strategies to survive despite being the "wrong" gender, end when she has established herself in the male-dominated musical world? I asked Saariaho how far she had to go in her career before she won an end to the attempts to subjugate her because of her gender: "They never ended; they never end. I cannot believe that they ever end. I am quite resigned to my destiny in that sense. Nowadays, bad treatment due to my gender happens, though less frequently. I thought that when I am old with many wrinkles, they would no longer dare try [laughter]. Sometimes I think that if a man were in this position, would he need to think of such things as I must just in order to cope? One cannot do anything but laugh. That's how it is." Saariaho's wish that her gendered position in music would become less stressful as she ages relates to the various discussions of the interrelatedness of woman's sexuality, age, and musical roles in other contexts such as, for example, in the ground-breaking anthology edited by Ellen Koskoff (1987). Age frees women from overtly gender-based prejudice and treatment. This may be due partly to achievements that can no longer be denied but also partly to the diminished sexual expectations placed on them. Older women in music (as in other domains) come to be treated more as human beings than as women—that is, as sexual objects.

Marcia Citron (1993, 156) argues that many women do not resist the gendered codes in music, codes that suggest women's acceptance of domination by men because of the way in which they are trained. In such a case, their compliance may lead to what Fetterley (1978; in Citron 1993, 156) calls "immasculation," taking the viewpoint of men and identifying oneself in distinction to other women. Even though Saariaho clearly dissociated from other women composers—and from "ordinary" women before becoming a mother—I do not interpret this as an extreme manifestation of immasculation. In my opinion, she never identified herself by denying aspects of her womanness (despite the short period at the age of twenty when she tried to smoke cigars and look like Sibelius). She has, for instance, felt insulted by listeners who attempted compliments by saying that they would never have believed that her work was composed by a woman.

Instead of attempting to identify with male composers, Saariaho tried to find a kind of gender-neutral position freeing her from the marginal position occupied by women composers. Neutralizing one's gender is one of the strategies a woman may use in male-dominated contexts.

As we know (see Citron 1993, 69), marginality and otherness may also be experienced as advantages by women composers. This was also the case with Saariaho:

> I never had to waste my time with Oedipal problems like many [male] colleagues did because I never had the possibility of identifying with my teacher. I have a feeling that some young male colleagues have quite unclear and uncertain musical identities. If you listen to compositions made by young composers, it sounds as if there is a little this and a little

that. You hear that this person is talented, but you wonder, what is his own style in music, how will his music be? I do not know if this is because they identify themselves completely with some composer they admire. I never had such an opportunity. I have never been an angry young man who needed to, at some point, break his ties with history.

It may be concluded that the outsider status a woman composer experiences in the male-dominated world of art music, the way she is treated as the Other and different, enables her to develop her individuality in a unique compositional style. This, in turn, may lead to marginality—if the style does not gain acceptance—but it may also lead to success, as has been the case with Saariaho. In my opinion, she has skillfully negotiated a new feminist subjectivity free from the restricting, conventional "womanness" without immasculating herself, without losing her positive individuality as a woman.

New Technology and Gender: Saariaho in Computer Studios

Tape music and music produced and controlled by computers were typical of Saariaho's works of the 1980s. In the early 1980s computer music was still a rather new phenomenon in Finland, one that elicited disdain from some critics: "Only the very weakest composers take support from 'computer crutches'; they are more interested in bustling with numbers and buttons than slowly scratching dazzling visions of sound on paper" (Seppo Heikinheimo, in *Helsingin Sanomat* 4 Oct. 1983).

Kaija Saariaho got her share of these prejudiced reviews. She was labeled both a woman composer and a computer composer. The combination of a woman composing with the help of computers was regarded as an astonishing, exotic oddity. Nevertheless, I think that computers somehow also enhanced Saariaho and lessened the extent to which her works were regarded as "feminized." In any case, Saariaho faced a double challenge in trying to overcome prejudices with regard to both her gender and the technology she used in her work: "My music can be categorized in whatever way, but I don't particularly like the term 'computer music,' just as I also do not like the concept of 'women's music.' Computers have been used already for such a long time that the means should not determine the result" (*Helsingin Sanomat* 10 Sept. 1987).

When Saariaho went to the IRCAM in 1982 to work in better-equipped computer studios, she obviously did not encounter prejudice against computers, but her gender combined with new technology formed an even bigger problem in social interaction with male studio workers. When I asked her about this interaction, she replied as follows:

> K.S.: During my first years in Paris, I was overlooked quite a lot because I was a woman. If one is a woman, a composer, and, in addition, working with the computers, it is to many a shocking combination. At the studio one must, in order to complete a composition, work with a technical assistant. They are always men, and their relationship with music is often problematic. Many of them would like to compose themselves. It may evoke awful conflicts if the composer under whom they work, that "creative being," is a woman.
>
> P.M.: How has that been apparent?
>
> K.S.: Women composing with computers are just so few that the way the male studio assistants related to me was, in the beginning, quite scary. They just wanted to ridicule me. I never had much interest in learning computer programming; I am interested in music and how I can use that equipment to make music. But that was not acceptable. However, if some well-known male composer wants only to contribute ideas and "the slaves" do the programming, that is regarded as quite normal. If I want to carry out some bigger ideas and I work with an assistant, it is an awfully complex relationship and a very delicate situation.
>
> P.M.: How have you dealt with that in practice?
>
> K.S. After a couple of catastrophic experiences, I became very friendly and careful, and I let them know all the time that I respect their work—which in fact is really true. And I have tried to formulate my words so that they do not sound commanding, because a man cannot accept such a situation.

As analyzed by the pioneering gender scholars in music, Ellen Koskoff (1987, 15) and Carol Robertson (1987, 242), power is undoubtedly always present in gender negotiations in music. Saariaho's experiences of studio work in Paris exemplify how power relates to gender and must be negotiated as a part of the gendered setting in all musical situations. In addition to being the one who is "creative," a composer in the studio is the one who has power and authority. Saariaho's strategy for coping with that unconventional situation (woman-composer-authority) has been to mask her authoritative position to achieve her goals, to enable the working relationship to work, to get her musical ideas realized.

Still, is it only the "inverse" power relation that makes the studio setting complicated? One possible interpretation is that the male studio assistants—

who, according to Saariaho, would themselves like to compose—cannot identify with a woman composer, and this distance makes a working relationship with her less fulfilling than one with a male composer whose work reinforces their male identity. The success of a male composer whose ideas they have helped to implement gives them a source of positive identification. Possibly, therefore, it is not only the unconventional power position but the impossibility of identifying with a woman composer that makes the studio relationship difficult.

Finnish National Pride and Gender in Interaction

Women composers negotiate their gender differences not only in male social settings but also in male-dominated media. Most music critics in Finland (and possibly outside Finland as well) are male, and music journalism as a whole—like other areas of Western art music— is based on male conventions and patriarchal ideology. The latter element, however, is much more important than the former. A preliminary analysis (Mämmelä 1997) of concert reviews of premieres published in the Finnish press between 1985 and 1995 supports the claim that the presence of sexist language and interpretations does not depend on the critic's gender. These phenomena are part of the language and ideology of Western art music.

Performers, new compositions, and their creators are perceived and evaluated from the male-dominated perspective of male-dominated musical life and publicity. What kind of reception can a woman composer expect in this context? The biographies of women composers through the ages support the claim that their works are primarily evaluated as works by women, that is, as curiosities, works made by someone not belonging to mainstream musical life (see, inter alia, Olson 1986 and Mitgang 1987). This was the same treatment that Saariaho received from the Finnish press at the beginning of her career, although the suspicion about her compositions was also partly due to her creation of computer-manipulated and tape music. The reviews of her early works were sour, if not harsh: "Kaija Saariaho attempts, in her work *Vers le blanc* (Toward white), to create, within the large and static overall form, micro processes so tiny that a listener does not recognize them. Indeed, one does not: the whole composition is an endless row of noise, in which absolutely nothing interesting happens" (Seppo Heikinheimo, in *Helsingin Sanomat* 4 Oct. 1983). This review could be interpreted as the reaction of a critic whose sympathies and understanding are not favorable either to minimalist processes or to computer music. A little later, however, in another review of Saariaho's works, the same critic asked, "Who would listen to Saariaho's compositions if she were an ugly woman?" which suggests that his attitudes toward women affected his evaluations of her works. Most of the articles and reviews of Saariaho's works of that time invoked her gender in one way or another. In addition, as Saariaho observed, the "feminine" vocabulary of reviews of her works is striking; "The reviews are influenced by the fact that I am a woman: 'She describes northern lights; she does this kind of feminine thing, veillike music, which has no structure; she does tone poems.' This is the pattern in which they push me, and it irritates me quite a lot, because I *am* interested in the musical form" (*Helsingin Sanomat* 20 Apr. 1991; emphasis added).

The "feminine" word and phrase choices made by journalists can be reinterpreted as sexist. How much "feminine" language is used depends on the reviewer in question, of course, and on the writer's style. An analysis of the sexism of the vocabulary used should be contextualized relative to other reviews written by the same author. As a rather general rule, however, feminine vocabulary has continued in descriptions of Saariaho in the Finnish press up to the present. Her latest premiere, *Château de l'âme* (The castle of the soul), was described with the help of adjectives such as "romantic," "sensitive," "glowing," "soft," "intimate," "beautiful" (*Helsingin Sanomat* 11 Aug. 1996). They make the reader question whether the reviews are able to perceive Saariaho's music only through particular lenses that exclude any other perception of her.

The emphasis placed on her gender was probably one of the main reasons Saariaho determinedly refused to discuss her gender in the media—at least when they let her do so. She wanted to be not a *woman* composer but a composer among other composers. She emphasized the abstract character of composing and thereby hoped to neutralize the gender of her public image. The new technology she used presumably helped her in this attempt.

Saariaho's reception in the Finnish press is affected not only by her gender, her works, and prejudice about computers as compositional tools but also by national factors. Since it is a small nation, Finland and its media have a tendency to look for heroes to promote national identity. In particular—possibly because of the role Sibelius played in the nation-building process—composers' and musicians' international successes attract the attention of the Finnish press.

The reviews written about the work *Verblendungen* (Delusions), which marked the beginning of Saariaho's breakthrough into international repute, are particularly revealing. *Verblendungen* (1982–84), a work for tape and orchestra, was commissioned by the Finnish Broadcasting Corporation and produced in collaboration with the French Radio Corporation. The tape material consists of tape noise and two sound types produced by violin: sforzando and pizzicato. The basic formal concept of the composition was a visual image giving the impression of a brushstroke, from *ffffff* to *ppppp*. In March 1984 Saariaho described the composition in her diary as "dazzling, distinct surfaces, fabrics, textures, depths. Symbolic blinding. Interpolations. Contre jour. Death. The sum of independent worlds. Shadowing, refracting colours" (brochure of the concert by the Finnish Radio Symphony Orchestra 10 Dec. 86). The Finnish reviewers from the two main newspapers were not impressed by this composition. In the light of the international success gained by *Verblendungen,* the following reviews make me wonder whether the reviewers were simply unable to recognize the work's value, whether they were insufficiently civilized to listen to its computer-manipulated microscopic nuances and the grand structure, or whether their ability to listen to and evaluate was shadowed by attitudes toward the composer's gender:

> As a composer, Kaija Saariaho has concentrated on studying long slow processes of noise, which are easiest to produce with the help of computers. *Vers le blanc,* heard last fall, was a particularly static and slow work. *Verblendungen,* premiered last Tuesday, included only two processes: the tape part moving in the opposite direction to the orchestra. Although the orchestral part had some distinct details, Kaija Saariaho's ideas seem, to me, still insufficient for such large-scale works requiring a large number of performers . . . boring it is to listen to such almost static noise, so very boring. (Seppo Heikinheimo, in *Helsingin Sanomat* 11 Apr. 1984)

> The pompous beginning of the new work promised more to the one-time listener of the sustained piece than earlier works by the dreamer-composer. However, when the imitation of the . . . bird song faded at the end, the impression of the whole remained flimsily slim. (Heikki Aaltoila, in *Uusi Suomi* 13 Apr. 1984)

Verblendungen was chosen to be performed at the festival of world music arranged by the International Society for Contemporary Music in the Netherlands in 1985, and it received the Kranichsteiner Musikpreis in Darmstadt in 1986. In their typical fashion, Finnish newspapers, journals, radio, and TV gave Saariaho considerable publicity after this success. She was also asked to comment on Finnish musical life from her perspective in Paris and to compare her experiences in Paris with those in Finland: "From a distance, Finnish musical life looks isolated and 'troubled by folk song.' Of course, we also have international composers. It is easy to be a composer in Finland: whatever kind of rubbish you write, there is always someone who performs it. Here [in Paris], it is the opposite; it is difficult to get anything performed. One performed work per year is an excellent achievement. The best thing in Paris, however, is the freedom. Here there is space for thoughts" (*Helsingin Sanomat* 24 Sept. 1986).

Because of her success abroad, Saariaho was no longer treated as a female threat to the male-dominated musical world. Instead she was seen as a "Finnish girl" who, despite her use of the newest technology, still maintained a highly admired, mythical relationship with Finnish nature. Her success induced reviewers to forgive computers and reduce the woman composer to a nature-loving girl: "Kaija Saariaho eagerly utilizes the possibilities provided by technology. They fascinate her. But one may probably still state in a slightly sentimental way that the nature-closeness of the Finnish girl has not disappeared from her. Technology and nature: perhaps there lies the secret of Kaija Saariaho's music" (Hannu-Ilari Lampila, in *Helsingin Sanomat* 22 Mar. 1987).

After her first wave of international recognition, Saariaho's career seemed to take wing. In 1988 she was awarded a Danish composition award and the Prix Italia for the radiophony *Stilleben* (Still life); in 1989 she won the Austrian Ars Electronica prize for *Stilleben* and *Io*. After establishing herself outside Finland, she could afford to assess critically the Finnish gender system, which in fact had been one of the main reasons she had left Finland to work in Paris:

> You can hardly envision a French woman as a composer. Here [in Paris] there is even more discrimination than with us. In Finland, we have an odd situation: on the one hand, we are equal; on the other, a completely patriarchal system governs. Every area must have some kind of a father figure, Kekkonen [the president of Finland for twenty-five years] or Kokkonen [one of the most prominent composers in Finland from the 1950s to 1980s]. There is something built in it; the whole system of upbringing leads to that. (*Uusi Suomi* 23 June 1988)

This kind of public criticism could no longer harm Saariaho's career as a composer in Finland. Even though she had, in the early 1980s, constantly emphasized that she did not want her gender to be a public issue and had firmly distanced herself from feminism, in the early 1990s she began to give interviews about her experiences as a woman composer and, after her first child was born, about the way she combines motherhood and composition. Some of her statements, such as the one just quoted, became critically feminist.

I suggest that, because of the international success that was much desired by a small nation, Saariaho's sex and gender were finally "forgiven" and accepted by the Finnish media. In 1991 she was one of three people who received special awards from the Finland Cultural Foundation. The way *Uusi Suomi,* one of the leading newspapers of the time, commented on this occasion is revealing:

> Composer Kaija Saariaho, 38, living in Paris, works in a traditionally male field; however, the Finnish Cultural Foundation hardly gave her the prize for such a trivial reason. It is, of course, just to say that Saariaho is our most famous woman composer and the only Finnish woman composer who has gained an international reputation. Presumably, it is more correct to see her simply as a composer (gender necessary but not crucial) who has consistently proceeded along her own path, avoided becoming bound by systems, by the dangers of "brain and paper music," and created music which impresses with its human content and which is well received everywhere. (*Uusi Suomi* 28 Feb. 1991)

Again on this occasion, Saariaho was asked to compare the cultural climate in France and in Finland, particularly with regard to their gender codes. She began to respond to these requests:

> All the important Finns are old men, including [in] music. It comes from Finnish mythology. Therefore, it is especially hard to become the only woman composer in Finland. There have always been Väinämöinens [Väinämöinen is the hero in Finnish national epics, *Kalevala*] who have the desire to rule. On the other hand, in France, discrimination is evident in public behavior more obviously than in Finland, as there are hand kisses and cheek kisses. In Finland, discrimination is hidden by the apparent equality. (Interview in *Neue Zeitschrift für Musik* Jan. 1991; in *Helsingin Sanomat* 20 Mar. 1991)

In the autumn of 1991 Saariaho took part in a special week-long "women and music" festival in Helsinki that had clear feminist aims. Ever since then, she has continued her critical assessments of gender imbalances in musical life. In addition, she freely gave me this opportunity to analyze gender as an aspect of her musical path. Her open and brave criticism regarding the Finnish gender system in music can no longer take away the national glory she has earned. The utmost praise Finnish media can possibly give to a composer is to relate her or his work to the mythical Kalevala spirit and the works of Sibelius, as in the review of one of Saariaho's latest compositions: "*Château de l'âme* is the composer's internal world which reveals its enormous treasures. The mythical level creates mantra-like, shamanistic pulsation. Has the Finnish shamanistic tradition awakened in Kaija Saariaho's music? An association with 'Luonnotar' by Sibelius and some other Kalevala-spirited works arises" (Hannu-Ilari Lampila, in *Helsingin Sanomat* 11 Aug. 1996).

Gender has long been—and perhaps still is—an obstacle in Kaija Saariaho's musical path, forcing her to negotiate her gender in socially acceptable ways within the male-dominated musical world. Saariaho's experiences demonstrate how, in order to survive, a woman composer, like a knight in an old fairy tale, must seek exactly the right strategies to overcome the obstacles put in her way simply because she is the "wrong" gender.

Gender in Music like Light Refracted by Crystal

This analysis interprets the history of a woman composer's experiences, experiences in collision with "woman" as a cultural concept in Finland. The basic premise of the analysis is that gender identity and female subjectivity are constructed at the crossroads of real-life experience and cultural representations of "woman," as much as between perceived differences between men and women, among women, and within oneself. As noted by Dorothy Smith (1987), experiences are born in relation to something, to other people, places, institutions, and practices. Furthermore, experience is a continuous process in which subjectivity is constructed: a woman localizes herself and she is localized into social reality (de Lauretis 1984, 159). Experiences relate to the process of becoming a feminist subject as well as to the cultural processes in which meanings are given or created. The gender of a "woman composer" (in fact, of any music maker) cannot be essentialized or taken for granted since it is discursively constructed, changeable, and fluid. Hence, interpretations of gender in music are in need of localization.

As a story of gender negotiation by a woman composer who has "made it," my interpretation may also be read as a story about the way in which a woman composer negotiates her gender with (but not within) the male-dominated system of Western art music and how her work becomes part of the canon.[9] As demonstrated by Marcia Citron, the works of a composer are not the only factor used to determine canonization; gender (among other things) also plays a part in this process.

In Saariaho's case the negotiation has required several strategies to overcome the Western patriarchal system's conventional gender obstacles and limitations with which she has struggled. This struggle has been situated within herself, in various sociomusical contexts, and in her interactions with people and the media. She has at specific moments neutralized, if not denied, her status as a woman in the sense in which her culture constructs the category and distanced herself from traditional gender roles, covering and masking her gender when necessary and seeking a new kind of gender position. Power is an inseparable part of these negotiations; "wrong" gender positions must be masked to achieve desired goals, and status gained provides the power to perform gender differently. The construction of new subject positions and new gender identities free from conventional constraints is a never-ending internally and externally conflicted process.

I claimed that Saariaho has negotiated her gender not "within" the male-dominated system but "with" it. In my understanding, when constructing her feminist subject position without immasculation and when, simultaneously, consistently and determinedly rejecting the "feminization" of her works and her subjectivity, she defined a new gender subject position that is not the conventional woman, not an imitation of a conventional man, and not gender neutral or androgynous; rather, it is the position of the nomadic subject. The nomadic subject position does not stay within the patriarchal art music system but instead changes it.

While I have been writing this article, I have listened to Saariaho's music intensively (see appendix B for discography). Among her works, one of my favorites is an orchestral work in two parts, *Du cristal . . . à la fumée,* which, in my opinion, provides an appropriate musical and textual metaphor for gender in relation to music: music and gender relate to each other as a crystal refracts and cuts light. Gender is performative, and gender performance is situational. In the context of music, gender performance reflects, reacts to, and interacts with the sociohistorical constraints of the music in question. Gender performance in music may also transgress the conventional gender boundaries. The metamorphosis of any conventional gender position into that of a nomad is like that from crystal to smoke. It is a metamorphosis from an organized and controlled entity into something that is unpredictable, flexible, and fluid.

Appendix A: Biographical Note

Kaija Saariaho (b. 1952) first studied visual arts, particularly graphics, before entering the Sibelius Academy, where she studied composition with Paavo Heininen from 1976 to 1981. She continued her music education in Freiburg with Brian Ferneyhough and Klaus Huberer, earning a diploma in 1983. Since 1982 she has lived in Paris, working frequently at IRCAM (Institut de Recherche et Coordination Acoustique/Musique). In 1984 she married the composer and director of the pedagogical department of the IRCAM Jean-Baptiste Barrière; the first of her two children was born in 1990.

Tape music and music produced and controlled by computer hold a central position in Saariaho's works of the 1980s, but new technology has been only one among many instrumental resources that she has used in her microscopic attention to and manipulations of sound. Timbre, harmony, and their interrelation especially interest her. According to English critic Robert Maycock, Saariaho is one of the few composers who have freed themselves from the tyranny of notes and metrics. The overall form of many compositions is based on visual ideas. Sound fields and sonic continuations are fundamental to the logic of her works, whereas melody and rhythm have played a less essential role.

Saariaho's compositions include so many kinds of compositional styles that it is quite impossible to give her work a single label. Her strongly unique style has found multiple ways to express itself. In her works of the 1990s, Saariaho turned more to acoustic instruments and melodic elements. One of her latest works, *Château de l'âme* (commissioned by the Salzburg Festival, where it premiered in August 1996), was purely acoustic.

Saariaho's compositions have achieved many international awards and recognitions, including the Kranichsteiner Musikpreis, given for *Verblendungen* in Darmstadt in 1986, which was followed by a Danish composition award (1988), the Prix Italia for the radiophony *Stilleben* (1988), the Austrian Ars Electronica prize for *Stilleben* and *Io* (1989), and the Finland Prize (1994). In 1988 she worked as a stipendiat in San Diego, California.

Over the years Saariaho has enjoyed successful concerts in several countries, for instance, in both France and England in 1989 and thereafter in Canada, Japan, and all mid-European countries. A 1992 Swiss music festival was dedicated to Saariaho and Elliot Carter, and she was one of the main composers at the music festival in Strasbourg in 1994, as well as at the Salzburg Festival in 1996. Many noted institutions have commissioned compositions from her; among others, a violin concerto entitled *Graal Théâtre* (1994), composed for Gidon Kremer, was commissioned by the BBC. In 1997 Kaija Saariaho was given an honorary title, Chevalier à l'Ordre des Arts et Lettres, in France. She is presently working on an opera that will premiere in Salzburg in 2000.

Appendix B: Selected Discography

Verblendungen, Jardin secret I, Laconisme de l'aile, . . . sah den Vögeln. Finnish Radio Symphony Orchestra, conducted by Esa-Pekka Salonen. BIS LP 307 (1986).

In Traume. Risto Poutanen, cello; Ilmo Ranta, Piano. Jase LP 00100 (1986).

Jardin Secret II. Jukka Tiensuu, harpsichord. Finlandia 1576533572 (FACD 357; 1987).

Lichtbogen. Endymion Ensemble. Finlandia 15765336 129 (FACD 361; 1989).

Verblendungen, Lichtbogen, Io, Stilleben. Avanti! Chamber Orchestra, cond. Esa-Pekka Salonen and Jukka-Pekka Saraste. Finlandia 1576533742 (FACD 374) (1989).

Jardin Secret I. Tape. Wergo WER 2025–2 (1990).

Petals. Anssi Karttunen, cello. Neuma Records 450–73 (1990).

Lichtbogen. Nouvel Ensemble Moderne. UMMUS UMM 102 (1990).

Suomenkielinen sekakuorokappale, Nej och inte. Tapiola Chamber Choir. Ondine ODE 796–2 (1992).

Maa. Several performers. Ondine ODE 791–2 (1992).

Monkey's Fingers, Velvet Hand. Aki Takahashi, piano. Eastwood TOCE-8021 (1992).

Adjö. Cluster Ensemble. Ondine ODE 808–2 (1993).

Du cristal . . . à la fumée, Nymphea (Jardin secret III). Los Angeles Philharmonic Orchestra; Kronos Quartet. Ondine ODE 804–2 (1993).

Petals. Anssi Karttunen, cello. Finlandia 4509–95767–2 (1993).

Jardin Secret II. Vivienne Spiteri, harpsichord. J and W CD 931 (1993).

Laconisme de l'aile. Pia Kaufmanas, flute. Dana Cord DACOCD 423 (1994).

Laconisme de l'aile. Manuela Wiesler, Flute. BIS-CD 689 (1995).

Nymphea. Arditti String Quartet. Disques Montaigne (1995).

Private Gardens. Ondine ODE 906 (1997).

Spins and Spells, Prés, Petals. Anssi Karttunen, cello. Petal 001 (1998).

NOTES

1. As the terms are used here, identity stems from unconscious processes, whereas political subjectivity is a conscious and deliberate position (Braidotti 1994, 166).

2. My position as author is that of a feminist ethnomusicologist with training in musicology. As Saariaho's contemporary, I have also worked in the male-dominated field of Finnish music and musicology.

3. See appendix A for a brief biographical note.

4. The interview with Kaija Saariaho was made in her childhood home in Helsinki, on 13 October 1995, when she was visiting Finland to make a speech for the fiftieth anniversary of the Finnish Composer's Union.

5. The data, which consist of close to 200 reviews and articles, are gathered from the major Finnish newspapers, *Helsingin Sanomat, Turun Sanomat, Huvudstadsbladet,* and *Uusi Suomi,* as well as from the music journals *Rondo, Synkooppi,* and *Finnish Music Quarterly.*

6. See appendix B for a selected discography.

7. When no other reference is given, the quotation is from the interview of 13 October 1995.

8. This anecdote illustrates how research is political and how the choices we make as scholars influence musical life, which in turn influences us. We are involved in musical life, and our responsibility is to be aware of—and communicate—our involvement.

9. Kaija Saariaho is without a doubt already a part of the Finnish canon of art music, and she may well be on her way to establishing herself as a part of the canon of Western contemporary music.

REFERENCES CITED

Braidotti, Rosi. 1991. *Patterns of Dissonance: A Study of Women in Contemporary Philosophy.* Cambridge, U.K.: Polity.

———. 1994. *Nomadic Subjects: Embodiment and Sexual Difference in Contemporary Feminist Theory.* New York: Columbia University Press.

Citron, Marcia. 1993. *Gender and the Musical Canon.* Cambridge: Cambridge University Press.

de Lauretis, Teresa. 1984. *Alice Doesn't: Feminism, Semiotics, Cinema.* London: Macmillan.

———. 1988. "The Essence of the Triangle; or, Taking the Essentialism Seriously." *differences* 1:3–37.

Foucault, Michel. 1984. "The Subject and Power." In *Art after Modernism: Rethinking Representation,* ed. Brian Wallis, 417–35. New York: New Museum of Contemporary Art; Boston: David R. Godine.

Koskoff, Ellen, ed. 1987. *Women and Music in Cross-Cultural Perspective.* Urbana: University of Illinois Press.

Mämmela, Paula. 1997. "Solea sopraano ja jylisevä basso" (Melodious soprano and thundering bass). M.A. thesis, Dept. of Musicology, Turku University.

Mitgang, Laura. 1987. "Germaine Tailleferre: Before, during, and after Les Six." In *The Musical Woman,* vol. 2, ed. Judith Lang Zaimont, 177–221. Westport, Conn.: Greenwood.

Moisala, Pirkko, and Riitta Valkeila. 1994. *Musiikin toinen sukupuoli* (The other sex of music). Helsinki: Otava.

Olson, Judith E. 1986. "Luise Adolpha le Beau: Composer in Late Nineteenth-Century Germany." In *Women Making Music: The Western Art Tradition, 1150–1950,* ed. by Jane Bowers and Judith Tick, 282–303. Urbana: University of Illinois Press.

Robertson, Carol E. 1987. "Power and Gender in the Musical Experiences of Women." In *Women and Music in Cross-Cultural Perspective,* ed. Ellen Koskoff, 225–44. Urbana: University of Illinois Press.

Smith, Dorothy. 1987. *The Everyday World as Problematic: A Feminist Sociology.* Boston: Northeastern University Press.

Margaret Myers

This essay mainly discusses the process of researching my doctoral dissertation, "Blowing Her Own Trumpet: European Ladies' Orchestras and Other Women Musicians 1870–1950 in Sweden" (Göteborg University, 1993). The research was carried out in various European countries during 1988–92. The sources used included documentary material (original historical sources and modern musicological sources, among others) and interviews with seventeen former musicians from some of the last surviving ladies' orchestras.

In this essay I will first illustrate what is meant by a "ladies' orchestra." Second, I will sketch some of the problems that arose during the process of carrying out research on this project. The structure of this essay thus works backward from the result to the research process. This is necessary since (for music-historical reasons that I hope will become evident) few people have any clear idea of the object studied: European ladies' orchestras during the eighty years from 1870 to 1950.

Overview of European Ladies' Orchestras

Origins, Distribution, and Decline

Independent, peripatetic European ladies' orchestras (*Damenorchestern/Damenkapellen*) first appeared in the German-speaking countries of central Europe around the middle of the nineteenth century. The activities and living conditions of ladies' and other peripatetic orchestras can be compared in many respects to those of traveling theater and circus troupes. Ladies' orchestras constituted a generally accepted category of entertainment orchestra (*Unterhaltungsorchester*). Sources indicate that they reached the height of their popularity early in the twentieth century and that they were then even more numerous than men's orchestras (*Herrenorchestern/Herrenkapellen*), another generally accepted category.

In my dissertation I identified a "first wave" of ladies' orchestras running from ca. 1870[1] until just after World War I, with a "second wave" stretching to the 1940s. These orchestras were a common and ubiquitous feature of European musical culture from the mid-nineteenth century until World War I.

Documentary sources clearly identify around two hundred ladies' orchestras during the 1890s. Their numbers peaked at around three hundred orchestras in the twentieth century's first decade.[2] Thousands of women instrumental musicians found employment in these orchestras. Ladies' orchestras must thus be regarded—along with music teaching—as a major source of employment for women instrumentalists until the end of World War I.

After the war their numbers decreased radically, as did those of other types of entertainment orchestras. Centralized music distribution (gramophone, radio, and sound films) was the major factor in reducing the demand for live music, and other economic factors made it no longer profitable for restaurants to hire orchestras. Duos, a pianist, or mechanical means of music reproduction replaced bands.

The Musicians' Social Background and Education

The members of the first wave of Damenkapellen came mainly from the lower-middle artisan class, often from families of musicians.[3] The members varied in age and civil status from prepubertal children (where possible, exploited as child prodigies) to married or unmarried middle-aged women. One or more male family members might be included, but they were in a clear minority in these orchestras. Apart from playing a musical role, they would have had a useful function in conducting the business side of the enterprise (compare Reich 1993, 130–32, 138).

Musicians were educated primarily by parents or other family connections (as with circus and theater families). They continued this education as apprentices, often in a family band (again like circus and theater families). Some complemented their education with private lessons from conservatory professors, and a few attended a conservatory. Some (how great a proportion is at present not established) learned their art at the special music school for orchestra musicians at Preßnitz, in Bohemia (Anonymous 1934). At least one other music school, at Graslitz, near Karlsbad, remains to be investigated.

The musicians in the second wave of ladies' orchestras had more varied social backgrounds. Factors concerned with World War I and new technology (the introduction of the gramophone and radio, and the movement of musicians from restaurants to the silent cinema) seem to have combined to break links with the older tradition of family bands. Family backgrounds in the "second wave" were still usually lower middle class but not necessarily musical. Music education might be acquired via private teachers or music schools, not, as formerly, through family connections.

The Hungarian violinist Lily Gyenes (b. 1904), whose twenty Hungarian Gypsy Girls created a sensation as they swept through the capitals of Europe in the 1930s, charming royalty and plebians alike, said of her education: "My mother didn't have the means as a girl to learn any music, but she decided that if she had a child, it would learn to play, and it would play the violin. I wasn't more than six years old when she bought a violin and forced me to learn it. . . . First, I attended a music school for small children, and I didn't want to practice. . . . Hungary is a musical country where 90 percent have (musical) aptitude. My mother didn't know whether I had aptitude or not" (see list of interviews in "References Cited").

Lily Gyenes sailed through the music school and was accepted at the Franz Liszt Academy in Budapest, where she acquired a thorough schooling. She was thus one of the few musicians in ladies' orchestras to attend a conservatory: "At the academy I took extra subjects—history, quartet, orchestra, chamber music . . . , not composition, but harmony, counterpoint, everything. I have credits in twelve subjects."

Some musicians of the second wave were largely self-taught. This was a consequence of the technical accessibility of new types of popular music as well as the relative cheapness of instruments and sound reproductions or sheet music. One of these autodidacts is the accordionist Maj Åhlén (b. 1925). She started her musical education as a small girl by attempting the difficult feat of playing tunes on her foster father's violin while accompanying herself with chords on the mouth organ. She tired of the violin, and her next step (at the age of fifteen) was to exchange it for an accordion, without asking her foster father's permission first. When she was twenty-one, she made friends with two girls—one a guitarist and the other an accordionist—whom she met in a music shop. They decided to continue their music making together, which they did, playing in public and learning as they went. As Åhlén later said: "I am completely self-taught, so I can't read music, unfortunately."

Apprenticeship in a family band was no longer the norm. Family orchestras with members from a wide age range became the exception, the rule being ensembles made up of individuals of the same age who found each other via advertisements, agencies, or personal contacts. Men still sometimes appeared in these ladies' bands. They were either relatives (usually husbands) of the musicians or—at least during the 1930s and 1940s—unattached males.

The Musical Status and Standards of Ladies' Orchestras

Musicians in European ladies' orchestras during both these periods were entertainers who often regarded themselves as artists (*Künstler*) and strove to uphold a reputation as such. This was also true of musicians in men's orchestras. The columns of *Der Artist* are filled with ladies' and men's orchestras using the word *Künstler* in their names, as emphasis and for safety's sake. Adult musicians in both types of orchestra had to be experienced and professional, both in their standards of performance and in their full-time practice of their vocation.

Even during the second wave, when jazz musicians no longer stressed that they were Künstler, ladies' bands still had to compete with all other bands. Some of the ladies' orchestra musicians whom I interviewed had the impression that they were judged negatively on account of their gender, but we must remember here that even some male musicians in entertainment orchestras were sensitive and uncertain about their status in the eyes of the world: "The general public looked down upon the professional musician, and socially he was not considered to rank particularly high. . . . To think of those great composers, and yet have to play jazz. . . . He should have played the violin or cello, or some other proper instrument. They were the true artists" (Abrahamsson 1945, 85, 110).

The pianist Asta Ek (b. 1912), despite being a successful musician in the 1930s, had no illusions. According to her, the Swedish Musicians' Union was negative to women: "Women musicians—they were worth nothing! . . . It was the tradition at that time to discriminate against women in all sorts of careers." Greta Sundell (b. 1901), a cellist, confirmed that male musicians in restaurant orchestras looked down on women musicians in general, believing themselves to be superior musicians: "At least they thought so themselves! Ladies' orchestras were nothing." One or two musicians were not aware of having met any prejudice, however, although this may have resulted from their youth and inexperience, as perhaps was the case with the saxophone player Elsa Ruda (b.1908), who said, "[I] didn't feel that anybody looked down on us."

Restaurants were the primary employers of entertainment orchestras, which they used to attract customers. Restaurants were often in severe competition with one another. Fashionable restaurants in Europe's famous watering places—spas, seaside resorts, or urban cultural centers—provided important meeting and mating grounds for the wealthy international upper crust. More modest hotel restaurants in large and small towns throughout Europe provided food, company, and music on a daily basis for a wider variety of clientele: bachelors, travelers, and families mostly from the middle classes. Summer concerts in hotel gardens, in parks, and on piers could attract all and sundry.

Engagements lasted at least one month and often several—perhaps a whole summer or winter season. The choice of band was vital, since a bad orchestra—like inferior food or unattractive premises—could drive off all the customers within a week. If this is not enough to convince the music historian of these groups' high musical standards, a glance at the repertory of any single orchestra will do so. About a thousand and sometimes up to two thousand works were currently performable. An orchestra with a repertory of only five hundred works was considered substandard. In addition, the music they played was technically demanding. Most of the pieces could be described as very difficult, difficult, or at least moderately difficult (see figure 7.1).[4]

A further factor to consider in this context is the work situation in which ladies' orchestras found themselves during both periods. Orchestras were on stage for up to six hours every day of the year, year after year. The only breaks were for traveling, plus a day or two each at Christmas and Easter, at least for the first-wave musicians. Later on a day off each week was introduced, thanks to campaigning by musicians' unions.

There was little if any time for rehearsal. New pieces were tried out early in the evenings before the main influx of customers. All this would have required good musicianship, including excellent sight-reading, stamina, good nerves, and experience. A missed repeat might temporarily sabotage a reputation. Also, musicians had to be prepared for the audiences' requests, which might involve taxing solos. When asked whether they had time for rehearsals, pianist Asta Ek answered with a raw laugh: "Never! Very, very seldom. It might happen on some rare occasion, if there was something special, something difficult, if, for example, we were to play a difficult overture, such as 'Orpheus in the Underground' [*sic*]. I played it straight off, however. I used to say when we were busy with something I'd never seen before: 'Can we hop over it so I can sit and read it in the interval.' So I read it through . . . (for) all the markings."

It was almost impossible to get the second-wave women musicians whom I interviewed to give a direct value judgment of their musical standards. Only one of them, Asta Ek, dared to say about her ensemble, Mary Aston's Ladies'

Figure 7.1. Excerpt of Saint-Saëns's *Samson et Dalila*, arranged by Ernest Alder; score courtesy of Inga Böckmann-Sandberg.

Trio, "We were good." For value judgments I had to rely on the music critics. The following two examples were typical. The first, from 1934, confirms Ek's comment: "During the whole of the present season, Mary Aston's Ladies' Trio has been responsible for the entertainment and has done so in a splendid way. The three young ladies do not only have musical feeling and ambition but also technical proficiency and besides that infectious good humour, which, especially on dance evenings, carries the public with them and enhances the party atmosphere" (Anonymous 1934). The second, from 1948, praises Britt Johnstone's White Ladies: "The band plays modern as well as older dance music equally brilliantly, and it masters the classical repertoire just as superbly. The three ladies are, moreover, pure quick-change artists, who one minute play one instrument and then the next cast themselves over another. The band's arsenal of instruments is truly impressive" (Anonymous 1948).

Orchestral Size and Instrumental Inventory

During the first wave ladies' orchestras varied in size from quartets or quintets to sixty-piece bands. The words *orchestra* and *band* (*Orchester* and *Kapelle*, respectively, were the original German terms) seem to have been used indiscriminately without reference to size or instrumental structure. As time went on, ensembles tended to diminish in size, so that by the 1920s a piano trio was the most common structure. The reasons behind this development were economic rather than musical.

Variations in instrumentation might depend on economic factors too, on which musicians or family members were available, or on the ensemble leader's taste and intentions. The basic instruments were violin, cello, and piano, and to these might be added any number of a wide range of string, woodwind, brass, and percussion instruments, as well as harmonium, according to convenience. Some bands consisted entirely of mixed wind or only brass instruments (e.g., *Damen-Blas-Orchestern* or *Damen-Trompeter-Korps*).

Just as the size of the bands changed, so also did their repertory and instrumentation. Repertory obviously influenced instrumentation. As early as the late nineteenth century, a few choruses and bands performing American and African American "Negro," or "nigger," music had begun to appear in Europe. Their members were usually black males (except in the choruses), and their numbers increased rapidly up to World War I.

The umbrella-term *jazz* was imported to cover the new African American music. Negro spirituals, tangos, Boston waltzes, Charlestons, shimmies, cakewalks, black bottoms, and Negro serenades became in turn all the rage, competing with and threatening to oust the older European repertory. Jazz required instruments different from those required by the old-fashioned art/ salon music repertory (I return to this issue later). Violinists, cellists, and even pianists had to learn second instruments and jazzy, syncopated, blue-note styles of playing. Soon all musicians were proficient on at least two instruments. Guitars, ukeleles, banjos, saxophones, jazz trumpets, trombones, clarinets, different types of percussion, plucked double basses, and accordions all found their ways into the hands of women musicians, especially those of the second wave.

The Repertory

Orchestras depended on demand. They had to be able to play the standard works expected of them. One category used within Western music during the nineteenth and early twentieth centuries was that of salon music (*Salonmusik*). This could include short pieces of both program music (including a large proportion of character pieces) and absolute music (see Myers 1993, 80–82, for a discussion of salon music). The diffuse term was often used pejoratively to mean light, trivial music. Its closest modern equivalent is perhaps "popular music," also an elastic category.

Both waves of entertainment orchestras, including ladies' orchestras, were sometimes accused of sinning against artistic expectations by playing too much salon music in the first case and too much jazz and too many popular hit tunes in the second. Their respective program contents varied to some extent from orchestra to orchestra, but the general impression given by the material collected is of balance between shorter pieces with great popular appeal and the more substantial works. As one journalist put it in 1916 in his review of Josef Pöschl's Damenorchester Walzertraum:

> When a band calls itself "The Waltz Dream," it appeals to the taste of that audience which principally wants to hear easily digestible, caressingly graceful, in a word, popular music of the day, from the concert tribune at a restaurant. The Waltz Dream Band's program also adheres to the popular style, but strangely enough, its great popularity everywhere it has had engagements has not arisen exclusively for this reason. Their repertoire in fact more than just fulfills what their name promises, for the leader, Pöschl, follows that which is a natural inclination for a full-blooded musician, to sacrifice not only to the profane but to the higher art. (*Restauratören* 1–2, no. 5 [1916]: 53)

As this review intimates, opinions sometimes differed as to program contents and the desirable proportion of lighter goods to the more serious stuff. The wishes of the proprietor, the audience, and the musicians had to be balanced against one another, and it was often the proprietor or the audience who demanded the lighter, shorter pieces. Asta Ek recounted an apparently unusual incident from the 1930s when some guests requested a long, serious work: "They requested the Valkyrie [selection]. We thought there was no danger in it, since there were no other guests, only them. It was so early in the afternoon, perhaps 4 P.M. . . . so we played the Valkyrie—the Alder trio [arrangement]. It was then that we started with the Alder trios. . . . Fantastic arrangements! . . . So I received an insane scolding from Director Claesson . . . that we were going to ruin his business!"

The heavy, locked music cupboards with which the first wave of ladies' orchestras traveled held a repertory consisting of up to two thousand pieces of varying length and technical and musical difficulty, all of which were currently programmable. "There was music by the kilo," as the double bass player Ally Pettersson (1910–98) expressed it. Twenty-minute-long opera or operetta overtures and fantasias/selections/potpourris (e.g., of Mozart, Beethoven, Weber, Wagner, Suppé, Strauss, Offenbach, Meyerbeer, Gounod, Bizet, Rossini, Verdi, Mascagni, Puccini, Donizetti, and Leoncavallo) were programmed along with shorter pieces. The latter were a mixture of dances (e.g., by Léhar, Strauss, and Waldteufel), marches (e.g., by Sousa, Teike, and Asch), and character pieces (e.g., by Schumann, Schubert, Grieg, Mendelssohn and most of the previously listed composers, to name but a few). These genres formed the core of the repertory. There existed a wealth of popular German arrangements for large salon orchestras (*grosses Salon-Orchester*), but as time went on Émile Tavan's and Ernest Alder's masterly piano trio arrangements of orchestral works became very popular. They were so skillfully done that they enabled a trio to mimic a whole orchestra. They also put greater pressure on each musician's technique. Each had now to be a soloist.

Works were often adapted or arranged by the musicians themselves, without being written down. One part might be omitted or doubled and another transposed for an instrument quite different from the one indicated. Musicians knew their craft and were flexible. The cellist Greta Sundell said in an interview that she often had a rough time, for her bandleader expected her to fill in "two bars of horn here" and to transpose at sight a difficult clarinet part there: "When I had played them, I threw [the pages of music] on the ground beside me. When I had played those potpourris, there

Table 7.1. The Most Popular Composers and Works, 1900s

Composer	Title	Type
Waldteufel	Ganz Allerliebst	Waltz
Waldteufel	Schlittschuläufer	Waltz
Waldteufel	Dolores	Waltz
Waldteufel	Sirenzauber	Waltz
Waldteufel	Estudiantina	Waltz
Waldteufel	Immer oder Nimmer	Waltz
Waldteufel	España	Waltz
Waldteufel	Goldregen	Waltz
Verdi	La Traviata	Fantasia
Verdi	Rigoletto	Fantasia
Verdi	Il Trovatore	Fantasia
Rossini	Guillaume Tell	Overture
Rossini	L'Italiana in Algeri	Overture
Rossini	Semiramide	Fantasia
Flotow	Martha	Fantasia
Flotow	Stradella	Fantasia
J. Strauss	Der Zigeunerbaron	Potpourri
J. Strauss	Wiener Blut	Waltz

Source: Myers 1993, 270.

was a whole sea of music lying there left behind. . . . One had to be very alert—very sharp!"

During the first wave, each printed evening concert program listed on average twelve pieces, with two intervals (see, e.g., figure 7.2). The concerts took place from 6 P.M. to 11 P.M. or later. Times varied. Matinees were often given on Sundays and sometimes on other days in the holiday season. As the twentieth century wore on, dance evenings became common and popular too (as indicated in the previously quoted reviews of Mary Aston and Britt Johnstone).

Ladies' orchestras, along with other types of entertainment orchestras, disseminated the newest pieces in the musical repertory. They reached out to many audiences, some of which had few other means of contact with professionally performed music before the days of gramophones and radios (especially people who lived in small provincial towns or rural areas). During the first wave concert halls and restaurants alike welcomed these orchestras all over Europe and elsewhere, whereas during the second wave they were more confined to restaurants and newly opened dance halls.

Repertory and Reputation

World War I (and then World War II) brought waves of Americans to Europe, and the popularity of jazz increased, although not with everyone. Jazz caused

Figure 7.2. Two programs from the Modell Ladies' Orchestra's visit to Jönköping, Sweden, in 1910.

havoc among classically schooled European musicians and music critics. They felt threatened by what they regarded as its low technical and musical level compared to the high-art European heritage, which they as artists felt themselves called to defend. Also, their jobs were in danger, since jazz music drew audiences, while European music in restaurants and on dance floors did so less and less. Most musicians were forced to compromise and play a mixture of old and new.

Jazz pushed even lighter salon pieces in the European repertory, such as Viennese waltzes, to the respectable side of the nineteenth-century art music (*Kunstmusik*)–entertainment music polarity. Bourgeois society turned a discreetly blind eye to the potently erotic associations of a large proportion of salon pieces, and the commercial aspect was not a matter of general aware-ness or discussion. Jazz, however, was overtly concerned with sex and com-mercialism and thus not at all respectable, though it was definitely popular. Also, it was seen as originating with an inferior species of human being.

The alignment and entanglement of the art music–entertainment mu-sic polarity with the polarity involving definitions of respectability versus nonrespectability put women musicians, whose moral respectability was a precondition for their employment at respectable establishments, modest or fashionable, in a difficult position (cf. Reich 1993, 132). To maintain their moral reputations, they had to perform art music and, if possible, prove themselves to be artists of the highest rank. To maintain their popularity, they had to play jazz, making efforts at the same time to avoid undermin-ing their respectability and their employment possibilities.

Many compromised, as did their male colleagues, but for women it was an especially tricky situation. One means of protecting themselves from calumny was to keep together, sharing rooms and acting as one another's chaperones. Another means was to emphasize their respectability in their publicity (see Reich 1993, 138). One of my interviewees, the violinist Astrid Steijer (b. 1909), was irritated by the emphasis put on respectability in a magazine article in 1932: "They kept on telling [the readers] that we were decent girls . . . , so it was really the case at the time that people didn't think it was really appropriate" (in Myers 1993, 364).

From the late 1920s onward some women's jazz bands did appear in Europe despite all the difficulties. In *Der Artist* in 1926, for example, we find E. Glotzbach's Damen-Jazz- und Stimmungs-Band typically advertising its services side by side with various more old-fashioned *Wiener-Damen-Orches-tern* (Viennese ladies orchestras), *Damen-Trompeter-Korps* (ladies' trumpet corps), and family bands, as well as many others of its own ilk (*Der Artist* 1926, no. 2091, 15:1).

Presentation and Reception

Like any band or individual musician, ladies' orchestras needed to attract attention to gain employment. High musical standards were not enough; visibility was vital, and appearance was an important factor. Sex, youth, eth-nicity, beauty, glamour, virtuosity, charisma, showmanship, and costume were all means widely exploited to gain attention. Daily newspapers and musical trade papers advertised many sorts of ensembles, including military bands; Tyrolean, Hungarian, Romanian, Russian, and Gypsy orchestras; children's orchestras; boys' bands; men's orchestras; and ladies' orchestras.

Ladies' orchestras, by virtue of their nomenclature, overtly used their members' sex as one of many eye-catching attributes. Costume was another attribute they exploited, in common with all other orchestras. Illustrations show ladies' orchestra musicians, both first and second wave, dressed in dazzling long evening dresses, with high necks and long sleeves, usually uniform or matching (see figure 7.3). Another variation was national dress. Both these types of clothing transmitted messages of respectability and serious professionalism.

As times and fashions changed, shorter skirts, shorter sleeves, and lower necklines became acceptable, as did special costumes including trousers (e.g., quasi-military uniforms and sailor suits; see figure 7.4). Even more exotic national costumes might be donned (e.g., Japanese). Evening dresses were still the norm, however. Ladies' orchestras always had several sets of concert clothes, sometimes one dress for each day of the week. Sometimes they even changed costume during a break in an evening performance. The cellist

Figure 7.3. Anny Wollman's Ladies' Orchestra, n.d. Photo courtesy of G. Fridell. Copied by András Bánovits and reproduced by kind permission.

Figure 7.4. Baby Stars, 1931–32. Photo courtesy of Astrid Steijer. Copied by András Bánovits and reproduced by kind permission.

Margareta Portnoff (b. 1914) shared the other interviewees' pleasure in their striking costumes: "We had Russian costumes . . . and long evening gowns. . . . We had a [different] dress for every day as well as starting to change during the evening to less formal . . . costumes, rather imaginative clothes which were more fun. . . . We had to look alike."

Ladies' orchestras performed in restaurants, a traditionally male public sphere. This had consequences for how they were perceived and received. Initially there was a good deal of skepticism among audiences and critics as to the possible qualities of a ladies' orchestra: "Since the beginning of the month, concert music is performed by Pöschl's Hungarian Ladies' Band. Our skepticism in the presence of the feminine [element] was subjugated when we heard the band play" (*Restauratören* 1–2, no. 5 [1916]: 53).

Attitudes to women performers in the public sphere were complex, to say the least. Women musicians had to live with a situation in which they were seen first as women, the sexual objects of men, and only second as musicians. Countless reviews and articles by male journalists and authors (there were few if any women journalists at this time) show this attitude, exemplified by statements from the critics quoted in this essay: "Rydberg with its Spanish ladies' orchestra is hardly in need of special recommendation—beautiful Spanish women are thus in great favour with Mr Stockholm and when they in addition to this are also able to play well, well then . . ." (Anonymous 1913). This sort of comment, focusing more on the sexual attractiveness of the musicians than on their musical skills, was commonplace. Nevertheless, the skills of ladies' orchestras could not be wholly ignored, and they were usually briefly, secondarily, and perhaps also slightly grudgingly acknowledged, as is the case here. Another example is offered by the Viennese Ladies' Orchestra led by Marie Schipek. It had about sixty members. In 1885 George Bernard Shaw attended a performance at Battersea's Albert Palace in his capacity as music critic:

> Fancy . . . the apparition in full sunlight of a charming person of the other sex in a crimson silk military tunic and white skirt. Fancy at her heels a string of nearly sixty instrumentalists, all more or less charming, and all in crimson tunics and white skirts. Fancy a conductor distinguished by a black silk skirt, and sleeves made somewhat shorter and wider than the others, so as to give free play to a plump wrist and arm. . . . The effect of the "lady orchestra" as a whole is novel and very pleasant. They are inferior to the Strauss band in precision and perfection of detail; but the Strauss impetuosity was forced, false, and often misplaced and vulgar: these Viennese ladies seem inspired by a feminine delight in dancing that makes them play dance music in a far more captivating fashion than their male rivals. They have grace, tenderness and moderation: qualities which are very refreshing after two months of the alternate sentimentality and self-assertiveness of Eduard Strauss, than whom, by the bye, Madame Marie Schipek, the conductor, is a much more dashing violinist. (Shaw 1981, 1:335–40)

As is well known, this assignment of particular (musical) characteristics to a particular gender is common. According to this system of gendered aesthetics, where the values applied to masculine and feminine qualities mirror the hierarchy between the sexes in real life, an especially good ladies' orchestra or woman musician might be accorded the highest conceivable praise of the day by being masculinized: "Directress Saro Bekker had it in her to use her bow in a truly masculine manner" (Johnsson 1908).

The musicians whom I interviewed also had this experience, for example, the violinist Astrid Steijer, who was complimented for her strong, full tone: "You play with masculine tone," she was told.

Negative—in fact, thoroughly impolite and ungentlemanly—comments on musicians' appearance were printed at times, too, although the musicians whom I have interviewed did not tell of any such incidents: "Older women in a ladies' orchestra have the effect of slight cloud in a sunny sky, and the best place that these can take is behind the double bass, which harmonises well with the solid, thick-set creature" (Johnsson 1908).

It has not been possible to gauge the degree to which awareness of these negative attitudes affected the musicians. Such comments were more the exception than the rule. Most critics treated ladies' orchestras with a basic respect, compelled by their musicianship, but this did not hinder a dissonant, sexually facetious overtone from sometimes creeping in. Women musicians were obviously aware of their position as women, as is evident in the following statement by the cellist Greta Sundell: "Lilly Ekström was a good pianist but very fat. A man might have three chins and a beer belly and that didn't mean a thing, but women had to look nice."

The Invisibility of Ladies' Orchestras as a Historical Phenomenon

First Inklings

The preceding material details some of the facts about ladies' orchestras I was able to establish, facts unknown to the scholarly world before my research. Looking at them now, so clear and self-apparent, I find it difficult to recall the state of ignorance and confusion in which I started systematically searching in 1986. The first impulse came when a librarian who knew I was a musicologist gave me a jolt by casually reporting that her mother and two maternal aunts had played in "ladies' orchestras."

I had never heard of such a category. Bearing in mind the ages of the librarian's mother and aunts, I assumed that they were pioneers in new careers that had opened up to women since the women's suffrage movement. The mother was dead, and at first I was told that the aunts were too old and deaf to be interviewed, although months later my librarian friend did interview them for me using an elementary questionnaire, since I hardly knew what to ask.

Initially I could not clearly identify my object and therefore did not know even how to focus my search, what to seek, or where to start looking for it. I was dealing with a phenomenon that had been invisible to me, although as I later discovered, it had been right under my nose—and for that matter, everybody else's noses, too—all the time.

Mechanisms of Invisibility

Why was the phenomenon of ladies' orchestras so invisible? First, there was no accepted definition of what constituted a ladies' orchestra. Second, sources on this subject had never been cataloged as such or collated. Tantalizing and contradictory sightings had been reported here and there, for example, in Carol Neuls-Bates's pioneer volume of source readings *Women in Music* (1982), in Cyril Ehrlich's study *The Music Profession in Britain since the Eighteenth Century* (1985), in George Bernard Shaw's (1981) nineteenth-century music criticism, and in Greta Kent's charming musical autobiography *A View from the Bandstand* (1983). Only Neuls-Bates was known to me when I started my search.

Third, ladies' orchestras landed on the "wrong" side of the great divide between art music and popular musics that developed during the nineteenth century in Western musical life. Orthodox musicology has not accorded popular musics much attention—that is, made them visible or audible to us—until quite recently. In this musicological negligence, a process of devaluation is quite clearly implied. Fourth, the same sort of musicological neglect and devaluation was applied consistently to women instrumental musicians in the public sphere until recently, when feminist musicology started to repair the damage and to correct some of the false assumptions of traditional musicology.

Later on in my search I came to the conclusion that the lack of definition and source cataloging and collation resulted from the combination of this musicological neglect and devaluation with the anomalous nature of the phenomenon itself. As historians of all categories know, anomalies and devalued categories tend to slip through the theoretical meshes of traditionally constructed historical nets.

I found that Simone de Beauvoir had articulated this problem helpfully in her classic study *The Second Sex* (1986 [1949]), where she describes anomalous woman as being seen as "the Other" in all historically and socially "significant" contexts. Recently theories of difference or the Other are being revalued and developed in the context of feminist and gay studies, as well as in ethnomusicology (see, e.g., McClary 1991; Solie 1993; Citron 1993).

Ladies' Orchestras: Some Contradictory Views

My initial problem with the phenomenon of ladies' orchestras was the vague and contradictory evidence. The contemporary nineteenth-century source reproduced by Neuls-Bates (1982, 193) gave the impression of sweet young things looking pretty and playing a limited range of instruments only fairly convincingly. Bernard Shaw, also a contemporaneous source, was amused by and gallantly praised the sixty-musician-strong Viennese band that played at the Albert Palace in Battersea, London, in 1885. He obviously reacted powerfully to the sheer sensation of the event, not to mention to the ladies' physical charms, especially those of their leader. He did, however, find the ladies' playing more musical than that of Eduard Strauss's orchestra, and he seems to have found them truly professional (Shaw 1981, 1:335–40), in contrast to the Viennese orchestra described in Neuls-Bates's book.

A literary sighting was Jean Anouilh's play *L'Orchestre. Pièce Concert* (1975 [1957]). Here the women members of the band are shown as unattractive, unmusicianly, and interested only in malicious gossip or the seduction of the only male in the band, the married pianist. The few comments I had found in Swedish musicological sources confirmed the view of ladies' orchestra musicians as musically worthless and morally questionable (e.g., Nyqvist 1983; Edström 1982).

Did I really want to spend years of my life rooting about in what seemed on balance to be a subject of depressing mediocrity? Would it not be more merciful to let sleeping dogs lie? My worst fears were confirmed by an article by Dorothea Kaufmann (1991) in which she commented that the disappearance of ladies' orchestras around the time of World War I was really nothing to be regretted, since their standards were so low and vulgar. A certain unease about this view of ladies' orchestras made me keep going, however. It did not tally with my intuition or with what I was learning from my librarian's aunts. Anyway, by that time I was committed to this study, for better or worse. Scientific integrity demanded completion of the project.

In the end I was compelled to explore the idea that the impression of ladies' orchestras that had been passed on to me (and to Dorothea Kaufmann) was informed by contemporary nineteenth-century ideas about the nature of women as received by the (invariably male) commentators and authors who had passed their views on to us. The latter-day Aristotelians—Schopenhauer, Nietzsche, Weininger, and in Sweden, Strindberg—were all the rage in the late nineteenth and early twentieth centuries. They were published and republished in cheap popular editions and quoted in daily newspapers and the popular press. Their ideas permeated most educated people's thinking. They were all thoroughly misogynist and denied women all creative and artistic capacity, as had their forefather, Aristotle, whose ideas had survived into modern times because they resonated with the ideas of the Church Fathers.

These misogynist ideas were projected on any woman who embarked on a public, professional career in occupations defined as masculine or creative. Such a woman had to be prepared for ridicule and castigation. She might be accused of being essentially male or essentially immoral. She might also be accused of being too feminine. Femininity was automatically classed as a weakness or a defect, since masculinity was strength and the norm for full humanity. Women working outside the home as artists—especially if they were exotic—were usually regarded as sexually "loose" and thus fair game for any man who might care to seduce, slander, or otherwise abuse them. For women during the period in question, seduction without marriage spelled ruin.

As soon as I had documented the sources of and the mechanisms behind the negative impression of ladies' orchestras that had initially reached me, as well as some of its forms of expression, I was able to proceed in a more hopeful and constructive spirit. The search for and examination of contemporary sources containing information about the orchestras constituted a major task.

Sources and the Search

Chance and intuition played a not insignificant role in the search for sources. Could I find sources that would let me piece together a coherent picture of ladies' orchestras (not to mention satisfy the requirements for a doctoral dissertation)? There were many questions to be answered apart from those about the nature of the object itself. How far did the temporal, geographical, and sociocultural limits extend? Did ladies' orchestras have any special musical significance? What music and instruments did their members play? What significance did they have as an area of professional musical activity for women? Was there a special market for ladies' orchestras? How did they differ from other entertainment orchestras, if they differed at all?

Musicologists whom I consulted had generally not considered this type of ensemble. I found only two articles mentioning historical ladies' orchestras—the one already mentioned, by Dorothea Kaufmann (1991), and one by Claudia Friedel (1990). Two literary sources that contain portraits of ladies' orchestras, Anouilh's play *L'Orchestre,* of which I was already aware, and one I discovered later, Oscar Straus's operetta *Ein Walzertraum* (1907), were interesting and amusing, but were they scientifically relevant?

Library catalogs in various countries where ladies' orchestras had been reported directly or indirectly were mainly unhelpful, first with regard to general categories (e.g., "café chantant," "Caféhausmusik," "Salonmusik," "Damenorchester," or "Unterhaltungsmusik") and later with regard to specific names (e.g., Wiener-Damen-Solist-Orchester, Perkêo, or the Biseras). As far as I remember, I never found any such references. Bibliographies, even those in modern musicological works that otherwise documented women musicians and composers, did not give much by way of leads either. Encyclopedias were no better.

I contacted Swedish evening newspapers in the search for more former musicians still living. This resulted in an unexpected response from about a dozen women. In the end I had seventeen Swedish survivors from the second wave of ladies' orchestras (post–World War I). I started interviewing them. They were certain that ladies' orchestras began in the 1920s to 1940s. Their certainty on this point initially convinced me that ladies' orchestras were indeed a postsuffrage phenomenon, bar the odd exception. The seventeen interviews contributed rich material that generally corroborated the deductions I was making based on the historical documentary sources.

Not until a different project drove me to start searching in a Swedish newspaper index (*Svenskt Press Register*, 1880–1900) that reached back into the 1880s did I understand that ladies' orchestras had been relatively common before 1900. I found a few references purely by chance. Only then did I realize the possible extent of the subject of ladies' orchestras. I had to work backward through years of Swedish daily papers, searching for references to ladies' orchestras until I reached a point in time where I found no more. The time span had quickly more than doubled, from thirty to at least seventy years.

I tested different types of literature for information. Memoirs; fiction; girls', women's, and "gentlemen's" magazines; trade papers; daily newspapers; posters; programs; trades union files; music conservatory registers; and other documents. Some of these sources contained slivers of useful information. The process was hermeneutic. The more slivers I juggled around, the clearer became the object I was trying to get into focus, and the clearer the object became, the easier it was to assess the significance of the individual slivers and to juggle them into place.

A major breakthrough occurred in 1990 when I tracked down the German trade paper *Der Artist* (see the reference list for the full title). It existed from 1883 and functioned at least from 1892 until 1941 as an international employment agency for performers of all types, from circus acrobats and theater companies to entertainment orchestras and virtuoso musicians. It proved a treasure trove, since it covered most of the period I was researching and documented the existence of hundreds of ladies' orchestras, giving details of their membership, instrumental structure, and travels (see figure 7.5). Information from *Der Artist* filled in a number of gaps, confirmed a number of theories, and helped in the identification of many already listed bands.

Figure 7.5. A page from *Der Artist* no. 1351, 1 January 1911.

Ladies' Orchestras: Defining the Reality

The juxtaposition of facts gleaned from such sources as posters, concert programs, trades union files, conservatory documents, and *Der Artist* with more subjective items such as newspaper reviews, memoirs, and interviews with musicians painted a picture of extremely professional, hard-working orchestras that, in competition with many others of similar capacity, succeeded in creating a year-round, economically viable, and sometimes even pleasurable living for their members, often within a family framework lasting several decades (at least during the first wave).

I perceived that, contrary to one of my earliest impressions, this life had not been one glamorous, amusing fête for the musicians in ladies' orchestras. They were obviously engaged in the same fight for a living as everyone else. There were many hardships to be endured or overcome: months or years far away from home; uncomfortable travel on smelly steamships across wintry seas or on cramped trains with heavy instruments and music cupboards; crowded living quarters, three or four to a room; long working hours and no holidays; smoky, noisy restaurants as working quarters; and sexual harassment from male guests or music critics.

This study shared with Cyril Ehrlich's the problem of giving "a general portrait of the profession" before "more work was done on individual cases" (Ehrlich 1985, 3). Like Ehrlich, I exercised caution by applying his "elementary safeguards": not generalizing from exceptional cases, not judging the merits of a musician only on the basis of institutionalized education, and not necessarily taking surviving records of a musician's social origins at face value, for they were sometimes distorted for various reasons—for example, to make her seem younger or more remarkable than she was.

The dangers of providing a lopsided or inadequately supported definition of ladies' orchestras has been countered by basing the study on a broad variety of sources instead of a narrow but closely scrutinized selection of sources, for example, on just a few orchestras.

Poststudium

The relative invisibility of ladies' orchestras in modern music history as well as in contemporary source materials was the first and overriding problem in the search for data for my study. The second problem was the contradictory nature of the sightings reported and thus the lack of a useful definition of the object. Third, sources were hard to trace because material was not cataloged or collated under relevant rubrics, for example, *"Damenkapellen."* I came to the conclusion that the musicological devaluation and neglect accruing to entertainment music (popular music, in modern terms) and also to women instrumental musicians had contributed to these inadequacies. The anomalousness of these groups further contributed to diverting scientific attention from ladies' orchestras.

I recently gained access to valuable sources that have allowed me to continue my research into ladies' orchestras. Comprehensive material concerning one of the orchestras in my study, the Modell orchestra (Myers 1993, 192, 268, 310–12), which first arrived in Sweden in the 1860s, has been put at my disposal by the heirs. It led to an archive in Bohemia, the Chomutov provincial archive at Kadan, in the Czech Republic, where I unearthed more material. These recent finds have already thrown more light on such questions as the geographic and historical origins of ladies' orchestras, their membership, and the education of musicians in them. Recent contact with Eveline Müller, who was born in Preßnitz and was a member of a Preßnitz musician family, has confirmed my findings (Müller 1994). Preßnitz is also briefly mentioned by Dorothea Kaufmann (1997, 21–28). She uses older sources however and does not appear to have known of Eveline Müller's work. The next step for me in my pursuit of ladies' orchestras therefore appears to be an individual case study of this particular orchestra. It was active for several generations, from about the 1860s until the time of World War I. Thus it existed during the entire period of the first wave of ladies' orchestras. Such a study has not been possible for me up to now on account of lack of material. It will complement my dissertation's horizontal approach to the earliest orchestras with a vertical, in-depth approach, thus, I hope, strengthening and confirming my conclusions.

NOTES

1. Recent research has pushed this date backward to ca. 1840.

2. These figures represent a minimum, since the indication is that far from all ladies' orchestras appeared in surviving documentary sources. Also, my major source, *Der Artist* (1883–1941) appeared every week with lists of Damenkapellen. I was unable to look at every number, having instead to limit myself to three or four numbers per year.

3. Nancy B. Reich (1993, 125–46) uses the term "artist-musician class," in which she includes "artisans." I suggest instead that the "artist-musician class" is a subgroup of the lower-middle craftsman or artisan class.

4. The skills required to play most of the music in the ladies' orchestras' reper-

tory are commensurate with those required to pass one of the two highest grades in the British Associated Board of the Royal Schools of Music examination system. The highest examination (grade 8) is a criterion for entrance to music colleges in Britain.

REFERENCES CITED

Interviews

Åhlen, Maj. Interviewed by Margaret Myers, Stockholm, 15 October 1987.
Ek, Asta. Interviewed by Margaret Myers, Vänersborg, 21 January 1988.
Gyenes, Lily. Interviewed by Margaret Myers, Stockholm, 22 December 1987.
Pettersson, Ally. Interviewed by Margaret Myers, Falköping, 1 October 1986.
Portnoff, Margareta. Interviewed by Margaret Myers, Stockholm, 15 October 1987.
Ruda, Elsa. Interviewed by Margaret Myers, Stockholm, 16 October 1987.
Steijer, Astrid. Interviewed by Margaret Myers, Stockholm, 14 October 1987.
Sundell, Greta. Interviewed by Margaret Myers, Stockholm, 13 March 1988.

Books and Articles

Abrahamsson, Gösta. 1945. *Vi äro musikanter* (We are musicians). Stockholm: Frilansen.
Anonymous. 1913. "Stockholms kafémusik" (Music in Stockholm's cafés). *Figaro*, 11 Oct.
Anonymous. 1934. "Restaurang Solfjädern." *Trelleborg Tidning*, 24 Aug.
Anonymous. 1948. Untitled newspaper review from engagement in Vänersborg. Cutting in Britt Johnstone's collection.
Anouilh, Jean. 1975 [1957]. *L'Orchestre. Pièce-concert.* Paris: Paris Table Ronde.
de Beauvoir, Simone. 1986 [1949]. *The Second Sex.* New York: Penguin Books.
Citron, Marcia. 1993. *Gender and the Musical Canon.* Cambridge: Cambridge University Press.
Der Artist. 1883–1941. Central-Organ zur Vermittlung des Verkehrs zwischen Direktoren und Künstlern des Cirkus, reisende Theater, Schaustellungen und Concert-Unternehmungen (Central organ for the mediation and communication between directors and artists in the branches of the circus, traveling theater, shows, and concerts). Düsseldorf.
Edström, Karl-Olof. 1982. *På begäran: Svenska musikerförbundet 1907–1982* (By request: the Swedish Musicians' Union, 1907–82). Stockholm: Tidens Förlag.
Ehrlich, Cyril. 1985. *The Music Profession in Britain since the Eighteenth Century: A Social History.* Oxford: Clarendon.
Friedel, Claudia. 1990. "Frauen Ensembles im 'Dritten Reich'" (Women's ensembles in the 'Third Reich'). *Info. Archivnachrichten* 19:1–5.
Johansson, C. E. ("Speljohan"). 1908. "Damkappellenas Dirigenter." *Nöjes Vännen* 3.

Kaufmann, Dorothea. 1991. "'Wenn Damen pfeifen gehen die Gracien flöten': Die Musikerin in der deutschen Tanz- und Unterhaltungsmusik des 19. Jahrhunderts" ("If women pipe, the Graces go up in smoke": lady musicians in German dance and entertainment music during the nineteenth century). *Worldbeat* 1:81–92.

———. 1997. *". . . routinierte Trommlerin gesucht." Musikerin in einer Damenkapelle. Zum Bild eines vergessenen Frauenberufes aus der Kaiserzeit* (". . . experienced drummer wanted." Women musicians in a ladies' orchestra. Toward a picture of a forgotten women's profession at the time of the Empire). Schriften zur Popularmusikforschung 3. Karben: Coda.

Kent, Greta. 1983. *A View from the Bandstand.* London: Sheba Feminist Publishers.

McClary, Susan. 1991. *Feminine Endings.* Minnesota: University of Minnesota Press.

Müller, Eveline. 1994. "Musiker aus Preßnitz in aller Welt" (Musicians from Preßnitz in the whole world). *Jahrbuch für sudetendeutsche Museen und Archive 1993–1994* (Yearbook of the Sudeten-German museums and archives 1993–94), ed. Jörg Kudlich, 193–218. Munich: Sudetendeutsches Archiv.

Myers, Margaret. 1993. "Blowing Her Own Trumpet: European Ladies' Orchestras and Other Women Musicians 1870–1950 in Sweden." Ph.D. diss., Göteborg University.

Neuls-Bates, Carol, ed. 1982. *Women in Music: An Anthology of Source Readings from the Middle Ages to the Present.* Boston: Northeastern University Press.

Nyqvist, Bengt. 1983. *Musik till middag: underhållningsmusiken i Sverige* (Music during dinner: entertainment music in Sweden). Stockholm: Almqvist och Wiksell Förlag.

Reich, Nancy B. "Women as Musicians: A Question of Class." In *Musicology and Difference: Gender and Sexuality in Music Scholarship,* ed. Ruth Solie, 125–46. Berkeley: University of California Press.

Shaw, George Bernard. 1981. *The Bodley Head Bernard Shaw: Shaw's Music. The Complete Musical Criticism.* 3 vols. (1876–1950). Ed. Dan H. Lawrence. London: Max Reinhardt at the Bodley Head.

Solie, Ruth, ed. 1993. *Musicology and Difference: Gender and Sexuality in Music Scholarship.* Berkeley: University of California Press.

Straus, Oscar. *Ein Walzertraum* (A waltz dream). Leipzig: Ludwig Doblinger.

Svenskt Press Register. 1880–1900 (vols. 1–5). Lund.

Part 3

Gendered Musical Sites in the Redefinition of Nations

Perceptions and symbolic constructions of nations as gendered are usually directly related to the hegemonic position of the nation vis-à-vis other nations. In our authors' dialogue, for example, Diamond reported a number of accounts in which Canada is gendered female relative to the United States, and Moisala observed the feminine imaging of Finland during World War II. The imagery may be paternal, maternal, avuncular, or regal (consider, for example, Uncle Sam, das Vaterland, or—extending beyond the concept of nationhood—Mother Earth).

Ceribašić deals directly with this relational aspect of the gendering of nations in her chapter in this anthology, but the terms are decidedly not parental but sexual. When, in the course of our dialogue, she spoke more informally and personally about her work on this topic, she described her growing awareness of the manipulation of gendered musical categories as "a manifold shock."

Instead of the (at least conceptual) equality of the sexes in socialist Yugoslavia, the [post-Soviet] idea, openly promoted, was a return to the traditional roles of men and women in patriarchal society. All of the formerly changeable, transitory, shifting, and numerous diversities were funneled into one irreconcilable opposition of Us and Them (first of all with regard to nationality). In this, all the pairs of notional opposites were abundantly used, including gender opposition. Theweleit's idea[1] of (our) good and (their) bad guys as well as (their) red armed women and (our) white nurses were explicit. Yugoslav "darling girls" in popular music started to be recognized as odious promiscuous "skirts" (to a much lesser degree, the male musicians from the enemy side were depicted as bullies) and separate male and female roles were imposed in domestic music.

A personal account such as this helps us understand that mappings of gender, nation, and music are historically specific constructions. It illustrates one instance in which both "genders" and "nations" have been fragile entities. Although the experience of this fragility is extensive, the academic discourse of nationalism as a fluid and contingent construction is substantially the product of the past couple of decades. Benedict Anderson's *Imagined Communities* (1983) was one highly influential work in this regard. In the wake of his arguments that communities and nations were invented or imagined, scholars began examining the mechanisms for achieving such inventions.

Since Anderson's work was first published, however, both the economic realities of globalization and political and social changes have radically disrupted stable concepts of nationhood. Some scholars have found it useful to articulate how aspects of "real" lifeways were objectified and commodified as representations of group or national identity. Others have interrogated the "level" of the nation within the complex interaction of the local and the global in contemporary society. As Homi Bhabha has explained, "nation" is now generally seen as a narrative strategy through which sovereignty and control are enacted. Furthermore, the erasure of people in transit—migrants or travelers—from constructions of this narrative are now revealed as integral parts of the picture. Bhabha (1994, 141) speaks of the "shadow of the nation" veiling the very "condition of exile." He identifies a phenomenon that has become a central theme in scholarly explorations of identity: the concept of diaspora, of people united by common histories and bonds to a place they perceive as "home."

Both ethnomusicology and feminist music scholarship have a rather complex place within this intellectual foment. Both music and feminism have been implicated in the discourses of colonialism and nation building in rather complex and sometimes conflicted ways. Music scholars, for example, have by and large accepted claims of certain traditions (e.g., German concert music of the seventeenth to nineteenth centuries) as "international" languages; some have participated uncritically in the collection of folk materials, collections that often served the representations of nationhood. Recent substantial contributions to the theorizing of nationhood in music have started to change this picture. Ethnomusicologists, for example, devoted an issue of the journal of the Society for Ethnomusicology to issues of nationalism in 1992 and focused, at their annual conferences, on issues of globalization (in 1995) and on nationalism and diasporic cultures (in 1996).

The three chapters in this section work within the context of "national" communities at moments of crisis, junctures where the stability of statehood is jeopardized. Two contributors (Ceribašić and Kimberlin) consider the particularly fragile constructions of gender and nationhood in times of, or as a result of, war. The third (Rüütel) explores a subnational community at a juncture where nationhood was achieved after the long shadow of Soviet rule. Their works move the understanding of the nexus of gender, music, and nationalism forward in several respects.

From its vantage point within the conflict zones of the former Yugoslavia, Ceribašić's 1993 study of the Croatian and Serbian appropriations of popular music emphasizes the strategic nature of the genderings of nationhood. Ceribašić clarifies the volatility of such constructions and the fluid mechanisms by which music may be used to control and reproduce gender definitions in the interests of state power.

Kimberlin, however, examines not the state's agency in gendering musical genres in the context of war but rather the effects of a long and devastating war in Ethiopia in the 1970s and 1980s on sociomusical roles and cultural practices. Whereas Ceribašić reports a tendency toward hard-line gender dichotomies in the region of the former Yugoslavia, Kimberlin outlines newly won equality (or at least an expanded range of female participation) for women musicians in Ethiopia and Eritrea. In this regard, her work mirrors the situation in Western countries during World War II, where women also assumed new roles and gained access to jobs that had previously been restricted to men. Kimberlin astutely asks whether the reversion to patriarchy following World War II will be mirrored in the Ethiopia and Eritrea of the late 1990s.

Rüütel describes the gendering of cultural responsibilities in the island communities of Kihnu, a part of Estonia. Comparing past and present, she refers frequently to the profound changes effected in the Soviet and post-Soviet periods and constructs an interpretation for women's increasing responsibility for maintaining musical practices.

In every case the tension between minorities that resist homogenization and the metaphors of nationhood that seek to assert totalizing narratives is articulated in the gendering of the musical practices.

NOTE

1. The reference is to Klaus Theweleit, "Mannerphantasien" (Masculine fantasies) (Frankfurt am Main: Verlag Roter Stern, 1979).

REFERENCES CITED

Anderson, Benedict. 1991 [1983]. *Imagined Communities: Reflections on the Origins and Spread of Nationalism*. Rev. ed. New York: Verso.

Bhabha, Homi K. 1994. *The Location of Culture*. London: Routledge.

8 Defining Women and Men in the Context of War: Images in Croatian Popular Music in the 1990s

Naila Ceribašić

Traditional values and concepts of desirability regarding gender in Southern Slav traditional cultures are marked by a sharp dichotomy whereby an individual is distinctly either masculine or feminine, belonging to one of two mutually exclusive categories. The objectives of this essay are to examine how gender has been defined through both Croatian and Serbian national discourses during the war, how gender opposition has been employed by both sides as a metaphoric device designed to uphold national and cultural stereotypes, and finally how male and female musicians in various popular music genres both negotiate and construct these notions of gender as cultural markers.

My insights concerning the Serbian perspective are based on radio and TV programs of the Serbian Krajina (i.e. the occupied Croatian territory), as well as ten audiocassettes by Serbian songwriters that emerged in the late 1980s and early 1990s. During the war I also read newspaper articles and other publications from Serbia, although such publications were often difficult to obtain given the political situation. I cannot judge whether the material I used is representative. Although I tried to include songs that seemed to interest the public, I cannot discuss their degree of popularity objectively. Since they were transmitted in the mass media, and the state exercised total control over the media space, those songs could be considered expressions of the dominant discourse.

As far as the Croatian perspective is concerned, the songs I will discuss were performed by prominent Croatian musicians, were often broadcast on Croatian radio and television, and were frequently requested by listeners or view-

---

Editors' note: This essay was received in September 1995. Although changes in the former Yugoslavia have occurred since that time, it should be emphasized that the author addresses a specific moment in the war between Serbs and Croats.

ers during phone-in programs. Nevertheless, at least in some cases, the prevalence of these songs may have resulted from state directives rather than genuine popular demand expressing the public's attitudes, tastes, and worldviews.

Thus, because of the impossibility of providing an equally comprehensive overview of these media from the Serbian side—I have no access to personal stories of Serbian participants in the war, and my knowledge concerning new musical production on the market under Serbian control is only general and often indirect—I can do no more than compare the two conflicting sides' ideas and the rhetorical apparatuses of their centers of political and mass media power. Those issues, coupled with the reality of living in Croatia during the war, carry the danger of bias. One's emotional submergence in the events of war reinforces the impossibility of "distanced scientific objectivity" and heightens the tendency to idealize the thoughts and actions of one's own community.

Researchers cannot assume an omniscient and/or neutral stance from which to observe the phenomena with which they deal "objectively." Instead they write, and in so doing, they create the object of their research through their personal viewpoint within the context of their own culture. This does not mean, of course, that I wish to provide an intentionally subjective review. Just the opposite. To quote Ian Hacking, "Although whichever propositions are true may depend on the data, the fact that they are candidates for being true is a consequence of an historical event" (in Rabinow 1986, 237). I have attempted to check my own subjectivity by monitoring various popular music genres and competing ways of giving meaning to the world, especially by taking into consideration the analyses of some authors on the Serbian side (Luković, Čolović, Prošić-Dvornić, and others). Culturally constructed, even fictional conceptions of gender are then confronted with realities of armed conflict, of existential and visceral peril.

Violence through Music

At the time of the relevant political changes (the breakdown of Yugoslavia and the outbreak of war), popular music (i.e., music in close relationship to the mass media [Manuel 1988, 3–4]) became a powerful point of differentiation between the competing discourses of the two mutually confrontational states. At the end of the 1980s the Serbian mass media had started a campaign of markedly favoring "newly composed folk music" (*novokomponirana narodna muzika*) at the expense of all other music genres. The genre in question was one of three main genres of popular music in the former Yugoslavia. It was described as a stereotypic but skillful and captivating mixture of the tonal relations and dance structures of Serbian traditional music, the melismatic melodies of Bosnian music, and the rhythmic organization of Macedonian traditional music (Kos 1972, 67). The texts wove traditional values and modern social processes, in particular the portrayal of relationships between the sexes (Simić 1976, 159–65; Rihtman-Auguštin 1978, 17; Povrzanović 1982, 30–31). Sociologists researching the uses of leisure time by and the interests of young people found that fans of newly composed folk music "were primarily rural youth by origin and domicile, farm workers . . . with relatively uneducated fathers, from Montenegro and Serbia, . . . and Montenegrins, Serbs, and Muslims" (Ilišin 1990, 93). According to an investigation carried out from 1 July 1981 to 31 June 1983, newly composed folk music constituted the largest part of Yugoslavian music production (57.75%). It was created mainly in Serbia: 78.6 percent was produced by three Serbian record companies, two of which published only newly composed folk music, and eight of the ten leading performers of newly composed folk music were Serbs (Hudelist 1984, 54–55).

According to Petar Luković (1993b, 12–13), a Serbian critic of Serbian policy, at the end of the 1980s "the *narodnjaci* [newly composed folk music performers] . . . spread the quasi-patriotic message . . . about Greater Serbia, the heavenly nation, [and] the Serbian son Milošević." Here one finds in action the three-dimensional concept of culture in which "each of the elements (extreme nationalism, fundamental Eastern Orthodoxy, and newly composed folk music) has its propaganda assignment: nationalism to convince us how we cannot ever live or want to live with others; Orthodoxy to convince us how this is in the sphere of spiritual history; and, finally, folk music to refresh us and cheer us up, and to fill us with strength" (Luković 1993a, 22–23; see also Čolović 1993, 99). In defining itself, the Serbian side adopted connotatively rich symbols from earlier times that managed to suggest themselves as both Serbian and Yugoslavian symbols: epic poems, the Kosovo myth, and Jovan Cvijić's belief in the superiority of the people of the Dinaric Mountains—stock raisers and warriors—of whom three-quarters were Serbian (Cvijić 1987, 337). According to Cvijić (1865–1927), the Dinaric people, who maintain a patriarchal social structure, are characterized by strong ties to nature, the honor they give to their ancestors, and individual and national pride. Throughout history the Dinarics have been known for their warrior-like qualities: "The Dinaric man burns with the desire to avenge 'Kosovo' [where the Serbian army was defeated by the Turks in 1389]. . . . This steadfastness and absolute faith in the national ideal is the main fact in his history. He sees himself as chosen by God to carry out the national task" (Cvijić 1987, 338). The Kosovo myth intertwines the notions of the victim, harmony and disharmony, heroism ("thanks to which the Serbs are undefeated even in defeat"), and "terrestrial defeat which is transformed into spiritual victory" (Naumović 1994, 107–8). The myth "unites within itself the important components of national self-awareness: the confirmation of the historical proto-origins and the representation of the victim" (Janjić 1994, 28). In the 1980s the Kosovo myth "was adapted 'on a daily media basis' for the requirements of ethnic mobilization" (ibid., 31).

The end of the 1980s saw the appearance of patriotic works exactly in this genre of newly composed folk music, songs bearing titles such as "Hey Serb, Awaken" and "Six Centuries Have Passed since the Kosovo Battle" (Dobriça Miletić Gera and the Zoran Pejković orchestra), "O Serbia of Three Parts, You Shall Be One Whole Again" (Stevanović duet and the Siniša Matejić orchestra; a reference to the situation before changes to the Serbian Constitution made in 1989 revoked the autonomy of the provinces of Kosovo and Vojvodina), and "Montenegro and Serbia Are Two Eyes in One Head" (Slađana Košutić and the Žarko Pavlović Valjevac orchestra; a reference to a well-known statement by Milošević). With the outbreak of war production of newly composed folk music functioned as a stimulus to and part of military campaigns. For example, Dragoslav Bokan, "convinced by his own experience and the experience of his comrades-at-arms," wrote an apologia for newly composed folk music, particularly the tape "Stop, Pashas and Ustashi" (by Baja Mali Knindža) in which he claimed that "the effectiveness of [the Serbian] battle would perhaps be 30 percent lower . . . without that tape" (in Prošić-Dvornić 1994, 195; originally published in *Our Ideas* [June 1993], a journal of the new Serbian Right).

Two main subgenres can be identified in the newly composed folk music produced during the war. One is made up of songs that are musically similar to songs from the 1980s, while their texts present new "quasi-patriotic" content, however, or celebrate and perpetuate the stereotypes of the brave Serbian soldier. Thus, for example, in the refrain of the song "Stop, Pashas and Ustashi," the lyricist says: "Stop, Pashas and Ustashi / don't touch that, it is ours / our hearts are like the lions' / we defend Orthodoxy." The second subgenre is made up of preexisting folk tunes arranged in the style of the newly composed folk music. These songs tell of the Chetniks (Serbian nationalistic warriors), while the melodies are of diverse origins, broadly disseminated in versions with other texts. The texts of these songs, which use traditional literary figures and vocabulary—even more so than do the texts of the first subgenre—celebrate heroic, intrepid fighters who remain undaunted even by almost certain death. As late as March 1995, relatives would mark the departure of their nearest and dearest into the Serbian army by requesting such songs on radio stations (recordings in Ceribašić 1994–95). Thus the song "The Chetnik Is Sitting upon a Stone," a variation on the melody of the World War II partisan song "From Ovčar and Kablar," describes a Chetnik fighter undaunted even by his mother's long wait for his return home, her "empty heart," the thought of his loved one, the death of his brother who "died in his arms," or even the possibility that he would be killed in battle "this very night" (ibid., IEF mgtf 2636/3).

In 1991 newly composed folk music, being a contemporary musical symbol of the Serbs, disappeared from Croatian television screens, radio programs, local entertainments, and weddings. According to Croatian perceptions, this genre revealed many of the stereotypes Croats attributed to individuals in eastern (particularly Serbian) culture, namely, laziness, untidiness, exaggerated emotion, arrogance, and an overbearing nature (Prica 1992, 95). The crucial fact, however, was that at the start of the war, the production of newly composed folk music was one of the strong points of Serbian expansionist policy; in addition, as the war went on displaced persons and individuals who had been prisoners in Serbian camps claimed that they had been tortured by, among other things, being forced to listen continuously to and even perform newly composed folk music inspired by the ideology of "Great Serbia" (material in Ceribašić 1994; Ceribašić and Pettan 1994). Moreover, it was not unusual for newly composed folk music to accompany incidents of rape, including forced anal and oral sex, and castration (Vlašić 1994, 16–17).

Some Serbian songwriters working in this genre presented the enemy through gender opposition. The enemy was represented as a promiscuous or whorish woman: like all women, she (Croatia) does not have her own world but is subject to the masculine sphere (Serbia). She is weak, with a nature inclined toward masochism, but also stubborn and capricious, openly offering herself (Žanić 1993, 98). Thus, Dragutin Knežević Krunica, in his song "Why Didn't Croatia Get Married" (from *Serbian Barricades*) uses the image of a Croatian divorcee who remains unwanted even though she "bares her calves and sashays through Europe" to mock Croatia's aspiration toward independence and deny the possibility of its achievement.[1] According to Čolović (1993, 73, 80–81): "Propagators of war . . . made fewer efforts to encourage love for the homeland but instead counted more on male conceit. They offered war as some type of brothel." If Croatia is a woman of low repute, then it is completely justifiable that she be condemned, punished, and tamed, for this is actually what she wants. In the middle to late 1980s, sociological research asserted that "people were frightened to express their ethnocentricism, because of fear of sanctions, but they were unhampered in expression of their sexism, their misesteem for women. This was a precursor of the flood of hatred for the Other. Today, that Other bears the name of another nation" (Vjeran Katunarić, in Rašeta 1993, 3). Therefore, it does not seem unreasonable to link songs such as Knežević's "Why Didn't Croatia Get Married" with a pornographic element in newly composed folk music of the 1980s. For instance, in the song "There'll Be Meat," by Mićo Popić, a woman yearns for a powerful "macho" type of man and "suffers without his 'meat'"; when she gets it, she guards him and his meat "like a drop of water in her hand." The phrase "there'll be meat," which appears in both the refrain and verses, is experienced in Croatia as a symbol of Serbian war crimes against Croatians: when entering conquered Vukovar, a Chetnik platoon sang, "Slobodan sent us salad, / there'll be meat, we'll butcher the Croats," which was filmed by TV cameras and broadcast on numerous TV news programs around the world. The attitude of Serbian superiority when entering Vukovar corresponds to Popić's "There'll Be Meat."

How to Be Different, Part 1

At the Croatian side, various discourses provided an interpretative frame through which explanations of the war were offered in terms of the opposition between Europe (the West, Croatia) and the Balkans (the East, Serbia). This implied further oppositional pairings, including democratic/totalitarian, bourgeois society/peasant society, peaceful/warlike, and female/male. This style of argumentation is reminiscent of the sociopsychological theories of Dinko Tomašić (1902–75). According to Tomašić *cooperative* (*zadružna*) culture is a farming culture, autarkic, peace loving, territorial, democratic, collectivistic, and nonpatriarchal, whereas *tribal* (*plemenska*) culture is a stock-raising culture, nomadic, competitive, rapacious, warlike, strongly familial, strictly exogamous, autocratic, individualistic, and patriarchal (see Tomašić 1937, 13–16, 18, 41; 1938, 106, 109, 133–34). Tribal culture maintains a strict division of labor according to sex and age: women, children, and old people do all the work around the stock, in the house, and in the fields, while the men spend their time either waging war and plundering or in idleness. In this model deadly weapons are synonymous with masculinity, and excellence in stealing and killing—"heroism"—is the ultimate male social value

(Tomašić 1993, 892–93). During 1991–92 an attempt was made to express the notion of Croatia as victim and Serbia as perpetrator through the opposition between cooperative and tribal cultures. Gradually this interpretative framework was suppressed, however, less because Croatia's own tribal, patriarchal cultural component became more obvious than because Croatia needed to build and confirm not just its position as victim but also its right to exist. In so doing, Croatia found itself in an unstable position. As the victim of Serbian aggression, it could not represent itself as an heir of tribal, patriarchal culture. On the other hand, as one who wants to win, it could represent itself only through a pattern of tribal, patriarchal culture, since that is the culture of those who by definition will emerge the winner. In other words, Croatia faced a problem: how to oppose the enemy effectively while not impairing its victim status and how to assert its status as a tribal, patriarchal culture yet still maintain its incomparability with the aggressor.

Therefore, in representing itself globally, Croatia sought simultaneously to maintain the patriarchal pattern, in which the status of women is analogous to the nation's "otherness" from the enemy and its victim status, and to exchange the patriarchal pattern for one of conflicting civilizations—in keeping with the need both to be different from the enemy and to win. On Croatian soil, however, the dominant discourse endeavors to maintain a patriarchal interpretative framework with respect to the modes of male and female engagement during the war.

The "femininity" of Croatia—its peacefulness and its victim status—is identified in the large number of songs written from a female perspective and in songs of pleading (pleas addressed to God, the Virgin Mary, or the international community), which are performed by both female and male performers. In addition, Croatian songs more frequently represent the soldier who defends his family (mother, wife, children, old folks, and home), whereas the model Serbian soldier primarily defends Serbian symbols and territory. The mother figure also differs: in Croatian popular music, the mother is proud of her son-defender, but she is also worried about him and would prefer that he return home safely, whereas the Serbian mother is relegated to a limited role in which she silently and without complaint gives all she has for Serbia. On the Croatian side, soldiers' personal stories contain admissions of fear, justifications of retreats by the army, descriptions of unfamiliar military skills, and pleas for leniency for deserters (see Čiča 1993). The Serbian side, however, identifies deserters with "mothers' lads." They are not only cowards and bad Serbs but also nonmen (Čolović 1993, 113–14). One should not, furthermore, ignore the differences between the Croatian and

Serbian constructions of war and peace. From the Serbian perspective, war is perceived almost as a natural state. Some song lyrics mention killing the enemy or even the subject's own death. In Croatian songs, however, the word *death* is avoided or replaced with euphemisms. Similarly, I have not encountered any Croatian statements in which a soldier boasts about killing, whereas on the Serbian side Ivan Čolović (1993, 64) cited the example of a soldier who bragged on TV that he had killed six Croats and would kill twice that number if it was necessary.

Within the framework of the music itself, Serbia's "masculine" and warlike self-representation and Croatia's "feminine," peaceful projection are best symbolized by the contrast between two musical instruments: the *gusle* (a bowed lute that accompanies the singing of epic songs), the Serbian national symbol, and the *tamburica* (a plucked lute, usually associated in tamburica ensembles), the Croatian national symbol. In a dichotomy that mimics Tomašić's previously mentioned opposition between cooperative and tribal culture, the gusle symbolizes the "tribal" and patriarchal world of the Balkan warrior-hero, whereas the tamburica evokes the world of the "cooperative," the farmer, the conscientious and peaceful laborer, and good, honest, and hospitable people (see Žanić 1993, 68; Cvijić 1987, 346).

How to Be Different, Part 2

Whereas the Serbian media were dominated by newly composed folk music, with the onset of a real state of war during the summer of 1991, Croatian Television (HTV) began to broadcast a series of diverse pieces of music: polished adaptations of traditional music presented by tamburica and choral groups, Croatian popular music standards, arias from Croatian operas (particularly from the national opera *Nikola Šubić Zrinski,* by Ivan Zajc), and new productions of various genres connected with the war. These included the contributions of various "Band-Aid" groups to responses to the war in rock, punk, dance, or rap music. Serbian aggression against Croatia prompted the creation of a sort of all-embracing homeland music that sought both to strengthen internal social cohesion and create national consensus (Lalić and Bulat 1992, 84, 90). Domestic production was supplemented with foreign popular music whose texts could be connected with the situation in Croatia,[2] and works from the domain of Western art music (particularly Albinoni's Adagio in G Minor and Beethoven's symphonies) were performed against a background of Croatian natural beauty, cultural monuments, and images of devastation in Croatia.[3]

From 1990 onward three distinct genres existed in Croatian popular music: *neotraditional tamburica music, entertainment* (zabavna) *music* of the middle European and Italian type, and *pop and rock music* of the Anglo-American type.

The tamburica is not a musical instrument universally recognized throughout Croatia. There is no common denominator of traditional music for all the country's regions. One can speak only of an aggregate of differing musical practices within different cultural milieux. Despite political attempts to establish them nationally between World War I and World War II, tamburica ensembles did not take root in the extensive regions of southern Croatia (Istria and the Croatian littoral, as well as Dalmatia and the mountainous Dalmatian hinterland). In recent years, however, the tamburica has again been imposed as a national instrument. There seem to be several reasons for the promotion of this instrument: tamburica music is diatonic, has firm meter and rhythm, and uses closed strophic forms that do not clash with popular music. Being allied to popular music, it becomes a means of integration of diverse Croatian traditional music practices. Furthermore, tamburica music evokes the world of farmers, hard-working and quiet laborers, and honest and hospitable people (the image that Croats wish to present both to themselves and to the international community). Moreover, the tamburica enacts a sharp contrast with the gusle, the Serbian national symbol. Therefore, recent neotraditional tamburica music functions as the most direct substitute for and counterpart to Serbian newly composed folk music. It is not surprising that the Croatian movement for the revival of old patriotic songs and the creation of new ones commenced precisely with the emergence of one of the neotraditional tamburica groups, the Zlatni dukati (Golden Ducats) (Bonifačić 1993, 190–91).

Entertainment music functions as another counterpart to Serbian newly composed folk music. Its simple rhythms, strophic forms, melodious refrains, moderate tempi, and "codified messages that move through a narrow circle of 'permissible' themes (patriotism; puritanism; unhappy, sentimental platonic love)" (Glavan et al. 1978, 19)—all of which show the influence of Italian and middle European *schlager*/light music—fit well with the contemporary political paradigm of Croatia's place in the Western cultural circle and of the image of Croatia as the bastion of Western civilization confronting incursions from the East (once the Turks and today the Serbs). This is corroborated by the fact that in the former Yugoslavia "entertainment and rock music elicited above average interest among the youth from Bosnia and Herzegovina, from Croatia, among Yugoslavs, student and school pupils, people living in urban centers and from the upper social strata" (Ilišin 1990, 93). According to a study by Darko Hudelist (1984, 55), from 1 July 1981 to 31 June 1983, Zagreb's Jugoton (today called Croatia Records) produced 86.2 percent of all recordings in the genre of entertainment music, whereas six of the ten leading performers of that genre were Croats. Finally, entertainment music is understood as a counterpart to Serbian newly composed folk music because during the war the former was largely engulfed by the latter both in Serbia and in territories under Serbian control.

The third main genre is pop or rock music (13.15% of total Yugoslavian production, whereas newly composed folk music constitutes 57.75% and entertainment music makes up 29.1% [see Hudelist 1984, 54]). Whereas the production of newly composed folk music and entertainment music reflected national divisions, rock music production was more homogeneous, with the two Zagreb record companies producing 58.2 percent of the total output and the Belgrade PGPRTB producing 27.5 percent, while of the ten leading performers, three were active in Serbia and four in Croatia (Hudelist 1984, 55). During the late 1970s and the 1980s, the youth rebellion against the adult system of values was recognized as the direct stimulus for the emergence of rock music. Music journalists had been emphasizing the influence of Anglo-American popular music and the social dimension of the phenomenon: urban themes, criticism of contradictions in the social system, and criticism of the ruling norms in art and society (Bobinsky 1985, 29–30, 58). It is thus understandable that in the context of war, Anglo-American-style pop and rock music in Croatia could function not only in contrast to but virtually separate from and incomparable to Serbian music promoted through Serbian mass media.[4] Musicians in this genre therefore needed not face the burden of differentiating themselves from the enemy (as Serbia was presenting itself through its dominant discourse), nor did they have to invoke, pathetically or militantly, mythical categories, history, the homeland, mother, the hearth, or God; they simply needed to cry out "for peace I lift my voice" (E.T.), "say Yo for Croatia, say No for the War" (H.C. Boxer and Montažstroj), or even more directly, "fuck Slobodan Milošević" (CLF) or "victory, victory, victory, victory" (Psihomodopop) (all from *Rock for Croatia!*). They also did not have to confirm their patriotism by expressing hatred toward others but indeed might even recall old friends (as in Jura Stublić's "Eh, My Belgrade Pal") now "on the other side of time" (Alka Vuica).

I have here paraphrased parts of several well-known Anglo-American-style songs produced in Croatia during the war. Because of their lack of aggression, the individualization of the expression, the human warmth, and the portrayal of the happier side of life in the former Yugoslavia (now irreplace-ably destroyed), the last two songs cited in previous paragraph are particu-larly interesting. It seems that this discourse could convince anyone "whose side justice is on." The first, the very popular song "Eh, My Belgrade Pal" (from *Rock for Croatia!* no. 2), does this through its text:

> You darling lasses from Belgrade,
> what splendid love you always made.
> I still recall the flaxen hair
> of my lass from Novi Sad.
> For the sake of that I often drove
> along the Danube and by Sava's shore,
> and I grew to love a hundred villages;
> oh, how happy I was.
> Eh, my Belgrade pal,
> all the Serbian songs we knew;
> before the war we sang
> "Hail, O Virgin, the Croats' Queen."
> Eh, my Belgrade pal,
> villages in Slavonia are all in flames;
> eh, my Belgrade pal,
> our sea itself is in thrall.
> Eh, my Belgrade pal,
> we'd meet on Sava's bank,
> you'd not recognize me,
> and you'd shoot at me.
> The first shot I'd leave to you,
> for you were always the first,
> the second I'd excuse to you,
> the third shot then is bound to miss.
> But I'd not aim my gun at you,
> and pray to God, that if I do,
> that I'd miss you,
> but I'll hit you.
> I'll mourn for you,
> and close your dying eyes withal.
> Oh, how sad I was,
> I lost my friend.

The persuasiveness of the second song (from *Alka Vu—Winnetou*) is con-tained in both its lyrics and music. This is a variant of the 1985 hit "On the Other Side of the Pillow," by the Belgrade singer and composer Momčilo

Bajagić Bajaga, who wrote the song and was formerly the boyfriend of Alka Vuica. Now he is no longer "on the other side of the pillow" but "on the other side of time."

The Fiction and Reality of Gender Roles during the War

I have already mentioned that the ruling Croatian discourse, in the way in which it has engaged the concepts of male and female during the war, has sought to retain the patriarchal cultural pattern. Activity, power, and fighting belong to the male world, and passivity, indulgence, tenderness, and warmth are characteristic of the female one (see Macdonald 1987, 20); during the war, male groups are on the front lines and women are in the rear. These conceptions were also supported by Croatian popular music, particularly in the genre of entertainment music.

Songs performed by female singers[5] that attained considerable popularity during the war almost without exception invoked some type of prayer. Thus, Tereza Kesovija, one of Croatia's most popular singers of entertainment music for decades, prayed to St. Blaise, the patron saint of Dubrovnik, Kesovija's hometown, to "defend us and freedom" (from *Song for Croatia*). Vana, the singer for the dance group E.T., performed "Prayer for Peace" (from *Rock 4 Cro*). Vera Svoboda, one of the most outstanding singers of neotraditional tamburica music, recorded the Croatian Marian songs (e.g., "Queen of All Croats, Pray for Us"). Finally, Josipa Lisac, the female center of the Croatian rock scene, performed "Ave Maria," the video for which incorporated a church ambience with images of activities of women from the Bedem ljubavi (Wall of Love) organization (recording in Marošević 1991, IEF video 181/1). The genre preferences accompanying the aforementioned worldviews can be seen here, for Anglo-American-style pop music has tended toward pragmatic demands for peace, whereas the entertainment music genre usually contains tearful pleas for help, most frequently directed toward the Virgin Mary.

The second, less publicized group of songs performed by women consists of those supporting and thanking Croatian soldiers, as well as expressing love for them and the hope that they will soon return home. The mother figure is proud but also worried for her son/defender.[6] The girlfriend represents a golden period of love, marriage, and Croatian freedom that will commence when he returns from the battlefield, as in the song "My Loved One Is in the National Guard," performed by Sanja Trumbić (from *Song for Croatia* no. 2):

My loved one is in the national guard,
driving out the enemy;
And I pray to God for his return,
and that he brings freedom with him.
When he returns, there will be a wedding,
and the real flag will fly on the roof:
the red, white, and blue [the Croatian flag].

In the entire body of popular music—being mainly created by men—the concepts of the homeland, the hearth, and mother belong to the same rhetorical group, one linked to the basic Christian values (New Testament faith, trust and love, and truth). With God's help, it is suggested, the Croatians are being defended by brave, self-sacrificing, devoted male protectors. Women, with tears in their eyes and a prayer on their lips, maintain morale back home and patiently wait for the return of their defenders and protectors.

All the genres of popular music in Croatia contain pairs of songs that delineate the different modes of deploying the concepts of masculinity and femininity during the war. Whatever the differences in genre, the performances from a male perspective are always rougher, more aggressive in sound, more pregnant rhythmically, and in brisker tempi, whereas the performances that delineate a female perspective (usually with a female lead singer) have a fuller sound and are more melodious, calmer, and more restrained. Within entertainment music such a relationship is shown, for example, in Đuka Čajić's "Ardent Croats" (Hrvatine) and Josipa Lisac's "Ave Maria"; in Anglo-American-style pop music, it is displayed by H. C. Boxer and Montažstroj's "Croatia in Flame" and E.T.'s "Prayer for Peace." In the latter, the male rapper's task is to explain the war situation rationally, whereas the female soul singer offers a kind of emotional scream for peace. According to Barbara Bradby (1993, 168) such "gendering of voices appears as a powerful restatement of traditional gender divisions: the association of men with culture, language, and technology, and of women with emotion, the body, sexuality." The model can be observed in the songs of a single performer: Marko Perković Thompson. In his song "Pray Little One," the female world is sketched with restrained sound, while the male world in the song "The Čavoglave Platoon" is accompanied by aggressive, warlike arrangements and production. Male-female differentiation in the songs is usually supported not only by the characteristics of musical style but also by the images in their videos. For example, in the video for the song "We're Gonna Be Free," performed by Guido Mineo and Josipa Lisac, two groups are contrasted: women, children, and old people on one side and male warriors on the other (recording in Marošević 1991, IEF video 183/54).

In such a way, popular music upholds the "appropriate" expression of male and female identities. In statements by people displaced from Vukovar, however, the sharp lines of demarcation between the masculine and feminine spheres are negated by their activities during military operations. In those circumstances, all people, male or female, fought in their own personal way, "the brave comforted those who were more frightened, but this was not divided by sex" (in Ceribašić and Pettan 1994). Women "broadened their role to inconceivable limits" and even took over men's jobs (in Ceribašić 1994). A similar phenomenon appeared on the Serbian side. One model of socialization exists on the basis of "the myth of the all-permeating patriarchy" (Sklevicky 1987, 54) and the Kosovo myth: soldiers have the "sacred and honorable duty to defend freedom and the fatherland, at the price of sacrificing their earthly existence"; women are expected "to bear children and raise soldier sons, . . . to mourn their deaths publicly and to exalt their exploits and sacrifice, or to give themselves up to quiet pain, dignity, and restraint" (Prošić-Dvornić 1994, 189). Reality, however, has another side to the coin. At the beginning of the war a group of parents of mobilized young men forced their way into the Serbian Parliament and demanded that their sons be allowed to return home, while women from the Knin area joined the army for a number of reasons, including the fact that "many healthy and fit young men left the Knin region and sought sanctuary in Serbia" (estimates put the success of the mobilization program at about 50%) (ibid., 189–92, 196).

Conclusion

After the intense warfare from 1993 onward, musical homogenization ebbed. On the Serbian side, the ruling authorities learned that their efforts to obtain formal international recognition following conquest were not best served by newly composed folk music. Thus, Mirjana Milošević, the Serbian president's wife, is interceding so that more space is given to the genres of Western-oriented popular music to demonstrate Serbian "openness and adherence to democracy." Songs that question the strict gender dichotomy engendered in the Kosovo myth are also appearing and gaining popularity. For example, Dragana Mirković's song "Is Love Only for Heroes?" an example of entertainment music, was at the top of the hit list on Serbian Radio Korenica in March 1995. Several hit songs demonstrate that the traits of newly composed folk music and recent Western dance music touch each other (consult recordings in Ceribašić 1994/95, IEF mgtf 2635/1–7). In Croatia songwriters are starting to speak out critically about problems in their own environment (e.g., Stublić's song about gangsters from Chicago, which alludes to current machinations with regard to the transformation of ownership), and there has been mention in the media of the return of Croatian "traitors" (the case of "Yugo-nostalgic" Branimir Johnny Štulić, one of the most popular Croatian songwriters during the 1980s) and opposition writers on the enemy side (Đorđe Balašević). Newly composed folk music (with texts dealing with subjects such as love and not with national themes), which existed on the margins of public life in Croatia during the war (Ceribašić 1993, 225), has started to be performed every day, for example, in fifteen Zagreb restaurants (Sabalić 1995).

Generally speaking, popular music on both sides has mainly reverted to its traditional themes of either happy or unrequited love. Despite its apparent conventionality, this reversal interrupts the picture of the unified national collective observed during the war. Instead of portraying the conflict-free biological and cultural dichotomy and complementary natures of men and women, as did the nationalistic discourse during the war (Milić 1994, 49), new music production builds on concepts of variety in relationships between women and men. Instead of perpetuating the sharp differentiation between spheres of activity found during the war, the idea of a static, essential identity, newer productions on both sides portray genders as a scale with multiple variations. Earlier insistence on the difference between the male and the female in fact delineates the wartime atmosphere of intolerance. Therefore, to locate masculinity and femininity along a continuum, and not as separate worlds, is to give peace a chance and to intercede for the values of a pluralistic world. Will these values prevail, and will music have the power to impose them? A rather utopian question, is it not?

NOTES

The lyrics for "Eh, My Belgrade Pal," performed by Jura Stublić, and for "My Loved One Is in the National Guard," performed by Sanja Trumbić, appear courtesy of Miroslav Lilić, president of the board of Croatia Records.

1. My thanks to Dr. Ivo Žanić, who let me listen to the audiocassettes of some Serbian songwriters, among them the cassette *Serbian Barricades,* by Dragutin Knežević Krunica.

2. In *Gardijada,* a TV musical program intended for soldiers, the troops were sent greetings and messages to the sounds of, for example, "Don't Give Up" (Pe-

ter Gabriel), "Nothing Compares to You" (Sinéad O'Connor), "You're Simply the Best" (Tina Turner), "All True Man" (Alexander O'Neil), "Jesus Loves You" (Boy George), "Wish You Were Here" (Pink Floyd), "Time Is on My Side" (the Rolling Stones), "Should I Stay or Should I Go" (the Clash), "We Will Rock You" and "We Are the Champions" (Queen), "Everything I Do I Do It for You" (Bryan Adams), "No Woman, No Cry" (Bob Marley), "Let It Be Love" (Simple Minds), "Wind of Change" (the Scorpions), "Knockin' on Heaven's Door" (Guns 'n' Roses), "Give Peace a Chance" (various artists), "War" and "My Father's House" (Bruce Springsteen), "Good Night, Saigon" (Billy Joel), and "Two Tribes" (Frankie Goes to Hollywood). These songs were broadcast in the second part of October 1991 (recordings in Marošević 1991, IEF video 180, 182).

3. Late in 1991 Dr. Grozdana Marošević followed and recorded Croatian TV broadcasts. My thanks to her for letting me use that extensive material (recordings in Marošević 1991, IEF video 180–199).

4. The same interpretative model appears in Serbian opposition discourse, not as the opposition between the two national communities, but as an opposition of two worldviews within one community. Thus Rambo Amadeus, a Serbian-Montenegrin rock musician, says: "It is very hard to push a man in a trench if you previously let him listen to Štulić, 'Stones' or any other music that is rebellious. To make a man be obedient, first you have to make an idiot out of him. . . . In surroundings where hatred is the main motif and a way of living, you can't cultivate rock 'n' roll" (in Jurišin 1993, 14–15). Supporting such representation, Croatian soldiers, particularly at the beginning of the war, nurtured the rocker image: "They wear black strips around their foreheads, earrings, Ray-Ban sunglasses and little crosses on their necklaces, wear jeans and tennis-shoes and T-shirts with different messages in English, their hair is cut in rock and punk styles" (Senjković 1992, 76).

5. In Croatian popular music women figure almost exclusively as performers, while lyricists, composers, arrangers, and producers are mostly men.

6. The motif of the mother who does not sleep at night because she worries about her son, who tells him to take care and not to play a hero and to try to come back as soon as possible, often appears in personal narratives of Croatian soldiers. The statements of deserters prove that mothers always support their sons in their unpopular decision (in Čiča 1993). Occasionally radio and TV broadcasts let women send messages to the defenders such as the following: "Let it all be finished as soon as possible, come home to your mothers and girlfriends"; "Take care of yourselves and think about us who think about you"; "Come home safe and sound as soon as possible." Other messages were more militant: "Persist and stay as brave as you are"; "Be courageous and strong, suffer it all, be persistent, full of hope, because you are fighting for a just cause" (messages of girls on Zagreb streets, broadcast in the middle of October 1991 on Croatian TV; in Marošević 1991, IEF video 180/24).

REFERENCES CITED

Bobinsky, Alenka. 1985. "'Novi val' u jugoslavenskom rocku: Analiza jednog specifičnog fenomena" (New wave in Yugoslavian rock: analysis of a specific phenomenon). Manuscript. Institute of Ethnology and Folklore Research, Zagreb, IEF rkp 1130.

Bonifačić, Ruža. 1993. "Uloga rodoljubnih pjesama i tamburaške glazbe u Hrvatskoj početkom 1990–ih: Primjer neotradicionalne grupe 'Zlatni dukati'" (The role of patriotic songs and tamburica music in Croatia at the beginning of the 1990s: the case of the neotraditional group Zlatni dukati [Golden Ducats]). *Arti Musices* 24, no. 2:185–222.

Bradby, Barbara. 1993. "Sampling Sexuality: Gender, Technology, and the Body in Dance Music." *Popular Music* 12, no. 2:155–76.

Ceribašić, Naila. 1993. "Glazbeni repertoar na svadbama u Slavonskoj Podravini (istočna Hrvatska) prije i poslije političkih promjena u Hrvatskoj 1990. Godine" (Musical repertory at weddings in the Slavonian Podravina [Drava River] region [eastern Croatia] prior and subsequent to the political changes in Croatia in 1990). *Arti Musices* 24, no. 2:223–28.

———. 1994. Razgovor s A.K., prognanicom iz Borova Naselja (Conversation with A.K., displaced person from Borovo Naselje). Audiotapes. Institute of Ethnology and Folklore Research, Zagreb, IEF mgtf 2579–80.

Ceribašić, Naila, and Svanibor Pettan. 1994. Razgovor s F. K. i S. Ž., prognanicima iz Vukovara (Conversation with F. K. and S. Ž., displaced persons from Vukovar). Audiotape. Institute of Ethnology and Folklore Research, Zagreb, IEF mgtf 2581.

Cvijić, Jovan. 1987 [1918]. *Balkansko poluostrvo* (Balkan Peninsula). Belgrade: SANU, Književne novine, Zavod za udžbenike i nastavna sredstva.

Čiča, Zoran. 1993. "Iskazi sudionika u ratu 1991/92" (Statements of the participants of the war, 1991–92). Manuscript. Institute of Ethnology and Folklore Research, Zagreb, IEF rkp 1413.

Čolović, Ivan. 1993. *Bordel ratnika: Folklor, politika i rat* (The brothel of the warriors: folklore, politics, and war). Belgrade: author.

Glavan, Darko, Velibor Jerbić, Stoja Lukić, and Vladimir Tomić. 1978. *Pop glazba i kultura mladih: Sondažno istraživanje publike rock-koncerata* (Pop music and youth culture: probing investigation into the audience of rock concerts). Zagreb: CDD SSOH.

Hudelist, Darko. 1984. "Jugoslavenska diskografska laž" (Lie of Yugoslavian recording companies). *Start*, 2 June, 50–55, 69.

Ilišin, Vlasta. 1990. "Slobodno vrijeme i struktura interesa" (Leisure time and the structure of interest). In *Ogledi o omladini osamdesetih,* ed. V. Ilišin, F. Radin, H. Štimac, and S. Vrcan, 61–109. Zagreb: Institut za društvena istraživanja Sveučilišta u Zagrebu.

Janjić, Dušan. 1994. "Od etniciteta ka nacionalizmu" (From ethnicity to nationalism). In *Kulture u tranziciji,* ed. M. Prošić-Dvornić, 15–33. Belgrade: Plato.

Jurišin, Pero. 1993. "Vreme je da izvadimo glave iz guzice" (It's time we get our heads out of our asses). Interview with Rambo Amadeus. *Feral Tribune,* 21 September, 14–15.

Kos, Koraljka. 1972. "New Dimensions in Folk Music: A Contribution to the Study of Musical Tastes in Contemporary Yugoslav Society." *International Review of the Aesthetics and Sociology of Music* 3, no. 1:61–73.

Lalić, Dražen, and Nenad Bulat. 1992. "Rat i mladi: Prema novoj generacijskoj kulturi" (Young people and war: toward a new generational culture). In *Sociologija i rat,* ed. O. Čaldarović, M. Mesić, and A. Štulhofer, 83–91. Zagreb: Hrvatsko sociološko društvo.

Luković, Petar. 1993a. "Estradija" (On estrade). *Vreme* 145:22–23.

———. 1993b. "Ne pevam gluposti i ne radim za režim" (I don't sing stupidities and I don't work for the regime). Interview with Momčilo Bajagić-Bajaga. *Feral Tribune,* 2 November, 12–13.

Macdonald, Sharon. 1987. "Drawing the Lines—Gender, Peace, and War: An Introduction." In *Images of Women in Peace and War: Cross-Cultural and Historical Perspectives,* ed. S. Macdonald, P. Holden, and S. Ardener, 1–21. Houndmills, Basingstoke, U.K.: Macmillan Education.

Manuel, Peter. 1988. *Popular Musics of the Non-Western World: An Introductory Survey.* New York: Oxford University Press.

Milić, Anđelka. 1994. "Nacionalizam i 'žensko pitanje' u Istočnoj Evropi" (Nationalism and "the women's issue" in eastern Europe). In *Kulture u tranziciji,* ed. M. Prošić-Dvornić, 47–56. Belgrade: Plato.

Naumović, Slobodan. 1994. "Upotreba tradicije: Politička tranzicija i promena odnosa prema nacionalnim vrednostima u Srbiji 1987–1990" (The use of tradition: political transition and change of relationship toward national values in Serbia, 1987–1990). In *Kulture u tranziciji,* ed. M. Prošić-Dvornić, 95–119. Belgrade: Plato.

Povrzanović, Maja. 1982. "Društvene vrijednosti izražene tekstovima 'novokomponiranih narodnih pjesama'" (Social values expressed in the text of "newly composed folk songs"). Manuscript. Institute of Ethnology and Folklore Research, Zagreb, IEF rkp 1077.

Prica, Ines. 1992. "Poetika otpora: Građa o običnom životu u ratu" (Poetics of resistance: notes on ordinary life in war). *Narodna umjetnost* 29:81–105.

Prošić-Dvornić, Mirjana. 1994. "'Druga Srbija'—mirovni i ženski pokreti" ("Another Serbia"—pacifist and women's movements). In *Kulture u tranziciji,* ed. M. Prošić-Dvornić, 179–99. Belgrade: Plato.

Rabinow, Paul. 1986. "Representations Are Social Facts: Modernity and Post-Modernity in Anthropology." In *Writing Culture: The Poetics and Politics of Eth-*

nography, ed. J. Clifford and G. E. Marcus, 234–61. Berkeley: University of California Press.

Rašeta, Boris. 1993. "Stiže li nas balkansko prokletstvo?" (Does the Balkan damnation come to us?). Interview with Vjeran Katunarić. *Feral Tribune,* 7 September, 2–3.

Rihtman-Auguštin, Dunja. 1978. "Od 'naroda' do folklornog kiča" (From "people" to folklore trash). *Zvuk* 3:13–19.

Sabalić, Ines. 1995. "Washingtonski sporazumi dramatično su izmijenili hrvatsku estradnu scenu: U Zagrebu je otvoreno 15 lokala s novokomponiranom glazbom" (Washington agreement has dramatically changed the Croatian Estrade: fifteen restaurants with newly composed music have been opened in Zagreb). *Globus,* 31 March, 56–59.

Senjković, Reana. 1992. "Poetika otpora: Na početku su bili grb, zastava i pleter" (Poetics of resistance: in the beginning there were a coat of arms, a flag, and wicker). *Narodna umjetnost* 29:63–80.

Simić, Andrei. 1976. "Country 'n' Western Yugoslav Style: Contemporary Folk Music as a Mirror of Social Sentiment." *Journal of Popular Culture* 10, no. 2: 156–66.

Sklevicky, Lydia. 1987. "Konji, žene, ratovi, itd.: Problem utemeljenja historije žena u Jugoslaviji" (Horses, women, wars, etc.: on the difficulties of founding women's history in Yugoslavia). In *Žena i društvo: Kultiviranje dijaloga,* ed. L. Sklevicky, 51–60. Zagreb: Sociološko društvo Hrvatske.

Tomašić, Dinko. 1937. *Društveni razvitak Hrvata: Rasprave i eseji* (The social development of Croats: papers and essays). Zagreb: Hrvatska naklada.

———. 1938. *Politički razvitak Hrvata* (The political development of Croats). Zagreb: Hrvatska književna naklada neovisnih književnika.

———. 1993 [1936]. "Plemenska kultura i njeni današnji ostaci" (Tribal culture and its present-day remnants). *Društvena istraživanja* 2, no. 6: 889–906.

Vlašić, Boris. 1994. "I ljude škope, zar ne?" (They castrate men, don't they?). *Feral Tribune,* 22 February, 16–17.

Žanić, Ivo. 1993. "Politički diskurs i folklorna matrica: Tradicijska kultura i politička komunikacija u Bosni i Hercegovini, Crnoj Gori, Hrvatskoj i Srbiji 1988–1992" (Political discourse and folklore matrix: traditional culture and political communication in Bosnia and Herzegovina, Montenegro, Croatia, and Serbia, 1988–1992). Ph.D. diss. University of Zagreb, Faculty of Arts. Institute of Ethnology and Folklore Research, Zagreb, IEF rkp 1465.

Recordings

Baja Mali K-328. n.d. (1991?). *Stan'te paše i ustaše [Stop, Pashas and Ustashi].* Ninatrade K-328.

Ceribašić, Naila, comp. 1994–95. "Želje i prozdravi slušatelja na Radio Korenici 11/1994, 2–3/1995" ("Wishes and greetings of listeners on the Radio Korenica"). Audiotapes. Institute of Ethnology and Folklore Research, Zagreb, IEF mgtf 2634–36.

Čajić, Đuka. 1991. *Hrvatine* (Ardent Croats). Orfej CAO 9502.

Knežević, Dragutin Krunica. n.d. (1990 or 1991). *Srpske barikade* (Serbian barricades). IKZ Grafosaund FI 5226.

Košutić, Slađana, and Žarko Pavlović Valjevac orchestra. n.d. (1989?). *Mlada sam, mlada sam* (I am young, I am young). Beograd ton K-109.

Marošević, Grozdana, comp. 1991. "Glazba emitirana na HTV tijekom domovinskog rata" ("The music broadcast on the Croatian TV during the Homeland War"). Videotapes. Institute of Ethnology and Folklore Research, Zagreb, IEF video 180–99.

Miletić, Dobriça Gera, and Zoran Pejković orchestra. 1989. *Šest vekova prođe od Kosovskog boja* (Six centuries have passed since the Kosovo Battle). Jugodisk BDN 3589.

Perković, Marko Thompson. 1992. *Bojna Čavoglave* (The Čavoglave platoon). Croatia Records MC-SG-D 3036775.

Popić, Mića. n.d. (1980s). *Bit će mesa* (There'll be meat). Eros 924.

Stevanović duet, and Siniša Matejić orchestra. n.d. (1989?). *Oj Srbijo iz tri dela, ponovo ćeš biti cela* (O Serbia of three parts, you shall be one whole again). Beograd ton K-105.

Svoboda, Vera. 1991. *Kraljice Hrvata, moli za nas: Marijanske pjesme* (Queen of all Croats, pray for us: Marian songs). Orfej MC-6 3034870.

Various artists. 1991. *Pjesma za Hrvatsku* (Song for Croatia). Croatia Records MC-6 3035563.

———. 1991. *Rock za Hrvatsku!* (Rock for Croatia!). Croatia Records MC-6 3035570.

———. 1991. *Rock za Hrvatsku!* br. 2 (Rock for Croatia! no. 2). Croatia Records MC-6–T 3035778.

———. 1992. *Pjesma za Hrvatsku* br. 2 (Song for Croatia, no. 2). Croatia Records MC-6 3036799.

———. 1992. *Rock 4 Cro!* Croatia Records MC-6 S 3036409.

Vuica, Alka. 1993. *Alka Vu—Winnetou*. Croatiaton MC CAH 0023.

9 Women, Music, and "Chains of the Mind": Eritrea and the Tigray Region of Ethiopia, 1972–93

Cynthia Tse Kimberlin

This essay looks at the changing social positions and roles of women—changes effected partially through the music they perform—from the Tigray region of Ethiopia and in the newly independent country of Eritrea.[1] The changing roles documented here occurred in the context of two major wars during and since the 1970s in Ethiopia and Eritrea. Two broad questions are addressed: how are ingrained attitudes about gender manifested in musical practices, and how has war helped women to redefine those attitudes and practices?

The first of the two major wars is the 1974 Ethiopian Revolution, which ultimately stemmed from university[2] students' unrest in the late 1960s. It led to the overthrow of Emperor Haile Selassie's forty-year monarchy in 1974 and continued with the seventeen-year reign of the Marxist-Leninist-oriented government of Lieutenant Colonel Mengistu Haile Mariam, ending with his abdication in May 1991. The second conflict is Ethiopia's ongoing thirty-plus-year civil war with its erstwhile province of Eritrea. Although the Eritreans actively worked for independence since 1962, the seeds of discontent were sown as early as 1895.[3] Today Ethiopia's and Eritrea's provisional governments are putting in place a more democratic form of governance. This essay focuses on the impact of the seventeen-year Mengistu regime and its aftermath with reference to the Ethiopian-Eritrean civil war.

The Mengistu regime ultimately provided the catalyst for improving the quality of life for Ethiopian and Eritrean women on a large scale. At the beginning of the 1974 revolution, the government called for women to participate in the war because there were not enough men. Implementing the decision to allow women into the military—which involved educating and training them to be soldiers—had to be done quickly, for their involvement was critical to winning.[4] Once they were allowed to work outside the home

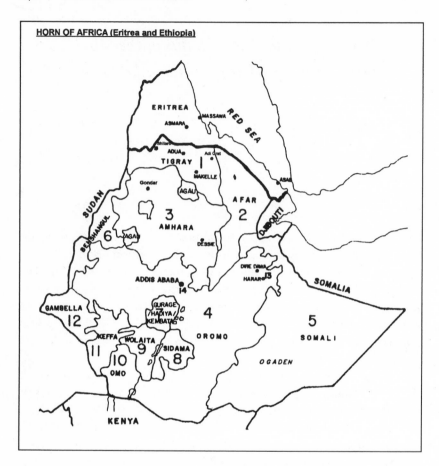

Map of Ethiopia and Eritrea

and assume new responsibilities, women wanted to continue and maintain their novel roles. Organizations and mandates were established to help achieve these recent gains. Especially after 1991, following four years of transitional government, Eritrea's vocal women's organizations have been instrumental in giving women the opportunity to establish precedents that would let them improve their position while a new constitution is put into place. Women's rights are slated to be written into this new constitution. Only time will tell the extent to which these rights will be implemented.

Although women's rights throughout Ethiopia and Eritrea have yet to be fully realized, a major impact of the revolution was the redefinition of female cultural roles in terms that benefited the entire society and gave

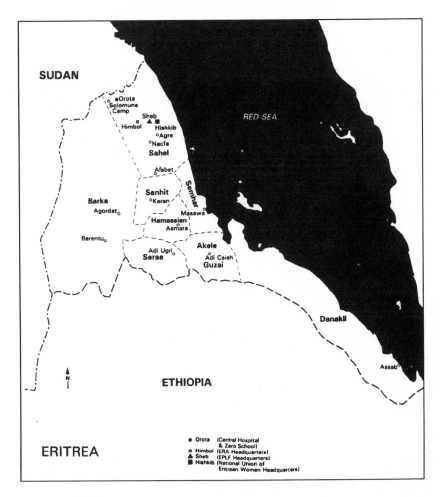

Enlarged map of Eritrea

women a chance to participate as full citizens. Assefa Tekeste, a senior government health official in Ethiopia who has studied the social consequences of the war and its aftermath, states that in the battlefield all individuals were equal, unusually so. People became a utopian society with a common psychology and shared goals (in Parmelee 1993, A:30).

The three most important gains women made were the rights to work outside the home, to obtain an education, and to own land. Twelve policies related to these rights were enacted during the course of the Mengistu regime. They are presented in order of their enactment:

Work in the Public Sphere

1. Women are encouraged to become soldiers.[5] The goal is for women to make up one-third of the armed forces.
2. Women soldiers have been permitted to marry since 1984.
3. Women may be employed outside the home. The goal is for women to make up one-third of the work force. This policy allows women to participate in elections and in the administration of their neighborhood councils.[6]

Education

4. Women may attend school. The goal is for girls and women to constitute one-third of the enrollment in coed schools.
5. Women should attain at least a sixth-grade literacy level.
6. Girls and women can no longer be circumcised.
7. Women can no longer bear the stigma of illegitimacy,[7] for the legal category has been abolished.
8. Women do not need to prove that they have not "provoked" rape if it occurs outside of marriage because of changes in the law regarding rape.

Land ownership[8]

9. A woman may own land when she is fifteen years of age.
10. A woman may marry whom she chooses when she is fifteen years of age.
11. Land ownership allows women to support themselves and their children if they become widows (e.g., if their husbands were soldiers killed in the war).
12. Women retain property ownership after a divorce. All property must be divided equally between wife and husband.

The changes in belief that these policy changes indicate were partly effected by means of musical performance. In this essay I chronicle changes in the position of women in five contexts (traditional performance venues for social commentary, refugee camps, schools, associations, and the public sphere). Examples will demonstrate how musical involvement challenged attitudes affecting women before, during, and after the revolution.

Methodology

The five contexts for music making will be explored using data gathered in Ethiopia in 1962, 1972, 1991, 1992, and 1993 and in Eritrea province in 1962–64 and Eritrea (the country) in 1993. Published and unpublished sources (especially Hammond 1989), as well as personal communication, expanded and confirmed primary data. With the exception of the refugee camps, these contexts and the circumstances underlying them existed before 1974, continue to exist, and overlap one another in time. For analytical purposes, however, each context is introduced in chronological sequence according to the height of its popularity (see table 9.1). Attitudes about women's position in society before, during, and after the revolution will be explored in each context. These beliefs have correlates in musical contexts. That is, beliefs are mirrored by musical performance.

Table 9.1

Context	Chronology
Traditional performance venues for social commentary by women musicians	Before revolution
Refugee camps in the Sudan	During revolution
Schools that include or are exclusively for girls and women	During and after revolution
Associations that include or are exclusively for women	During and after revolution
Public sphere	During and after revolution

Traditional Performance Venues for Social Commentary by Women Musicians

Individual women who performed music received virtually no mention by name in published written historical accounts related to the revolution, but oral histories contain evidence of their participation (Hammond 1989, 42). As my fieldwork shows, women composed not only proverbs, stories, and poetry but also song texts on every conceivable subject. Because men are viewed as the primary practitioners of music in both private and public spheres, music and its specific relationship to women have not been given wide attention. Women have been discouraged from performing in public or from becoming professional musicians.[9] Men have been reluctant to have their women interact with outsiders. Women's public musical performance has been associated with prostitution. In the private sphere, however, women perform without these constraints.

There are exceptions to this gendered dichotomy of private and public spheres, however. Although it was customary for women to keep their opinions to themselves before 1975, on Emperor Haile Selassie's birthday in 1972, following his speech, about a half-dozen women began singing in alternation the *shillela,* a body of songs meant to arouse or prepare people for war.

All wore what looked like old military uniforms of medium-dark khaki. For this occasion their songs described past exploits of female and male heroes who died defending their country (Kimberlin 1972).

Furthermore, some traditional musical roles were open to women. *Melkesti,* professional poet-singers and social commentators (including women), were engaged at all social levels to sing the *melkes,* or funeral ritual.[10] After the formalities of celebrating the life and achievements of the deceased, they were free to criticize publicly any aspect of society without reprisal (an example is the melkes chant in Hammond 1989, 35). A rebuttal could be presented by the opposing side, which engaged its own musicians to present a counterview. Famous female melkesti at the courts of well-known feudal lords included Maskale, at the court of Ras Seyoum, and Weyzoro Tekle and Weyzoro Te'ebey, in the service of Dej Gebreselassie (Hammond 1989, 32).

A second traditional role open to women was that of the *hamien,* who formed distinct communities and traveled around the country to practice sorcery and perpetuate superstitious beliefs, often in revenge for offenses or injuries. These women and men are said to possess special powers over individuals and to be skilled at a particular form of poetry and song that allows them to criticize. The women are accompanied by men on the *masinqo* (a single string bowed spike lute). One example of this song/poem type describes a hamien poet who uses her skills to beg (Hammond 1989, 93). Other songs composed by ordinary women prior to 1975 indicate women's social and sexual inequality by talking about the vagina, or *hemsi,* for men and women were taught that the vagina was a curse (Hammond 1989, 32–33).[11] Other topics include plowing the fields, an activity that symbolizes male economic power through crop production and land ownership. Since most ordinary women in Tigray were not allowed to own land, they were excluded from this major source of economic livelihood. A further pre-1975 plowing song openly expresses resistance to conditions of daily life (Hammond 1989, 90). Similarly the woman singing at her grindstone, a symbol of the hard labor and isolation of women, became a metaphor for inequity, including the community's relation with the landowner (see the example in Hammond 1989, 30).

After 1975 some of these practices decreased as new outlets for expression became available. Hammond (1989, 40, 94) reports that superstitious beliefs were suppressed in some areas by the Tigrayan People's Liberation Front (TPLF)[12] within the first two years of the revolution.[13]

Refugee Camps in the Sudan

Ninety-nine percent of the over five million African refugees remain on the continent. Many Eritreans sought to escape the war in the Sudanese camps of Tawawa and Um Gulja, in Khartoum and Gedaref, respectively, hoping to survive there until they could return home. According to Salem Mekuria (1991)[14] two million fled war and famine. Almost seven hundred thousand live in settlement camps. Five thousand refugees from the Tigray and Gondar regions of Ethiopia live in the Gulja, a camp located in the eastern Sudan (Salem 1991, 1993). The refugee camps are alleged to be temporary ghettos, separated physically and culturally from the mainstream population of the host country. Although the refugees built their own "towns," the native populations ostracized and denigrated them and withheld all rights. Conditions were such that assimilation was discouraged. Although various relief agencies tried to help the refugees eke out a living, their overriding concern was to survive and keep their families intact until they could return home. Home meant both a geographical place and a psychological state; returning home meant returning to their own country or settling in a country where they would be welcomed, made to feel safe, and allowed to make choices and take responsibility for their futures.

Salem Mekuria's *SIDET: Forced Exile,* filmed on location during May and June 1990, vividly portrays life in these refugee camps by focusing on three Ethiopian and Eritrean women living in the Sudanese camps. Her intent was to heighten the visibility and complexity of women's experiences in exile, to demonstrate the relevance of relief programs in the context of the daily experience of families and individuals living in exile, and to show the consequences of political discord that uproot and disrupt the lives of women and children. Most important, she focused on the refugees themselves, the individuals who were most affected by the catastrophic events that led them to embrace a precarious existence in a poor and frequently hostile land. The film illustrates how a host country can affect the internal conditions of the refugees, but at the same time it reveals how refugees can affect the economy and stability of the host country (Salem 1993).

Women living under such constantly shifting conditions felt a strong need to express their feelings; they composed new texts to existing melodies. Hunger, poverty, and war were recurring themes.[15] The two songs heard in the film give women the opportunity to voice their isolation, state of limbo, despair, poverty, and resignation. Song text 1 (appendix A) is an example of Adeyi Abrehet singing of her hunger, poverty, and despair. She accompanies herself on a five-stringed plucked lyre (*krar*), playing a melody in the mode (*q_ñ_t*) *ambas_l*. Although song text 2 is a complaint about locusts destroying grain that is used to feed chickens, the locusts also symbolize the suffering and dislocation to which women were subjected.

Schools That Include or Are Exclusively for Girls and Women

In the refugee camps the women also indicated that education, learning to read and acquiring other practical skills, was important for their survival and their futures. In response some schools were set up exclusively for women, whereas other new schools were coed.[16] These schools advocated literacy, new skills and training for jobs previously held by men and encouraged belief in parity for women in the military and politics. Hammond (1989, 80) estimates 30 to 40 percent of the students in coed schools in Tigray during the late 1980s were female.

The schools fall into four types: the regime schools (e.g., in the Katan region of Eritrea), the Marta School (in Ethiopia), the March 8 School (also in Ethiopia), and the Zero School (in Eritrea). The first type was established by Mengistu's government. The other three schools were established in the 1980s in reaction and as a challenge to the policies of the Mengistu regime.

Some regime schools were established to carry out policies of reeducation, collective learning, and indoctrination advocated by the *Derg*.[17] Attendance was mandatory for those who were recruited. Music was used as a teaching aid to indoctrinate the children into the prevailing ideology. An example of this type of school is found in Eritrea's Katan region, camouflaged between the towns of Himbol and Apollo, where boys and girls from different ethnic groups throughout the country were recruited and forced to attend. For thirteen years, from the time the schools were established around 1978 until 1991, group songs, dances, and theater (all replete with repetitive, jargonistic slogans) were used to instruct the children in Mengistu's revolutionary ideology.

Two other types of school were established as a direct result of the first TPLF Women Fighter's Conference, held in 1983. The March 8 School and Marta School were camouflaged for security reasons, for schools have been prime targets for destruction by the opposition. Established in 1984 in Tigray, both are schools for girls and women that focus their curricula on women's issues. Students were recruited from both the civilian and military population. Song and poetry were important means of raising consciousness. The March 8

School, believed to be located near the town of Shilaro, was named after International Women's Day, celebrated every year in parts of Africa, Europe, and elsewhere.[18] The name was originally selected by Clara Zetkin, a German Marxist, during the Second International Women's Day meeting in 1910 commemorating a women garment workers' strike in the United States. The school's motto is "knowledge is power." Hammond (1989, 79) has published the text of a Tigrayan International Women's Day song text about March 8.

The Marta School, believed to be located in or near Adi Grat, was established to educate female soldiers. Although the curriculum includes political education about women's issues, its primary purpose is to teach practical and theoretical skills to be passed on to women in the communities after they graduate. For instance, women have been taught how to recycle objects of war for peacetime use or how to convert ammunition boxes into satchels for carrying schoolbooks. At Arota medicine was stored in cabinets made of old ammunition boxes, old artillery shells were made into kitchen pots and pans, and cannibalized military equipment parts were converted into furniture. The ubiquitous black rubber sandals continued to be produced from discarded vehicle tires. Light switches seen dangling from trees were impro-

Young male who maintains a "timeline" using an empty gasoline tank as a drum joins female drummers in Apollo, Sahel region, Eritrea, 24 April 1993. Photo by Cynthia Tse Kimberlin.

vised from used hypodermic syringes (Kinnock 1988, 10, 32). People in general did not waste anything.

Even musical instruments were made from such nonmusical objects. Church bells were made from army tank components, and drums were fashioned out of gasoline tanks from vehicles. Graduates have become a vanguard in the villages against the taboos and superstitions that have traditionally oppressed women, as illustrated in song texts published by Hammond (1989, 41, 55).

The Marta[19] School advocates sixth-grade literacy, and it teaches students how to control their biology rather than be controlled by it; to be proud of menstruation, not ashamed; to appreciate the nutritional value of vegetables; and to design and build cooking stoves that use less wood and require less cooking time. The school also trains women in home economics, rural science, health care, child care, agriculture, and women's health, and it prepares women fighters to be politically conscious by teaching them about various types of oppression they have experienced or will experience. Women at the Marta School have refused to let men do anything that requires strength and fitness, such as killing a chicken for a meal. The women at the school learn to make their own houses, kitchens, clinics, and stores (Hammond 1989, 85). The following song text further illustrates the power of women's strength to benefit the whole country. It says:

> The mountains scrape the sky
> but we can climb them.
> The rivers boil in flood
> But we can cross them.
> Our strength is in our people and our politics
> And we will not submit. (Hammond 1989, 134)

The Zero School is carefully concealed somewhere in the area of Arota, Eritrea. It was set up to accommodate four thousand girls and boys, with the specific purpose of teaching them chemistry, history, English, mathematics, sports, music, and the region's two main languages, Tigrinya and Tigre. Wolde Giorgis Andeberhan, regional director of Eritrean education, says the Eritreans are not interested in disseminating political theory or ideology at the Zero School; rather, they want to maintain academic standards and the children's cultural and national identities. The school is considered to be a model for Eritrea's new educational system. Its classrooms consist of sticks and foliage, or else they are merely areas under rocks or near ditches and slit trenches, where pupils can run for shelter if they hear the sound of aircraft

(Hammond 1989, 47; Kinnock 1988, 35). Such camouflaged classrooms at the Zero School are part of a larger school complex dotted along a twelve-kilometer valley. Girls and boys, it seems, are given equal opportunities. The school resists conventional gender roles; for example, one female student at the Zero School named Awet later joined the front-line troops of the Eritrean People's Liberation Front (EPLF). She was encouraged to be interested in subject areas more traditionally reserved for boys. "Engineer, scientist, doctor, teacher are words that don't have a sex, aren't they?" said one EPLF woman. The unpaid instructors are intent on teaching a cooperative, non-competitive approach to problems (Kinnock 1988, 36).

The Zero School's cultural activities include the school band. Kinnock witnessed two women playing guitar and oboe as part of a five-piece band that performed in public on the day she visited. The band, its members playing a saxophone, trumpet, two guitars, and an oboe donated by Italians of Eritrean origin, offered a medley including songs by the Beatles' John Lennon and Paul McCartney, Bob Dylan, and George Gershwin. According to Kinnock (1988, 40) the students never heard of the Beatles. What is distinctive about the female band members is that they were wearing not dresses but slacks and T-shirts, their hair was not arranged in plaited braids but left free in "afros," they were performing with male band members, they were playing Western musical instruments, and they were performing in public.

These schools allowed women greater access to education, but it also showed them that working collectively gave them a greater voice in their community. It also gave them the impetus to form new women's organizations and to improve existing women' organizations to work more actively, for example, by educating women in the intricacies of the political arena. In addition, they learned that there are others, not only in the community, but in other parts of the world, who are working toward similar goals.

Associations That Include or Are Exclusively for Women

A fundamental tenet of the revolution, part of an overall strategy for gaining women's equality, was the right of women to organize within separate associations. Although women's associations existed before the revolution, they were primarily social bodies that offered their members mutual assistance (Yewoubdar 1994). Associations established later during the revolution focused specifically on promoting equality and women's rights. Separate organizations and special educational provisions helped to accelerate women's capacity to use circumstances generated by the revolution to their advantage (Hammond 1989, 134–35). Associations were a way of using individual experience to inform a shared political analysis of long-term oppression by the government. Even so, attitudes from the past still persisted. Older women found it hard to overcome years of prohibition on speaking in public that left them able to do little more than smile and cover their faces with their *shamma*.[20] For example, prior to the revolution women could not be called as eyewitnesses in legal cases or to participate in political activities (Hammond 1989, 33, 40, 74). After women were allowed to have equal rights to land, however, which gave them an economic base from the age of fifteen regardless of their marital status, they became much more active in the political arena. In the 1990s there are many women in politics, although there are still more men at every level. Their rights to land, to education, and to medical facilities are all arranged through their associations, which attend to any complaints in these areas (Hammond 1989, 116, 136). Women's association meetings deal with political issues such as literacy, preventive health, and the burdens of women's work, always with a belief in parity for women (Hammond 1989, 71).[21]

In Shilaro an active women's association used music as a propaganda tool for advocating improving conditions and rights. One morning just before the elections, at 8:30, they put on a demonstration for a visiting delegation of which I was part,[22] singing, dancing, and chanting slogans for the TPLF and against the Ethiopian Democratic Union (EDU). Group musical performances symbolized the collective spirit supporting political reforms between 1974 and 1992 more effectively than solo performance could. In fact, when questions were posed to special interest groups regarding the upcoming elections, they often responded with group songs. Because of the political and cultural environment during Mengistu's regime, it was difficult for individuals and groups to refrain from answering in prepared jargonistic slogans, usually in a call-and-response format; such was the case in Shilaro. In answer to one question about the future of Ethiopian women, the women responded by singing a song. It was frustrating to receive responses to questions in the form of prepared slogans, but it was done in conformity to the politics of the time.

Three organizations for women or including them are especially notable. The first is Baito (people's party), a grass-roots organization that administers all the people's activities. It elects its own members and is run by the people at the local level (Kimberlin 1972; Hammond 1989, 137–38). Second is the National Union of Eritrean Women, an organization led by Askalu Menkarios and formerly headquartered in Hishkib, Eritrea (Kinnock 1988,

74). In 1993 some of its members were transferred to Asmara. This organization believes that women's active participation plays an important part in discussions and decisions in Eritrea. Together with the Eritrean People's Liberation Front, it has accomplished much to improve the situation of Eritrean women. For example, mothers now spend a lot of time looking after one another's children, which produces a strong sense of confidence for the mothers and security for the children. Songs (see, e.g., Hammond 1989, 70) demonstrate a mother's concern for her child on the battlefield.

The third notable women's organization is the Women Fighters Association of Tigray (WFAT), which seeks to raise women's consciousness so that women will be aware of the traditional social mores that prevent them from exercising their options and participating equally with men. Indeed, women soldiers—this group's constitutents—are at the forefront of efforts to overcome gender stereotypes and limitations. Their female counterparts in Eritrea also espouse equality; TPLF women command tanks and hold high rank in the army. They make up one-third of the forces at the front. At the Arota hospital one could see female soldiers who were wounded by bullets and shrapnel at Afabet, clearly showing that women fought alongside the men.

These political organizations have forged links outside Ethiopia and Eritrea. TPLF organizations are found worldwide, particularly in Europe, the United States, Canada, the Middle East, and elsewhere in Africa, as illustrated in the TPLF song "Beyond Tigray" (Hammond 1989, 159). In the past twenty years over two million Ethiopians have left Ethiopia and are living abroad.[23] The EPLF has continually relied on contributions from Eritreans living outside the country. It sent musicians on concert tours around the world to raise money for the liberation movement. Some of this money bought arms, but some helped to set up factories, build roads, establish schools and factories, and provide food to the people, trucking it through the Sudan. "Beyond Tigray" talks about this network of worldwide support.

The Public Sphere

Some women worked in the public sphere prior to the revolution, but they were for the most part either wealthy and elite or single, poor, and uneducated. The greatest change that took place during and after the revolution was that greater numbers of women between these two poles began working outside the home, although still not in the same proportion as their male counterparts. Both the TPLF and EPLF advocate that all women should have the option of working in the public sphere. The fact that women were able

Woman drumming on election day in Maychew, Ethiopia, 22 June 1992. Photo by Cynthia Tse Kimberlin.

Women drumming in celebration of the Eritrean Referendum in Asmara, Eritrea, 27 April 1993. Photo by Cynthia Tse Kimberlin.

to observe female soldiers working outside the home made a great impact. Eysa Mohammed, an Afar from Endele, in eastern Tigray, describes the women soldiers: "I understood their movement from things I saw. . . . The men cooked their food; the women cooked their food; men spoke at the associations and so did women, equally. The men had guns; so did the women fighters. I saw that they gained their equality through the struggle. In fighting they affirmed their equality" (in Hammond 1989, 104).

Public musical performance was highly visible evidence of the change. Examples of such public performance by persons from different age groups and martial status include unmarried girls in Apollo who sang and played *kabaro* (double-headed barrel-shaped drums) and girls flirting with unmarried boys while dancing to the boys' drum accompaniment. I witnessed a young man join the female drummers, using an empty automobile gasoline tank as a drum and managing to produce three distinct pitches from it.

Major changes in attitude toward women and work allowed them to perform traditional drumming (formerly a male symbol and prerogative) in public, as witnessed throughout the "democratic" local and regional elections in Ethiopia and for the Eritrean referendum. The fact that most women in Ethiopia and Eritrea had not previously drummed in public was confirmed by some of my colleagues who lived in Ethiopia and Eritrea before 1974. I was surprised to see so many women playing the drums in public: in Maychew, Ethiopia, in 1992; in Eritrea in 1993, where young and older women were observed drumming and making music in the streets of Asmara during the April 1993 referendum proceedings and celebration; and in Apollo and Korara. Women played the drums wherever I traveled in the Sahel, even in public in the company of boys and men. If drumming by women in public continues to be a common occurrence in the 1990s, it will indicate that ordinary women can now speak out, perform music, and be seen in public in their own right.

Some women joined cultural troupes while they were soldiers in the field. Atsede Teklai, a bass guitar player, was assigned to the cultural troupe for her brigade.[24] An excerpt from an account of her transformation follows:

> There were flute players among our neighbors, and I was very interested to hear these instruments played by the fighters. . . . When I was a child I was more interested in the TPLF than marriage and 10 years ago when I was 12 years old, I went to a TPLF camp and began making tea for them. After 3 years of training I was accepted into the TPLF. My brigade was organizing a cultural troupe and I was assigned to that. I started to sing for the first time openly in front of the brigade. It was a song I made up

about my AK 47. "You have thirty children to fight with you!—the AK 47 has thirty bullets." Then I started acting in cultural dramas. As there are many possible roles, I decided to be a peasant child because that's what I knew most about.

A friend who was a player began to teach me the bass guitar. It was the policy to have more women instrument players, so a plastic guitar was purchased for me from Addis. It was destroyed in an air raid after 3 months, and that was the first time I'd ever cried as a fighter. I wrote to the Cultural Arts Department to try and get another guitar. They assigned me and another fighter a guitar and we started to learn it properly. I played the bass guitar because there was another woman playing the guitar. I was very pleased about this, because I was the first student to play it. The first time I played, the people really accepted me, and clapped.

I married an Amhara fighter, a POW from Gondar. I am pleased to be a woman musician in the revolution. I write songs and I act in dramas. I write and read poems and I compose music—very easy cultural songs. I know I am armed with a bass guitar and am serving the revolution as much as the comrades on the war front with their bullets. I know that art is war by itself. (in Hammond 1989, 139–41)

The career of the internationally successful Ethiopian recording artist Aster Aweke illustrates some of the challenges facing women who were pioneers in public performance. Because Ethiopians believed women should not perform music in public, Aster left her community and later her country during the height of the revolution, when romantic songs, one of her specialties, were forbidden in public (Nelson and Kaplan 1981, 288). Since then she has performed in other parts of Africa, the United States, Europe, and Asia. She holds contracts with recording companies in England, the United States, and Japan.

Aster, one of nine children, was born in Gondar, Ethiopia, and raised in Addis Ababa; in the mid-1990s she was in her late thirties. Derk Richardson interviewed Aster in 1991 before a concert in Oakland, California. Aster said she had liked to sing since she was a child, but she immediately felt the pressure of a society where women rarely took high-profile roles in music: "It was only [the force of] culture. . . . Nobody would come and tell me, 'You're not supposed to sing this.' It was only my family, really, who didn't agree with me, so I had to leave home. When my family found out about it, I had to go. They didn't tell me to go, but I was scared to face them. Women singers were not welcome before. But I kept on doing it, and here I am today. That's the only thing I wanted to do in life" (in Richardson 1991, 11).

When she began performing professionally, she sang pop music in night-

Aster Aweke performing at the Festival of the Lake in Oakland, California, 2 June 1991. Photo by Cynthia Tse Kimberlin.

clubs for five years and then began making cassette recordings in Ethiopia. Bootleg copies showed up in Europe. To further her education, she traveled to Oakland to study English and typing. Her mother told her, "Now you're coming back to your senses." She moved to Washington, D.C., in 1983 at the urging of her sister and attended Northern Virginia Community College to continue her education.

It was by accident that Aster was discovered in Europe. Lucy Duran, who worked for the British Archives at the time, said she picked up some cassettes imported by an Ethiopian souvenir salesman (Kimberlin 1992). She took a tape to Triple Earth Records, where the owners, Iain Scott and Bunt Stafford Clark, tried to trace the remarkable singer through the Ethiopian importer, but they had no idea where she was. Coincidentally, a woman who knew Aster from Washington was traveling in London; she met the importer and heard that the recording company was searching for Aster.

Triple Earth considered issuing a compilation of Aster's best work from her eleven Ethiopian cassettes, but her voice had matured, and Aster wanted to do them over again. The songs were thus recut in London with an eight-piece band of Ethiopian and British musicians and released with the title *aster aweke*. Several tracks with relatively dense instrumental arrangements are attempts at pop crossover. The sparser arrangements, though, such as the traditional-style ballad "Tizita" (Memories) and the piano-accompanied "Y'Shebellu" (the name of a river), are showcases for her vocal talents: "When [audiences are] mixed, they seem to enjoy it a lot. If they're Americans, they're searching for a meaning in what I'm talking about, and they don't know how to dance or what to do. But if there are Ethiopians among them, the Americans try to do what they do—the way they clap, the way that they dance. And I love it when they try to do that. That's the most exciting part, really. You can see their eyes go here and there—they can tell I'm singing from the bottom of my heart" (in Richardson 1991, 11).

Aster collaborated with Ethiopians and non-Ethiopians in recordings and for concerts (Scott and Clark 1991; Richardson 1991), breaking from the traditional pattern in which solo songs are primarily composed by the performer. Listening to the songs on the later recordings, it is easy to discern which songs involve only Ethiopian collaboration and which utilize both Ethiopian and non-Ethiopian collaborators. For instance, Aster is solely responsible for the lyrics and melody of "Tizita." It is interesting that only this song is accompanied by the traditional Ethiopian six-string krar, perhaps because Western technology and instruments could not capture the song's modal and melodic essence.

Nevertheless, advances in technology supported Aster in disseminating her songs by enabling her to be heard internationally, introduce new sounds, and integrate musical collaboration from different sources and people—for example, using a drum machine to establish the now overt time line.[25] On a larger scale, technology has enhanced the position of women in the public sphere by letting them perform as a group even when they are not all present in the same place at the same time; by expanding their local musical environment to the international arena; by allowing indigenous and foreign record producers and distributors to communicate more efficiently, giving women greater access to outsiders who can provide input into the process of music making and dissemination; and by producing a historical record of their actions in the form of recorded musical events and songs. It is often the accumulation of these numerous and sometimes discordant actions in music that encourage women to speak out.

Summary and Conclusions

In this essay I have demonstrated how the musical practices of Ethiopian and Eritrean women over the past twenty-five years were instrumental in changing beliefs about the social value and societal roles of women. Table 9.2 summarizes these changes.

Music served to influence and change attitudes not only because local communities considered music necessary for their well-being but also because music was effective as a teaching tool and as a socially sanctioned way of communicating information, no matter how sensitive or controversial. To this end communities maintained their own musicians to help them commemorate notable events. Schools incorporated music as part of their curricula. The TPLF Cultural Department used skilled performing arts troupes not only to write and present plays, poems, and songs but also to research traditional cultural practices. New songs were (and are) composed to mark important events, and some reflect the importance of women in working for positive changes. Music served to convey what ordinary speech and other forms of communication could not. It acted as a barometer of change and documented the quality of people's lives. These functions manifested themselves with greater clarity during wartime because of the urgency of the cause and the importance of timing, which is crucial to winning. Events during wartime are condensed into a shortened time frame, and as a result, the parallels between music performance and cultural attitudes could be more clearly seen.

The concept of struggle often appears in the performance contexts and song texts described in this essay. For Ethiopian and Eritrean women, struggle is a broader concept than military confrontation with the government. It is more a state of determination, a habit of mind aimed at change, whatever the short-term costs. The women I met in Shilaro, Ethiopia, called it a struggle against the "chains of the mind,"[26] in this case the conditions that lessen the quality of women's lives. In spite of advances, however, traditions are still slow to change. After the war the differences between men and women were still apparent. In Eritrea, for example, single women returning to civilian society found their chances of marrying or remarrying almost nil, unlike the single male fighters, who are now sought after as husbands.[27] The examples described in this essay are symptomatic of changes throughout both countries, but they are partial because documentation has not been conducted comprehensively throughout both countries. At this point one can only speculate as to the extent of these changes.

For the most part, improving the condition of people in general and women in particular has been a major goal for Ethiopia and Eritrea, and according to Yohannes Petros, Ethiopia's constitution of 1987 is the first to recognize that women and men have equal rights and to require the state

Table 9.2

Prevailing Beliefs before 1974	Music Examples Relating to Change in Beliefs
1. Women from nonaffluent families worked essentially in the private sphere. Community social pressures, not laws, excluded women from working in public.	Some men and women now share domestic chores. Society became more permissive in allowing women to work outside the home. For example, women and men played drums in public in towns visited during 1992 and 1993.
2. Middle-class and peasant women were not encouraged to work or speak out in public.	The first song text composed in the 1970s by Kasu (a.k.a. "Marta"), the first female freedom fighter, became a rallying cry for female soldiers.
3. Women as individuals were not encouraged to voice complaints in public.	The Women's Association in Shilaro, Ethiopia, continually voiced complaints in group singing during the 1992 election proceedings.
4. A girl can marry at nine years of age.	The provisional government's policy changed the minimum age of marriage for females to fifteen. At fifteen a woman also can own property. These two factors allow her to pursue her own interests, such as becoming a soldier. Such was the case of Atsede Teklai, who wanted to be a soldier when she was twelve, joined the Tigrayan People's Liberation Front (TPLF) when she was fifteen, and at twenty-two was still a member of a cultural troupe she joined while a soldier in the field.
5. A woman must either marry or be born into an influential family to retain or advance her social status.	Traditional markers of social status were sometimes ignored and other aspects of identity were presented: for example, the female fighters' "afro" rather than the traditional plaited hair style; direct eye contact instead of downcast eyes; dress that signified a new status, including "rock" and "heavy metal" T-shirts to signify membership in the TPLF.
6. A woman must marry to become economically secure.	Since women are now discouraged from marrying before the age of fifteen and can own property at fifteen, they are more likely to pursue interests such as music performance without fear of reprimand or accusation of social inferiority.
7. Women were rarely mentioned in written published accounts about the revolution.	Song texts document women's exploits before, during, and after the revolution.
8. Women need little formal education.	Schools (e.g., Marta and March 8) were established specifically for girls and women to improve their positions in society. Music was part of the curriculum that helped raise consciousness and trained girls to voice their opinions.
9. Although Emperor Haile Selassie I was a pioneer in advocating women's concerns, he promoted and enacted women's rights at too slow a pace.	The environment of the Mengistu regime created enormous opportunities for women and allowed changes to occur within a shorter time span than previously. Mengistu's repressive policies led to a sudden increase in women's organizations. These organizations routinely used music performance to educate women and communicate their views.

to provide special support toward this end (Yohannes 1989, 38). Eritrea's EPLF party incorporated four elements in its agenda: unity, participation by women, development of rural areas, and self-reliance (Kessler 1992). The government is currently monitoring and evaluating policies affecting women (Gebre Hiwet 1993, 35). Isseyas Afeworki, president of the Provisional Government of Eritrea (PGE), made clear the importance of recognizing women in the EPLF's work: "It would be stupid to ignore such a formidable force. Eritrea will never be liberated without 50 percent of the population" (in Kinnock 1988, 75).[28]

Finally, it is important to bear in mind that the issues relating to women's social roles, status, and opportunity are closely linked to efforts to build a shared national identity. Here, too, music is often implicated. The following case illustrates this important point. John Sorenson's book *Imagining Ethiopia* is a study not only of Western representations of Africa but of ways these representations are linked to indigenous invention and construction of certain images, histories, and identities (Sorenson 1993, 4–5). The cover photograph, taken by the author in 1986, is a photograph of Mama Zeinab[29] when she stayed in a camp for internally displaced people. Today she is known as Eritrea's "national poet" and is revered by the Eritrean people throughout the world. In my experience, the terms for poetry and music are used interchangeably in the region. Hence Mama Zeinab is also a vocalist who sings her own poetry and whose songs are disseminated by others. The fact that her photograph, her name, and her title of "poet" appear on a publication available internationally is notable. The decision that she, a Tigre and Muslim woman, is portrayed on the annual EPLF publicity poster in 1988 demonstrates the changing role of women in Eritrean nationalist discourse (Sorenson 1993, 53). She is a member of the older generation who has lived through the Haile Selassie and Mengistu eras and witnessed the changes within the past forty years. She is part of a generation that was forbidden to speak out in public. Who she is today and what she represents symbolizes hope for the future.

APPENDIX A: SONGS FROM SALEM 1991

SIDET: Forced Exile, by Salem Mekuria
Khartoum and Gedaref, Sudan
Um Gulja Refugee camp in the eastern Sudan
Woman playing a five-string plucked lyre (krar) in ambas_l q_ñ_t (mode)
Song text translations by Salem Mekuria; transcriptions by C. Tse Kimberlin.

Song Text 1
I'm thirsty, my sister.
I'm hungry, my mother.
Who can I tell this to?
I'm in exile.
Oh me, oh my . . .
In silence all season.

I have nothing at all
except old age and my poverty
hunger and poverty united together . . .

[krar interlude]

I am crying and I am sick.
As I cry about my poverty,
give me one injera.[30]
I will eat it standing.
Since there is no respect
for one in exile.
Exiles don't raise their heads to look straight.
People in trouble never have enough.
Poor people don't give ingera to other people . . .

Song Text 2
Note: The women in the camp see locusts as symbols of their suffering and dislocation.

Oh grain, powdered grain,
you make us quack like chickens.
You made us exiles without judgment.

Refrain: That was what we sang in the time of the locusts.

APPENDIX B: SONGS FROM *ASTER AWEKE* (1989)

Song Text 3
"Tizita" (Memories)
"Tizita" is sung by Aster Aweke in Amharic, accompanied by Kassa Admassu on the six-string krar, or lyre. The following is an approximate English translation:

They're your memories, just as you are a memory.
Promising to come and yet not being there.
The melody of my song is only sound to you.
Memory is love . . . it's a longing you should know.

Song Text 4
"Shebebu" (My excuse)
"Shebebu" is accompanied by Abegas Kebrework Shiota on the keyboards, Henok Temesgen playing bass, George Jones on the drums, Ray Carless on the saxophone, and Colin Graham on trumpet and flugelhorn. The following is an approximate English translation:

Because you're the cloak that protects me,
you're the only thing that the world sees.
Even if you think I'm cold,
don't ask for anyone else.

Note: The recording entitled *aster aweke* includes the following credits: cover photograph of Aster by Julien Broad; cover textile photographs by Jak Kilby; page layout and typesetting by Diacritic; basic tracks recorded by Chris Murphy at Omega Studios, Rockville, Maryland; vocals, horns, and the song "Tizita" recorded by Hugo Nicolson at Townhouse Studios, London.

NOTES

1. The Tigray region is located in the northern highlands of Ethiopia, but its Tigre-speaking inhabitants have cultural links to the Tigrinnya-speaking peoples of Eritrea. Unlike the latter, who wanted their independence, the Tigre did not reject Ethiopian identity.

2. These students were primarily those from what was formerly called Haile Selassie University in Addis Ababa and is now called Addis Ababa University.

3. The published sources cited in this essay include Eritrea as part of Ethiopia. Eritrea officially became an independent country in 1993. Because this essay describes situations and conditions before and after May 1993, conclusions drawn reflect both countries unless otherwise stated.

4. Eritrean nationalism is based on a shared identity that first emerged during the period of Italian colonization starting in 1895. Italy attempted to colonize Ethiopia but was defeated by Emperor Menelik II's forces in 1896. The Italian defeat and the subsequent Treaty of Addis Ababa established the boundaries of Eritrea as an Italian colony, distinct from the Ethiopian Empire. This colonization caused Eritrea to develop differently from Ethiopia and to maintain those differences. By the mid-1940s Eritreans, now under British administration, had formed political organizations and trade unions. The United Nations voted to federate Eritrea with Ethiopia in 1950, but Emperor Haile Selassie voided the Eritrean Constitution and ended the federal status of Eritrea in 1962. Following the May 1991 fall of the Mengistu government, Eritrea became a de facto independent state and officially became an independent country on 27 April 1993 (African American Institute [1994], 10).

5. According to estimates, Ethiopia had 220,000 uniformed soldiers and Eritrea had 70,000–90,000 (Nelson and Kaplan 1981, 245; Parmelee 1993). Women are said to make up one-third of each of the armed forces.

6. In Eritrea women are to hold at least 20 percent of the positions in government; in Ethiopia, 20 to 30 percent.

7. Illegitimacy (7) and rape (8) are complex subjects. Although the law may support women in some instances, it is the community itself and its underlying social code that continue to play a defining role in setting the boundaries and influencing the outcome of specific cases.

8. Land ownership is a complex subject. In some cases women have rights to land and property ownership, but there are differences between who owns the land and who can collect taxes on produce grown on the land. For example, *rist* land is hereditary, whereas *gult* land, defined by who can collect taxes on it, is not (Lipsky 1962, 242). Although there are some groups—such as the Amhara—whose upper-class women have considerable property and inheritance rights, the generally depressed status of Amhara peasant women reflects the low opinion commonly held of them (Levine 1965, 79). According to Lulseged Kumsa, among the pagan Wollomo tribe, a married woman cannot possess anything of her own. Everything she acquires goes to her husband (Lord 1963, 65). Thus, rules of land tenure vary throughout the country largely according to local custom, type of agriculture, and degree of governmental influence.

9. For reasons, see Kimberlin 1983a on the status of Ethiopian musicians.

10. In Amhara traditional society funeral songs were usually performed by women, and it was only the women who were allowed to cry openly at funerals, although men were allowed to cry first during the mourning period, which can last up to seven days (Yewoubdar 1994).

11. Not only were some women circumcised, but they had their vaginas sewn shut after delivering each child. After 1975 women were educated to learn that the vagina is a blessing for their protection.

12. The TPLF is the majority political party in the Tigray region.

13. The TPLF Cultural Department has a collection of hamien poems.

14. Because Ethiopian and Eritreans are addressed by first name, I cite them by their first names in the text and also alphabetize using those names in the reference list.

15. Dawit Wolde Giorgis, a former head of Ethiopia's relief agency, stated in 1987 that "hunger and war were intertwined, and the most seriously affected areas were Eritrea, Tigray, and Wollo—the areas where the major insurgent movements operate" (Dawit 1989; in Hammond 1989, 122).

16. During Emperor Haile Selassie I's reign, three girls' schools were established in Ethiopia, in Addis Ababa, Harrar, and Nazareth (Yewoubdar 1994).

17. *Derg* is the Amharic word for "committee." It also refers to the Mengistu regime.

18. For instance, in 1992 it was celebrated as a major holiday in Asmara, where thousands of women paraded down the main street and filled a stadium for a celebration.

19. Who was Marta? There were two. The first Marta attended Addis Ababa University and was a prominent member of the student movement. She fought during the early stages of the Ethiopian and Tigrayan wars. In 1972 she and other university students tried to hijack a plane. They failed and were arrested by Haile Selassie's police; she was later executed. When the revolution began in 1974, it marked the beginning of an increase in the number of the women soldiers. The first female fighter in the revolution was named Kasu. The other fighters renamed her Marta in memory of the university student. This Marta grew up in Adi Grat, worked in a factory in Asmara, and eventually joined the revolution. She was illiterate when she joined but learned to read and write. She was killed in 1980. The school was named mainly for her but indirectly for the first Marta.

20. The shamma is the traditional finely woven cotton embroidered dress that is accompanied by a type of shawl that can be used to cover the head.

21. A 1989 issue of *Mekalih,* a magazine for soldiers, contains information about family planning, abortion, and organizing women (Hammond 1989, 99). Given impetus by women's organizations, the EPLF produced and distributed sanitary napkins, a commonplace necessity for women that is often overlooked as a priority product (Kinnock 1988, 75).

22. At that time I was a member of the official U.S. delegation invited to Ethiopia to observe and evaluate the first democratic election process in 1992. Hans Alles, a delegate from Holland, and I were assigned to the Tigray region in northern Ethiopia, where we visited and evaluated seventeen villages over nearly three weeks. In Shilaro the women's association conducted a demonstration on our behalf advocating voting for TPLF.

23. In the United States there is the recently established Center for Ethiopian Arts and Culture in Washington, D.C. (*Center for Ethiopian Arts and Culture Newsletter* May 1994), which was incorporated December 1991. It claims that over 100,000 Ethiopians now live in the United States and approximately 40,000 reside in the greater metropolitan Washington, D.C., area where Ethiopians run restaurants, nightclubs, social service centers, radio and TV stations, churches, publications, and various businesses. The Adams Morgan area attests to this presence, with over fifteen Ethiopian restaurants and markets lining the streets (ibid.).

24. Atsede Teklai, in her early twenties at the time, is from Adua Awaraja, in Edaga Arabi.

25. The time line plays an important function in instrumental ensemble and solo music. It can be an external or internal repeated rhythmic pattern played or felt throughout. It functions as the basic pulse or rhythmic referent to which all other instruments relate. Until the advent of the drum machine, a covert, not overt, time line was used, and this allowed for greater elasticity in the way rhyth-

mic patterns were articulated. One could get behind, so to speak, and catch up at crucial points—resulting in what is known as the rubato effect. This use of "elastic time" between crucial pulses is a major characteristic of traditional musical performances. With the drum machine, this elasticity is not very apparent, and rhythmic patterns appear more rigid (Kimberlin 1983b).

26. Hammond (1989, 80) also heard this explanation for the term *struggle*.

27. Most women are married by age twenty. Some women did not marry and bear children during the war, spending their marriageable age on the battle lines. In 1993 Askalu Menkarios wrote a critical editorial in the government-run newspaper where she cited cases of male fighters divorcing the wives they had married in the field for younger women who cooked, wore their hair long, and were more often the virgins that Eritrean and Ethiopian society prefers as brides (Parmelee 1993).

28. My recent fieldwork suggests the presence of a paradigm shift from a belief in the government as the major force for improving conditions for women to a greater reliance on grass-roots forces as the basis for change affecting women in Ethiopia and Eritrea.

29. In many cultures it is customary to refer to countries using feminine forms (e.g., *she* or *her*). Although one could say Mama Zeinab validates this reference, what is unique is that a photograph of one identified woman, not a drawing of an anonymous woman, was reproduced on the 1988 poster and on Sorenson's book cover.

30. Injera is a pancake-like fermented flat bread made of t'eff or barley.

REFERENCES CITED

African American Institute. [1994]. *Eritrea Referendum on Independence April 23–25, 1993*. Washington, D.C.: African American Institute.

Aweke, Aster. 1989. *aster aweke*. Triple Earth Records (U.K.), LP Terra 107.

Dawit Wolde Giorgis. 1989. *Red Tears: War, Famine, and Revolution in Ethiopia*. Trenton, N.J.: Red Sea.

Gebre Hiwet Tesfagiorgis, ed. 1993. *Emergent Eritrea*. Trenton, N.J.: Red Sea.

Hammond, Jenny. 1989. *Sweeter Than Honey: Testimonies of Tigrayan Women*. Oxford: Third World First.

Kessler, Wayne. 1992. Personal correspondence with former Peace Corps volunteers who served in Eritrea.

Kimberlin, Cynthia Mei-Ling. 1972. Unpublished field notes.

Kimberlin, Cynthia Tse. 1983a. "The Music of Ethiopia." In *The Musics of Many Cultures*, ed. Elizabeth May, 232–52. Los Angeles: University of California Press.

———. 1983b. Liner notes to *The Music of Nigeria: Igbo Music* (record 3). Barenreiter Musicaphon, UNESCO collection, BM 30L 2311.

Kinnock, Glenys. 1988. *Eritrea: Images of War and Peace.* Chatto and Windus: London.

Levine, Donald. 1965. *Wax and Gold.* Chicago: University of Chicago Press.

Lipsky, George. 1962. *Ethiopia.* New Haven, Conn.: Hraf Press under the auspices of the American University.

Lord, Edith. 1963. *Cultural Patterns in Ethiopia.* Washington, D.C.: Department of State, Agency for International Development.

Nelson, Harold D., and Irving Kaplan, eds. 1981. *Ethiopia: A Country Study.* Washington D.C.: Foreign Area Studies, American University.

Parmelee, Jennifer. 1993. "Eritrean Women Who Fought in the Trenches Now Battle Tradition." *Washington Post* 25 June, A:30.

Richardson, Derk. 1991. "The Best of All Worlds." *The East Bay* [Oakland, Calif.] *Guardian*, May.

Salem Mekuria, producer and director. 1991. *SIDET: Forced Exile.* Videotape. Mekuria Productions.

———. 1993. Unpublished descriptive sheet for *SIDET: Forced Exile,* prepared for author, May.

Scott, Iain, and Bunt Stafford Clark. 1989. Liner notes to *aster aweke.* Triple Earth Records (U.K.), LP Terra 107.

Sorenson, John. 1993. *Imagining Ethiopia: Struggles for History and Identity in the Horn of Africa.* New Brunswick, N.J.: Rutgers University Press.

Yewoubdar Beyene. 1994. Personal communication, May.

Yohannes Petros. 1989. *Constitutional History of Ethiopia.* Studies in Ethiopian Politics: Social Science Monograph Series, Discussion Paper 2. London: Ethio-International Center of Translation.

10   *Past and Present Gender Roles in the Traditional Community on Kihnu Island in Estonia*

Ingrid Rüütel

Kihnu is a small island near the eastern Estonian coast that has to an extent retained its traditional culture and way of life up to the present day. The first data about its population derive from the fifteenth century, but the island was probably consistently populated from the end of the thirteenth or the beginning of the fourteenth century. Most of its population appears to have originated in the Estonian islands Saaremaa and Muhu, both of which were populated by northern Estonian tribes since prehistoric times. Inhabitants of Kihnu Island have also had close contact with communities on the western Estonian coast, where they worked on farms during summers and traded (exchanging fish for corn) in winter. Kihnu's linguistic and cultural dialect thus represents a transitional form between the dialects of the islands and those of the western Estonian coast. In addition to occupying themselves with fishing and sealing, the men engaged in shipbuilding (both on Kihnu and outside) and navigation, especially before World War I.

Despite these interactions, the island itself remained considerably closed and isolated from the outside world. The Kihnu community preserved an extremely conservative way of life. Ancient forms of traditional culture, both material and spiritual, have been maintained up to the present. Some new cultural phenomena penetrated the island from the second half of the nineteenth century on, but they did not replace the older ones, and different cultural layers coexist there even in the 1990s.

With regard to musical styles, for example, one may observe

1. archaic, pre-Christian traditions (the wedding ceremony), alliterative songs in *Kalevala* meter[1] with an ancient musical style, and round dances;
2. newer folk song styles (rhymed songs in strophic form) with a newer musical style influenced by European folk music of the eighteenth and nineteenth centuries, couple dances, and other country dances;

3. songs from the Orthodox, Baptist, and other church traditions;
4. old and new popular songs of literary origin and newer social dances; and
5. contemporary disco music and dances, as well as other forms of current popular and mass culture.

The unique cultural situation of Kihnu has elicited the keen interest of ethnologists and folklorists. From the beginning of this century, the island has been a site of numerous fieldwork expeditions. Estonian folklore and ethnographic archives contain rich collections of folklore, folk music transcriptions and ethnographic descriptions, as well as sound recordings, photos, films, and videos.

I started my fieldwork in Kihnu toward the end of the 1950s when I was a young folklore student at Tartu University, where the title of my first student essay was "The Folk Music of the Islands of Kihnu and Ruhnu." At the beginning I had only pen and paper, so I could do only transcriptions. Later I started working with a tape recorder and managed to record many songs and instrumental pieces, as well as interviews describing context. I have also made numerous recordings during traditional wedding ceremonies. In more recent years I have been assisted by a camera operator, thus providing the collections of the Estonian Folklore Archives with numerous videorecordings. In cooperation with Estonian TV, I have made twelve TV documentaries about Kihnu Island, its inhabitants, and its culture.

Kihnu traditional culture has also been the subject of a number of my monographs and articles. So far I have discussed mainly song melodies and wedding ceremonies (Rüütel 1956, 1977, 1992, 1995). In this essay I examine a special aspect of the traditional spiritual culture of Kihnu—namely, its feminization during the last hundred years. I have tried to bring forth different aspects of this process and to search for the reasons behind it.

Traditional Gender Roles in Kihnu Communities

When speaking about the gender roles in a culture, one must take into consideration changes in lifestyle over time. Because a Kihnu family traditionally got its main income from fishing, sealing, and navigation, all the men spent plenty of time away from home and the household; consequently, cattle breeding and tillage (including plowing, traditionally a man's job) were women's tasks in Kihnu. The father's role as the head of the family was therefore not as essential there as on the Estonian mainland, and the real leader of the farmstead was his wife.

Table 10.1. The Basic Pattern of the Kihnu Wedding

Bride's Home	Groom's Home
Day 1	
The relatives arrive.	The relatives arrive.
The groom's procession is welcomed festively (the bride is hidden).	
The guests are treated to food and drink; the bride is brought to the table (the ritual headwear *uig* covers her face).	
The bride is ceremonially seen off from the parental home.	The young couple is welcomed festively.
	The *uig* is removed in a ceremony.
	The guests are treated to food and drink.
	The bride's relatives arrive with the dowry chest; the "brother's smoke" ritual is performed.
	The dowry is distributed to the groom's relatives.
	The bride is dressed and adorned in a married woman's clothes (an apron and a special coif are the signs of a married woman).
	The bride dances with relatives and guests.
Days 2 and 3[a]	
	The "bride's bread and wine" is distributed (a custom of collecting money for the young couple).
	Members of the wedding party tell jokes and dance.
The young couple and the groom's relatives are greeted and treated to food and drink.	
Money is collected in a ritual accompanied by jokes and dancing.	
The young couple and the groom's relatives leave the house of the bride's parents.	
Guests are treated to food and drink once more and then are sent off.	Guests are treated to food and drink once more and then are sent off.

a. In the past, the second day probably began with the arrival of the bride's relatives at the groom's farmstead with the dowry chest.

Generally in Estonia, when a man named his eldest son as the heir to his farm, he lost his rights as head of the household and, together with his wife, became a dependent of that son. In Kihnu, where a farm was distributed among all the sons, the former mistress of the household continued in her role as the main manager of housekeeping. She also had a significant role in bringing up grandchildren and transmitting spiritual values and traditions. In Kihnu, as in Estonian peasant society in general, children were traditionally educated in large part by participating in work-related activities. From their early years, boys accompanied the older men to sea to fish. Girls helped their mother and grandmother in housekeeping and farming.

The most important skill for a girl was considered to be handicrafts. She would start to prepare her dowry chest in early childhood. She learned such skills from her mother and grandmother, although the village girls' handicraft evenings (the so-called *ülaljõstmised*) also played a significant role.

After a young couple became engaged, the bride's girlfriends were asked to gather at the bridal house (*nuorikumaja*) to help the bride prepare her dowry chest. In the nuorikumaja the making of handicrafts was always accompanied by collective singing, as was customary during other handicraft evenings as well. Dancing started when the boys came with a musician (a fiddle or *harmonica*[2] player). The song repertory for handicraft evenings was not fixed. Old alliterative songs, newer rhymed folk songs, and various popular songs were sung. Collective singing was also an inseparable part of the farmstead carding bees, which are sometimes arranged even in the 1990s.

The wedding ceremony is the most essential event in Kihnu, bringing together various genres and forms of traditional culture and preserving them to the present day (see table 10.1). The Kihnu wedding confirms the agreement between two different lineages. It probably originates from the clan system, and its basic features are common to all Balto-Finnic people. The so-called two-end or two-part wedding is celebrated separately at the farmsteads of both the bride and the bridegroom, but the main events take place with both sides participating. The main ceremonies are accompanied by the old ritual songs of alliterative verse.

Until recent times only relatives were invited to weddings, and traditional figures of the ceremony belonged to the nearest kin of the bride and the bridegroom. Women were the principal figures in the ceremony, but some men had significant roles as well. Among the most essential figures of the wedding ceremony were (and still are, in the case of traditional weddings) the following male relatives:

FROM THE GROOM'S KIN

The **groomsman** (*peiupoiss*) is a young unmarried man whose task is to assist (or replace) the groom.

—The groomsman is the first to come to the bride's house announcing the arrival of the wedding procession. He gives a mitten with beads to the bride's mother, who replaces these with some coins as a sign that the groom's procession is welcome.

—He rides on horseback (nowadays usually on a motorcycle) in front of the procession (both on the way to the bride's home and on the way back to the groom's home).

—He dances with the bride for her first dance as a married woman.

—He encourages the guests to gather to collect money for the young couple (a special ritual enabling the bridegroom's kin to pay for the bride's dowry).

—He carries out some rituals for neutralizing the power of evil forces (e.g., he makes three crosses with his sword on the door jamb).

The **Iron Hand** (*raudkäsi*) is a married relative of the groom whose task is to protect the bride until she becomes a married woman.

—The Iron Hand takes third position in the wedding procession, and the bride sits atop his knee on the way to the groom's house.

—Together with the bride's brother, he brings the bride from hiding to the table (i.e., to the groom and his relatives).

—He brings the bride to the dowry chest.

—He guards the bride from being stolen and protects her from any other misfortune (including evil forces).

FROM THE BRIDE'S KIN

The **bride's brother** (*veli*)

—Together with the Iron Hand, the bride's brother brings the bride from hiding to the table.

—He accompanies the bride to the groom's house.

—He advances to meet the dowry chest and strikes it three times with his sword.

—He makes the "brother's smoke" for the bride's relatives when they arrive at the groom's house.

—He guards the wedding flag.

The **bride's father**

—The bride's father brings the dowry chest into the groom's farmstead (as a rule, he sits on the chest en route from his house to the groom's).

Instrumental musicians were also men (without exception in the past), and they were the initiators of wedding jokes coming from both the bride's and the groom's kin.

Female ceremonial figures included the following:

The **bride's mother**
—The bride's mother gives permission to the groom's procession to enter.
—She leads the hospitality and other activities in her house.
—She sends the bride off to her new home.
—She holds the candle near the dowry chest while the dowry is distributed.

The **groom's mother**
—The groom's mother leads the treating and other activities in her house.
—She welcomes the bride while standing at the door of her house and covers the doorsteps with white cloth.
—She removes the ritual headwear (*uig*) that covers the bride's face.
—She holds the candle near the dowry chest.

The **Iron Hand's wife**
—The Iron Hand's wife dresses the bride in a married woman's clothes (an apron and a coif);
—She assists the bride in the ceremony of distributing the "bride's bread and wine."

The **bride's girlfriends** (*umbrukad*)
—The bride's girlfriends help to do different chores in both the bride's and the groom's houses (set the table, wash the dishes, etc.).
—They tie a waistband on the well of the first farmstead in the bride's (and groom's) village on the arrival of the wedding procession.
—They assist in distributing the dowry.
—They start the third dance (after the two dances with the bride), which is joined by the rest of the wedding guests.

Thus, *women have the most essential roles in the wedding ceremony as leaders of the central rituals.*

The wedding singers were and are women without exception. There are traditionally two wedding choirs, one from the bridal lineage and the other from the groom's lineage. They accompany (and in many cases lead) the most essential events of the wedding ceremony.

Wedding songs were performed (1) while walking or sitting in the carriage during the wedding processions; (2) while moving in a closed circle (singers of the bride's clan performed special songs at the bridegroom's farm—e.g., at the ceremony of the "brother's smoke"—and vice versa); and (3) while

Singers from the groom's clan arrived at the bride's yard, 1986. (The author is on the left.)

Sending off the bride from the parental home, 1954.

The mother-in-law is removing the *uig*, 1975.

Singing in a circle under the triumphal gateway of the wedding, 1959.

Adorning the bride, n.d.

Dancing with the bride,
n.d.

standing in a half-circle, stamping from foot to foot and swaying the body, usually holding one another by the arms or some other way. This last method was the most common way to perform the old wedding songs in the arrival ceremony of the groom's clan's wedding procession to the bride's yard, at the table while the guests were treated to food and drink (both at the bride's and the groom's farm), during the ceremony of sending off the bride from the parental home, and when the newlyweds were greeted at the groom's farm, as well as when the dowry was distributed at the groom's house.

There used to be only one melody for all songs, which varied noticeably when performed by different singers as well as within a single performance. The performance is monophonic, although heterophony may arise from the simultaneous sounding of different variants. No accompaniment by any musical instruments was used (as in the runic song tradition in general).

Traditional musical instruments played at weddings—probably foremost the bagpipe (judging by the tunes), followed by the fiddle and then the harmonica, which is nowadays mostly replaced by the modern accordion—were generally used for accompanying social dances of more recent origin, danced for recreation by the wedding guests and having no direct relationship to the wedding ceremony. Still, two special dances belong to the ritual: (1) the dance with the bride, the first presentation of her to the groom's kin; and (2) a special old round dance performed in an open circle by all the participants of the wedding. In the latter, the dancers moved around the farmstead, passing through all of its main places. This dance is evidently older than the bride's dance (which was a couple dance) and probably had special significance connected with magic powers in the past.

The old Kihnu wedding customs are without doubt pre-Christian in origin, containing animistic features and other traits of ancient traditional beliefs as well as tribal practices (see Rüütel 1995). Although people long ago abandoned such ancient beliefs, their symbolic meaning has been preserved, helping to strengthen the alliance formed by the marriage. In addition, such symbolic actions help to prepare the bride for her new social status and to integrate her into the new family, thus facilitating future cohabitation. Belief (even if subconscious) in the power of words and the effect of a ritual has been preserved for a longer time than the beliefs underlying them.

Other song genres preserved and passed down in family circles up to the present day are lullabies and nursery rhymes, both of which are as a rule also sung by women (mothers and grandmothers). Nevertheless, in Kihnu as well as on other Estonian islands, older men (grandfathers) who no longer went to sea spent most of their time at home, where they also used to take care of children and sing nursery rhymes to them.

What about collective singing by men on Kihnu? It existed until the beginning of this century. There is little data about men's songs using alliterative verse. The men's runic song tradition had already begun to ebb by the first half of the nineteenth century. The more recent folk song style, the strophic rhymed songs that were disseminated on Kihnu at the end of the nineteenth and beginning of the twentieth centuries, contained mainly men's songs (sailor songs, humorous village songs, etc.).

Contemporary Gender Roles in Kihnu Communities

In the latter decades of the twentieth century, men no longer sing even the newer folk songs; they survive only in women's repertories and memories. Although women have preserved a great deal of their traditional song lore, men rarely sing at all today. Furthermore, even the instrumentalists are nowadays often girls or women. They do not play the fiddle (this instrumental tradition died when the last fiddle players died in recent decades), but some women play harmonica and modern accordion. None of them, however, master the harmonica as well as the best male musicians did in the past, as is evident from recordings.

Women have also occupied some other special roles and functions that traditionally belonged to men. Some of these roles occur within the Greek Orthodox faith, which the Kihnu islanders have followed since the middle of the last century, when they and certain other Estonians converted to the (Russian) "czar's religion" in hopes of gaining land. During the Soviet period, however, there was no priest on the island. A priest from the mainland visits the island occasionally. For many years an old woman, Marina Rooslaid, supplemented the work of the priest. Her activities were formally accepted by the Orthodox church authorities, and she had official status as the priest's assistant. She carried out the church ceremonies during calendric feasts, she buried the deceased, and sometimes she even baptized children. She also rang the church bell and directed a group of women who sang religious songs during the church services, as well as folk or popular songs during secular feasts in the Kihnu community center and elsewhere. The same women also acted as wedding singers at this time, when Rooslaid was the director of many wedding ceremonies.

Women have assumed traditional male roles as song composers, too. As do other Estonian islands, Kihnu has a tradition of composing songs on topical themes, such as village life or sailors' adventures. These songs belong to the newer rhymed, strophic style mentioned previously. The song makers were usually men, but today Kihnu's best-known song maker is an elderly woman, Virve Köster. She composes her songs in her head, the melody and words simultaneously, and later writes the words into her songbooks. These are lyrical songs or lyrical narratives about her own life, composed in the style of popular songs from the 1930s to 1960s. Her songs are first performed in her family circle; she sings them with her granddaughters and daughters, who accompany her on the guitar or accordion. Some of her songs, however, are also known and sung by other islanders. She has even been commissioned to compose a special song for the ceremony of seeing off the bride from the parental home during the wedding ceremony.

One of her songs ("The Feast of the Sea") is included in the repertory of the popular folk music group "Kukerpillid" (a group that, incidentally, consists only of men—architects and musicians from the capital city of Tallinn), who learned it from the author on Kihnu. The song became popular in the whole of Estonia and could be heard frequently on Estonian radio and TV programs some years ago. This group has visited Kihnu Island several times, playing the old Kihnu songs and dance pieces in the Kihnu community center. Consequently, old dances were revived in the context of social dances at village parties, held in the community center; for a long time before that, these had been performed only at home during weddings. In recent years some new popular folk music groups (such as Väikeste lõõtspillide ühing [Association of small harmonicas] in Pärnu, Untsakad in Viljandi, and others) have been founded by young people (mostly young men) in towns. Their repertory has included a number of the Kihnu songs and dance tunes. They visit the island, often singing and playing together with the Kihnu girls during common parties as well as in official festivals in Estonia and abroad. Because of all these activities, the recognition of Kihnu traditional songs and music has increased on both Kihnu Island and the Estonian mainland.

The Feminization of Kihnu Culture

What caused the feminization of Kihnu culture? There are general historical and cultural reasons as well as local and specific ones.

1. In the traditional Kihnu family, women (especially the eldest matriarch) play an essential role and enjoy high status. Because men spent a lot of time outside the home and off the island, Kihnu to a large extent developed as a women's community.

2. The absence of political and economic independence during the Soviet period affected men more than women. Men's freedom was considerably more restricted, for the men were not allowed to go to sea or invest money in enterprises when they pleased. After the small Kihnu collective farm was merged into the giant Pärnu fishing *kolkhoz* (collective) a number of Kihnu men even became unemployed—a rather rare situation during Soviet times. The fate of Kihnu islanders was similar to that of other small indigenous communities in the Soviet Union (as well as in America) whose residents lost their freedom to carry out their traditional ways of life and livelihood. Ironically, Kihnu fishermen who belonged to the official kolkhoz fishing team earned more money than ever before.

As a result of this economic disparity, traditional values decayed, and men appeared to be spiritually weaker than women in this process. Women carried and transmitted traditional values more than men did and thus were perceived as mentally stronger throughout this period.

I asked Marina Rooslaid why men do not attend church services and why they have forgotten even the traditional secular songs. She answered:

M.R.: The men do not do much more but drink.

I.R.: When did it start and why?

M.R.: During the kolkhoz time. They got so much money with their *kakuams* (a special kind of fishing net) and then the drinking began.

I.R.: In some other places people also earn much money but do not drink as heavily. Why just here in Kihnu?

M.R.: I do not know what is the matter. They have also too much free time now. In earlier times, they left the island in spring and returned in autumn. Now they are at home a lot helping the women, and they have too much free time. But there are still men who keep their living standard and do not drink. There was also a lack of a strong leader in Kihnu who would guide the people. There must always be a strong leader. The guidance happened to be too weak.

Rooslaid was still hoping that things would turn for the better. Today there are young men who are eager to change their lifestyle and are actively participating in every aspect of their community life.

3. Another cause for the disappearance of men's traditional singing is the fact that, in more recent times, traditional singing has been concentrated mainly around weddings, and wedding songs have always been women's songs. Other customs and occasions for collective singing have disappeared.

Men thus began to regard singing as a woman's affair. Even in male drinking parties, conversation is much more usual than singing.

Still, in amateur folklore groups that perform traditional songs and dances during modern festive events at the Kihnu community center, as well as on different occasions off the island, boys and young men participate together with girls and women. They dance folk dances and sing traditional songs but unfortunately do not play traditional instruments. Again, women and girls play more active roles in those groups, usually acting as group leaders.

4. Men have always introduced elements of innovation to Kihnu society. They introduced the newer folk song styles to the island and started to wear modern clothes a long time ago, whereas women have preserved their traditional Kihnu striped skirts in everyday use up to the present day.

In recent times young men have also played in amateur groups that perform modern music for dance and entertainment in the Kihnu community center and at weddings. Nevertheless, leading singers of such groups (the musicians may vary) are usually young women who live in Tallinn and visit home during summer holidays, as all the young people who study or work on the mainland usually do. Change and cultural innovation concern the young people, boys and girls who are studying in towns and come to the island in the summer. And of course, radio and TV programs, movies, and films—the commercial standards of the transnational media industries—are the main factors influencing cultural change and weakening the traditional songs and music of Kihnu. The situation where "the adherence to one's own culture . . . is often eroded by the impact of the industrialized culture purveyed by the mass media" (UNESCO 1989, 5) is evident today both on Kihnu and in Estonia in general.

It is notable that women are preserving traditional cultural values even in this modern situation, acting on different cultural levels: the same old women sing ancient wedding songs in pre-Christian rituals and Orthodox songs for the church tradition; girls and young women participate both in making modern music and as umbrukad, who sing old wedding songs at wedding ceremonies. Women occupy essential positions both in the church and as cultural leaders in the community center, where different layers of music and dance are performed.

Women are also active in private enterprises. A young woman, Annely Akermann, is the manager of the recently founded tourist firm Kihnu Rand ("the Kihnu Coast"), which organizes tours to the island. She also acts as a guide. The tour includes, besides sightseeing, a folk music and dance presentation. Akermann is also leading the project "The Way of Kihnu to the Open Society," which started in 1998 with financial support of the Open Estonian Foundation. Katrin Kumpan should also be mentioned. She came to the island from the mainland city of Pärnu as a young girl to work as a teacher and leader of a folklore group. Later, after graduating from the Theater Department of the Tallinn Conservatory, she worked for a number of years as an actress in Tallinn, still often visiting the island and leading the folk music group Kihnumua. She recently returned to Kihnu Island, and in 1996 she was the director of the community center. Kumpan and Akermann together organize the biggest cultural summer event in Kihnu, called "Kihnu Days," where both local groups and mainland guests participate.

Nevertheless, men have not given up their leading positions in production areas and as formal administrative leaders. Bear in mind that Kihnu islanders have always obtained their main income from men's jobs—fishing, sealing, the building of boats, organizing boat cooperatives, and so on. Furthermore, the clan chief, later the leader of the village community, was a man. During the Soviet period leaders of production (chairman of the kolkhoz or its departments) as well as formal administrative leaders were also men. Nowadays men occupy leading positions as chairman of the fishing cooperative, manager of the fishing industry, chief magistrate of the parish, and chairman of the parish council.

Thus, one could say that traditional Estonian society (distinct from today's situation, where things are still a bit different) has not known and recognized female politicians or administrative leaders. Nonetheless, women lead the spiritual sphere, preserving and carrying on traditional values both at home and in the traditional rural society.

NOTES

1. The older Estonian folk songs belong to the ancient Balto-Finnic songlore (referred to in the literature usually as *runic songs, Kalevala-meter songs,* or *alliterative songs* but in oral tradition referred to mostly as "old songs"). They are based on alliteration, syntactical parallelism, and eight-syllable verses of quantitative meter (i.e., regular alternation of long and short syllables with changing positions of stress). This poetical form probably dates back to the era when the Balto-Finnic tribes had not yet branched off and used the same Balto-Finnic proto-language, which constituted the original basis of the song form.

2. This is a traditional type of village accordion.

REFERENCES CITED

Rüütel, Ingrid. 1956. "Kihnu ja Ruhnu rahvaviisidest" (About the folk music of the islands Kihnu and Ruhnu). *Sirp ja Vasar,* 3 Aug.

———. 1977. "Opornaya sistema i zakonomernosti var'irovania mobil'nyh elementov kak strukturnye priznaki tipologii narodnyh melodii" (The basic tones and legitimacies of the mobile elements of a melody as the structural principles of the typology of folk tunes). In *Problemy taksonomii estonskih runicheskih napevov* (Taxonomic problems of Estonian runotunes), ed. M. Rummel, 80–117. Tallinn: Akademia nauk Estonskoi SSR.

———. 1992. "Tradition and Innovation in Estonian Folk Music Today: On the Kihnu Traditional Culture." In *European Studies in Ethnomusicology: Historical Developments and Recent Trends: Selected Papers,* ed. Max Peter Bauman, Artur Simon, and Ulrich Wegner, 237–44. Intercultural Music Studies, 4. Berlin: F. Noetzel Verlag.

———. 1995. "Wedding traditions of the Isle of Kihnu—Roots and Developments." In *Folk Belief Today,* ed. Mall Hiiemäc and Mare Kõiva, 377–405. Tartu: Estonian Academy of Sciences, Institute of the Estonian Language and Estonian Museum of Literature.

UNESCO. 1989. "Recommendations on the Safeguarding of Traditional Culture and Folklore Adopted by the General Conference." Report of the Twenty-fifth session of the General Conference, 15 Nov., Paris.

Part 4

Technologies in Gendered Motion

Perhaps it is not surprising that our authors' dialogue about issues of gender, music, and technology related both to the extension of self and to the loss of self. Sandstrom, for example, found that the "neutralizing" effect of technology rendered her both genderless and raceless, enabling her to work across traditional identity boundaries and identities in ways she might not otherwise have used: "As I set out to learn the field, I did not appreciate that I would be one of the few women mix engineers in this country. The men owned the companies; they weren't hiring unless you had experience and the only way to get experience was to work with your friends' bands which were all male. Therefore, men had access to the experience. I didn't realize it at the time, but through my association with sound equipment and my role as a mix engineer, I became somewhat gender neutral and to a certain extent race/ethnic neutral." Although this journey, which enabled her to meet musicians from many ethnocultural communities, was an exciting one, in the end she regretted the necessity of "losing your gender because of your job."

Moisala's experience, however, casts a shadow on illusions of "neutrality." The composer Kaija Saariaho, about whom Moisala writes in her contribution, confided that she "experienced difficulties in working with male sound engineers because the power positions were 'wrong.'" Moisala also describes the "framing" of gendered expectations she encountered in the course of fieldwork in Nepal: "My first field trip in Nepal I made with my husband. Western people, particularly American colleagues, all assumed that he had done all the technical things/decisions and he was asked how we solved such technical problems as photographing in the bright mountain light, developing films in mountain villages where there was no electricity nor pure water, or recording singing accompanied by loud drumming."

The assumptions of male subjectivity—indeed, the erasures of female participation in technological pursuits—was strongly reinforced by Andra McCartney's account (quoted in the introduction) of being treated as either alien or absent in a MIDI users' group in Peterborough, Ontario: "Although I persisted for a year in attending meetings, I never felt completely accepted. Even the language seemed strange. Although I was familiar with computer language, the terminology of this group seemed even more concerned with size, speed, power, and control than business computer language."

Dusman describes her own early "fear of electronics," a fear not shared by her male colleagues, or at least one they did not acknowledge. She remains unsure of the ratio of enculturative experience and enculturative self-esteem mechanisms: "Perhaps it was just that my father never involved me in repairs, tools, carpentry, etc. the way he had involved my brothers. What I am trying to say is that I think for those of us who were young girls in the 50s and 60s in traditional white middle-class American families, there were cultural discriminations at work that our parents and teachers were unaware of at the time, and so we were too."

Several contributors commented on the special (al)lure that technology held for them. An early motivation for Sandstrom to study technology was to feel equal to men. She also comments on the similarity between sound engineering and conducting, another role in the music business she found particularly attractive. Pegley describes her own initial positive experiences in the Technology in Music Programme, which she describes in her essay as "seduction": "I recognize that initially I was seduced by both the volume and complexity of the technology."

Nevertheless, she proceeds to present a cogent analysis of the "down" side of digital technologies, particularly regarding the loss of bodily awareness.

> Several program initiatives had led to this dilemma: first, the choir had been cut, and while singing did take place at some music stations in the room, it (predictably) was avoided by many students who preferred to work and communicate via headphones. Second the instrumental music programme was terminated (although students could perform MIDI wind instruments at one centre). I was not convinced that their limited time on the MIDI wind replaced playing other wind instruments. Having suffered from bronchitis and its related breathing problems as a child, I believe playing a brass instrument helped expand my capacity to breathe and "take up space" both physically and mentally. The MIDI wind found in classrooms are not so demanding on the body and I have to wonder

about the drawbacks and gains of that technology to the exclusion of all other instruments.

Pegley proceeds to identify other problems—limited screen size and restricted arm movements, leading to less socially active and more disruptive students. She observes that the relationship to gender is marked: "The students who excelled at the technology and demonstrated less physical awareness all were boys. Girls generally were more cautious and questioning of the technology, sought alternative means of expressing their creativity, and were more aware of the need for expanded physical expressions."

Kisliuk also offers a critique of hegemonic implications that the use of technology carries:

> In Central Africa, I tried to downplay my relationship with machines. I did not want camcorders and tape recorders to stand between me and other people, and I wanted to distance myself from the colonial legacy of "taking" and "shooting" and "collecting" (the link to patriarchy and colonialism should not be lost here either). But I did use those machines as tools from time to time, after I had been living locally for many months. Once, when I did bring out my video camera and recorded informally the mayor of the village of Bagandou, when I played back for him his own image, he exclaimed in amazement that "white people are gods." When I protested that I did not even understand how the machine works and that it was made in Japan, he was not interested. He preferred to see the technology as a justification of long-term domination by Europeans. Thus, although for me, perhaps especially as a female, I found the technology to be somewhat alienating, for many local people in Central Africa the connection of technology with gender was superseded by its association with European domination.

It is not clear whether these anecdotes offer support for the highly influential social critique of Donna Haraway (1991), who suggests that women who use technology must somehow bridge identities to be "cyborgs," at once human and machine, subject and object. The anecdotes related by the contributors do not in any way deny the humanity of female computer users; rather, they tell a story that is simultaneously extremely painful and pleasurable, "dear and dangerous," to use a phrase from McCartney's essay.

The four chapters in this section address issues of gender and music technology from four different perspectives, those of the sound engineer, the educator, the composer, and the listener. In every case the contributors avoid essentialist conclusions while nevertheless recognizing the power of socially reinforced, essentializing gender constructions.

Boden Sandstrom interviewed her fellow sound engineers to learn about their career paths, aesthetic strategies, and styles of professional social interaction. She queries how gender affects access to the field, interactions with musicians, and aesthetic decisions.

Karen Pegley writes about a specially devised technology program in a Canadian elementary school where she served as a guest consultant. The strength of her approach undoubtedly lies in the rich ethnographic detail about the restructuring of physical space and its impact on the relative empowerment of boys and girls in the music program. She ascertains the preferences of students for activity centers that encourage individual or cooperative work, arguing that these centers are "multilocal"—that is, evocative of plural responses.

Andra McCartney describes both the creation of an electroacoustic work—the Canadian composer Hildegard Westerkamp's *Breathing Room*—as well as gendered responses to it. Her essay focuses on the contradictions and ironies encountered, in particular, on the use of breathing as a symbolically charged acoustic basis.

As an American composer, Linda Dusman, like McCartney, also considers electroacoustic music from the dual perspective of composer and listener. She posits that the absence of live performers in concerts of "acousmatic" (tape) music alters the bases on which listeners construct their gendered selves. Influenced by recent work from queer theorists in musicology, she argues that tape performance creates a more intense awareness of the body and a resultant "homosexualizing threat" to the audience. The focus of her exploration is the reception of Pauline Oliveros's *II of IV*.

These four essays engage some global critical issues, but they should be read with an awareness of their position, historically and nationally. Tools have always and everywhere been socially delimited and culturally defined. The technologies under consideration deal with a small range of such tools: digital technology for sound manipulation in the 1990s. As such, they are associated with certain aspects of contemporary science that—at least in North America—are marketed as leading edge for those who are or who aspire to be economically privileged. The recognition made by the phrase, "at least in North America" is significant. If our small sample of contributors (as well as the dialogue participants in this part of the questionnaire) is indicative, the analysis of the symbolism of this specific technological juncture is North American–centered. We invite our readers to be aware that these perspectives are shaped by experience in the part of the world that controls a large proportion of the transnational media.

Reference Cited

Haraway, Donna. 1991. *Simians, Cyborgs, and Women: The Reinvention of Nature.* New York: Routledge.

Boden Sandstrom

Sound and recording engineering[1] plays an integral part in the creation of music today. Most of the music we hear has been electronically altered, perhaps several times. In fact, the recent trend for major popular musical groups in the United States to perform "unplugged"—with lesser but varying degrees of electronic amplification—is an attempt to get back to the basics. It indicates the pervasiveness of electronic alteration, enhancement, or amplification of sound.

The manipulation of sound is fairly obvious to everyone when we think of popular music around the world but not at all obvious when we think of ethnographic recordings done in the field. Even as ethnomusicologists attempt to free themselves from notions of objectivity in research, we still seem stuck in a position of trying to present authenticity in our sound recordings, videos, and films.

The myth of the purity, authenticity, or even sanctity of field recordings was blown apart with Steven Feld's revelations, both in the article "From Schizophonia to Schismogenesis" and in his conversations with Charlie Keil in *Music Grooves* (1994), that he had used complicated technological means to enhance the sounds of the jungle based on his understanding of "lift-up-over sounding" of the Kaluli and their environment[2] (Keil and Feld 1994, 278–84, 328–29). Feld is doubtless not the first scholar to have done something like this. In fact, such techniques as changing speeds, filtering, and analyzing by tracks have been used for years. Feld's discussions of his creative process to recreate the Kaluli sounds helped bring this issue to the forefront.

It is rather ironic to think that performers, perhaps seeking to be more authentic, are turning off their microphones and amplifiers, just when ethnomusicologists are admitting to tinkering with music recorded or filmed in the field. Is this a ceremonial inversion of the notions of authenticity, property, or priorities?

How, then, are ethnomusicologists to deal with a colleague who comes to ethnomusicology with a long background in sound engineering? Can this somehow inform the winds of change in our various understandings of authenticity? More important, can it bring a greater degree of honesty to the research process and product? I argue that it can.

When a mix engineer manipulates sound, whether live or in a recording, the implication is that he or she is assuming a certain degree of creative control. Issues of power and control are inherent in access to this technology in any situation, and it is important to ask whether these issues are gendered,[3] and if so, how.

What is a mix engineer? A mix engineer is one who controls the sound mix during the recording process or a live performance. The mix engineer may either try to reproduce the sound heard with as little alteration as possible or to enhance or change the sound as much as might be desired within the limitations of the existing equipment. During recording the process is usually one of capturing sound onto some medium such as tape and then altering it later; in a live performance situation, the manipulation of sound takes place in real time and is usually referred to as "sound reinforcement." To have one's hands on the knobs or faders of a mixing board is to exercise considerable control. The sound engineer also controls the volume in the performance area and the way the sound covers that area in addition to controlling the actual mix. The sound reinforcement engineer has a one-shot chance to create the mix, whereas the recording engineer's mix can be repeated over and over again until everyone involved is satisfied. Usually the musicians involved and their producers have a great deal to say about the final mix during a recording session, but it is the engineer who controls the sound. Is this process gendered?

Methodology

In exploring sound engineering as a gendered field, it is important to say that the primary issue is power; all other issues are merely aspects of power. I will consider three aspects to this question: (1) the issue of power in relation to access to the field; (2) power, gender, and differences in mixing; and (3) sound engineers as sound mediators in relationship to the participants, whether performers, business staff, audiences, or others.

First, it is of absolute importance to locate myself and the period in his-

Leslie Ann Jones at a mixing board. Photo by Irene Young, used by permission.

tory that I am discussing.[4] This research is based on my experience as a white middle-class feminist entering the field of sound engineering during the 1970s women's rights' movement in the United States. My observations and conclusions were then discussed with four other white women engineers with whom I worked during that period, one of whom I trained. We worked with each other at different times at the Michigan Womyn's Music Festival (MWMF).[5] It was no coincidence that most of the few female sound engineers working during this time met each other at this festival. Professionals who worked with us during that period, 1975–85, were also consulted.[6]

The conclusions drawn from this research are intended not to essentialize what it is to be either a male or female mix engineer but to look at a socially constructed gendered field in a particular period of time in order to contextualize the possibility that women might handle the power of sound differently than men do and to consider the implications of this possibility.[7] Even in the 1990s in the United States, after two decades of Western feminism's struggle toward equality of all women, sound engineering remains a gendered field. In the Washington, D.C., area, where I have been working as a sound engineer for over twenty years, the number of female engineers mixing can still be counted on one's fingers.

Historical Context

The Michigan Womyn's Music Festival was started in 1976, a year after I founded Woman Sound, my sound company. These two women-operated organizations were created during one of the most active periods of the second wave of the women's rights movement. One feminist ideology that developed during this wave was cultural feminism. Cultural feminism involved the idea that the personal is the political, thereby adding importance to individual empowerment for women. As Ruth Scovill (1981, 148–49) points out: "A structure was needed with a woman-identified consciousness to support [women's] music, both spiritually and financially. . . . All-women feminist events offered an opportunity for women to get together on a larger and more supportive scale. . . . This . . . allowed women to interact and grow with each other, without outside . . . criticism."

In addition, the notion developed in feminist circles that women need not only to gain political power but also to regain their own spiritual and cultural life. Through the second wave of the feminist movement, notions of women's ways, women's rights, women's duties, and other aspects of a women's culture were being consciously created, negotiated, and brokered.

There was great interest in creating alternative ways of relating and exploring women's culture in 1970s. Women's music festivals were created as an environment in which to hear the new music called "women's music." What is women's music? It can be music sung by a woman, composed by a woman, or about a woman, but a fairly universally agreed on characteristic is that the music is "women-identified."

Within this new movement, women were experimenting with many different forms for reinventing every aspect of their lives. Cultural feminism concentrated on the importance of the whole. In everything that women created, they considered carefully how each part fit with the others and how they would be accountable to each other in conscious avoidance of hierarchical schemes. Simultaneously, a political movement within the feminist community emphasized the importance of enabling women to gain economic power. For women to be truly equal, it was necessary for us to become economically equal. During the late 1970s women started all kinds of businesses to control the means of production as well as the product. Lesbians were in the forefront, both in creating women's music and in starting women's businesses. Women started to control the economic production of their new women's culture. Within the cultural feminist movement, this translated into, among other things, being in charge of the entire production of a musical event: the sound, the lights, the management, and the promotion.

The purpose of women's music festivals, however, was not only to achieve economic control but also to create a women-identified environment, safe and comfortable to all women. It was important to women not only to have economic control in their lives but also to be able to exercise that control for the benefit of women, since the music was created for women by women. It was within this context that I and the other engineers mentioned here learned our skills.

It was also in this context that the Michigan Womyn's Music Festival was born. The festival was created from a need for a women-only space in which women could take charge of every aspect of their lives to hear women's music. In this space the musicians, producers, technicians, workers, and audience worked together to make this happen. The context becomes critical because of the emphasis that this women's community places on integration and wholeness. It is almost impossible to separate a performance of women's music, including sound engineers or performers, from its environment and context.

The Power of Sound Engineers: Access to the Field

In the music industry a mix engineer is in a position of power. This power involves control of the mix and overall sound, which affects the final product and thus helps to sell records and tickets. If we look at the source of this power and note that males have dominated production, it is easier to understand the origin of the exclusion of women in this industry. In the United States men—especially white men—hold the most power and have the most wealth. Prior to the 1970s technology and business in the music industry were a man's domain. The field of sound and recording was most definitely controlled by men, reflecting the dynamics of the whole industry. Women had to struggle for a place in the music scene, whether as artists or as workers in the business and technical part of the industry. Women musicians were relegated to certain types of music and instruments, and women in the business part of the field were pretty much invisible until recently.[8]

Since women mix engineers started entering this formerly male domain, the gender of the person who mixes the sound became an issue of control vis-à-vis performers. Performers tend to develop preferences about the way their concert performances are mixed, and some have specific requirements for their sound engineers.

The established and advertised image of a performer needs to be replicated in live performances just as it is controlled in studio recordings. For example, during the summer of 1994 I attended a Billy Joel–Elton John concert at a football arena in Washington, D.C. These artists have the resources to create any sound they want. Even though they both performed through the same sound system, the two acts differed radically in the quality of their sound.

The sound for both was loud beyond human tolerance, approaching over 110 decibels, with an overwhelming emphasis on the kick drum and bass guitar, much to the detriment of what I would consider a good musical mix.[9] Elton John's sound was so loud and heavy that his piano and vocals were completely drowned out, whereas Billy Joel's sound was mixed much more "musically": the different instruments were distinguishable, and his piano playing and vocals stood out. Nevertheless, this is not necessarily a case of one engineer doing a better job than the other. Both were creating the sounds that sell these particular artists. Elton John, though an incredible singer, songwriter, and piano player, has made his money by performing at huge rock concerts where an overwhelming sound is what sells tickets and the products.

In this context the issue of who controls the sound becomes important. The right sound can help to sell the product. Controlling an artist's sound makes the mix engineer feel powerful and therefore want to guard this position carefully. Most men in these positions were not willing to share this power.

The stories of the women featured in two industry magazines articles in 1987 and 1994[10] exhibit many of the patterns of exclusion other female mix engineers felt in the 1970s and early 1980s. Shockingly, the field has not changed a great deal, except that women now have a few role models to inspire them to enter the field. Once in, they are taken more seriously. The systems of exclusion were experienced throughout the industry by women attempting to enter the field. Sometimes male musicians in the studio or union theater would refuse to work when the engineer was a woman.

In the live concert world, it was impossible to become an apprentice of any kind without having the ability to lift heavy objects at a grueling pace while staying up all night. In the studio the system of hazing involved constant troubleshooting and being able to repair the gear by oneself. When I was just beginning to learn the trade, the one company that would even talk to me used to invite me to the shop at all hours to load the tractor trailer before a tour. Similarly, Andrea Weatherhead[11] comments: "I think the physical aspect of the 'load-in' is particularly sexist, and the equipment itself in design is only now becoming light enough for women to do the job alone.

They were always loading racks with several amplifiers, etc. In the studio, the big thing was 'troubleshooting.' Because that level is a little easier to compete (it just takes brains), it wasn't quite as obviously gender based." Margot McFedries observes: "I suspect it's harder to be a female working in a studio. The atmosphere tends to be more stressful anyway, and all that stress brings out the worst in people. I don't think sexism is anywhere near dead, so even though it's still true everywhere that for a woman to be thought of as half as good she has to be twice as good, probably in a studio she has to be three times as good."

When I first started working with a female mix engineer as a peer, which occurred at the MWMF, we had so thoroughly adopted this male competitive approach to mixing that we spent our first night of work engaged in a power struggle. All night we invented tasks related to the equipment to see who could outlast the other. We both instinctively knew that the one whose hands were on the mixing board last that night would be the one in charge and in control in the morning. It took us several years to start to relax and collaborate. Eventually we started mixing together.

When I was first trying to obtain employment mixing in the world of rock, which is quite different from mixing at festivals and political rallies, it was often quite difficult to get work. In the 1980s one of the old movie theaters in Washington, D.C., was just starting to be used for rock concerts by a new promoter in town. The hall's size was perfect for the sound equipment I owned, so I tried to convince the producer to hire me based on my other successes. He kept coming up with excuses. He finally admitted the real reason: he could not risk what the male rock musicians would think about having their sound mixed by a woman's sound company. Some of my male friends in town were in the rock industry and treated me as a peer. One of them was the stage manager for that particular theater, and he called in sick on the day of a big show, explaining that he would not come to work until the promoter gave me an opportunity. The promoter gave me a chance, after which I started mixing his shows on a regular basis, doing such groups as the Police and Bobbi Humphries.

Differences in Mixing

Gender and Mixing

Do men and women mix differently? None of the people I interviewed thought that women by their nature mix differently than men do. Rather, they believed that women generally listen better and are more sensitive to the needs of the performers and the music. McFedries stated: "I think *everyone* mixes differently. I think there are infinite variations on a mix, a large number of which may be equally as good. I imagine women do mix differently than men, but I'm not fast to say women mix better than men as I've seen some very sensitive mixing by men and some rather poor mixing by women. I think it has to do with hearing, and not necessarily what an audiologist might call 'good hearing' but something more intangible. And, of course, women are known to be better at listening." Carlos Arrien, a musician said, "I don't know that [a gender-based difference in mixing styles] to be the case, but I can say that female engineers have a great sensibility and a good feel for mixing."

What exactly is "mixing musically"? My bias is that great mixing consists of mixing musically, as a conductor would conduct an orchestra or a musician would interpret his or her music to fit the aesthetics of the genre. Mixing better could be interpreted as possessing greater musical talent.[12] It is also listening to the desires of both the artist and audience and negotiating this in the mix. Some of the musicians interviewed stated that often women engineers listen to their needs better than men do. According to Jeanne Mackey, a singer, "Female engineers are somewhat more sensitive to what I ask for—more responsive." In some instances the complaint was that men mix too loudly and without subtlety. Nevertheless, Pablo Maldonado, a producer, thought that gender makes no difference in mixing. He thought what is important is an individual's respect for the music, performers, and other cultures.

Leslie Ann Jones told a story about an Oscar-winning music producer with whom she worked. He said that in his earlier experience in theater, women were always better board operators because of their sensitivity to "the scene." He was commenting on the importance of being sensitive to the drama and action of the scene in order to mix well. Andrea Weatherhead perceived it this way: "I think I hear the 'world' through a different mind set in the first place—since the music must filter through the psyche, it's clear that my experience of the world as a woman affects how I hear music. When I was recording music, I tended to create 'warmer' mixes than my male counterparts." A warmer mix can actually be documented by observing the differences in the board and equalizer settings, as well as the choice of speakers and equipment. What are these people talking about? Listening differently as a mix engineer in this context refers to differences in communication that partially result from differences in gender socialization. In discussing the issue of listening differently, we need to focus in addition on the mix engineer's response to different agendas: those of the musicians, the audience, or the industry.

Training and learning the trade constitute one aspect of this socialization. Most male sound engineers learn through an apprenticeship, which usually begins with unloading and loading trucks as well as setting up the equipment. Another route for many American men is to purchase sound gear while in a band and later decide to start a sound company. Most women did not have the opportunity to be in bands or have the money to own the sound gear in the 1970s. Instead most emphasized academic training in the field. It was much harder for women to receive hands-on experience as apprentices.

Women who wanted to mix thus found themselves in a position where it was necessary to seek out classes on the science of sound as well as "how-to" classes. This actually worked in their favor since they ended up knowing more, scientifically and technically, than many men and could handle the electronic and acoustic problems better. This acoustic knowledge can result in better control of the sound during a performance or recording. Women discovered that to be employed and noticed, they needed to work more intelligently and from a broader base of knowledge. Questions about training elicited the following responses:

> I had to learn in the academic sense as opposed to the "hands-on hang around the guys" sense. I'm glad I learned from books because my knowledge is more firmly based. (Andrea Weatherhead)

> My learning process was very different from males who were learning at the same time, as well as very different from women who are learning now. When I was learning, I didn't have access to the technical world of rock and roll that males had. (Margot McFedries)

At the time being discussed, the various women's music concerts and festivals, particularly the Michigan Womyn's Music Festival, provided great training grounds for women. The performances were a constant learning and growing process. These spaces became the training ground for the first wave of women engineers, including myself. Women were trained to be responsive to the needs of all three components of a performance: the musicians, the audience, and the producers. The flow of information was circular, from the performer through the technicians to the audience and back around. In the woman-identified music of this period, there was much emphasis on the message delivered through the words of a song. The blend of the musicians and being able to hear every instrument and note was also extremely important. These concerns influenced how these women mixed. Much attention was paid to the quality and articulation of the mix. The engineers also practiced how to mix together and collaborate on what sounded good.

One of the women's music producers whom I interviewed said that engineers trained in this circuit were empowered and therefore, in her words, "beyond equal to men." The concept of being empowered by training in the women's music circuit should be explained further.

At women's music festivals, beginning in the 1970s and continuing to today, women create and build everything needed for the music to be heard. This is part of the process of empowerment. Women with the necessary skills are brought in. Women who worked in male-dominated fields were called because of their skills. This process of women building and creating their own environment started to break down the powerlessness that women had systematically been made to feel. I will never forget the first phone call that I received from a women's music festival producer, asking me to organize the sound for five stages and to mix on the main stage. It was the first time that I did not have to fight for every ounce of recognition.

Women mix engineers at the Michigan Womyn's Music Festival, 1985; Myrna Johnston, center, and Boden Sandstrom, far right. Photo by Joan E. Biren, used by permission.

This difference in training contributed to these women's skills and priorities when mixing. Jann Darsie, a mainstream concert promoter, stated that she preferred me as a sound engineer because I was "willing to go the extra mile and take more care than probably any man would do." Rhiannon, a singer who is a women's music circuit favorite known both for her solo work and her dynamic jazz group Alive!, had just finished a tour with Bobby McFerron when I consulted with her. She said it was hard to answer my questions since McFerron's male engineer was excellent, but her overall experience has been that the best engineers are women, and she prefers working with them. She prefers the camaraderie, the desire to work together, and the lack of intimidation. She thinks that because of their training in women's music, these engineers can hear instruments better, can make voices articulate, and can mix a cappella voices well.

Life in the Middle:

Chris Noyes described her experience working with Andrea Weatherhead while recording her album as being similar to her experience of giving birth with a midwife. She has three children, two of whom were delivered by midwives. She said she made the comparison because she felt she was safe and could share her emotions during this recording process. She thought that women are more sensitive to the creative rhythms of the process of recording.

Acting rather like a midwife, a mix engineer mediates the sound between the performers and the audience. This group of women engineers, because of their training and listening capabilities, saw themselves as mediators, attempting to transfer sound to the audience while taking into account what is important to both the musicians and the audience. This approach to mixing is appropriate in a performance at which the audience and musicians have come together for the music or the message. Engineers in the role of mediator resolve conflicts differently and deal with differences more adeptly than do others. Andrea Weatherhead observed: "I did not sit in judgment of my clients they way I know lots of male engineers did. My African American clients related to me, I believe, in a very equal level sort of like mutual understanding of being a minority. This produced great simpatico." Margot McFedries claimed: "Women relate to people differently than men do. Again, we listen better to what people say to us, so it follows we would be ahead of the game in understanding a director's or artist's concept. I think relating to other cultures also involves a class and cultural awareness, and maybe women

Boden Sandstrom, mix engineer, at Gay Pride Day, Washington D.C., 1978. Photo by Joan E. Biren, used by permission.

are quicker to broaden their minds, but I'm a little leery of making sweeping generalizations about this."

Another element of the process of communication these women experienced through mixing was their identities as marginalized persons relating to other marginalized people. Often the musicians from the many cultures with whom I worked as a mix engineer were not necessarily marginalized in their countries of birth but were marginalized in the United States. Through the technology of sound equipment and the art of mixing, a very special communication was created between sound engineers and the performers. Our experiences as members of a marginalized group helped us not only to identify with the performers' need to communicate their music and its meaning but also, as sound mediators, to contribute to the process to the best of our abilities. In response to my question whether it is better to have a person of the culture mix the music, Darsie stated that she believed "anyone with true cultural sensitivity can do the task. Of course this implies prior knowledge and study in addition to appreciating the diversity of cultural expression."

As women mix engineers in a predominantly male environment, we experienced the breakdown of gender identities. We were often viewed as genderless. Jones said: "Most of my clients see me as genderless as far as my work. But I will always be seen [by the profession] as a 'female engineer.'"

Other women ethnomusicologists have written about similar experiences while in the field.[13] Stretching female gender roles when in the field provides new access to communication and information and continues to dismantle the insider/outsider classifications. When mixing their own music, women engineers are on the inside; when mixing in a male-oriented world, however, they are still more on the inside than on the outside because of being perceived as genderless. When one gender crosses over into the role of another, the construction of that gender sometimes disappears, and for the duration of the crossover there may be no gender, or else a new one is perceived.

I experienced this often when participating in a basically male context as a mix engineer. I communicated with male groups and in cultural situations I otherwise could not have approached. A mix engineer who is involved in the creative process has a unique basis of communication. Knowledge of technology allows women the opportunity to participate where they would normally be excluded. Mixing has the potential of being a form of technological communication among people within and between cultures.

Technology and its interconnectedness to so many aspects of contemporary cultures have dramatically changed the nature of fieldwork. Technology has created the opportunity for a new medium of intercultural dialogue: transculturation of music and communication about this music. The use of technology creates the possibility for greater equality in this process of understanding, but it also can limit access to the discussion and the processes of world creativity. Access and the use of technology are gendered. As performance acts out the gender relations in culture, the use of technology reveals existing gender differences. Even in our postmodern world, we are not yet gender-neutral cyborgs,[14] nor does everyone wish to be one in this diverse world. Issues of agency and technology go hand and hand with performance. Use of technology has the ironic ability both to exaggerate existing gender differences and to neutralize them. This irony exists in the performance of sound engineering.

APPENDIX 1: PROFESSIONALS CONSULTED

Carlos Arrien: former program director for DC Commission on the Arts and Humanities, Washington, D.C.; formerly member of Andean music group Rumisonko.

Michelle Crone: former producer of the women's music festival Rhythmfest.

Jann Darsie: fund-raising specialist; former program director for D.C. Commission on the Arts and Humanities, Washington, D.C.

Myrna Johnston: sound engineer and owner, MJA (Myrna Johnston Audio), Boston, Mass.

Leslie Ann Jones: former recording engineer, Capitol Studios, Los Angeles, Calif.; director of music recording and scoring, Skywalker Sound, Calif.

Jeanne Mackey: vocalist, guitarist, and instructor, Ann Arbor, Mich.; former member of the women's band Lifeline.

Pablo Maldonado: director of Marketing and Communications Division, Creative Associates International, Inc., Washington, D.C.

Margot McFedries: sound engineer for International Alliance of Theatrical Stage Employees; currently head of Department of Sound Engineering, Kuran Theater, San Francisco, Calif.

Chris Noyes: singer-songwriter, Claiborne, Md.

Rhiannon: singer-songwriter, Inverness, Calif.; former member of the women's band Alive!

Andrea Weatherhead: associate producer, Microsoft Network, Seattle, Wash.; former recording engineer, Roar Productions, Columbia, Md.

NOTES

I would like to acknowledge the support of Drs. Marcia Herndon and Carolina Robertson for both inspiring and editing this essay.

1. In this essay, *sound engineering* refers to sound reinforcement, that is, mixing in live situations for an audience, whereas *recording engineering* refers to mixing in a recording studio or in the field for recording purposes. When referring to both I will use *mix engineering*.

2. Feld first addressed the dialogic nature of recording in the field with the Kaluli in his article "Dialogic Editing" (1987).

3. Gender is a social construct. In this essay I focus on the two accepted genders in Western (particularly U.S.) culture: woman and man. Two comprehensive resources on gender origins and consequences are Bem's *Lenses of Gender* (1993) and Lorber's *Paradoxes of Gender* (1994). Bem analyzes three gender lenses through which Westerners view the world, and Lorber challenges the validity, permanence, and necessity of gender.

Two excellent works on the interrelationship between technology and race, gender, and class are Zimmerman 1983 and Wajcman 1991. Zimmerman's collection *The Technological Woman* contains essays by feminists on the political ramifications of what was then the new technology. Wajcman's *Feminism Confronts Technology* deconstructs science and knowledge from a feminist perspective. She explores the power base and gendered character of technology. For a historical perspective see Joan Rothschild 1981, 1982.

4. While Western feminism of the 1970s was relevant to the times, its proponents made many of the same mistakes as the patriarchal culture that we were criticizing; in particular, we failed to realize the differences among women. First-wave feminism was dominated by white middle-class women who attempted to speak for all women. Dominant cultures tend to speak from a privileged position. Adrienne Rich (1986) and subsequent postmodernists address the need to deconstruct privilege by locating one's self. For an excellent compilation of essays on feminism and postmodern thought, see Nicholson's *Feminism/Postmodernism* (1990). In the article "The Postmodernist Turn in Anthropology" (Mascia-Lees, Sharpe, and Cohen 1989) the authors caution against carrying the deconstruction of feminism too far and abandoning a political viewpoint. For a more international perspective on feminism, see *Third World Women and the Politics of Feminism* (Mohanty, Russo, and Torres 1991).

5. The spelling of *womyn* for *women* is one of many feminist alternative spellings to eliminate *man* or *men* from the root of the word. In this article the festival will also be referred to as the MWMF.

6. Consultations were conducted via questionnaire and telephone.

7. I want to make it clear that I acknowledge the talents and sensitivity of my male engineer colleagues.

8. For a thorough comprehensive discussion of the exclusion of women in the music industry, see Garr 1992.

9. Judgments about what constitutes a "musical mix" are socially constructed as well. My minimum requirements are that I can hear each instrument and follow its part and understand the vocals. The mix also needs to fit the aesthetics of the music—and one could argue that both these mix engineers were doing exactly that.

10. See "Women in Sound Reinforcement: Four Success Stories," by George Petersen (1987), and "Women in Audio," by Sally Dorgan Potts (1994).

11. A list of informants appears at the end of this essay as appendix 1.

12. Musical talent and musicality are also socially constructed concepts. Henry Kingsbury tackles this difficult subject from a Western point of view in *Music, Talent, and Performance* (1988).

13. *World of Music* 3, no. 2 (1991) contains several good articles written by women ethnomusicologists on experiencing a different gender identity while doing their fieldwork, particularly, the article by Cynthia Tse Kimberlin, "What Am I to Be? Female, Male, Neuter, Invisible." Bell, Caplan, and Karim's *Gendered Fields: Women, Men and Ethnography* (1993) and Whitehead and Conaway's *Self, Sex and Gender in Cross-Cultural Fieldwork* (1986) are excellent resources.

14. "A cyborg is a cybernetic organism, a hybrid of machine and organism, a creature of social reality as well as a creature of fiction. Social reality is lived so-

cial relations, our most important political construction, a world-changing fiction. The international women's movements have constructed 'women's experience,' as well as uncovered or discovered this crucial collective object. This experience is a fiction and fact of the most crucial, political kind. . . . The cyborg is a creature in a postgender world" (Haraway 1991, 149, 150). In *Simians, Cyborgs and Women* (1991) Donna Haraway takes a creative hard look at the destabilizing effect that women and feminists have had in the field of science and on Western evolutionary, technological, and biological narratives.

References Cited

Bell, Diane, Pat Caplan, and Wazir Jahan Karim, eds. 1993. *Gendered Fields: Women, Men, and Ethnography.* London: Routledge.

Bem, Sondra Lipsitz. 1993. *Lenses of Gender: Transforming the Debate on Sexual Inequality.* New Haven, Conn.: Yale University Press.

Garr, Gillian G. 1992. *She's a Rebel: The History of Women in Rock and Roll.* Seattle: Seal.

Haraway, Donna. 1991. *Simians, Cyborgs, and Women: The Reinvention of Nature.* New York: Routledge.

Keil, Charles, and Steven Feld. 1994. *Music Grooves: Essays and Dialogues.* Chicago: University of Chicago Press.

Kimberlin, Cynthia Tse. 1991. "What Am I to Be? Female, Male, Neuter, Invisible . . . Gender Roles and Ethnomusicological Field Work in Africa." *World of Music* 33, no. 2:14–34.

Kingsbury, Henry. 1988. *Music, Talent, and Performance: A Conservatory Cultural System.* Philadelphia: Temple University Press.

Lorber, Judith. 1994. *Paradoxes of Gender.* New Haven, Conn.: Yale University Press.

Mascia-Lees, Frances E., Patricia Sharpe, and Colleen Ballerino Cohen. 1989. "The Postmodernist Turn in Anthropology: Cautions from a Feminist Perspective." *Signs: Journal of Women in Culture and Society* 15, no. 11:7–33.

Mohanty, Chandra Talpade, Ann Russo, and Lourdes Torres, eds. 1991. *Third World Women and the Politics of Feminism.* Bloomington: Indiana University Press.

Nicholson, Linda J., ed. 1990. *Feminism/Postmodernism.* New York: Routledge.

Potts, Sally Dorgan. 1994. "Women in Audio." *EQ,* May, 50–57.

Petersen, George. 1987. "Women in Sound Reinforcement: Four Success Stories." *Mix: The Recording Industry Magazine,* June, 46–120.

Rich, Adrienne. 1986. "Notes toward a Politics of Location." *Blood, Bread, and Poetry: Selected Prose 1979–1985.* New York: Norton.

Rothschild, Joan. 1981. "Feminist Perspective on Technology and the Future." *Women's Studies International Quarterly* 4, no. 1:65–74.

————. 1982. *Women, Technology and Innovation.* New York: Pergamon.

Scovill, Ruth. 1981. "Women's Music." In *Women's Culture: The Women's Renaissance of the Seventies,* ed. Gayle Kimball, 148–62. Metuchen, N.J.: Scarecrow.

Wajcman, Judy. 1991. *Feminism Confronts Technology.* University Park: Pennsylvannia State University Press.

Whitehead, Tony L., and Mary Ellen Conaway, eds. 1986. *Self, Sex, and Gender in Cross-Cultural Fieldwork.* Urbana: University of Illinois Press.

Zimmerman, Jan, ed. 1983. *The Technological Woman: Interfacing with Tomorrow.* New York: Praeger.

Gender, Voice, and Place: Issues of Negotiation in a "Technology in Music Program"

Karen Pegley

> Women and men do not receive an equal education because outside the classroom women are perceived not as sovereign beings but as prey. . . . The undermining of self, of a woman's sense of her right to occupy space and walk freely in the world, is deeply relevant to education . . . [because the] capacity to think independently, to take intellectual risks, to assert ourselves mentally, is inseparable from our physical way of being in the world . . .
>
> —Adrienne Rich

Over the past several years technology has played a significant role in redefining many North American music classrooms. Studies exploring computer-assisted instruction within music education have focused largely on the effect of computers on students' musical literacy and creativity. One perhaps less obvious ramification of technology yet to be explored is the restructuring of physical space within the classroom and its impact on students' musical expression. This oversight is not surprising, however, for within anthropological theory, the issue of space received little critical attention until the 1990s.[1] As Michel Foucault stated: "A critique could be carried out of [the] devaluation of space that has prevailed for generations. . . . Space was treated as the dead, the fixed, the undialectical, the immobile. . . . They didn't understand that to trace . . . the organization of domains meant the throwing into relief of processes—historical ones, needless to say—of power" (Foucault 1980, 70).

In this essay I explore how technology can affect the physical space of a music room and students' subsequent sense of place within it. The particular room to be analyzed was part of a school located near Toronto, Ontario, Canada's largest urban metropolis. The children who attended the school were largely from upper-middle-class families and predominantly of British lineage. Although these demographics were representative of this southern Ontario town, the children here did not attend a "typical" suburban school: in 1988 it was designated as a "center for innovation" by the educational foundation of a major computer company. The classrooms were subsequently restructured into technology-driven configurations: an influx of computers initially brought the schoolwide student:computer ratio to approximately twelve to one. The "computer room" (an area in which all students spent time four out of six days) had an impressive one-to-one ratio. The music room became the base for a new curriculum initiative entitled the "Technology in Music Programme" and was furnished with microcomputers, sequencers, drum machines, and other musical instrument digital interface (MIDI) devices and software, in addition to a sound editing and production facility.

I came to the school initially to assess the program's success in meeting the objectives of the school board's general curriculum.[2] To this end, the Music Readiness Assessment—a test to establish aptitude for and attitude to music—was given to thirty-three randomly selected students (ages thirteen to fifteen) at the outset of the study. Over the next several months these students were interviewed on their responses to the program and the technologies it featured. Most important, the study included a program of observation as the selected students worked individually and in groups throughout the year. These observations were documented by means of written notes, audiotape, and videotape.

As I collected my data, however, I recognized an unusual—and sometimes disturbing—interactive pattern: girls' and boys' negotiative styles appeared to alter as their groups moved between the different music technology areas. For example, what seemed to be a cooperative small group dynamic in one setting, with each student fulfilling a unique and valuable role, would inexplicably alter at the next location. Even more puzzling was that this shift did not appear to be related to the students' level of comfort with the new hardware and software. These observations prompted me to move beyond the original assessment and ask two additional questions: first, why would girls and boys suddenly shift negotiative strategies, particularly when they rotated with the same group of people, and second, how might the different physical locations influence their communication styles? By recounting how students in one class responded to their new technological spaces, I will examine possible reasons for their interactive styles within them. I then will focus my analysis on the musical output of one girl and one boy ("Meghan" and "Nicholas") and provide evidence to support the hypothesis that the musical expressions of these two individuals—their musical voices—were shaped by their personal constructions of place. Ultimately, I will argue that their highly complex and sometimes contradictory constructions of gender hinged on their empowered—or disempowered—sense of being in the room.

To begin, I will clarify my use of four words that appear in this essay: *space, place, location,* and *landscape.* Edward Relph (1976, 2) has defined space as a context within which places are constructed. A school, for example, may be considered an institutional space. Joseph May has noted that place differs from space because the former has a unique perceptual unity that marks one place as different from other places (in Relph 1976, 4). Place, then, is phenomenological, for its meanings are based on peoples' lived experiences (Relph 1976, 3). The music room of a school may be an important place for some students, or on a micro level, the music room itself might be considered a large space within which students construct personalized places. In this essay I use the word *location* for specific places. There are six technology centers within the room to be considered here; I thus call these individual places "locations." Finally, the physical component of place—what the individual views or inhabits—will be identified as the "landscape." It is the landscape of music rooms that has been most radically reshaped by synthesizers, computer monitors, and other technological hardware.

Anthropologist Margaret Rodman has emphasized the importance of understanding place as something more than a neutral framework. In particular, she has demonstrated the complexity of place by revealing the plurality of meanings possible within a single location. According to Rodman (1992, 647): "Places, like voices, are local and multiple. For each inhabitant, a place has a unique reality." She uses the term *multilocality* to reflect these pluralistic responses to places. A multilocal landscape will often hold a unique meaning of place for the individual, and as a result, a single place may be experienced very differently by two people occupying it at the same time (ibid.). Multilocality may also refer, as Rodman (1992, 646) puts it, to "reflexive relationships with places." For example, an individual unfamiliar with a landscape is likely to view that landscape in relation to a more familiar one (ibid.). I will argue that in the music classroom to be discussed here, multilocal reflexivity (viewing each new place in relation to a more familiar one) is a powerful strategy for children as they attempt to negotiate within unknown technological territory.

How then can a multilocality framework illuminate the impact of technology on girls and boys within the Technology in Music classroom? First, let us examine the room. Figure 12.1 indicates the room's general layout and contents. The room was divided into six centers that focused on literacy, sequencing, composing, MIDI wind performance, recording, and integrated arts performance (centers 1 through 6, respectively). It was divided into several areas: the literacy, integrated arts, and recording centers at the bottom of the figure each were self-contained and separate from the main music room, which housed the sequencing, composition, and MIDI wind centers; the teacher spent much of his time in this main room. The sequencing, recording, and integrated arts centers involved the most interaction between the students. At the sequencing center students worked at computers arranged in a cluster, where they were encouraged to play alone or in groups of two or three. The primary activities here included songwriting, sequencing, assembling, and editing, in addition to improvising on the keyboard. The lines between the individual stations represent a headphone network system that facilitated group work. At the recording center each student

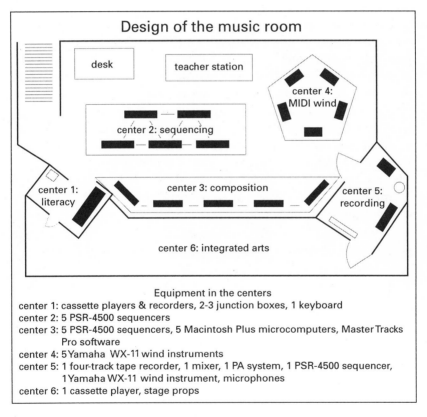

Figure 12.1. Design of the music room.

played a specific functional role (producer, director, etc.) so that a collaborative environment would be established. Here students made final decisions on their projects, adjusted their work on a mixer, and produced a tape. Finally, they entered the integrated arts center, where they worked together to integrate their music with movement, dance, mime, and drama. As one student reported: "[At the integrated arts center] I learned how to put movement to music and express myself." At the other end of this cooperative continuum was the composition center, where the computer arrangement separated the students by having them sit side by side and focus on their own projects. At this location ensemble work was encouraged at the ends of sessions, when students were invited to share their individual projects.

How did the boys and girls respond to these different centers? The students filled out a questionnaire in which they ranked the centers from "most favorite" (1) to "least favorite" (6). Table 12.1 provides a breakdown of the responses.

The boys' favorite location was the composition center, followed by the sequencing and recording centers. Most girls identified the recording center as their favorite location, followed by the integrated arts, sequencing, and the composition centers. The literacy and MIDI wind centers, which focused on musicianship and music appreciation, were ranked as least favorite by both groups. A brief description of these centers may help explain these negative responses. The literacy center housed cassette players and recorders, junction boxes, and a keyboard. Here students were directed to sing back pitches heard on the keyboard, build chords with their voices, and practice comparing and contrasting different musical styles and genres heard on the cassette players. At the MIDI wind center students practiced reading staff notation, improved their tone on the instruments, and blended their sounds in an ensemble setting. Generally, none of the objectives from the two centers elicited an enthusiastic response from the students: most reported feel-

Table 12.1. Ratings of Individual Centers by Boys and Girls

Boys		Girls	
Center	Rating[a]	Center	Rating[a]
Composition	2.3	Recording	1.8
Sequencing	2.5	Integrated arts	3.1
Recording	2.6	Sequencing	3.3
Integrated arts	3.9	Composition	3.4
MIDI wind	4.1	Literacy	4.5
Literacy	5.7	MIDI wind	4.8

a. Highest possible rating = 6.

ing restless and without direction, and eight students reported having learned little or nothing. The fact that the curriculum was not yet well developed for either center, combined with changing technology during the year, may explain their negative responses. As a result, I will exclude these two centers from my analysis.

At first glance the findings in table 12.1 seem to suggest that the girls preferred the centers that involved less manipulation of computer software and more personal interaction, whereas the boys enjoyed the more technologically based centers that featured individual activities. Various factors might explain why each group felt empowered at some centers and not at others, such as attitudes toward technology, differences in girls' and boys' familiarity with computers, and interpersonal styles. Instead of looking for sweeping engendered explanations for this preference imbalance, however, I searched for solutions by observing two "talented" students (a label provided by the music teacher) in more detail to identify how they were motivated and empowered at each center. I traced Nicholas's and Meghan's individual progress through the sequence of centers, paying particular attention to their styles of interaction at each center. I sought to understand how the individual centers functioned as multilocalities, that is, how they functioned differently for these two students separate from the rest of the class, as well as how Nicholas and Meghan responded uniquely to each center. These students were well matched for a comparative analysis: they reported a similar musical profile, each with several years of private keyboard instruction, and both students scored above 90 percent on the Music Readiness Assessment. The most notable difference between the two students was in their attitudes toward technology. When asked whether they liked using computers to learn music a lot, a bit, or not at all, Nicholas responded that he liked using them "a lot." Meghan, however, said that she did not like them at all. As she stated: "[I] liked learning the old way."

Did Nicholas's and Meghan's preferences mirror those of the other boys and girls? Their responses are shown in table 12.2. Nicholas's favorite site was the recording center, followed by the sequencing and then the composition centers. Meghan most favored the composition center, followed by the recording and sequencing centers. In short, their preferences were more similar to those identified by the other sex than to those identified by their own. These responses, however, seem incongruent with their earlier statements on their attitude toward technology. Meghan, for example, stated that she did not like computers, yet she enjoyed working in isolation at the center with the most computer hardware and software. Could their comments

Table 12.2. Preferred Centers of Nicholas and Meghan

Nicholas	Meghan
Recording	Composition
Sequencing	Recording
Composition	Sequencing
Integrated arts	Integrated arts

reflect Nicholas's preference simply to work more cooperatively and Meghan's to work more independently? Furthermore, could these reversed negotiation styles (within this class, at least) result in more interactively balanced students who were then more successful within the room?

Both students were observed closely at each center. Nicholas took full advantage of headphone networking within the main room and indeed appeared to thrive in a cooperative environment. When asked to identify what he had learned at the sequencing center, for example, he stated that he enjoyed "composing music with a group of people" (a comment more frequently made by the girls in the class). When I listened in during a group project, however, I noticed that Nicholas had a unique formula for negotiating with his peers. He enjoyed working within the group while at the first four centers, occasionally borrowing and developing ideas provided by other students. A significant change in his negotiating style occurred in the recording center, however, a completely enclosed booth where crucial decisions regarding projects were discussed. Rather than work within the fold at the recording center, Nicholas instead asserted his ideas and enthusiastically took control of the project as both director and producer. Once the group reached the integrated arts center to perform their project, Nicholas was often the most visible participant. In a performance of "Supply Teacher Rap," for example, Nicholas was both lead rapper and apparently the group organizer, having designated two boys to perform a choreography behind him and two more to provide the musical accompaniment on the synthesizers. The song's lyrics—also written by Nicholas—recount a day of comedic interactions with a substitute teacher. The song's text, part of which follows, evidences his self-assurance and sense of humor:

"Supply Teacher Rap"

Yesterday in School the teacher was a supply,
Because of her I laughed so hard I almost cried,

Sit down and let me try to explain
The supply teacher made me laugh again and again.

[instrumental]

I was on my way to class looking down the hall,
When I bumped into a teacher and saw her fall,
Offered her a hand and she said to me "No! . . ."
As I ran to class I thought "Oh great!
Because I bumped into her I'm gonna be late . . ."

To both the class and teacher, Nicholas appeared to be the mastermind behind the group project during both the performance and the question session that followed. In actuality, however, Nicholas did not contribute significantly to the musical component, having instead focused on writing the lyrics. In the recording center he chose to orchestrate the group's musical ideas into a rap, a genre that often foregrounds lyrics and performance over musical sonorities. To this end he shaped the others' musical ideas to become background to his creative text. By then taking the role of lead rapper in the final performance, Nicholas presented himself as a critical contributor to the entire process and subsequently was commended for its overall success.

Meghan, by contrast, preferred to work alone at the first few centers in the room, carefully developing her ideas. Then she entered the recording booth. Like Nicholas, the booth became the location at which her style of negotiation altered, but in the reverse direction. Her pattern was to distribute her ideas, thus diluting her creative talents with those of the other members of the group. This strategy allowed her to avoid unwanted praise and attention when they performed the song in front of the class. Meghan's end-of-term arrangement of "I Still Believe in Santa Claus,"[3] a ballad recorded by New Kids on the Block, was indicative of her creative process. The song likely appealed to her because the music was accessible yet challenging to arrange and because the lyrics reflected a gentle appreciation for play and imagination. The opening stanza follows:

"I Still Believe in Santa Claus"

I still believe in Santa Claus,
Maybe that's just because I'm still a child . . . at heart.
And I still believe in old St. Nick,
Then again, maybe that's a trick we need, we need to retrieve
From a world of make believe.

With this work Meghan displayed her strength at the synthesizer by arranging (by ear) a drum track, a bass line, a chordal organ accompaniment, and an arpeggiated piano line. She recorded the instrumental tracks diligently on her own at the composition center; when she moved into the recording booth, however, she preferred to play back her recorded arrangement while she practiced the vocal lines with the other girls. By prerecording the music track, Meghan was able to blend easily with the other girls, share ownership of the vocal and choreographic performance, and erase her leadership role in arranging the music.

For these two students, then, the recording center functioned as a location unlike the others in the room. Whereas Nicholas viewed working there as an opportunity to select other students' ideas and creatively orchestrate them, Meghan chose to yield control over her compositions, opting for a unison rather than a solo texture. The recording center was a multilocal landscape: it held contrasting meanings for these two students and was experienced differently by each of them. Because it was self-enclosed and often unsupervised and contained complex music technology, it also functioned as a foreign landscape for both of them. As a result, it became a reflexive location to which they responded by engaging in an interactive style familiar to them from other settings more so than they did at other openly visible centers. Although their negotiation strategies appeared to be unique at the first four centers, their interactions at the recording center and final performances in the integrated arts area demonstrated that Nicholas and Meghan were not unlike the other students in the class after all.

Both Nicholas's leadership style and Meghan's ability to distribute her power can, of course, be effective and rewarding methods of negotiation. It is important, however, that they are made aware of their interactive frameworks. This is particularly critical for Meghan, who, because of her negotiative style, unknowingly may experience bias in current technology-based programs. In the Technology in Music curriculum, for example, technology is defined as a tool that "must support the spectrum of teaching/learning styles, from teacher-directed learning, to co-operative group learning, to independent, self-directed learning" (Alger 1989, 4). An implicit message here is that self-directed learning is the more valued activity and that the ability to work and share ideas cooperatively is not necessarily an asset.

One additional problem for both girls and boys evident here and within many other technology-based programs is the attempt made by designers to forge a "nonsexist" environment. By treating students as one neutral gender when they use technology, curriculum developers and educators have in the past often ignored the social realities beyond the classroom. Feminist educator Linda Briskin (1990, 14) noted a danger with this strategy when she observed that under these "nonsexist" conditions students will often not only perpetuate stereotypes but strengthen them (a possibility I noted regarding the recording center). What is required is an "antisexist" strategy that, to paraphrase Briskin, makes conscious and legitimizes the multiplicity of experiences based on gender, and, by extension, class, ethnicity, race, and sexual orientation (ibid.). If technology continues to be treated as a neutral tool and the gendered approaches of the students are not challenged as they enter the classroom, current patterns will be perpetuated easily through headphones and behind closed doors. If the teacher cannot be with the students, she or he needs to listen more carefully to their voices—musical and otherwise—to explore with them the numerous colors available for painting their musical landscapes.

To conclude, I refer to Adrienne Rich's statement quoted at the opening, where she connects women's empowerment inside the classroom to that on the outside. Here I have made the parallel argument for the importance of understanding girls' empowerment at different locations within one classroom. Teachers, of course, cannot be responsible for students' senses of place once they leave the schoolyard. They can, however, create an environment within which students can explore music and movement both as individuals and as members of cooperative groups and help them to implement a wide variety of interactive styles. Only then it will be possible to transform the music room from a series of technological spaces into a sequence of empowering places.

NOTES

An abridged version of this paper was presented at the Feminist Theory and Music II conference at the Eastman School of Music, Rochester, N.Y., in June 1993 and published in *The Recorder: The Ontario Journal of Music Education* 37:55–59. This research was supported by the Social Sciences and Humanities Research Council of Canada. The opening epigraph is from Adrienne Rich, "Taking Women Students Seriously" (in Briskin 1990, 3).

1. There are, however, several earlier ethnomusicological writings that consider the correlation between music and social organization. Anthony Seeger (1987), for example, examined how the Suyá of Central Brazil marked different spaces within their environment through singing or by observing silence. Carol Robertson (1979) has addressed the discrepancy between Argentine Mapuche wom-

en's travel restrictions in the lived world and their use of extended psychic travel in their performance of a vocal genre called *tayil*. Marina Roseman (1987) also
has pointed out the inversions between daily life and ritual in the female performance mobility of the Malaysian Temiar. Although these authors address issues
of spatial control on the microcosmic level, the patterns they illuminate reflect
power structures that dominate even larger public domains.

2. This material is drawn from Clarkson and Pegley 1991.

3. "I Still Believe in Santa Claus" appeared on the New Kids on the Block's 1989
Christmas album *Merry Merry Christmas* (Sony 45280).

REFERENCES CITED

Alger, Brian. 1989. "Electronic Instrumental Music Pilot Project: Draft Copy."
Halton Board of Education, Milton, Ont.

Briskin, Linda. 1990. *Feminist Pedagogy: Teaching and Learning Liberation.* Ottawa,
Ont.: Canadian Research Institute for the Advancement of Women.

Clarkson, Austin, and Karen Pegley. 1991. *An Assessment of a Technology in Music
Programme.* Toronto, Ont.: York University, Centre for the Study of Computers in Education.

Foucault, Michel. 1980. *Power/Knowledge.* Brighton, U.K.: Harvester.

Relph, Edward. 1976. *Place and Placelessness.* London: Pion.

Robertson, Carol. 1979. "Pulling the Ancestors: Performance Practice and Praxis
in Mapuche Ordering." *Ethnomusicology* 23, no. 3:395–416.

Rodman, Margaret. 1992. "Empowering Place: Multilocality and Multivocality."
American Anthropologist 94, no. 3: 640–56.

Roseman, Marina. 1987. "Inversion and Conjuncture: Male and Female Performance among the Temiar of Peninsular Malaysia." In *Women and Music in
Cross-Cultural Perspective,* ed. Ellen Koskoff, 131–49. Urbana: University of Illinois Press.

Seeger, Anthony. 1987. *Why Suyá Sing: A Musical Anthropology of an Amazonian
People.* Cambridge: Cambridge University Press.

13 Cyborg Experiences: Contradictions and Tensions of Technology, Nature, and the Body in Hildegard Westerkamp's "Breathing Room"

Andra McCartney

Theorists in the areas of feminist aesthetics and epistemology discuss a contradictory stance that characterizes feminist work with technology. Teresa de Lauretis, in her discussion of feminist cinema, claims that a contradictory stance is specific to feminism. She describes it as "a twofold pressure, a simultaneous pull in opposite directions, a tension toward the positivity of politics, or affirmative action on behalf of women as social subjects, on one front, and the negativity inherent in the radical critique of patriarchal, bourgeois culture, on the other. It is also the contradiction of women in language, as we attempt to speak as subjects of discourses which negate or objectify us through their representations" (de Lauretis 1987, 127). As de Lauretis describes it, feminist artists are in a constant state of tension, pulled equally in two directions, attempting to affirm a range of different creative approaches while criticizing existing cultural assumptions that are represented in contemporary language.

The discourses of technology are particularly objectifying, representing the relationship between artist and work as one of gendered power and control. I have written elsewhere about the way music technology magazines use stereotypically masculine imagery related to sports and war to define their community (McCartney 1995). Working within this technologically musical community puts women composers of electroacoustic music in a seemingly contradictory—and often uncomfortable—position: they are at once represented as the object of control and the subject exerting it.

What can such composers do in this uncomfortable situation? One way to resolve the contradiction would be to sway one way or another: to take a stereotypically masculine position of control over the world, and deny a connection with femininity, or to take a stereotypically feminine position of connection with the world, and deny a connection with masculinity. Neither position can work for long, since these composers are still women working with technology that is represented as facilitating control over the world. There is another alternative. In her "Cyborg Manifesto" Donna Haraway (1991, 149) says that the strategy of irony acknowledges contradictions without attempting to resolve them: "Irony is about contradictions that do not resolve into larger wholes, even dialectically, about the tension of holding incompatible things together because both or all are necessary and true. Irony is about humour and serious play. It is also a rhetorical strategy and a political method. . . . At the centre of my ironic faith . . . is the image of the cyborg." Haraway's cyborg is a mythical being, part organic and part cybernetic. It cannot dream, as humans sometimes do, of a return to organic wholeness, because that is not its history. It is fashioned from both machine and organism, which Western philosophy trains us to imagine as radically separate: man and machine, nature and culture. The cybernetic and organic parts of a cyborg's being must somehow exist together.

Westerkamp's Approach to Electroacoustic Music: "Breathing Room"

The image of an ironic cyborg is evident in a recent work by the Vancouver composer Hildegard Westerkamp.[1] "Breathing Room" is explicitly concerned with breathing, for it is structured around the breath, bringing together bird sounds, water sounds, and machine sounds in a piece that is constructed technologically.

Westerkamp's ambivalent feelings about technology are evident when she speaks of the electroacoustic studio. On the one hand, she describes it as a place protected from the outside world where she can give her creative voices room to breathe. She says:

> The studio environment has provided me with a "niche" where I could find my own creative voice without interference from the surrounding social, cultural context. . . . Since it has always been hard for me not to give external voices more power than my own inner voice, this was an important stage for me—and, given my socio-cultural background, this separateness may to some extent always remain an important part of my creative process. The sound studio has taught me to be in touch with that inner voice and to believe in it. In my electroacoustic compositions my inner voices speak. . . . I would go as far as saying that these isolated places are perhaps the urban person's replacements for wilderness experience, places where one can play/work undisturbed and uninterrupted—at a distance from daily life. (Westerkamp 1988, 133–34)

Particularly intriguing in this quotation is her description of the studio as resembling a wilderness setting in its peace and privacy—a natural image applied to a technological location. At the same time, Westerkamp also speaks of the studio as a stifling environment where she finds it difficult to breathe:

> I really hate to go into studios, because of that health aspect. . . . You know, my back aches afterwards, I'm not breathing properly, I just simply feel very tired and exhausted. And I actually experience it as a huge contradiction to what I'm trying to do in the pieces. It's the same with the . . . performance spaces . . . , [which are] controlled environments. And yet when the pieces are playing, they open something up in the audience, they open something up in me. They're saying something about place, about environment, about ecology, and about acoustic balance in our lives. . . . And yet the contradiction is not gone. (interview with author, 1993)

So the studio, for Westerkamp, is at once an expansive and an enclosing space where her creative voices have room to speak but where she eventually has trouble breathing. Susan McClary (1991, 137) writes that Laurie Anderson, too, is at the same time fascinated with technology *and* critical of its alienating influence. Other women composers whom I have interviewed make similar comments.[2] They speak of pleasure in studio work and possibilities for developing new languages of expression, but at the same time they criticize the patriarchal ordering of the studio, where minds command sound and bodies are neglected.

This ambivalent stance toward technology is given voice in "Breathing Room." This piece is particularly important as an index of Westerkamp's style because of the request that the producers made of the participants on the CD for which the piece was written. Each composer was asked to create a three-minute piece that would encapsulate his or her compositional style. Westerkamp, one of two women out of the twenty-five composers involved in the project, composed "Breathing Room" in answer to this request.

Westerkamp's style is influenced both by her association with the World Soundscape Project in the 1970s and by her association with American experimental composer Pauline Oliveros. Westerkamp describes herself as a soundscape composer, that is, one who works with sounds in context. The concept of an environment of sound is the basis of the word *soundscape,* a term credited to composer R. Murray Schafer, who directed the World Soundscape Project at Simon Fraser University, Vancouver, in the 1970s. He defines it as "the sonic environment. Technically, any portion of the sonic environment regarded as a field for study. The term may refer to actual environments, or to abstract constructions such as musical compositions and tape montages, particularly when considered as an environment" (Schafer 1977, 275). By *sonic environment* Schafer (ibid.) means "the ever-present array of noises, pleasant and unpleasant, loud and soft, heard or ignored, that we all live with," an acceptance of all sounds similar to that espoused by John Cage (1961, 4), who said that the use of electronic instruments "will make available for musical purposes any and all sounds that can be heard." Recording equipment makes any sound in the world available: it can be isolated from its context and treated as a sound object, or the interplay of sounds within a specific environmental context can be the focus of attention. Schafer's statement that abstract constructions such as musical compositions are soundscapes *particularly when considered as an environment* underscores the importance of context in soundscape composition. This makes soundscape composition quite different from musique concrète, in which sounds are isolated from their original context in studio work.

Westerkamp insists on her bodily presence through her work. In the liner notes for "Breathing Room," Westerkamp (1990) says: "Music as breath-like nourishment. Breathing as nourishing musical space. The breath—my breath—is heard throughout the three minutes. All sorts of musical/acoustic things happen as I breathe in and out. Each breath makes its own, unique statement, creates a specific place in time. Meanwhile the heart beats on, propelling time from one breath to the next." Her desire to create a breathing environment within musical space is influenced by her contact with American experimental composer Pauline Oliveros. She says: "The first time I encountered Pauline was when she was advertised to give a concert. The concert was us doing sonic meditations all evening and her sitting in the centre listening."[3] Westerkamp was astounded and delighted by this overturning of everyone's roles: composer as listener, audience as performers. Later she was impressed by the breathing environment that Oliveros creates: "When I hear her play the accordion and the way she uses processing in concerts, it is a breathing type of environment, providing a place for the listener to breathe in and for herself—to breathe in while she's playing. The way she develops some of the technology is particularly with that in mind" (interview with author, 1993).

Westerkamp began to integrate Oliveros's sonic meditations, and her own transformations of them, in her electroacoustic studio teaching at Simon Fraser University in the 1980s. She found that students started to learn how to equalize and filter frequencies with their own bodies and how to incorporate technology rather than see it as an alien structure:

Sonic meditations . . . give you a chance to breathe, to get to know your voice and to experiment. . . . And the techniques that they learned about equalizing and filtering in the studio, mike techniques—they heard that they could do very similar things with their own voices. So it wasn't just the equipment that was altering their voices or their sounds, but they themselves could alter their voices so that their body became an equalizing and filtering body—changing sound quality, sound colour, rhythms. . . . There was a very interesting interaction going on between the studio techniques, and the body as an instrument, and group work. . . . [We were finding] a way to work with [technology] that makes sense to incorporate it into one's life and into teaching life, so that it's not such an alien structure any more. (interview with author, 1993)

Westerkamp's approach to the use of sonic meditations emphasizes the interaction of technological and bodily processes of making music, providing a bridge between the roles of humans and machines.

Breathing in the Studio

The request to encapsulate her style in a three-minute piece created a difficult task. Complicating matters, at around the same time she had been commissioned to create another piece. This one was to be a response to the 1989 Montréal Massacre, in which a sole gunman killed fourteen women engineering students at the École Polytechnique, an engineering college in Montreal, calling them feminists. Westerkamp's schedule at this point was frantic, and she found the Montréal Massacre an important and difficult subject. Both commissions initially seemed challenging.

Westerkamp responded by creating breathing room within these difficult demands. One day she lay down on the studio floor and breathed deeply for nine minutes. She recorded this interlude of relaxed breathing and then used it to form a rhythmic structure, adding a mechanical, repetitive pulse. Over these rhythmic pulses she layered reworked material from earlier pieces, using this opportunity to reflect on her previous work.[4] This method then formed "Électroclip" and later became the basis for the beginning and end sections of her piece about the Montréal Massacre, "L'École Polytechnique," in which breathing is gradually interrupted by more and more ominous sounds and then eventually returns in hope for continuing life at the end.

The choice of one's own breath as a compositional structure is a radical one for a number of reasons. Frances Dyson (1994, 175) points out that philosophers since Plato have insisted that proper voice can be produced only by "barring" the breath: "The coming and going of life which the breath represents brings the inevitable mortality of the body too close to the voice. . . . It interferes with the smooth functioning of the voice of the mind—that bodiless instrument which continues to speculate and reflect uninterrupted in the mind's I/eye for all eternity. It allows death, absence, to touch the light of reason and the vision of the soul." The sound of breath is a constant reminder of our mortality, our physicality. Susan McClary (1991, 136) notes that "a very strong tradition of Western musical thought has been devoted to defining music as the sound itself, to erasing the physicality involved in both the making and the reception of music." Electronic composition, with its ability to eliminate performers, can potentially form the extreme of this idealist trajectory. In "Breathing Room," however, the composer insists on her bodily presence through her own voice.[5] With each breath she creates the illusion that she is breathing in sounds—the sounds of water gurgling, birds singing, an airplane passing overhead, or wind chimes. The mechanical "heartbeat" pulse, fading in after about thirty seconds, continues throughout, moving from foreground to background at different points in the piece but never disappearing.

The use of breathing as a compositional structure reflects Westerkamp's respect for the acoustic environment as being active, alive, and in dialogue with the composer. By creating the illusion of breathing in sounds, Westerkamp makes tangible the function of the breathing tract as a conduit between the body and the environment. Robert Fried (1990, 8) says: "Breathing brings us into intimate communion with our environment. We can think of the lungs as *external organs,* always exposed to the atmosphere." Westerkamp expresses her sense of respect for the environment through refusing to think of sound as merely a compositional resource:

> I do feel that sounds have their own integrity and feel that they need to be treated with a great deal of care. . . . It did take me two years to dare to compose with that cricket's recording [for the composition "Cricket Voice"], as it had been such a magical moment of recording, such a gift. I could not just "manipulate" it. It had to be a new sonic journey to retain the level of magic for me. And I remember a moment at which I said "Stop." The journey was beginning to turn into electronic experimentation and the cricket was being obliterated. Same experience with the raven in "Beneath the Forest Floor." I tried to make it into a regularly beating drum . . . [but] it simply wouldn't let me. So I returned to the shape of the original full call, slowed that down and received from it a drum-like

sound. It took a whole day to fly off into electronicland and return to the raven call. (Westerkamp, personal communication, 26 March 1995)

In thus describing her way of working sounds, Westerkamp offers remarks strikingly similar to Lorraine Code's account of the epistemological positions of three women research scientists. Code (1991, 150–51) says that their work is marked by

> i) a respect that resists the temptation to know primarily in order to control. . . . The work is ii) oriented toward letting the "objects" of study speak for themselves; hence it is wary of imposing preconceived ideas and theoretical structures. Yet this openness is not theory-neutral. Rather, it is an attitude aware of the constraints of theory-ladenness and thus governed by reflexive, self-critical imperatives. The approach is iii) non-reductive, adding to the first two features a recognition of an irreducible complexity in nature. . . . In all of the features there is iv) a sense of the knowing subject's position in, and accountability to, the world she studies. That sense manifests itself in a mode of observation that is immersed and engaged, not manipulative, voyeuristic, or distanced.

Westerkamp speaks of letting the raven sound speak for itself, about caring for the cricket sound and not wanting to obliterate it. She wishes to leave these sounds recognizable, not to distance them from their roots in the world. She questions her compositional decisions and wants sounds to retain their complexity, not to be simplified or obscured through her work. Her engagement with the sounds is reflected in her choice of language: the cricket voice was a magical gift, and with the raven sound, she flew. At the same time, she is not limiting herself to documenting nature. Her studio work is a dialogue between the original sound in context and her imaginary constructions. Above all, her language reflects a responsibility to the natural world and a desire to avoid completely effacing it with technology, allowing sounds to breathe within their own environments while creating imaginary constructs that juxtapose different contexts.

Analysis through Listening

When I first heard "Breathing Room," I was struck by the feeling of intimacy that I experienced on hearing close-up breathing. The interplay of environmental sounds intrigued me, as did the gradual movement from air to water and the complexity and density of the sound world that was produced. I also felt vaguely anxious.

This last sensation confused me somewhat, leading to a decision to analyze the piece, approaching it simultaneously in two ways. I used James Tenney's (1992) method of analysis, which considers all parameters of music by following the principles of gestalt perception. Unlike methods of analysis that rely on a written score, this method is based on focused listening to a piece. My listening resulted in a graphic representation of the piece as well as the description in appendix A.

I also solicited the responses to "Breathing Room" from various listeners, wanting to compare my initial reaction to the piece with those of others. Some of these listeners were Canadian composers, both men and women. Some were people who said that they rarely listened to electroacoustic music. The individuals in both groups listened to the piece on tape in their homes and wrote open-ended responses to it. I also played it for four university classes: a graduate class in women's studies, a graduate class in music, an undergraduate listening class for non–music majors, and an undergraduate class in electroacoustic composition. Only some listeners decided to submit their responses. Each of the class members wrote open-ended responses on paper. These listeners were given no program notes until after listening. I asked the listeners to complete a questionnaire giving me details about their gender, ethnic identity, age, and background in electroacoustic music. These thirty-one listener responses are shown in appendix B, which includes any such information that the listeners gave me (not all of them answered my questions). The comments that follow are drawn from these listeners' responses and from my analysis.

Two listeners, both from the women's studies class, described this piece as gendered female. One respondent said: "Birds, breathing, decidedly a female gendered piece." I wonder whether a piece structured by a man's breathing would be described as gendered male, or whether these listeners were reacting to the dangerous essentialist equation "body = woman or bodily sounds = gendered female"? Later the same listener asked whether the essentialism is intentional. A discussion regarding essentialism followed in this class, with discussants noting that a woman composer working with environmental sounds risks being described as essentialist, whereas a male composer would not. On the other hand, another listener (a man in the undergraduate music class) heard the breathing as a man's: "Vietnam, swamps, birds, soldier—in pain or feeling really exhausted . . . suspenseful and scary atmosphere . . . he is a survivor." His image of a soldier in the jungle perhaps led him to hear a man's breathing rather than a woman's.

Several listeners interpreted the use of natural and bodily sounds as more generally stereotyped or hackneyed, creating an essentialized nature. One male composition student praised Westerkamp's layering and spatial composition but then added: "Cliché sounds of birds and breathing hindered the piece." Another male composition student said: "Is this a *Solitudes* tape? Touristy New Age . . . back to Nature."[6]

Interestingly these listeners did not comment on the sounds of airplanes that recur several times during the piece. *Solitudes* tapes would never include such urban sounds. Neither would they include the sound of a person's breathing, since the title suggests their intent: to create a purified wilderness, devoid of any sounds of humans or cities. Westerkamp does adjust volume levels and frequency bias to idealize her sonic world—the airplanes become quieter than the crickets—but they are never erased. The urban world does not disappear completely but is brought into her idea of balance.

Although many listeners liked hearing the relaxed breathing and felt connected to it, others described it as annoying or disruptive. One composer said that it disrupted his own breathing pattern. A female composition student said that the breathing "hits you right in the chest." A male composition student reported, "The breathing aspect gets very annoying very quick—sounds superficial." It is interesting that all these descriptions of annoyance or disruption came from people involved in electroacoustic composition (although not all composers have this reaction); the other listeners did not mention such reactions. Perhaps, as Frances Dyson (1994) notes with regard to the development of the contemporary radio voice, the sound of the body is still not considered acceptable by many in the electroacoustic studio.

Sometimes the breathing was perceived as threatening. A women's studies student said: "Threatening, relaxation, relief (i.e. hearing relief in the expulsion of breath, but also my own sense of relief that what had sounded like the beginnings of a threatening phone call, i.e. a heavy breather, was in fact, simply an amplified track of someone breathing"). This last reaction puzzled me until I realized that most often, when we hear *amplified* breathing, it is stressed breath, either through a threatening phone call or in the context of television or film soundtracks, where it is often a sign of danger or excitement. The amplification of *relaxed* breathing—something we rarely hear— establishes an intimacy between performer and listener, creating the feeling that we are right next to the composer as she breathes.

Those who enjoy the breathing, and I include myself in this group, mentioned that listening to the work produced a heightened awareness of their own breathing. One listener in the women's studies class said: "The breath is like surf, inevitable and always but never the same." Several others described the breathing as relaxed, sensual, or meditative. The breathing is thus a source of either tension or relaxation.

Not all the sounds are introduced by breaths. Another source of tension for some listeners is the mechanical pulse, which Westerkamp refers to as a heartbeat. A student in the undergraduate listening course juxtaposed words as follows: "outside—river: power plant? heartbeat? illness, impending doom, struggle, extinct." A male composition student says: "Pulse in background creating tension from the foreground relaxation. As the pulse gets louder it creates a worry and stress within."

More extended listening reveals reasons for this worry and stress. Again, several listeners, including Westerkamp, have referred to the pulse as a heartbeat. This is a mechanical heartbeat, however, with a regular rhythm, unlike organic hearts. The heartbeat of a relaxed individual rises slightly with every inhalation and falls with each exhalation (Fried 1990, 156). Pulse rate tends to be more regular in stressed breathing, and a very regular heartbeat is considered a symptom of heart disease. The regularity of the mechanical heart can thus be interpreted as a sign of stress.

Also, there are only fifteen breaths in the three-minute piece, a very relaxed breathing rate. The pulse is much faster, however, 140 beats per minute, suggesting much more activity. The pulse is insistent once it begins—it never completely disappears, and the tempo never changes. It fluctuates only in volume. As I listen to the piece, I find that my feeling of tension is directly related to the pulse's volume and proximity to the foreground. A male composition student commented: "My heart beats seem to get quicker. Feeling very anxious, waiting for something to happen." (As I type this, I notice that my computer is producing a regular pulse that becomes louder as I listen. How is my body responding?)

Abstracted or processed sounds are the last to be introduced to the piece, starting at around thirty-five seconds. These sounds come from two sources: a fiddle and a truck brake. They have been slowed down to alter their character completely, producing gradual evolutions in timbre and pitch and a feeling of amorphous shifting through space. Only one listener referred to these sounds, saying: "Superimposed pitches create a feeling of expectation." Perhaps listeners who hear the piece only a few times do not comment on these sounds because of their subtle presence: they are rarely foregrounded.

On repeated listening and analysis, however, these sounds seem more important. They form a harmonic bridge between the mechanical beat and the environmental sounds, at times forming restful octaves and fifths and at other times producing more complex harmonies (see appendix A). They also form polyrhythms with the mechanical beat, making it seem less relentless. Although they continue between the breaths, some of the shorter processed sounds join dynamically with the environmental sounds and are inhaled. Westerkamp considers work with sounds such as the truck brake to be a political act:

> When you know a sound, or when you know how something works and how it affects you, it is already the beginning of action. Then you can begin to deal with it. Then you can decide whether or not you want to wear ear plugs . . . When I hear a truck brake and I say, "that's fantastic, I want to record it," then I'm not as disturbed by it. When there is a political issue and you don't want to know about it, it's actually much more energy to block it out, than to . . . take it on and begin to act. It's like breathing again. (in Young 1984, 7)

Westerkamp metaphorically inhales and exhales environmental sounds, creating a sonic construct of her relationship with the world around her. There is a sense here of an interaction with a living, breathing world, where she can learn from ravens, crickets, and truck brakes, representing what she learns in compositional dialogue with the environment: "Music as breath-like nourishment. Breathing as nourishing musical space." In "Breathing Room" Westerkamp creates a cyborg body, with her own human breath taking in and singing the world around her, propelled by a mechanical heart. This is not a border skirmish between human and machine or human and environment. Haraway (1991, 180) says: "The machine is us, our processes, an aspect of our embodiment. . . . We are responsible for boundaries, we are they." Westerkamp uses technology to create a body of work that makes audible the breathing connections between inner and outer worlds.

At the same time, this cyborg body is still ironic. The mechanical heart, for instance, while metaphorically part of this body, is more rigid and less organic than the other sounds. Thus, although it forms part of the cyborg body, its rhythms seem somewhat alien: mechanical heart and organic breath coexist in an uneasy tension. Listeners hear both relaxation and stress, what one respondent referred to as "the dear and the dangerous," and those contradictions never resolve.

APPENDIX A: "BREATHING ROOM" ANALYSIS

General Description

"Breathing Room" is a three-minute tape piece using acoustic and synthetic sounds (see figures 13.1 and 13.2). It has an approximate pitch range of four octaves, and noisy (unpitched or timbrally complex) sounds predominate. It moves at a slow tempo, and the dynamics encompass a medium range (*piano* to *forte*). It is structured by the irregular rhythm of the fifteen breaths that continue throughout the piece. Each breath is followed by a space without breath (at first silence and later processed and synthetic sound). The piece becomes denser and thicker in texture, reaching a point of maximum density at the tenth breath and decreasing in timbral diversity and density after this point. In this respect, its shape can be said to resemble that of a single breath. The work includes four types of sounds: breathing, taped acoustic sounds (relatively unprocessed), processed tape sounds, and a mechanical beat.

Breath 1 (0.01)

This section has a narrow pitch range (three octaves), which is higher than that in later sections. There are only three different timbres (breath, water, birds), followed by silence. The timbral content of the section is more noisy than pitched, since only the bird sounds have defined pitch, while the breath and water sounds are more complex. Volume ranges from *piano* to *mezzopiano*. The breath has a quiet inhalation and an open-mouthed exhalation that is louder and rises in pitch. The point of greatest dynamic/timbral diversity/vertical density comes

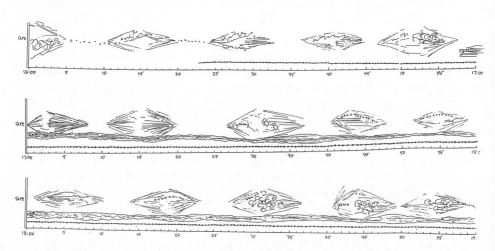

Figure 13.1. "Breathing Room": Westerkamp's score.

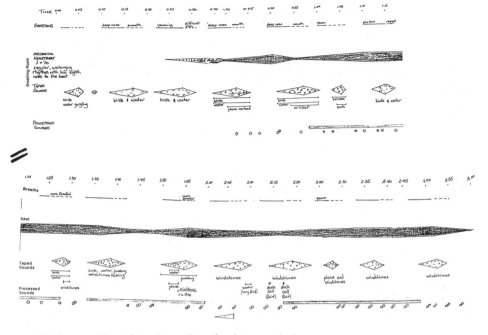

Figure 13.2. "Breathing Room": author's transcription.

toward the end of the inhalation. The inhalation is short (two seconds), followed by a longer exhalation (four seconds) and four seconds of silence.

Breath 4 (0:35)
This breath has a broader pitch range (approximately four and one-half octaves) and more pitched material (processed sounds, birds, airplane, mechanical beat). There are two noisy sounds: breath and water. There are six different timbres, so the breath is denser. The inhalation is loud and long (five seconds), followed by a quieter, shorter exhalation (four seconds). This breath is less audible than the first, and the other sounds are louder. It is followed by five seconds of just the mechanical beat and short processed sounds. The mechanical beat maintains a pitch of $E\flat_2$ throughout. The airplane is just above E_3 and short processed sounds $E\flat_4$–E_4. The bird sounds are clustered in a range from two to three octaves higher than the other sounds.

Breath 10 (1:50)
The pitch range is approximately the same as that of breath 4. This breath has the greatest timbral diversity, with nine different sounds: breath, mechanical beat, water, June bug, airplane, wind chimes, rattle, and long and short processed

sounds. This exhalation also has the greatest number of sounds (seven). The breath is loud on both the inhalation and exhalation, with the mouth moving on the exhalation, where the pitch rises. The inhalation is four seconds long; the exhalation, three seconds; and there is a four-second section with only processed and mechanical sounds. This is the only time the rattle appears in the piece. The wind chimes are in the same approximate pitch range as the earlier bird sounds.

Breath 15 (2:47)

Here the timbral diversity has again been reduced to four sounds: breath, mechanical beat, wind chimes, and short processed sounds. The pitch range is about the same as for the fourth breath. There is a long, quiet inhalation (five seconds) followed by a shorter, quiet exhalation (four seconds) and a section with just the mechanical beat and short processed sounds. The mechanical beat continues to maintain the pitch of $E\flat_2$. The airplane is between $E\flat_3$ and E_3. The long processed sound is at A_4, while the short processed sounds are close to it in pitch, rising from F_3 to $G\flat_3$. The wind chimes are several octaves higher, in the same pitch range as the earlier bird sounds.

APPENDIX B: LISTENER RESPONSES TO "BREATHING ROOM"

Note: Listeners self-identified by choosing a pseudonym and describing themselves using the labels or phrases in parentheses.

Kate (female occasional listener, Anglo, twenty-four): "new age . . . springtime—waking up—nature . . . cool, not too elitist . . . superimposed pitches creating feeling of expectation."

X [undergraduate music class]: "someone waking up . . . tension. We're travelling like the air, from inside the beings to the outside backyard."

Y [undergraduate music class]: "outside—river: power plant? heartbeat? illness, impending doom, struggle, extinct."

Zel (male listener, undergraduate music class): "Vietnam, swamps, birds, soldier—in pain or feeling really exhausted . . . suspenseful and scary atmosphere . . . he is a survivor."

Albert (male composer, Euro, twenty-eight): "Hildegard has combined a beautiful treatment of material (the birds are something else) with a dominant structure which makes me either forget to breathe or yawn, both due to her disrupting my own breathing pattern. Unfortunately the breath must be there to shape the stuff within the breath."

Eve Angeline (female occasional listener, Euro, twenty-seven, women's studies class): "excellent opening image. 'life within woman.' had a real presence. inner world piece, sounds very gendered female."

Women's studies 1: "Threatening, relaxation, relief (i.e. hearing relief in the expulsion of breath, but also my own sense of relief that what had sounded like the beginnings of a threatening phone call, i.e. a heavy breather, was in fact, simply an amplified track of someone breathing). Life. Tension or urgency of the rhythm belied by the breath. Labour contractions (somewhat like the point during labour where your whole existence is focussed on your body and breathing becomes the focal point of your concentration)."

Women's Studies 2:

> Waking up in a tent up north
> Birch Island
> Railroad tracks cross
> between tent and water
> Cross over Mother Earth
>
> Steaming breath of night in tent
> Steaming between us and the Water Being
> The insects nearby buzz
> Drowning out the train
>
> Perspective
> The near and far
> The dear and the dangerous
> Open the flap—the train has passed
> Sun rises over water—waves
> I breathe in the shining breeze.

Shona (female occasional listener): "In the womb. . . . There is a heartbeat in the background, even the odd gurgle of water, just like a stomach churning. These really are quite like the sounds I must have heard . . . and yet I am hearing this with all of me, not just my head. . . . THERE'S SOMETHING OUTSIDE! . . . the breath is like surf, inevitable and always but never the same."

Rusty (mostly male composer, white, twenty-six): "I like the opening a lot . . . balanced strength, forces aligning and combining harmoniously. . . . there's a human spirit here among other spirits—yawns show how breathing, which summons, is grounded."

Max (bisexual female composition student, Euro-U.S., twenty-one): "This piece would make me feel bad if I were on any type of illegal drug. Very 'deep' sounding. The breathing hits you right in the chest."

Jean (female composer, white, forty-two): "Immediately I felt a sensation of being brought back into my body after having to have left it previously in order to survive. I felt taken care of, that I didn't have to put up my defences. The piece created a process that moved through me. Discreet layers of sound were audible, each layer discernible, and through the development of the piece there was a sensation of accumulated energy."

Biff (heterosexual male composition student, white, twenty-two): "Is this a *Soli-*

tudes tape? Touristy New Age . . . back to Nature. The breathing aspect gets very annoying very quick—sounds superficial."

Dave (male composition student, Canadian, twenty): "relaxing by a brook . . . ominous pulsing . . . importance of self-awareness and inner purity."

Jane (bisexual female composition student, Caucasian/unknown, twenty): "hot sun and water in the forest by a river. Someone with heat stroke having an auditory hallucination. I really liked it. It kind of teases you but never delivers, making me want to hear it again and again."

Mark (heterosexual male composition student, Austrian, twenty-four): "Natural, like swimming . . . underwater then up into the air. Menacing, almost Jaws music. Insistent rhythm, a heartbeat."

Seal (male composition student, Canadian, thirty-five): "Breathing very sensual. Pulse in background creating tension from the foreground relaxation. As pulse gets louder it creates a worry and stress within."

James (heterosexual male composition student, Euro, twenty) "Multi-layering and spatial composition were tastefully done. Cliché sounds of birds and breathing hindered the piece."

Elizabeth (female composition student, white, twenty-one): "Good 'jungle' sounds but more could be done with them to make it more interesting. Not particularly fond of breathing sounds. Background drum interesting. . . . fairly boring."

Charles (male composition student, Asian-white, twenty): "an open field, blowing grass. I liked it very much because it created space. It felt like it was building somewhere, but it seemed like it ended too soon."

Zubian (heterosexual male composition student, Roman Catholic, twenty): "Makes me want to yawn! My heart beats seem to get quicker. Feeling very anxious, waiting for something to happen."

Madame X (female occasional listener, Euro, forty-one): "walking through the woods focusing on my own breath. A sense of peacefulness, relaxation. Yawning, taking up and sensing the space around me."

Ric (both [genders], occasional listener, thirty, women's studies class): "Birds, breathing, decidedly a female gendered piece. Birds and nature and women again, more essentialisms. Intentional?"

Sam (male occasional listener, thirty-seven): "early morning in a rustic setting."

Liz (female occasional listener, white, twenty-eight): "Nature, relaxed breath, fatigue, at ease."

Elizabeth (female composition student, Canadian, twenty-one): "ocean, floating . . . reeds that blow lightly in the sun. It is now getting darker as the clouds come in and there are animals swimming through the reeds."

Yorgay (female occasional listener, Canadian, twenty-five): "me in my bed back on the prairies . . . spring sunlight. Shadows, undergrowth as I advance into the tall deciduous forest. Unafraid presence of other beings or spirits."

X [no identification]: "At the seaside. When someone's falling asleep, she or her starting to have a kind of nightmare."

Ishmael (male listener, Euro, thirty-six): "Pre-natal exercises in the woods (send in the loons). No. Make that Margaret Atwood Murders in the Dark soundtrack. Nope. I dunno. It's off-putting."

Larry (composer): "nice beginning. Simple but evocative. Has the advantage of being short."

David (very female composer, very white, thirty): "Reminds me of Q[i]-gong meditation: breathe in and imagine lotus flower in your stomach open, and radiating light to your inner organs, esp. heart. Energy to the lotus when it opens (lotus closes when you breathe out). Your pores opening up when inhaling and all kinds of light and energy entering."

APPENDIX C: HILDEGARD WESTERKAMP DISCOGRAPHY

Harangue II. 1998. "Gently Penetrating beneath the Sounding Surfaces of Another Place." earsay (Vancouver), CD.

Harangue I. 1998. "Talking Rain." earsay (Vancouver), CD.

Transformations. 1996. empreintes DIGITALes (Montreal), CD.

Électroclips. 1990. "Breathing Room." empreintes DIGITALes (Montreal), CD.

Electroacoustic Music. 1990. "Cricket Voice." Anthology of Music in Canada 37. Radio Canada International (Montreal), CD.

The Aerial 2. 1990. "Cricket Voice." Nonsequitur, CD.

Inside the Soundscape. 1986. Hildegard Westerkamp and Norbert Ruebsaat. Cassettes 1–5. 1: "Fantasie for Horns I and II"; 2: "A Walk through the City," "Whisper Study," "Street Music"; 3: "Cordillera," "Zone of Silence Story"; 4: "Voices for the Wilderness"; 5: "Harbour Symphony." Inside the Soundscape (685 W. Nineteenth Ave. Vancouver, B.C., Canada V5Z 1W9).

Women Voicing. 1985. Excerpts from "Collage of Desert Plant Sounds," "Cricket Nightsong," "His Master's Voice." Musicworks (Toronto) MW 31.

A Walk Through the City. 1984. Excerpts from "Cool Drool," "A Walk Through the City," "When There Is No Sound." Musicworks (Toronto) MW 26.

NOTES

1. Born in Germany, Westerkamp moved to Vancouver in 1968. Her association with the World Soundscape Project inspired her to explore the possibilities of composing with environmental sounds in the recording studio. She has also worked extensively with Vancouver Cooperative Radio and taught acoustic communication at Simon Fraser University for several years. She is a founding member of the World Forum for Acoustic Ecology and coordinating editor of their *Soundscape Newsletter* (School of Communication, Simon Fraser University, Burn-

aby, B.C. V5A 1S6). As well as composing, she travels internationally to present workshops on acoustic ecology.

2. For my master's thesis research through York University's graduate program in music (McCartney 1994), I interviewed fourteen Canadian women composers of electroacoustic music. All these interviews took place between February and November 1993, usually in the composer's home or private studio.

3. Oliveros's *Sonic Meditations* (Baltimore, M.D.: Smith, 1974) contains listening and sound-making meditation exercises that focus on the relationship between listeners and their environments.

4. For a more detailed analysis of "Breathing Room," see appendix A.

5. This strategy was dismissed by one reviewer in a Toronto newspaper, who says that Westerkamp "shapes her Breathing Room with exhalations and heartbeats, a strategy that seems more interesting in theory than in her practice (Everett-Green 1990, C4). This is the only negative comment in the entire review, which ignores the only other woman on the compilation by twenty-five composers and praises several of the male composers' work as "aggressive," "fiercely protean," or "hefty."

6. *Solitudes* is the brand name of an extensive series of relaxation tapes and CDs produced in Toronto, Ontario, by Dan Gibson. The majority of these productions combine environmental (usually wilderness) sounds with classical music played on a synthesizer. They are marketed in tourist shops, garden centers, and record stores.

References Cited

Cage, John. 1961. *Silence.* Cambridge, Mass.: MIT Press.

Code, Lorraine. 1991. *What Can She Know? Feminist Theory and the Construction of Knowledge.* Ithaca, N.Y: Cornell University Press.

de Lauretis, Teresa. 1987. *Technologies of Gender: Essays on Theory, Film, and Fiction.* Bloomington: Indiana University Press.

Dyson, Frances. 1994. "The Genealogy of the Radio Voice." In *Radio Rethink: Art, Sound, and Transmission,* ed. Daina Augaitis and Dan Lander, 167–88. Banff, Alta.: Walter Phillips Gallery.

Everett-Green, Robert. 1990. "'Snapshots' That Stimulate." *Globe and Mail,* 26 November, C4.

Fried, Robert. 1990. *The Breath Connection.* New York: Plenum.

Haraway, Donna. 1991. *Simians, Cyborgs, and Women: The Reinvention of Nature.* New York: Routledge.

McCartney, Andra. 1994. "Creating Worlds for My Music to Exist: How Women Composers of Electroacoustic Music Make Place for Their Voices." M.A. thesis, York University.

———. 1995. "Inventing Images: Constructing and Contesting Gender in Thinking about Electroacoustic Music." *Leonardo Music Journal* 5:57–66.

McClary, Susan. 1991. *Feminine Endings: Music, Gender, and Sexuality.* Minneapolis: University of Minnesota Press.

Schafer, R. Murray. 1977. *The Tuning of the World.* Toronto: McClelland Stewart.

Tenney, James. 1992 [1964]. *Meta+Hodos: A Phenomenology of 20th-Century Musical Materials and an Approach to the Study of Form.* Hanover, N.H.: Frog Peak.

Westerkamp, Hildegard. 1974. "Soundwalking." *Sound Heritage* 3, no. 4:18–27.

———. 1988. "Listening and Soundmaking: A Study of Music-As-Environment." M.A. thesis, Simon Fraser University.

Young, Gayle. 1984. "Composing with Environmental Sound." *Musicworks* 26 (Winter): 4–8.

14   No Bodies There: Absence and Presence in Acousmatic Performance

Linda Dusman

In an article entitled "Unheard-of: Music as Performance and the Reception of the New," published in *Perspectives of New Music* (Dusman 1994), I argued for the identification of new music as "other" within the cultural context of the so-called art music or classical music community. The performance of new music subverts the historical context assumed by a culture identified by repeated, reifying performances of old music. In the same article I also used Peggy Phelan's ontology of performance as articulated in *Unmarked*[1] (1993) to critique historical music performance as a primarily reproductive performance genre, for attending audiences know most works from years of repetition in recording, broadcast, and performance. Such performances do not generate a musical "present" and so can never truly be experienced as performance as Phelan defined it; rather, most symphony orchestra concerts are live reproductions. In the art music scene, performing new rather than old music embodies the "nonreproductive present" essential for Phelan's performative experience, for performances of those works have rarely been heard and are seldom available on commercial recordings.

In this essay I will continue to theorize music as performance by focusing on a particular site in the domain of new music, that of tape music performance, or what has more recently been dubbed "acousmatic" music, a term Pierre Schaefer used for sound without a source or music performed via loudspeakers. This performance genre was created with the simultaneous development of electronic music studios and the tape recorder in the early 1950s, when composers working in electronic studios recorded their compositions on tape to be played back in performance venues. After the initial fascination waned, performances in which one sits in an audience facing a pair of audio speakers for an entire evening became a much reviled and contested form. Audiences understandably tired of never seeing a human performer, and tape music concerts, mostly located at universities, became a medium for specialists and students.

I have several reasons for choosing this site. Most important, it eliminates one-third of a complicated triangle of musical experience constituted by composer, performer, and audience and so allows me in the beginning stages of this project to focus exclusively on sonic experience.[2] Another reason is that by eliminating the performer, tape music inherently subverts the concert music tradition and as a result has been marginalized by the music community. As such, it provides a view from the extreme of what identifies music performance, a vantage point that can ultimately illuminate more mainstream genres.

A third reason is its persistence. When synthesizers became smaller, computers became portable, and the development of MIDI (musical instrument digital interface) allowed for interaction between performer and synthetic sound, many believed the genre of tape music would disappear, since the necessity of its perceived disadvantages had been eliminated. This is far from the case. In fact, the tape music genre has expanded exponentially in the last few years. A number of reasons could be cited for this—the economic difficulty of hiring performers for a sufficient rehearsal schedule during a period of severe arts funding cuts, the drop in price of computers, and the proliferation of inexpensive software and "shareware" for sound synthesis and processing. Also, the psychological and cultural state of the composer in recent times may contribute to this boom. New music has been systematically ignored or slandered by the musicological community, and so retreating into a marginalized performance genre allows composers to support one another while maintaining relative freedom from criticism. This arena also allows relative freedom from the confines of the business and politics of music composing—that of commissions, higher-profile performances, publication, and the press.

From the perspective of cultural analysts, the idea of defining recorded sound as performative is curious. In the classical music community, a music culture where recordings have become a substitute for performance, recordings are often thought of as "representations" of performance (consider the "live" recording, for example). As a result, in our particular historical moment, what is actually experienced in music performances is a live reproduction of recorded sound, not performance per se. In tape music performances, recorded sound, a medium largely understood as representational by the music community at large, has been claimed as performative by a marginalized group. Thus one way to view this medium might be to see it as a representational genre that creates a performative present in contrast to the representational present created by historical performance genres, the more common musical performative experience. In other words, the paradox of this type of performance is that recorded sound might offer the listener a performative moment, as defined by Phelan, whereas a performance of Mozart's G Minor Symphony (K550) is unlikely to do so.

Alternatively, tape music may provide music history its first possibility of a nonperformative musical genre—that is, works not necessarily intended by their creators to be performed in a traditional concert venue. Though these works are often performed, they can exist without performance; the sound is already there and accessible in each composer's desktop computer. Though the nonperformative music genre has been successful in popular music for years in the form of the highly edited CD, it has arguably not yet become part of the mainstream consciousness in classical music circles.

Any analysis of music reception must acknowledge musical desire as the prime feature that distinguishes audiences for music from those for the other performing arts. A love of the musical indicates a specific kind of sonic pleasure, and the fascination with sound is a particular human experience that appears long before language acquisition in infants. We learn to pay attention to sound early in life, for both its pleasurable and its meaningful aspects. Music thus becomes an object of contemplation, and as a result it has been objectified and subjected to the same patriarchal oppressions experienced in other art forms. As a primarily sensory experience devoid of representational meanings, however, music is particularly associated with the body, not as an object of experience, but as the source of the experience itself. As such, it is especially vulnerable to the societal oppressions that originate in Western European associations with the body, namely misogyny, homophobia, and racism. Feminist theorists and queer theorists in music are laying important groundwork for the connections between music and the body in our culture. I have found the queer theorists to be particularly useful in thinking through the experience of acousmatic performance, an inherently subversive performance form.

In "Music, Essentialism, and the Closet" Philip Brett (1994) presents an insightful exegesis of the body connection in music, the resultant feminization of the art form, and the consequent homosexual panic particularly among male musicians. "Modernism, when it arrived," Brett (1994, 13) states, "simply intensified the principle of abstraction by eliminating from music all imitative 'expression,' thus removing it further in the direction of pure form and pattern."

Given Brett's formulation, it is no coincidence that tape music as a performative possibility was conceived at the height of modernism. In its elimination of the performer's body, the connection with the body of the composer became even more remote; moreover, particularly since many of the sounds used in early synthesis were quite obviously "machinelike," there are many ways in which this music could sound distant as a human expression. Algorithmic composition, often employed in computer music, involves writing a computer program that selects at least some specific sonic content, making the composer's body one step farther removed. Computer music in many ways achieves the "pure form and pattern" Brett cites.

But the body of the audience member, not the composer, is perhaps the most critical role in acoustic performance. With no performer on which to focus one's attention, no interpreter or mediator stands between the sound of the music itself and the body of the listener. I believe this constitutes part of the unacknowledged threat of this music in the classical music community: not only does the absence of the performer break with the historical tradition, but it also makes the listener's body present in a public setting through a listening mode that is customarily private. I am much more aware of my own self in tape music performances, because I have no performer's body to which to attend. Particularly in works that involve a tremendous amount of silence, the bodily awareness is extreme. This is not the sensual pleasure of lush warm colors of sound but rather the coarse imposition of my own physical presence into an arena—that of listening to recorded sound—in which I am accustomed to being transported away from that everyday awareness.

That this performance happens solely in the ears of the audience, that the listener must supply the emotional, physical, and intellectual understanding of the sonic object, with no performer to buffer the implications of that involvement, presents another important facet of this kind of performance. One does not know when this music is about to begin or exactly when it will end. This music "happens to us," and we have no idea what kinds of sounds to expect (for there are no instruments that parade on stage along with their performers). As the final trial, we are the sole interpreters of the work. Without a performer there to instruct my listening via facial expressions, body movements, and the shaping of the sound itself—and then to smile at me at the end of the process—I have no idea whether I have successfully negotiated this sonic terrain. It is up to the listeners to know for themselves, a weighty responsibility for the average concertgoer.

To continue with the metaphor of terrain, the rocky territory that listeners find in tape compositions includes the sounds themselves. Our culture defines musical sounds as existing in naturalized and unnaturalized states, as Elizabeth Wood illustrated in her article "Sapphonics" (1994). She created this term not only to describe the mode of articulation of erotic and emotional relationships between female singers and female listeners but also to describe the human vocal instrument in its female ranges, including such voices as the male falsetto and the boy soprano, among others. Many of these sounds were described by listeners as "unnatural" and "not properly housed in the human body," and the attendant homosexual overtones have been well documented by Wayne Koestenbaum in *The Queen's Throat* (1994).

I think the connection with computer-generated sound as unnatural is obvious. Although music listeners are accustomed to combinations of vocal and instrumental sound, sounds from a computer are not natural, whether they are synthetic or concrete. Beyond using them to produce the basic sounds themselves, composers often turn to the computer precisely because it is not limited by human technical ability—compared to human beings, it can make sound move faster and slower, higher and lower, and louder and softer, and in addition it can simulate movement in space. Computer-generated sound is most certainly "not housed in the human body."

From these vantage points, acousmatic performance produces a double bind for its audience. As Brett suggests, music is of the body and as such is effeminized. It is also naturalized in that bodily state—there are certain kinds of sounds that are most acceptable because they are emitted by "natural" human beings, as Wood and Koestenbaum make clear. Removing the body from both sonic production and performance creates a doubly unnatural performance experience. From the audience's perspective, while tape music obviously does not originate in the body of a performer, it would at least be more natural if it did. Moreover, listening to this unnatural music while having one's own body rather than the body of the missing performer foregrounded doubles the effeminizing and homosexualizing threat. In acousmatic performance there is no body on which to transfer that anxiety, no possibility of the safety of voyeurism. To use a metaphor of sexuality, the only possible mode of engagement is autoerotic.

How then is the average concertgoer to gain access to this rich and ever-proliferating repertory? Here, of course, I am speaking not yet of the specific experience of an individual work but rather of general strategies for listening to a performance genre that is far from the "normal" concert experience. Clearly concertgoers must have greater access to understanding the body in performance—information usually reserved for performers. But queer theorists in musicology have also begun to reflect on the physical musical experience. For example, Suzanne Cusick outlines a lesbian listening experience in "On a Lesbian Relationship with Music" (1994) that is useful in thinking about the body of the audience member in performance.

Cusick assumes that because sexuality and musical listening are both of the body, they are analogous. This analogy is perhaps easier to accept from a lesbian perspective, partly because our culture has had such a difficult time providing a fixed definition of what lesbian sex is. Cusick (1994, 73) describes lesbian sexuality as a site which "channels pleasure . . . much more diffusely than the phallic economy, admitting as sexual . . . pleasures and sites of pleasure beyond the usual ones." She says the word *lesbian* denotes not an identity but rather a preferred behavior, an organization of one's relationship to the world in a "power/pleasure/intimacy triad."[3] Cusick summarizes her lesbian aesthetic response as a preference for musics that invite and allow participation as one chooses, musics with which one may experience a continuous circulation of power even when the music is "on top" (Cusick 1994, 76).[4]

Though Cusick is not necessarily addressing the experience of music in a performance context, I believe the tape music concert falls within her preferred category of musical experience that upsets the balance of power relations. Again, I am speaking not of the music itself here but rather of this performance genre generally, one that places an extreme demand on the audience to "be on top," to be the sole source of engagement and interpretation. The listeners in this performative context must exert power to achieve the musical pleasure and performative intimacy they come to concerts to find—not to do so would in many ways turn the concert experience of this music into prerecorded background music. Allowing this to happen, allowing this music to exist purely as a recording in acousmatic concerts, creates extreme discomfort, for it negates the fundamental premise of the event: that we are there to experience music being created. Tape music cannot be created, we cannot experience a performative present, without imagining the performance into existence ourselves. Once "on top," we can then engage with the music itself in a circulation of power: we can participate with it or not as the music invites or not. But the listener must assume a position of power before that interpretive act can even begin. This is an experience akin to one Umberto Eco (1989, 18) described in *The Open Work,* in which he speaks of listening to new music as a condition "where the listener is not faced by an absolute conditioning center of reference, [requiring] him to constitute his own system of auditory relationships." My hunch is that for most concertgoers the "conditioning center of reference" in performance is the performer, not the music. In a tape music performance that center shifts, of necessity, to the audience members themselves.

Thinking of music listening as analogous to sexuality is viable because musical engagement originates in physical activity, as does sexual engagement—in the age of recording, a body must still be present in music listening, although it is not necessarily physically there in music production. The act of musical engagement for the listener has no meaning in and of itself; the difference comes when we begin to attach language and other sensations to that act, when we begin to respond, to define, analyze, and emote.

Since queer sex is fundamentally nonreproductive, it may illuminate the experience of new music performance: a nonreproductive music in nonreproductive performance. This nonreproductive aspect of the queer experience has been discussed by many queer theorists. Sue-Ellen Case, for example, constructs her queer theory at the site of ontology, "challenging the Platonic parameters of Being—the borders of life and death." For her, "the lethal offshoot of Plato's organicism has been its association with the natural. Life/death becomes the binary of the 'natural' limits of Being: the organic is the natural. In contrast, the queer has been historically constituted as unnatural" (Case 1991, 3). In this way, heterosexual sex, even though it is often nonreproductive, is always associated with its reproductive function and so is seen as natural, whereas homosexual sex, being nonreproductive, is its unnatural counterpart. Analogously, the performance of historical music is inherently reproductive,[5] and so it has a culturally understood meaning as "natural" even before it is performed. New music does not suffer from that luxury. In its unnatural state of newness, when performed, it has no context within which it can be understood a priori, nor is it doomed to constant repetition. It subverts the reproduction of the historical as natural, as queer sexuality subverts reproductive sexuality as the natural.

Pauline Oliveros's *II of IV* (1966)[6] is one example of an electroacoustic work that clearly expresses a performative mode. Oliveros composed this piece in real time at the Electronic Music Studio at the University of Toronto, using a configuration of twelve Lafayette signal generators. Eleven of these generators were set in the superaudio range (from 30kHz to 60kHz), and one was set to the subaudio range, with the resultant combination tones and the bias frequency of the tape machines amplified for audibility. Tape delay was employed, with the tape running between two Ampex 351 tape machines.[7] On first hearing the piece, I experienced it as a physical work, as did a colleague who also attended the concert. He remarked that as he listened to the piece, he had powerful memories of the physical sensation of sitting in front of a Buchla synthesizer creating his own music, an experience I had never had. My experience of the work's physicality occurred on a number of different levels. For one, the omnipresence of the delay technique provides a constant "echo," a transfer of sound from one place in time to another by a distance of almost eight seconds, and the accumulative experience of the seventeen-minute work embeds this physical movement of sound from one tape recorder to another in the listener's consciousness. On another level, one can sense Oliveros's careful yet exuberant sensitivity to the tones created by the sub- and superaudio generators and the rhythmic ride of their color changes throughout the frequency range. The rapid glissandi back and forth through registral extremes that begins five minutes into the piece give a "drawn" quality to these areas, as if etched into the sonic landscape. Throughout its performance, the series of clearly defined sonic shapes is constantly reinforced and unified by the omnipresent echo of the tape delay. Though it is difficult to put into words, *II of IV* does not "sound" (as an active verb) as a recording, as a repetitive act. Oliveros has captured the presence of the performative in spite of her use of an inherently reproductive venue.

How can this paradox of presence during absence in the acousmatic experience be explained, and why are some works more successful at initiating a performative response in listeners than others? Is there some corporeality actually present—perhaps as echo or shadow—of the creator of the work?[8] Again, lesbian theory provides a useful model to examine this "ghosting," this presence of absence. In reference to Greta Garbo in *The Apparitional Lesbian*, Terry Castle (1993, 2) remarks: "When it comes to lesbians . . . many people have trouble seeing what's in front of them. The lesbian remains a kind of 'ghost effect' in the cinema world of modern life: elusive, vaporous, difficult to spot—even when she is there, in plain view, mortal and magnificent, at the very center of the screen. Some may even deny that she exists at all." *II of IV* is remarkable for its own kind of "ghost effect," for from its very inception, Oliveros set out to make what is inaudible audible via her super- and subaudio generators and her amplification of their combination tones. The sudden cut to silence, an abrupt gesture that concludes what is generally a smoothly flowing composition, makes the presence of absence palpable at its close. Oliveros's fascination with amplification of the inaudible already characterized her work with dancers, as illustrated by *The Bath* (1966), a composition for Ann Halprin's Dancers' Workshop "in which the dancers' movements and vocalizations as well as environmental ambience were utilized as sound sources, and the tape recorders as modifiers, during a live performance" (Oliveros 1984, 39–40). During these performances Oliveros "performed" the technology, and her presence as the performer of her music (along with the audience) is an important element of her current identity and performance mode. In many of her current performances, she is at the "center of the screen," apparitional as a lesbian, perhaps, but clearly the composer-performer. In her emphasis on the physicality of the music that is *II of IV,* she is present as well—though apparitional—and it is this aspect of the piece that makes it succeed in performance in a way that many tape works do not.

I have attended tape music concerts in two guises, as annoyed, bored listener, relegating the music to Muzak and hating it, and as its aggressive partner, demanding that performance happen. I am not always in control of which position I take, for some of this music is better than others in evoking a performative response. Indeed, some tape music is not performative in the least and perhaps should be heard in a home environment or else should serve as a kind of sonic "diary" for the composer. As such, this music really is not intended for a broader audience response. In our age of technology and its accompanying travels on the edge of the performative, creating music does not necessarily create performance, for either composers or audiences.

NOTES

1. See Phelan 1993; chap. 7, "The Ontology of Performance" Representation without Reproduction," is especially important to this discussion.

2. There are some theorists doing excellent work on the performing musician, mainly Suzanne Cusick and Marion Guck, and I refer you to their articles in the "Feminist Forum" section of recent issues of *Perspectives of New Music* (31 and 32: 1993–94).

3. Cusick illustrates, in what could initially sound like a disclaimer of lesbian identity, the primacy of the relationship with music for "music lovers," both amateur and professional. As I mentioned earlier, an attachment to sound for both its pleasurable and its meaningful aspects occurs early in human development, and the subsequent identification of children as "musical" becomes a powerful identity for those of us who are musical. This identity is often grounded and nurtured by familial, educational, social, and religious institutions long before a child takes on a sexual identity, and whether or not that musical identity gets expressed ultimately as an adult profession, the primary identification with musical experience remains. I contend, then, that for those who are "musical," sexual identity is secondary to an identification as a musician or music lover. For

many, "being musical" was a very early source of identity and thus is more fundamental than even sexual identity.

4. "On top" is a term used in the American lesbian vernacular to describe the sexual partner who is providing pleasure to the other partner "on the bottom," in reference to the heterosexual stereotypic "missionary position." Allowing the music to be "on top" is thus analogous to a more common expression—"losing oneself" in the music. In this situation, one "submits" to the power of the music.

5. See Dusman 1994 for a complete discussion of this concept.

6. Available through Smith Publications, Baltimore, Md. A CD recording is available as *II of IV, Electroacoustic Music V,* Neuma Records 450–92.

7. Electronic communication from Pauline Oliveros, 15 November 1995. A complete diagram of the technical setup for *I of IV* is included in Oliveros 1984, 44. Both *I of IV* and *II of IV* use the same setup.

8. I am grateful to Elizabeth Wood for bringing this point to my attention.

References Cited

Brett, Philip. 1994. "Music, Essentialism, and the Closet." In *Queering the Pitch: The New Gay and Lesbian Musicology,* ed. Philip Brett, Elizabeth Wood, and Gary C. Thomas, 9–26. New York: Routledge.

Case, Sue-Ellen. 1991. "Tracking the Vampire." *Differences: A Journal of Feminist Cultural Studies* 3, no. 2: 1–20.

Castle, Terry. 1993. *The Apparitional Lesbian: Female Homosexuality and Modern Culture.* New York: Columbia University Press.

Cusick, Suzanne. 1994. "On a Lesbian Relationship with Music." In *Queering the Pitch: The New Gay and Lesbian Musicology,* ed. Philip Brett, Elizabeth Wood, and Gary C. Thomas, 67–83. New York: Routledge.

Dusman, Linda. 1994. "Unheard-of: Music as Performance and the Reception of the New." *Perspectives of New Music* 32, no. 2:130–46.

Eco, Umberto. 1989. *The Open Work.* London: Hutchinson, Radius.

Koestenbaum, Wayne. 1994 [1993]. *The Queen's Throat: Opera, Homosexuality, and the Mystery of Desire.* New York: Vintage.

Phelan, Peggy. 1993. *Unmarked: The Politics of Performance.* London: Routledge.

Oliveros, Pauline. 1984. *Software for People.* Baltimore: Smith.

Wood, Elizabeth. 1994. "Sapphonics." In *Queering the Pitch: The New Gay and Lesbian Musicology,* ed. Philip Brett, Elizabeth Wood, and Gary C. Thomas, 27–66. New York: Routledge.

Epilogue
The Place of Gender within Complex, Dynamic Musical Systems

Marcia Herndon

The inclusion of gender as an essential aspect of all ethnomusicological research is far from becoming a reality. In fact, gendered considerations of music, along with what Moisala (1996) suggests as "musical genders," have yet to be recognized as a useful tool either in the scholarly dialogue across cultures or in the discourse within them. The situation results in no small part from a determined lack of interest and understanding among theorists who prefer to focus their research efforts only on men instead of grappling with the complexities of whole, functioning musical systems.

Many ethnomusicologists have been slow to realize that studying "gender" as it relates to music is not the same thing as studying "women's music." Gender studies includes women's music, of course, along with men's music and the music of all gender categories recognized by the particular society being investigated, documented, or otherwise considered. In addition, an insidious American and European ethnocentrism has, among other things, left most ethnomusicologists presuming that Western dichotomies of "homosexual" and "heterosexual" transfer unchanged to all other cultures; this is simply not so.

Over a decade ago a few ethnomusicologists began a discussion about the need to include gender in all musical analysis. These discussions led to a petition to the International Council for Traditional Music that it recognize the Study Group on Music and Gender. The study group has produced a number of papers and meetings; the book *Music, Gender, and Culture* (Herndon and Ziegler 1990), which is an official publication of the study group; and a special issue of the *World of Music* entitled *Women in Music and Music Research* (Herndon and Ziegler 1991), which includes a bibliography on women in music, five reviews of books on women in music, and four articles. Since then members have continued to study, research, and publish in this area, slowly developing insights and methods.

Most of the approaches to music and gender thus far have been less theoretical than descriptive, definitional, and methodological. The study group's initial efforts often focused on women's music, or women's roles in music cultures, because this information had often been neglected in the past, whether the scholar was male or female. Considerable time and effort were also expended in distinguishing sex from gender, as well as in exploring concepts of androgyny and more ambiguous areas of gender blurring. Now that scholars have filled in some of the gaps, particularly with reference to the women "missing" from the literature on various music cultures, this volume begins to situate gender in its proper place as a major factor in musical exegesis and analysis.

Before attempting to position gender within musical scholarship, it would be well to take note of the kinds of work now being done in some of our cognate disciplines. In particular, I would like to consider trends in musicology and anthropology. My review is limited to North America, because I am more familiar with work in anthropology and musicology in my home area.

New Musicology

Discussions of gender in what is being called the "new musicology" in the United States have been enlivened in recent years by a group of scholars who have mixed their interpretations of Theodor Adorno with the ideas of Michel Foucault, Antonio Gramsci, and Mikhail Bakhtin, among others. The result has been to merge musicological discourse with the matter and manner of cultural studies and literary criticism.

In terms of musicology and gender, American musicologist Susan McClary led the way in 1991 with her book *Feminine Endings,* a modified poststructuralist manifesto for feminist musical analysis. For her, music exists only as an ever-changing illusion or dream in the minds of socially particularized listeners. At the same time, however, she declares gender to be an unambiguous and intrinsic presence in the very musical fabric whose aesthetic independence she denies. She never backs her assertions with careful evidentiary proof; at least, she fails to provide evidence of the sort ethnomusicologists prefer. One fears that McClary and the other new musicologists may have simply exchanged one kind of ideological fog for another, replacing the formalist theoretical generalities with unsubstantiated assertions about sex and gender. Whatever the case may be, the new musicologists have stirred strong emotions, enlivened debate, and generally signaled a revolution whose end is not yet in sight.

Musicology and Difference, an anthology edited by Ruth Solie (1993), and *Queering the Pitch,* edited by Philip Brett, Elizabeth Wood, and Gary C. Thomas (1994), exemplify some of the problems particular to new musicology in the United States and its divergence from ethnomusicology. The difficulty with both volumes lies in the dearth of empirical data in historical explorations, although the Solie volume does include contributions from two ethnomusicologists among its sixteen chapters. For historical musicologists, however, the metaphorical whimsies and personal vendettas of nineteenth-century commentators or earlier sources have already skewed the picture of things long before their twentieth-century successors even begin their own analyses. This problem is compounded by modern musicological writings' general inattention to differences of culture, time, and concepts of gender.

Reinventing Anthropology

Unlike those in musicology, discussions of gender in anthropology have tended to focus on two related issues, both of which are homeostatic: (1) the control of women's sexuality and (2) the relationship of women's power to public and private spheres of social life. These issues, including anthropologists' general acceptance of a peculiarly limited and unexamined view of marriage, have vexed anthropology for the past twenty years.

More recently, the control of women's sexuality has been addressed in many articles, including Michael Herzfeld's "Honour and Shame: Problems in the Comparative Analysis of Moral Systems" (1990) and Brinkley Messick's "Subordinate Discourse: Women, Weaving, and Gender Relations in North Africa" (1988). Women's power issues have been the focus of numerous books and articles, including *The Poetics of Gender* (Miller 1986) and Ruth Mandel's "Sacrifice at the Bridge of Arta: Sex Roles and the Manipulation of Power" (1983).

Anthropologists in the United States have also chosen to pay considerable attention to feminist writings. In 1984 Peggy Reeves Sanday organized a conference session to challenge Simone de Beauvoir's concept of women as the second sex and its implicit assumption of universal male dominance. The authors in the resultant book, titled *Beyond the Second Sex: New Directions in the Anthropology of Gender* (Sanday and Goodenough 1990), question the traditional view of gender ideologies as unitary, hegemonic systems of belief imposed by dominant groups on subordinates. They also initiate the notion of gender roles as diverse and variable, contested rather than shared, noting that specific situational variables may elicit or inhibit the expression of different aspects of gender ideology.

Within the last five years anthropologists have recognized the need to understand the gendered perspectives of non-Western people in their own words and to acknowledge individual variation. Serena Nanda's *Neither Man nor Woman: The Hijras of India* (1990) is a good example of ethnography that allows for socially and culturally based gender definitions that change from one society to another. In addition, anthropologists have moved toward the thesis that religion is a critical factor in the social definition as well as the valuation of gender variance. There has also been a trend toward self-examination, or reflexivity, and various attempts at a dialogic approach, as in Micaela di Leonardo's collection *Gender at the Crossroads of Knowledge: Feminist Anthropology in the Postmodern Era* (1991). In Deborah Heath's "Politics of Appropriateness and Appropriation: Recontextualizing Women's Dance in Urban Senegal" (1994), the reflexivity seems focused more on the ethnographer than on her research subjects and skirts dangerously close to ethical issues about when, and whether, the researcher should become part of the web of performance.

Gender Dynamics and Analysis

Beyond being subjected to these rather tentative approaches in musicology and wider advances in anthropology, gender ought to be studied with full recognition of the potential variances that might be found in particular places, times, and occasions. Shifting contexts of boundaries, representations, negotiations, and conflicts are to be expected in the mediation and negotiation characteristic of a living culture. Gender, then, should be regarded as a basic, dynamic field within which meaning may vary.

The world is a dynamic place, and much of what we call research, analysis, or investigation has been driven by our desire to understand dynamic phenomena. In the humanities and social sciences, we have tended to copy the classic Baconian "scientific method" as far as possible. In the past we have incorporated a philosophical microreductionist stance, looking for static patterns, hierarchies, and relationships on which to create synthetic models and systems. Our styles of analysis have followed trends in both related and nonrelated fields of study, as have our notions of methodology.

Given that there are fads and fallacies in the pursuit of theory, we do well to remind ourselves that ideally we should let theory emerge from data rather than collect data only to support hypotheses and theories. Methodology is somewhat driven by technology, especially in ethnomusicology, but technology is adapted to serve current questions that have been generated in a subfield of study. There are at least three (and probably more) levels of analysis to which methodology applies and from which theory can emerge or be discussed.

1. *Primary analysis* attempts to be rigorous about the data it collects. Ethnomusicologists' practices of collecting, recording, and initially analyzing data in the field distinguish us from scholars in the other branches of music research and relate us to the ethnographic methods of anthropology. Although the notion that the researcher is totally objective has faded, and at least some scholars are trying to evaluate the impact of their own backgrounds, gender, biases, and personalities on their research, the ideal of empirical research remains. We are no longer trying to discover and illuminate a singular truth about "what really happens" in music and musical systems, but we still assume that there is a real world out there with which we interact and about which we can discover a certain (or uncertain) amount.

2. *Secondary analysis* operates from a distance on collected and recorded data, using one or more models or styles of analysis. Secondary analysis provides local generalizations, which may be taken as common sense, rejected as contrary to it, or obscured by jargon. Model construction, which often proceeds from the collection of data, suggests causal connections or attempts to identify other patterns and links.

3. *Tertiary analysis* attempts to be rigorous about the logic of its concepts and is the originating level for most secondary analysis in ethnomusicology, although ideally tertiary analysis should arise out of secondary analysis if we are to maintain ethnographic integrity. Tertiary analysis has a use in selecting or rejecting certain questions for analysis and in attempting to create conceptual frameworks for the examination of comparative data. It represents the highest and most generalized level of abstraction.

Examining Whole Systems

At the risk of violating ethnographic integrity, I want to put forward several possible approaches to theoretical thinking about gender and music that originate from a tertiary level rather than directly from a primary one. Rather than emphasize description, or center on the music of women or men, can we not profit from a focus on whole systems? Adopting this approach seems to me to be much more informative than using deterministic (cause-effect) models, equilibrium (diffusion) models, or generative (modified cause-effect) models. Given that the world is complex and dynamic, I want to examine complex and dynamic approaches that might inform research on music and gender.

My rationale in taking this rather contrarian approach to the development of gender theory in ethnomusicology stems from the position of gender in human life. It is axiomatic within the social sciences that the basic division of labor in any society is by sex. This division of labor by sex is ameliorated by and filtered through that society's range and number of gender roles. Thus gender is a high-level discriminant in society. As such, it seems only appropriate that some preliminary notions and concepts should originate at the tertiary level of analysis rather than at the primary one. Note, however, that this is so only because a good amount of primary work has already been done and is freely available to researchers.

I offer two tertiary-level questions, then, along with my own thoughts about them, to encourage dialogue about the issues they confront and imply.

Question 1: Are gender roles self-organizing dynamic systems that respond to the amount of specificity in a particular society's division of labor by sex? For example, it seems to me that if there is a high degree of specificity in the way a particular society defines its sex roles, it will also allow for those individuals whose personalities and inclinations cannot fit into those sex roles to occupy other gender categories. A case in point is the North American Plains Indian tribes and bands, whose division of labor by sex included very rigid rules of behavior for men and women. Given the rigidity of definition of sex roles in these societies, it is quite understandable that they developed additional gender roles, including what researchers call the *berdache* for males and the *manly hearted woman.* These two additional gender roles have been described many times in the anthropological literature. Often, they appear under the rubric of kinship domains or social institutions rather than gender categories. Sometimes they are discussed as if these and other gender categories of the tribes in this area were not fluid and context sensitive.

I suggest that gender roles are self-organizing dynamic systems. They, rather than kinship, are the first and most general divisions created and recognized by every society, no matter how that society defines these divisions and no matter what other cultural sanctions or notions may be attached to them.

If gender roles are self-organizing dynamic systems, then under what circumstances do they organize themselves? In some societies gender systems are quite rigid and unchanging or at least seem to be. In others gender schemes are ordered but exhibit some possible fluidity, while in still others they may appear to be turbulent. Gender roles, then, may organize them-selves into rigid, ordered, or turbulent dynamic systems; since they are part of the living culture of a group of people, they may change through time. The analyst needs to discover whether these gender categories are separated by permeable barriers, dislocations, or other cultural constraints.

Assuming that gender roles are indeed self-organizing dynamic systems, we need to determine whether musicians copy their particular societies' gender roles, parody them, or selectively use them in other ways. We also need to note whether gender roles of musicians in a particular society re-spond in distinctive ways to the degree of specificity the society places on gender roles generally.

How do we determine the amount of specificity with regard to gender roles? For musical information, the work may be relatively easy. Among other things, we need to know (1) how many gender roles the society recognizes; (2) who has access to learning the different types of music in the society; (3) who has access to instruments, instrument making, documentation, or other technology; (4) who can perform and under what constraints; and (5) how, and by whom, performance is evaluated.

My second tertiary-level question generates even more questions than the first.

Question 2: Do gender roles operate, respond, and act in a systemic con-text in relation to other gender roles within that society? The key word here is *systemic,* for it presupposes an awareness of all possible gender roles with-in a society, as well as their interaction. Together, interacting gender elements perform as a complex whole.

That is, do gender roles affect the entire sociocultural "body"? Can we assume that if a society is to perform properly, no one gender role can be missing? Is it possible that one or more gender roles can be "missing" in a society's self-construction without threatening its flexibility or its very exis-tence?

A line from an old popular song called "Love and Marriage" comes to mind here: "You can't have one without the other." In terms of love and marriage, you obviously can have love without marriage or marriage with-out love. In terms of gender roles, however, it is *impossible* to have a full, continuing society with only one sex and one gender. Subgroups of a soci-ety have managed to create single-sex associations or gender-specific calen-drical ceremonials, but no would-be human society has yet managed to ex-ist for long in the absence of either sex.

Society requires two sexes to reproduce and continue for many generations—at least it has until now. Given two sexes and the division of labor that this distinction produces, there will be at least two genders. So let us assume, for the moment, that gender roles operate in a systemic context and examine some of the ways in which they might interact within a system.

Do different genders within a society compete with one another for finite resources, or do they cooperate? If genders compete with one another for finite resources, would any of the following models taken from evolutionary biology be useful? Each stresses different aspects of dynamic change.

Van Valen's Red Queen Hypothesis

In the book *Alice in Wonderland,* the Red Queen says: "It takes all the running you can do to stay in the same place. If you want to get somewhere else, you must run at least twice as fast as that." In the real world, a Red Queen situation is one in which the benefit of increased competitive energies is minimal or even produces diminishing returns as energies are dissipated. The "winner" is the one who stays in the running while competitors have dropped out (Vrba 1993). A possible nonevolutionary example of this is explored by Jennifer Robertson in an article entitled "The Politics of Androgyny in Japan: Sexuality and Subversion in the Theater and Beyond" (1992). As she points out, much has been written about the all-male Kabuki theater in Japan, but very little attention has been paid to the Takarazuka Revue, an all-female theater. Robertson sketches the history of the Takarazuka Revue while examining how the scrambling of gender markers in performance both undermines the stability of a sex-gender system premised on a male-female dichotomy and retains that dichotomy by either juxtaposing or blending its elements. Importantly, she demonstrates how in Japan the body of the androgyne has changed from male to female over the last three hundred years. It was embodied by the *onnagata,* the male Kabuki actor specializing in girl's and women's roles, from 1603 (when the shogunate banned women from the public stage) through 1868, but since 1910 (when women returned to the stage) the androgyne has been embodied by the *otokoysku,* the female Takarazuka Revue actor specializing in boys' and men's roles.

The Takarazuka Revue has been the focus of heated debates about the construction and performance of gender. The positions fueling these debates ranged from Buddhist teachings about bodily transformation or metamorphosis to claims about the transformation that precedes a male actor's becoming female and then acting in a role. The Takarazuka Revue was, from its inception, closely linked to nationalism, state formation, and the notion that theater, as an agent of the state, helps orchestrate and regulate gender.

In a Red Queen situation, the stimulus for change is not the physical environment but the social one. Change depends on the interaction of gender roles within a given social system. There is competition between genders in what social scientists call a zero-sum environment. That is, irrespective of time and change in the system, genders will still be ranked in the same order based on their "fitness," or the ways in which the society perceives them to relate to one another.

The Takarazuka Revue seems to be a good example of the Red Queen situation, particularly in the change Jennifer Robertson reports as to which gender constructs, performs, and embodies the androgyne in Japan. The Red Queen situation could well be a useful tool in the examination of perceived gender roles and their mediation through performance elsewhere.

The Punctuated Equilibrium Model

In a punctuated equilibrium model, the stimulus for change is a modification of the physical or social environment. The systemic characteristics include homeostasis and a lack of overt competition between genders in a stable, established cultural system. Such situations will produce long periods in which there is little or no change in gender roles, along with bursts of change following alterations in the physical or social environment.

For example, the transport of slaves from Africa to the Americas, even when people of different tribal origins were not thrown together at their destination sites, caused gender-role changes, as well as musical changes. Any situation in which there is fairly rapid dominance of one society by another, or in which cataclysmic physical change has taken place, may be said to produce effects consistent with a punctuated equilibrium model in both musical and gender systems.

A musical example of the punctuated equilibrium model appears in a paper I wrote some years ago (Herndon 1979) on the relationship of Cherokee myth and stories to musical styles and of both to the potential for musical "play": a point in the flow of time where the possibility of the retention, change, or elimination of a form and its social explanations might occur. As I suggested in that paper: "There is the choice of retaining or eliminating a form and its explanation; a form is introduced, becomes rigid, then becomes susceptible to play. This construct might also be used to explain the progressional development of any explanatory myth, and perhaps of any kind of myth, among North American Indians" (Herndon 1979, 129). When might the cultural baggage of a gender role be subject to play and thus change? The easy answer would be to say that music provides that impetus. Perhaps this is so in some cases, but if the stimulus for change is a modification of the physical or social environment, it is likely that the catalyst is peculiar in nature, whether it comes from natural disaster or a conflict among cultures or other social groups.

The "Nice" Theory

Somewhere between the notions of competition and cooperation is the so-called nice theory of evolutionary biology, which states that if all competitors have to spend the same amount of time on competition, another factor decides who wins. That is, if all trees can grow equally tall in principle, the one that best fits the soil type (or some other "nice" dimension) will win. This leads to the following question: if the male gender role in a society is defined by competition, and the males spend maximum time competing with one another, whereas the female gender role is defined by cooperation, will the female gender role ultimately prevail?

If genders cooperate with one another for finite resources, or appear to do so, what are the implications for the development of gender theory? The notion of gender complementarity in a cooperative system, which might be defined as mutual dependence and ideal equality, seems to imply a stable symbiotic totality.

Note, however, that relationship does not mean that the ideal of equality and gender complementarity is achieved in everyday life. The Eastern Cherokee have the *ideal* of gender balance and went very far in the direction of attaining gender equality; nevertheless, men historically did most of the singing and playing of musical instruments because of the perceived power of sound and the need to balance the innate power of women's reproductive capacity, on the one hand, and their menstrual blood, on the other.

Instead of looking at competition or cooperation or ideals of complementarity, perhaps we should focus on the notion that gender identities are contested, with members of each gender continually called to witness and perform the attributes of their genders. If this is so, we need to examine whether the negotiation is constant or intermittent. We may assume, for working purposes, that there will be changes in the ways genders are signaled as well as in the social roles to which individuals of a given gender may aspire.

Given the ambiguity inherent in most musical performance, it seems that the enactments of gender in musical contexts provide the best locus for understanding the dynamics of contested identities. The first performance of contested, or blurred, gender identities is often to be found not in musical sound or texts but in the musicians, whether in performance or in their everyday lives. Also, specific situational variables may elicit or inhibit the expression of different aspects of gender ideology.

Perhaps we should assume, at the outset of any cross-cultural study, that gender identities are always potentially contested identities, requiring continual performance, revision, and restatement. Further, we may also assume that each gender role, as a component of a system, acts in its own self-interest and toward the goal of preserving its own prerogatives.

The "nice" theory suggests that we pay careful attention to the early identification of those areas of behavior or material culture that constitute competition within a musical culture, in addition to the factors that constitute success, mastery, triumph, accomplishment, achievement, or triumph. Then, if all competitors have to spend the same amount of time on competition within a musical system, a factor other than those elements that constitute the social arena of competition will be decisive as to who "wins."

Conclusion

What can we now identify as initial directions toward a unified methodology or a more theoretical approach to gender studies? The inclusion of gender as an essential aspect of all ethnomusicological research is related to a determined group of theorists who prefer to focus their research efforts mainly, or only, on men instead of wrestling with the complexities of whole, living musical systems.

One way to distinguish ethnomusicologists from musicologists is through the fact that ethnomusicologists deal with living musics in a synchronic way, whereas musicologists deal with historical musics in a diachronic way. As musicologists begin to add information about the cultural context of the performers or composers they are studying, and as ethnomusicologists venture more often into art music topics and historical contexts of current musics, it is possible that the two fields of study may yet merge.

For both musicologists and ethnomusicologists, however, the addition of a new aspect complicates the process of analysis. It is natural, then, to suggest that music scholars tend to resist what they believe might muddle their theoretical and methodological processes. Gender information, although not particularly difficult to discover, may threaten to complicate unduly the theoretical and methodological processes of musical analysis. That is, struggling with the complexities of whole, functioning musical systems may seem a daunting and unrewarding process.

A trio of general assumptions based on the two questions I raised earlier should be considered: (1) gender roles are self-organizing dynamic systems that respond to the amount of specificity in a particular society's division of labor by sex; (2) any given gender role acts in relation to other gender roles within that society; and (3) gender identities are contested identities.

If we take these assumptions as our main assumptions about gender and add to them the knowledge bases about specific music cultures, our assumptions can be tested against data already available. We already have sufficient primary and secondary ethnographic materials that constitute a substantial base on which to identify, agree on, and test tertiary questions that can focus the development of theory and method for gender studies in ethnomusicology.

REFERENCES CITED

Brett, Philip, Elizabeth Wood, and Gary C. Thomas, eds. 1994. *Queering the Pitch: The New Gay and Lesbian Musicology.* New York: Routledge.

di Leonardo, Micaela, ed. 1991. *Gender at the Crossroads of Knowledge: Feminist Anthropology in the Postmodern Era.* Berkeley: University of California Press.

Heath, Deborah. 1994. "The Politics of Appropriateness and Appropriation: Recontextualizing Women's Dance in Urban Senegal." *American Ethnologist* 21, no. 1:88–104.

Herndon, Marcia. 1979. "Play Elements in the Myth of North American Indians." In *Forms of Play of Native North Americans: 1977 Proceedings of the American Ethnological Society,* ed. Edward Norbeck and Claire R. Farrer, 121–32. St. Paul, Minn.: West.

Herndon, Marcia, and Susanne Ziegler, eds. 1990. *Music, Gender, and Culture.* Intercultural Music Studies, 1. Wilhelmshaven, Germany: F. Noetzel Verlag.

Herndon, Marcia, and Susanne Ziegler, eds. 1991. *Women in Music and Music Research.* Special issue of *World of Music* 33, no. 2.

Herzfeld, Michael. 1990. "Honour and Shame: Problems in the Comparative Analysis of Moral Systems." *Man,* n.s., 15:339–51.

Mandel, Ruth. 1983. "Sacrifice at the Bridge of Arta: Sex Roles and the Manipulation of Power." *Journal of Modern Greek Studies* 1:173–83.

McClary, Susan. 1991. *Feminine Endings: Music, Gender, and Sexuality.* Minneapolis: University of Minessota Press.

Messick, Brinkley. 1988. "Subordinate Discourse: Women, Weaving, and Gender Relations in North Africa." *American Ethnologist* 14:210–25.

Miller, N. K., ed. 1986. *The Poetics of Gender.* New York: Columbia University Press.

Moisala, Pirkko. 1996. "Music Education Experienced and Interpreted from the Point of View of Gender." Unpublished paper presented at the Gender, Music, and Pedagogy conference, Gothenburg.

Nanda, Serena. 1990. *Neither Man nor Woman: The Hijras of India.* Belmont, Calif.: Wadsworth.

Robertson, Jennifer. 1992. "The Politics of Androgyny in Japan: Sexuality and Subversion in the Theater and Beyond." *American Ethnologist* 19, no. 3:419–39.

Sanday, Peggy Reeves, and Ruth Gallagher Goodenough, eds. 1990. *Beyond the Second Sex: New Directions in the Anthropology of Gender.* Philadelphia: University of Pennsylvania Press.

Solie, Ruth, ed. 1993. *Musicology and Difference: Gender and Sexuality in Music Scholarship.* Berkeley: University of California Press.

Vrba, Elisabeth L. 1993. "Turnover-Pulses, The Red Queen, and Related Topics." *American Journal of Science* 292-A:418–52.

Contributors

Jane Bowers, a professor of music history and literature at the University of Wisconsin at Milwaukee, has been researching women in music for more than twenty years. Coeditor of the ASCAP–Deems Taylor award–winning book *Women Making Music: The Western Art Tradition, 1150–1950* (1986) and the author of numerous articles, including a recent survey of women's lamenting traditions worldwide (in *Woman and Music: A Journal of Gender and Culture* 2 [1998]), she is completing a biography and repertory study of Chicago blues singer Estelle "Mama" Yancey.

Naila Ceribašić holds a Ph.D. degree in ethnomusicology and is an assistant at the Institute of Ethnology and Folklore Research in Zagreb, Croatia. She has published many articles, mainly in Croatian journals. Her research focuses on music in Croatia, especially the relationship between norm and individuation, gender issues, and the impact of politics and war on music.

Beverley Diamond is a Canadian ethnomusicologist at York University. Her research focuses on Native American music cultures, feminist musicology, and Canadian music historiography. She coauthored *Visions of Sound: Musical Instruments of First Nations Communities in Northeastern America* (1994) and coedited *Canadian Music: Issues of Hegemony and Identity* (1994).

Linda Dusman is a composer, theorist, and educator whose works have been performed across the United States and in Europe, Asia, and South America. Among her awards and grants are those from the Swiss Women's Music Forum, the International Electroacoustic Music Competition of Sao Paulo, the Ucross Foundation, and the D.C. Council on the Arts. Her music is available on the Neuma and Maximalist Music labels, and her theoretical work has been published in *Interface* and *Perspectives of New Music*.

Marcia Herndon, one of the pioneers in gender studies within ethnomusicology, taught at the University of Texas at Austin, the University of California at Berkeley, and the University of Maryland at College Park. Her publications include a special issue of *Worlds of Music* (1993) on gender, the coauthored *Music as Culture* (1981), and the coedited *Music, Gender, and Culture* (1991). From 1987 until her death in 1997 she was the cochair of the Music and Gender Study Group of the International Council for Traditional Music.

Helmi Järviluoma, an associate professor of musicology at the University of Turku (Finland), studied ethnomusicology and sociology at the University of Tampere and at Goldsmiths College, London. She has written and edited several books, including *Music and Identity at Grassroots Level* (Finnish, 1997), *Music, Social Movements, Restraints* (Finnish, 1986), *Soundscapes: Essays on Vroom and Moo* (English, 1994), the coauthored *Music on Show: Issues of Performance* (English, 1998), and the coedited *Yearbook of Soundscape Studies* (English, 1998).

Cynthia Tse Kimberlin, who received a Ph.D. degree in ethnomusicology from the University of California at Los Angeles, is the executive director of the Music Research Institute in Richmond, California, and has taught at San Francisco State University, the University of California at Berkeley, the University of Ife (Nigeria), and Addis Ababa University (Ethiopia). She is coeditor of a series on intercultural music focusing on twentieth-century music and has published widely on various aspects of Ethiopian and Eritrean music.

Michelle Kisliuk teaches at the University of Virginia and specializes in the ethnography of performance, integrating theory with practice. Since 1986 she has researched the music, dance, daily life, and social politics among forest people (BaAka) from Central Africa. She has written about urban music and about dance and modernity in Central Africa and about the socioaesthetics of jam sessions at bluegrass festivals in the United States.

Andra McCartney, a multimedia soundscape composer, completed a doctoral dissertation in music at York University and a CD-ROM about Vancouver soundscape composer Hildegard Westerkamp. McCartney's work is available on CDs produced by the Canadian Electroacoustic Community, Terra Nova, and Entartete Kunst. Abstracts of her published and online writings are available on the Worldwide Web through the research link at <http://www.finearts.yorku.ca/andra/>. She teaches at Concordia University, Montreal.

Pirkko Moisala, a professor of musicology at the Åbo Akademi University (Finland), studied ethnomusicology at the University of Helsinki, the University of London (SOAS), and the University of California at Berkeley. She specializes in cultural studies of all kinds of music, particularly in Nepal and Finland. Her publications include *Cultural Cognition in Music: Continuity and Change in the Gurung*

Music Culture of Nepal (1991) and the coauthored book *The Other Sex of Music* (Finnish, 1994). Since 1993 she has been the cochair of the Music and Gender Study Group of the International Council for Traditional Music.

Margaret Myers grew up in South Africa and was educated in England. She took her B.A. Honours at Southampton University in 1968 and her M. Music at King's College, London University, in 1972. Her doctoral dissertation at Göteborg University (1993) is on European ladies' orchestras. She teaches music history and analysis at Göteborg University and Halmstad University.

Karen Pegley teaches in the Department of Fine Arts at Atkinson College, York University, and has published articles on youth cultures, music consumption practices and identity formation, and feminist operatic criticism, including "Femme Fatale and Lesbian Representation in Alban Berg's *Lulu*" (in *Encrypted Messages in Alban Berg's Music* [1998]). Her doctoral research (Ph.D., York University, 1999) focused on the construction of gender, race, and nationality within Canadian and American music television formats.

Ursula Reinhard conducted fieldwork in Turkey from 1956 to 1973. She is the coauthor, with Kurt Reinhard, of *Turquie: Les Traditions Musicales* (1969) and *Auf der Fiedel mein . . . : Volkslieder von der Osttürkischen Schwarzmeerküste* (1968) and the author of *Vor seinen Häusern eine Weide: Volksliedtexte aus der Südtürkei* (1965), *Music der Türkei: Die Kunstmusik* (vol. 1) and *Die Volksmusik* (vol. 2) (1984).

Ingrid Rüütel, head of the folk music department of the Institute of Estonian Language and the sound archive at the Literary Museum, has numerous publications on the traditional music of the Estonians and other Finno-Ugric peoples and on folk music typology. Her ongoing research deals with the roles and functions of contemporary Estonian folk music.

Boden Sandstrom is a lecturer in ethnomusicology at the University of Maryland and a sound engineer at RFK Stadium in Washington, D.C. She has degrees from the American University, the University of Michigan, and St. Lawrence University. From 1975 to 1988 she owned and served as chief sound engineer for Woman Sound, Inc. Her research interests include world popular music, gender studies, women in music, and technology.

Index

Note: The editors wish to thank Heather
Sparling for her assistance in compiling
this index.

Typeset in 9/13 Stone Serif
with Braganza display
Designed by Paula Newcomb
Composed by Jim Proefrock
at the University of Illinois Press
Manufactured by Thomson-Shore, Inc.

University of Illinois Press
1325 South Oak Street
Champaign, IL 61820-6903
www.press.uillinois.edu